Arms
and
the Self

Arms and

the Self

War, the Military, and Autobiographical Writing

Edited by

ALEX VERNON

The Kent State University Press

Kent and London

Library of Congress Catalog Card Number 2004017496
ISBN 0-87338-812-7

Manufactured in the United States of America

08   07   06   05   5   4   3   2   1

"The Life Writing of a Military Child" by Jennifer Sinor was first published as "Inscribing Ordinary Trauma in the Diary of a Military Child" in *Biography: An Interdisciplinary Quarterly* 26, no. 3 (Summer 2003). Copyright © 2003 Biographical Research Center.

"War Elegy" by Pat C. Hoy II was first published in the *Sewanee Review* 106, no. 3 (Summer 1998). Copyright © 1998 University of the South. Reprinted by permission of the editor and author.

Library of Congress Cataloging-in-Publication Data
Arms and the self : war, the military, and autobiographical writing / edited by Alex Vernon.
     p. cm.
   Includes bibliographical references and index.
   ISBN 0-87338-812-7 (hardcover : alk. paper) ∞

   1. Soldiers' writings, English—History and criticism. 2. Soldiers—English-speaking countries—Biography—History and criticism. 3. Soldiers' writings, American—History and criticism. 4. American prose literature—History and criticism. 5. English prose literature—History and criticism. 6. Military art and science—Historiography. 7. War—Historiography. 8. Autobiography. I. Vernon, Alex, 1967–

PR120.S64A89 2004
820.9'921355—DC22   2004017496

British Library Cataloging-in-Publication data are available.

My war is virtually synonymous with my life. I entered the war when I was nineteen, and I have been in it ever since.

—Paul Fussell, "My War"
The Boy Scout Handbook and Other Essays

Contents

Preface

This collection of essays hopes to add significantly to the critical canon by introducing the reader to a range of primary and secondary texts through different interpretive approaches. Attempting to capture narratives from all historical armed conflicts, from all parties to these conflicts, from the many kinds of participants, from military periods other than war, and from all possible genres would be impossibly, exhaustively inclusive; instead, this collection provides an eclectic, suggestive perspective. A collection of bibliographic essays would certainly have its advantages, but it too would have severe problems in terms of inclusion, and it would lack the compelling nature of critical minds imaginatively engaged. As for the gaps created by the book's eclecticism, the hope is that reviewers will remark on neglected texts, authors, military periods, and other approaches so that the book and its reviews will together constitute an even richer resource from which scholars can draw.

The primary problem with the volume, as a glance at the table of contents will reveal, is its Anglo American focus (with a few exceptions). This is understandable given the Anglo American heritage of our contributors; our neglect of works not available in English will not bother most readers. Still, other voices deserve to be heard for their own sake and also, incidentally, as correctives for how Western culture sees itself, as well as for the very idea of "otherness." The absence of those voices is regretted. Other notable absences include narratives by naval combatants (literary scholars tend to privilege the foot soldier), irregular combatants, noncombatant military personnel, war protestors, deserters, refugees, journalists, people who as children suffered from war, and I'm sure many other "categories" of authors. Only two of the twelve essays cover authors who lived, witnessed war, and wrote prior to the twentieth century—prior to the explosion of literate soldiers and the memoir and autobiography genres.

Despite these absences, the essays in this volume cover a variety of participants and genres in autobiographical writing about war, armed conflict, and military service. I hope that this book will encourage more scholarly work in the field. Several volumes like this one are in order, because we all need help understanding the most vital and valuable documents available about the human experience of war and the military.

Introduction

No Genre's Land

The Problem of Genre in War Memoirs and Military Autobiographies

Alex Vernon

What we value in any text reveals as much about ourselves as it does about the studied text, as evidenced by two reviews of Nathaniel Tripp's 1997 memoir *Father, Soldier, Son: Memoir of a Platoon Leader in Vietnam*. The *Washington Post Book World* called Tripp's book "a complex and beautiful meditation" that "discovers and presents" both "subjective and universal truths" and achieves the worthiness of "art," whereas *Army*, the monthly magazine of the Association of the United States Army, fixed bayonet and slashed away:

> A military reader is not likely to find much worth emulating in the author's narrative. . . . [His] introspective thoughts about his own considerable personal baggage take up so much of the narrative that it is fair to say the book is only incidentally about soldiering in a platoon, and never about platoon leadership. . . . [The book] demeans the faithful service of the hundreds of platoon leaders, living and dead, who actually led their platoons and who gave a damn about their mission.[1]

Regardless of how we evaluate the merits of Tripp's memoir, it meets the primary qualifying criteria for readers and critics alike: it was written by one who was there, whether in the trenches or in the bush. Samuel Hynes's *The Soldiers' Tale: Bearing Witness to Modern War* (1997), arguably the first critical work to attempt to shape a definition of the first-person nonfiction war narrative genre (and the most cited text in this volume), shares the literary preference for narratives by battlefield soldiers and in the process demonstrates the difficulties involved with and ideologies encountered

1

in any effort to define the war narrative genre. Of the texts his book considers—from soldiers who served in World War I and World War II to the U.S. war in Vietnam—some

> were written by men who were, or later became, established professional writers . . . but I also look at the one-book men, who told their stories and then settled quietly back into their lives. . . . The test, for me, is not how literary a book is (what does literary mean, anyway, except writing that gives a reader pleasure?), or how prominent the author became, but whether the book speaks with a voice that is stubbornly distinct, telling us what it was like, for this man, in his war.

Hynes excludes accounts written by "generals and other senior officers," because "in modern wars, commanders don't usually do the fighting, or live with the troops, or get themselves shot at."[2] Hynes subtly narrows his genre even further by including only narratives by those who *have done the fighting.* Memoirs by military personnel who never fought in combat units thus do not fall under his critical purview. Of course, one must limit the field somehow, and this limitation makes sense; the term "war memoir" for most of us instantly produces images of line combat, not desk duty.

This limitation also reveals Hynes's own autobiographical background as a U.S. Marine combat pilot in World War II. Military and veteran culture tends to judge its members according to a hierarchy not of military rank but of proximity to and experience with the enemy. Another World War II veteran turned literary scholar, Paul Fussell, whose works include *The Great War and Modern Memory* (1975) and *Wartime: Understanding and Behavior in the Second World War* (1989), uses the proximity and experience standard to dismiss generalizations made about soldiers in J. Glenn Gray's *The Warriors: Reflections on Men in Battle* (1959). Gray, an intelligence officer, normally "resided at division or even corps headquarters" located "miles—miles—behind the places where soldiers suffer abject terror and madness and relieve the pressure by crazy brutality and sadism. . . . Despite his sensitivity and intelligence, Gray's optimistic and congratulatory view of nature never underwent testing on the line."[3]

Yet think of all the lives affected by war and that affected warfare (in whatever minor way) neglected by such a narrow definition: military and civilian, men and women, at the front and elsewhere—support soldiers, nurses, wives, children, refugees, correspondents, siblings, parents, relief workers, partisans, and so on. One study of nonfiction narratives by American soldiers from Vietnam acknowledges that due to its omission of texts written by anyone above company grade (the U.S. Army's rank of captain), by sailors and airmen, and by soldiers in support roles who did not see combat, it attends to "less than 5 percent of all the GIs connected with the tragedy of Vietnam."[4] It is a historical axiom that the more professional and modern a military organization, the lower its tooth-to-tail ratio—that is, the fewer people, equipment, and resources devoted to fighting in relation to those needed for logistical and technical support. Thus Fussell's correct observation that only a very small percentage of soldiers "actually encountered the enemy" during World War II[5] ironically suggests that Gray's experience of being a soldier is more typical than Fussell's own. Indeed, as most war narratives are written by combat veterans, they collectively misrepresent warfare as actually experienced by most people in uniform. Personal narratives by male noncombatant military persons—white males especially—are easily the most neglected of all military life writing in Anglo American criticism, because they are ignored both by scholars who concentrate on the combat memoir and by those who focus on historically marginalized voices (women and minorities).

Moreover, as most casualties in large twentieth-century conflicts have been inflicted by artillery—even in the direct-engagement branches like the infantry—and as the range of artillery (to include aerial bombardment) has increased dramatically over the century, war's most prevalent danger has become a much more equal-opportunity experience. Hynes would call the story of a German civilian victim of the Dresden firebombing a "sufferer's tale," as if the supplying of munitions and clothing and sons to the military did not constitute active participation in the war effort (and as if soldiers do not qualify as "sufferers"). Allowing ourselves as literary scholars to consider narratives by military personnel not assigned to ground, sea, or air combat units, narratives by local civilians displaced or otherwise affected, and narratives by the soldier's beloved back home would be a very slight and reasonable loosening of the restriction on who qualifies as an author of a war story. Once we make that easy interpretive move, nearly every other exclusionary criterion quickly falls aside. The definition of war stories that includes only (male) combat narratives is not *wrong*, critically speaking, but it should be understood for what it is—a *sub*genre of autobiographical writing about war, armed conflict, military service, and the involved societies and cultures.[6]

On the other end of the spectrum from Hynes and Fussell's male combat narratives sits Susan Griffin's *A Chorus of Stones: The Private Life of War* (1992), a finalist for both a Pulitzer Prize and a National Book Critics Circle Award. Griffin never served in the military, much less in a theater of combat operations. She did not have a parent, sibling, spouse, or lover who served. Nevertheless, *A Chorus of Stones* is an extended personal essay on the intersection of culture, war, history, and the individual. Griffin's birth in 1945, the year the United States dropped atomic bombs on Hiroshima and Nagasaki, coincided with the birth of the atomic age and the Cold War. Her book weaves together her family history with the lives of people she interviewed or read about, from Appalachian coal miners to soldiers used as experimental subjects during atomic bomb tests in the 1950s, from her anti-Semitic grandfather to Heinrich Himmler, one of the Holocaust's architects. "I do not see my life as separate from history," she writes—or, as we might put it for our present purposes, "military history":

> In my mind my family secrets mingle with the secrets of statesmen and bombers. . . . I am beginning to believe that we know everything, that all history, including the history of each family, is part of us, such that, when we hear any secret revealed, a secret about a grandfather, or an uncle, or a secret about the battle of Dresden in 1945, our lives are made suddenly clearer to us, as the unnatural heaviness of unspoken truth is dispersed. For perhaps we are like stones; our own history and the history of the world embedded in us, we hold a sorrow deep within and cannot weep until that history is sung. . . . I was born and brought up in a nation that participated in the bombing of Dresden, and in the civilization that planned the extermination of a whole people. We are not used to associating our private lives with public events. Yet the histories of families cannot be separated from the histories of nations. To divide them is part of our denial.

Her last chapter, "Notes toward a Sketch for a Work in Progress," juxtaposes fragments from what she presents as a diary recorded during the 1990–91 Persian Gulf War with other bits—with, for example, thoughts about the German painter Charlotte Salomon, the American writer Ernest Hemingway, and her own composing process: "What I am seeking is the effect of a work in progress, a work that still continues off the page, and is only completed in the imagination. . . . I want the boundaries of the book to be opened, letting in the atmosphere of contemporary events."[7] Griffin wants the boundaries opened between people and events; she demands that we expand our appreciation of all the lives that touch and are touched by war. Remoteness from the battlefield is not a condition she recognizes. Hers is not a voice to be denied.

Especially now. If the events of September 11, 2001, the preceding decade of terrorism throughout the world, and the subsequent war on terrorism (including the recent regime-change campaigns in Afghanistan and Iraq) have taught us anything, they have taught us how much we are all implicated and involved whenever and wherever violence against a society's representatives—civilians included—occurs.[8]

Literary scholarship of autobiographical writing related to war and the military has moved beyond studying only the combat memoir. These days, alongside literary-confessional texts like Tripp's *Father, Soldier, Son* and more canonical works like Robert Graves's *Good-bye to All That* (1929),[9] we study less belletristic but equally significant and revealing material— namely, letters, diaries, and memoirs by writers without literary ambition. We consider texts authored by combatants and noncombatants, by men and women, at the front and elsewhere.

War, armed conflict in general, military service, and their aftereffects have likely inspired more textual testimonies than have any other kind of human event. It would require a small army of scholars on an extended campaign to locate and catalogue the published primary material alone, much less provide any synthesizing analysis. Unpublished personal nonfiction accounts, scattered around the world in libraries, private collections, and attics, magnify the issue tremendously. Book-length scholarly studies of this vast body of work, however, do not begin to do it justice. Charles V. Genthe's 1969 *American War Narratives 1917–1918: A Study and Bibliography* stood alone until Fussell's 1975 *The Great War and Modern Memory* joined it, though Fussell's book is only partly about war narratives. If we conceive of Hynes's *The Soldiers' Tale* as addressing only a subgenre of this large body of autobiographical material, it sits next to other critical works that similarly consider small subsets of texts, like Craig Howes's *Voices of the Vietnam POWs: Witnesses to Their Fight* (1993) and Penny Summerfield's *Reconstructing Women's Wartime Lives: Discourse and Subjectivity in Oral Histories of the Second World War* (1998).[10]

Given the vast quantity of material and the varied historical and personal circumstances in which each was produced, autobiographical writings about war and the military pose enormous critical challenges. Attempts at generic taxonomy are doomed from the outset. Whom do we "count" as war participants or as career military personnel? What even counts as combat, war, or military service? How do we handle the problem of war memoirs camouflaged as fiction? How do we classify first-person nonfiction texts that run the gamut from literary-confessional, history, propaganda, and journalism to training manuals, collected and edited oral histories, poetry, and documentaries—and that combine these various and often competing genres (and motivations) into single texts? How do the complexities of class, nationality, gender and sexuality, race and ethnicity,[11] and nationality figure into our interpretations?

Wars themselves shatter every boundary imaginable, from national boundaries to bodily ones, often confusing distinctions between social castes as well as between friends and foes, men and women, humans and animals, humans and machines, the living and the dead. Writes Eric J. Leed in his important 1979 work *No Man's Land: Combat and Identity in World War I,* "War experience is nothing if not a transgression of categories. In providing bridges between the visible and the invisible, the known and the unknown, the human and the inhuman, war offered numerous occasions for the shattering of distinctions that were essential to orderly thought, communicable experience, and normal human relations."[12]

This blurring of boundaries in war bleeds into its narrative representations; indeed, making sense of genre distinctions among war and military service narratives is as befuddling as trying to make sense of what happened on a particular battlefield. For Laura Marcus, autobiography is an inherently instable, hybrid, and transgressive genre, "a site of struggle."[13] Accounts of the interaction between self and a militant culture epitomize this characterization, as the textual sites of struggle depict actual moments of life-and-death struggles in the extremely ambivalent moral context that is war.

As a mechanism for exploring the variety of kinds of texts and authors out there, the remainder of this introduction will examine further the troublesome issue of genre through two perspectives: the status and the intention of the author, and the form of the text.

Authorial Status and Intention

Let me begin with a famous example—Ernest Hemingway, who, as scholars are quick to assert at academic conferences and in print, was never even a soldier, never a veteran. Those six weeks in 1918 as a Red Cross ambulance driver on the Italian front lines, the argument goes, no more qualify him than does his time as a war correspondent (and occasional combatant) in the next world war. But compare Hemingway's Great War experience with that of Edward W. Wood Jr., a World War II soldier and author of the memoir *On Being Wounded.* A nineteen-year-old enlisted infantryman, Private Eddie Wood "shipped out" to France in August 1944, where he joined Patton's Third Army driving toward Germany after the liberation of Paris. Eddie reached the front, just west of the Moselle River, on September 6—and on September 6 Eddie left the front and the war for good, shrapnel from an artillery shell having penetrated into his brain and blown off a large portion of his rear end. He had fired one round from his rifle into a haze in the vague direction of the enemy. He had been in-country less than a month and in combat a matter of minutes, less time in both cases than Hemingway, yet we would never dispute Private Wood's status as a soldier, or that of the multitudes of armed service members who never found themselves within range of enemy guns.[14]

Hemingway's later role as war correspondent in the Spanish Civil War and World War II can also be read against his experiences in the Great War. His was an identity so much formed in war that he could look at later wars only as a soldier and veteran—and the personal nature of his war dispatches has long been recognized. Similarly, Anthony Lloyd's first-person, book-length reportage of the 1990s Balkan wars, *My War Gone By I Miss It So* (1999), is as much about his experience fighting—or rather of not fighting—in the Persian Gulf War. War correspondents are firsthand witnesses *and participants:* they interact with the soldiers, form relationships with them; they risk their lives; they observe events from a different vantage; they sometimes get involved in the action, tending to the wounded, getting in the way, even sometimes firing off a couple of rounds (Hemingway and Michael Herr both admitted to firing weapons as correspondents).[15] The line between journalists and soldiers is particularly complicated when the journalist wears a military uniform, as was the case with most American correspondents in World War II (Hemingway included); such journalism can slip or be pushed into propaganda (another kind of weapon).

We can also consider journalism as a form of memoir even when it does not employ a first-person voice, if we recognize the piece's ultimate subjectivity and if we observe the convention that memoirs always concern others. Gloria Emerson's journalistic *Winners and Losers: Battles, Retreats, Gains, Losses, and Ruins from the Vietnam War* (winner of the 1978 National Book Award) gathers and narrates Emerson's interviews with American and Vietnamese participants and witnesses, then recasts them as third-person prose stories, without ever sacrificing her own voice, opinions, and persona. A particularly poignant instance of the autobiographical nature of a war reporter's dispatches involves the only change an editor made to Ernie Pyle's famous report on the death of Captain Waskow.

Watching the soldiers in Waskow's company come down the mountain in Italy and pay their respects, one by one, to the leader they had loved, had moved Pyle to write a sentence that was stricken prior to publication: "You feel ashamed to be alive."

Along with the noncombatant war correspondent, the person in uniform who did not see combat, perhaps never even deployed to the theater of operations, also confuses and blurs the division between soldier and civilian. Daniel Hoffman's *Zone of the Interior: A Memoir, 1942–1947* (2000) recounts his World War II stateside assignment producing air force technical manuals while, off duty, studying to become a poet. The cover of the book shows the young Lieutenant Hoffman in his khaki uniform at his desk, writing, inkwell before him, cigarette in his mouth. Should we "count" Hoffman's book as a war memoir? A passage near the end of the book exhibits the war's influence on his sense of himself:

> While they were having their mettle and manhood tested in these terrible circumstances, seeing men blown to pieces, luckily surviving the deaths of their comrades, I had held a desk job in Ohio. I'd heard of the guilt felt by those who survived battles in which their buddies had died. Inevitably, a portion of guilt attached to my thoughts of how I'd been untested, untoughened, and unscathed. I felt the need to justify, if only to myself, my assignment, convince myself . . . that what I had done, too, had a part, however slight, in winning the war. Was what I had done as useful as what I might have been ordered and, perhaps, been able to do, had I, like these veterans, been in a combat unit? Perhaps as a rifleman or a fighter pilot I'd have had little or no effect on the outcome of battle. There was of course no way to know. I could not help but feel that my service in the Zone of the Interior had kept me from initiation into a maturity shared by some of my friends and many of my generation. There was a certain spiritual space between those who had been under fire, had seen men killed, had had to kill enemies, had tasted fear and survived, and those who had no such experiences. . . .
>
> I drew some consolation from the thought that I'd been placed in charge of a journal of knowledge essential to the Air Force's conduct of the war, helping to make possible the development of its planes, weapons, and all their systems. . . . This, I told myself, this must have counted for something [even if] my duties were essentially civilian in nature, harnessed to military needs.[16]

This passage from a man in uniform who supported the war brings to mind the writings of the 1980s by American men who had not gone to Vietnam and who now wondered whether, as the poet Michael Blumenthal has asked, the veterans "didn't turn out to be better *men*, in the best sense of the word." Milton J. Bates identifies such personal writing as a "genre"—"Viet Guilt Chic"—and locates it in the larger context of a generational "crisis of masculinity."[17] Does Hoffman's anxiety about his manhood follow this generation's lead—his memoir came out more than a decade later—or does it accurately record the feelings of his generation of male noncombatants and thus serve as evidence that this subgenre of war writing has a tradition of historical depth? How might autobiographical accounts by deserters—Terry Whitmore's *Memphis-Nam-Sweden: The Autobiography of a Black American Exile* (1971) or Jack Todd's *Desertion* (2001)—participate in this genre? Might these authors instead have found masculine agency and courage in the very act of obeying their principles and refusing to fight?[18]

Other wartime jobs that share the ambiguous position of the soldier-journalist and the home-front soldier are found in medical and religious services. Medical professionals might feel a conflict between their commitment to the preservation of life and the easing of suffering, and their service in an institution committed to the exact opposite. Military chaplains face a similar moral dilemma. In World War I, able-bodied American men working as ambulance drivers or nurses were very much considered "unmanly," and their association with "womanly" enterprises caused their sexual orientation to be questioned. On the other side of gender ambiguity during war are the narratives by women close to the front and by women who fought. In *The Cavalry Maiden* (1936), Nadezhda Dúrova tells her story of pretending to be a boy in order to fight in the Napoleonic Wars; *An Uncommon Soldier: The Civil War Letters of Sarah Rosetta Wakeman, Alias Private Lyons Wakeman, 153rd Regiment, New York State Volunteers* (1995) offers a North American instance of soldierly gender-passing.[19]

The lives and identities of civilians in the contested region, be they innocent citizens or relief workers or others, are often as affected by warfare raging around them, destroying their homes, killing family members, and displacing them, as exhibited by Nuha Al-Radi's *Baghdad Diaries: A Woman's Chronicle of War and Exile* (2003). Le Ly Haslip's *When Heaven and Earth Changed Places: A Vietnamese Woman's Journey from War to Peace* (1989) records her childhood and young adulthood in war-torn Vietnam; her *Child of War, Woman of Peace* (1993) is her postwar memoir. Other first-person nonfiction narratives of wartime childhood are Elizabeth Kim's *Ten Thousand Sorrows: The Extraordinary Journey of a Korean War Orphan* (2000), Loung Ung's *First They Killed My Father: A Daughter of Cambodia Remembers* (2000), Chanrithy Him's *When Broken Glass Floats: Growing Up under the Khmer Rouge* (2000), Magda Denes's *Castles Burning: A Child's Life in War* (1997), Gudrun M. Gsell's *A Time to Laugh, A Time to Weep: History Experienced: My Childhood Memories of Growing up during the Third Reich, World War II, and Foreign Military* (1998), and Carol Bly's *An Adolescent's Christmas: 1944* (1999).

Personal narratives by male soldiers' wives or beloveds probably constitute the most common kind of writing from people connected to war and the military by association. In general, the older the text of this kind, the more it is about the man and the less about the author herself. Examples of the wife's tale include Elizabeth Custer's *Boots and Saddles* (1885), Zoe Townshend's *An Officer's Wife* (1932), Vijaya Naravene's *The Uniform and I* (1969), and Doe Nair's *I Married the Army* (1991). In this volume, Bettina Hofmann's essay "American Women Writing Their Lives on the Vietnam War" discusses two other wife's tales, Marian Faye Novak's *Lonely Girls with Burning Eyes* (1991) and Sybil Stockdale's *In Love and War* (1990), cowritten with her husband Jim. Jennifer Sinor's included essay, "The Life Writing of a Military Child," tackles the peculiar problem of the American military child, whom she rhetorically treats as a "conscript" because the child did not volunteer to belong to the military culture. One of the most central themes of life writing, the writer's relationship to home, is absent for the military child, who moves every several years. Sinor's essay, which combines scholarly inquiry with personal reflections on her military childhood, reinforces the inextricability of the military child's identity with the military parent.

As a daughter of a U.S. Navy admiral and a student of mine in the late 1990s wrote in an essay:

> Our military ID was a free ticket almost anywhere on base. Without it you might as well just stay at home. To buy groceries, to buy gas, to go bowling, to go to the movies, to buy a sweatshirt, to go swimming; you showed your ID. Ironically, the ID card was not much of an identification of who you were, but who your father was. It had your father's name. It had your father's rank. It had your father's social security number. But it had your picture. In the military you were your father.

A number of autobiographical texts, notably James Carroll's *An American Requiem: God, My Father, and the War That Came between Us* (1996), revolve around the civilian child's relationship with the military parent. Mary Palevsky's *Atomic Fragments: A Daughter's Questions* (2000) explores Palevsky's search for answers about her parents' involvement in the development of the atomic bomb during World War II; in its inquiry into the lives of her parents, it resembles Mary Gordon's *The Shadow Man* (1996), which traces Gordon's investigation into the life of her father, a spy during World War II and the Cold War.[20] Often the child of a military parent joins the military, and their autobiographies, like Lewis B. Puller Jr.'s Pulitzer-winning *Fortunate Son* (1990) and Pat Conroy's *My Losing Season* (2002), are simultaneously narratives of the military child and of the soldier.

Who else? There are those civilians at the home front without a spouse, child, or parent in the war who nevertheless write about their experiences of the war—Mary McCarthy's collected personal essays on Vietnam, *The Seventeenth Degree* (1974); and Norman Mailer's third-person autobiographical *Armies of the Night* (1968). We also have veterans themselves writing autobiographically about experiences not in wartime, for surely the war has colored their ideas about themselves. Samuel Hynes is the perfect example here. His *The Growing Seasons: An American Boyhood before the War* (2003) appeared after his war memoir *Flights of Passage: Reflections of a WWII Aviator* (1998), not to mention his two books of criticism about war, *A War Imagined: The First World War and English Culture* (1992) and of course *The Soldiers' Tale* (1997).

Do the narratives of spies "count"? War protestors? Terrorists? Participants in the thirty-year-old international U.S. war on drugs? Survivors, witnesses, and rescuers of the September 11 attacks? In January 2002 President George W. Bush signed into law the Victims of Terrorism Relief Act, which provides substantial tax relief to families of those killed in the September 11 attacks and in the Oklahoma City bombing, the latter an act of "domestic terrorism" perpetrated by Timothy McVeigh. That these tax benefits are similar to those granted to families of American military personnel is perhaps the first official U.S. act that blurs the line between soldier and civilian. Terrorism, of course, is a phenomenon with which other parts of the globe are much more intimate. In order to establish whom we can consider commentators on war, armed conflict, or military service, we have to establish what we can consider as war, armed conflict, and military service. The answers to this question are usually political; one group's war is another group's terrorism, one group's professional army is another group's guerilla band. These distinctions matter—it should matter to our reading, for example, if the author of a war narrative was a conscript, draftee, volunteer, or mercenary. The role of the author and the conflict or period of service just might influence the form the writing takes.

The author's intention and purpose for the work also contribute to his or her narrative's shape and form. Samuel Hynes, for example, does not bother to distinguish between memoir and autobiography; instead, he places all forms under the umbrella term "personal narrative." But he does recognize "two principal kinds" of personal war narratives, "correspond[ing] to two quite different needs: the need to report and the need to remember." He then associates each of these needs with particular prose forms: "The reporting instinct operates as war happens, and appears in journals and diaries and letters. . . . Memoirs are another, more complex kind of personal narrative: reflective, selective, more self-consciously constructed than the immediate reports, an old self looking back."[21] Objections to this scheme leap to mind. First, not all memoirs are complex, reflective, or self-conscious, and memoirs written soon after the experience hardly qualify as those of "an old self looking back." Indeed this definition does not address the traditional distinction between memoir and autobiography, the former being "only an anecdotal depiction of people and events" without much introspection and the latter an "evocation of a life as a totality" (though this distinction has its problems too, as discussed later).[22] Second, the prose forms that Hynes associates with the need to report—journals, diaries, and letters—we could easily associate instead with the need to remember. Such writing can be selective, and it can certainly be reflective and self-conscious. A line from one of my own letters from the Persian Gulf War is maddeningly self-conscious and selective: "I will not describe what happened these last few days."

I do agree, however, with Hynes's instinct to associate genres with authorial intent (whatever form the text takes). An aspiring young author freshly home from war, for example, might see his or her memoir as a writing career's first step, as a way of getting published, of getting noticed, of getting practice—of preparing for the next book. Robert Graves, as Fussell notes, wrote *Good-bye to All That* to pave the way financially for his next books, and that motivation very much shaped its content and style, as in it Graves tried to include "the 'ingredients' of a popular memoir."[23] T. E. Lawrence's *Revolt in the Desert* was also intended in part as a moneymaker (see Terry Reilly's essay, "T. E. Lawrence, Modernism, and Cultural Poetics," in this volume). Anthony Swofford, a graduate of the famed Iowa Writer's Workshop, drew on his experiences in the first Gulf War for his first book *Jarhead* (2003). As Elisabeth Piedmont-Marton demonstrates in this volume, Swofford's memoir struggles to free itself from the style of Vietnam narratives.[24] It can only be assumed that General Fred Franks agreed to coauthor his Gulf War memoir *Into the Storm: A Study in Command* (1997) with Tom Clancy, a fiction writer whose work had been extremely successful commercially, in order to make his retirement from the military financially more comfortable. Franks, who holds an M.A. degree in English from Columbia University, could have easily written his story himself and would done a much better job; the result of his collaboration with Clancy is a bumbling mess, poorly written by any standards, the two supposedly separate voices often bizarrely conflated.[25]

Into the Storm also reflects another purpose of the military memoir—setting straight the historical record. Franks had received a lot of criticism for the slowness of the advance of his VII Corps into Iraq, and in his book he hoped to explain and justify his actions and to confute his critics. In writing his story, he was attempting to write history. Indeed generals and civilian leaders know their narratives will be heavily scrutinized by their peers and by future historians. So while these authors enjoy the advantage over the common soldier of having infinitely more information, especially the kind that is of value to historians, they also have agendas. They can comment on debates over strategy, they can reveal military secrets, but they also attempt to make, protect, or correct their reputations. Often the battle narratives written by leaders suggest a coherence, order, and cause-effect linearity that—given the chaos of battle—hints at a degree of imposed fictionality. As far back as Caesar, as John Keegan's *The Face of Battle* (1976) observes, the "historical" accounts written by leaders have simplified battles, out of the practical necessity of command and control (and for political and self-promoting reasons). As historical sources, their memoirs are paradoxically both invaluable and unreliable. And, they rarely undergo the literary critic's scrutiny; we prefer the more expressive and personal writing—also invaluable and unreliable—of the men and women who were there.

Literary scholars ignore leaders' texts for any number of reasons. That in recent years some of these books appear to have been produced for mass consumption and so verge on being "mere" popular literature hardly explains the critical neglect. There are deeper reasons. Hynes omits them from his study because he is interested in the men who do the fighting, and in modern war, certainly, the leaders do not often make it to the front; besides, "the story of command is its own subject" (xvi). (For a classic exception, we have Xenophon's *Anabasis*, on which see, in this volume, John Lee's "Xenophon and the Origins of Military Lifewriting"; Jeffrey Loeb's essay briefly touches on Colin Powell's 1995 *An American Journey*.) Leaders' texts typically offer themselves as historical documents rather than personal narratives; to the literary scholar the historical debates and issues, and the language itself, can be foreign. Such works do not seem to qualify as expressive works deserving of humanist attention; we would prefer to valorize the relatively powerless and voiceless majority that has borne the lion's share of war's tragedies. Sympathizing with the suffering of the common participant is also politically safer, analogous to "supporting the troops" without supporting or even having a solid opinion (or understanding) of the operation. Yet leaders' memoirs can be studied for their rhetorical and literary interest. What is Robert McNamara's *In Retrospect* (1995), after all, but an apologia, a political version of Augustine's *Confessions?*

As for Hynes's "soldiers' tale" genre, the soldiers fighting the battles also frequently write to correct the official histories. Their memoirs regularly accuse superiors of not understanding the battlefield situation. The stories told by frontline troops have the authenticity of the work of amateur writers without literary or historical reputations to make or protect; the authenticity of attempts to express what cannot *not* be told; the authenticity of the special knowledge of people who have faced death.[26] These authors rarely have knowledge beyond their fields of vision, and their narratives suffer the limitations of human memory operating through the fog of battle and the haze of years. Yet to imply that they lack the motivation, investment, or ability to craft narratives, to spin both the presented facts and the presented self, not only seems the height of educated arrogance but reinforces the image of these men as passive-vessel memoirists. Like the leader's tale, the soldier's autobiographical account often tries to explain and justify actions, to testify how history actually unfolded—as exemplified in the detailed subtitle of Robert E. Gajdusek's *Resurrection, a War Journey: A Chronicle of Events during and following the Attack on Fort Jeanne d'Arc at Metz, France, by F Company of the 379th Regiment of the 95th Infantry Division, November 14–21, 1944* (1997).

Also, of course, the author's intended audience makes a difference. It matters whether one's account is serialized in *Ladies Home Journal*, appears in a veteran's magazine like *The Southern Bivouac* or an online discussion forum read primarily by other veterans, or is targeted at children, like *Farewell to Manzanar* (1973), Jeanne Wakatsuki's account of her internment as a Japanese American.[27] Other significant audiences include other and future members of the military and of the corporate world—I make this odd pairing because in both cases the authors want to communicate lessons learned, to share valuable professional insights and tips. My own war produced a number of examples of each, such as Joseph C. Barto III's first-person account *Task Force 2–4 Cav—"First In, Last Out": The History of the 2d Squadron, 4th Cavalry Regiment during Operation Desert Storm*, published by the U.S. Army's Combat Studies Institute (1993). There were also a slew of articles based on personal experience in professional military journals, as well as books like General William G. Pagonis's *Moving Mountains: Lessons in Leadership and Logistics from the Gulf War* (1992), published by the Harvard Business School Press. Behind Pagonis's war "memoir," written for business people, is the practical sensibility that drives much military retrospection, reducing experience to instructive vignettes and applicable principles. In some cases, the author does not write solely for a military readership and future combatants, yet the text seems fated for such use. Over recent decades, U.S. military cadets and officers have read Charles MacDonald's *Company Commander* (1947) and James McDonough's *Platoon Leader* (1985), texts few literary critics have read, much less analyzed. It is as if members of the literary culture and the military culture inevitably read and value different sets of personal war narratives.

If the author's intention for the work helps shape its form, knowledge of personal narrative forms and their conventions also shapes intentions and content. Healthy criticism must consider both constitutive dimensions of the autobiographical text.

The Form of the Text

The unpublished personal narrative of a great uncle of mine, mostly treating his military service in World War I, begins with a dedication to his wife followed by a two-page letter to his grandson, complete with block addresses, date, salutation, and signature. Near the end of this letter portion of the manuscript, he tells his grandson his purpose in writing:

> If you find an occasional event that seems to indicate good common horse sense, perhaps these will make this account worth reading. This possibility is one of the main reasons for writing this chronicle. Another is the belief that every person is entitled to know something

of those who have preceded him up the family tree. We live too far apart for you to learn much about me through daily association, so I offer this letter as a substitute. . . . I wish you luck, patience and a certain amount of pleasure in the reading.

On the next page, the main text body opens with the memoir form's conventional statement about the time and circumstances of the author's birth. One hundred seventeen single-spaced, typed, legal-sized pages later, it ends by slipping back into correspondence mode:

It is good that you and Ralph are coming out this summer for a longer visit than you usually can make. . . . In another five years when your dad becomes eligible for another long vacation, we might not be able to get together. You will be fifteen, and Fay and I will be crowding eighty. So we are planning to make the most of our opportunities this summer.

Ever since you can remember, we have had brief glimpses of each other when we came to visit you at Christmas and when [you] came out here during the summer. I am hoping this letter may help to fill in some of the blank spaces in your knowledge of your granddad, what he was like and how he got to be the way he is today.

The final line, "So long," is followed, again as in a letter, by the author's signature.

Do we consider this narrative a memoir or a letter? The distinction is finally impossible, because it's neither and it's both. There are probably hundreds if not thousands of similar documents around the world. As with any literary genre, autobiographical forms blend, overlap, and sometimes defy generic classification altogether. Uncle Clint's narrative is a conspicuous example; most texts are more subtle in form, and narratives about war and military experience especially confuse the issue. A piece of journalism can look a lot like propaganda or a lot like a personal essay, while a memoir by a general or diplomat can concern itself mostly with historical rather than personal matters (presuming for the sake of this argument that we can make such a distinction)—think of Caesar's histories. Frequently survivors turn their wartime diaries, journals, and letters into memoirs, making for a peculiar blend of the diurnal and the reflective.

Given the inevitable blurring of genres, one must assay distinctions anyway. A war correspondent's collection of published dispatches is not the same thing as a war correspondent's continuous postwar memory and reflection. A memoir is not an oral history, and we cannot analyze them in terms of each other without accounting for the differences in the occasion of their creation (primarily between the motivation and control of the memoirist and those of the oral historian). To treat such texts identically is truly to compare narrative apples and oranges.

Autobiography and Memoir

The genesis for this book occurred when I was asked to write an entry for "Military Autobiography" for Margaretta Jolly's *Encyclopedia of Life Writing* (2001). This would seem a relatively straightforward assignment, except that the encyclopedia was to have a separate entry for "War Memoir," and I had therefore somehow to distinguish the two.[28] The "Military Autobiography" genre fell under the encyclopedia's larger categorization of "Career" narratives, and while we do have a few narratives that encompass the life and career of a professional member of the military (like Debra J. Dickerson's *An American Story* [2000] and Len Maffiolo's *Grown Gray in War: The Len Maffioli Story* [1997, with Bruce H. Norton]), the vast majority of primary material focuses, naturally, on wartime experiences. One might think, for example, that Omar Bradley's *A Soldier's Story* would address his entire career in uniform; instead, it recounts only his role in World War II.

The traditional distinction cited above sees autobiography as "evocation of a life as a totality" and memoir as "only an anecdotal depiction of people and events," without much introspection.[29] The inadequacies of this general distinction are well established, and they trouble war and military personal narratives as well. To read General Winfield Scott's *Memoirs* (1864), you would hardly know the man was married or had a life outside the army; his text covers his lifetime of military service but in the end reads as merely anecdotal. Any number of autobiographies by career soldiers share this lack of totality. Conversely, a fair portion of memoirs— like Tim O'Brien's meditative *If I Die in a Combat Zone, Box Me Up and Ship Me Home* (1975)—do much more than anecdotally depict people and events. This traditional distinction also tends to limit the memoir to a specific period of time as opposed to autobiography's life in totality; this distinction poses not only a general problem for classifying texts but a notable problem for war writings. Using this distinction, neither the entry "War Memoir" nor "Military Autobiography" would capture the postwar war memoir—like Henriette Roosenburg's *The Walls Came Down* (1957), which recounts the journey of four political prisoners, liberated by the Soviet army at the end of World War II, from Germany to their Holland home; or

Dana Sach's *The House on Dream Street: Memoir of an American Woman in Vietnam* (2000), which one reviewer has described as an "artfully written, anecdotal account of three separate visits to Hanoi before relations between Vietnam and the United States were normalized in 1995." The account possesses, the reviewer believes, a peculiar tension: "Sach persists in reminding us of the war even as she fails to find vestiges of its legacy either in her personal life or in present-day Hanoi."[30] Also, neither "War Memoir" nor "Military Autobiography" by title alone implies inclusion of accounts of relatively short periods of military service other than war, like Henry O. Flipper's *The Colored Cadet at West Point* (1878),[31] autobiographies by one-war citizen-soldiers, accounts by associational military members (that is, spouses and children), or autobiographies by civilians profoundly affected by a war.

In defining "Military Autobiography" as distinct from "War Memoir," I took advantage of Hynes's observation in *The Soldiers' Tale* that war memoirs frequently treat the war as a discontinuity in the author's life, an episode disconnected from what came before and what followed after. Any work that provides significant treatment of a person's life beyond the temporal bounds of the war and that somehow involves military service, then, become fair game. The resulting definition: military autobiography "consists of those continuous nonfiction personal narratives that present a life lived largely in or around professional military service; that include a short-term military experience as an important element of a life not otherwise spent in or around the military; or that recount experiences of military life other than war."[32] This solution allowed me to capture most narratives not understood strictly as war memoirs, yet it too has its shortcomings. It obviously excludes alternate forms of life writing (letters, diaries, oral histories) covering nonwar periods, and it has trouble dealing with texts like Indian-captivity narratives and texts by irregular soldiers (guerillas, resistance fighters, partisans, rebels, terrorists).

To the extent that memoirs conventionally record lives of others as opposed to the first-person authors, they very nearly become biographies (or even journalistic accounts). Since at least the turn of the twentieth century, literary critics have also been aware of the degree to which standard biographies have autobiographical dimensions; expressions of the biographer's subjectivity and idiosyncrasies cannot but be present. W. D. Ehrhart's 1999 *Ordinary Lives: Platoon 1005 and the Vietnam War* is "a series of profiles that follows, through Vietnam and beyond, the lives of those young Marines with whom Ehrhart trained at Parris Island in 1966,"[33] and thus it clearly and consciously blurs the line between biography and autobiography as well as between war memoir and military autobiography. In a sense, Ehrhart's book participates and extends the older, pre-twentieth-century memoir tradition. As Helen M. Buss notes, "In the 18th century memoirs were seen as more biographical than they are today . . . [such that] memoir and biography were not always distinguished from one another . . . [j]ust as in the nineteenth century . . . memoirs were more aligned with historical discourses, and the memoirs of generals, explorers, and politicians were often accepted as histories."[34] The development of military autobiography naturally parallels the development of autobiography in general, which did not fully flower until the twentieth century. As Robert Lawson-Peebles discusses in his essay "Style Wars: The Problems of Writing Military Autobiography in the Eighteenth Century," in this volume, authors of that period worked with an entirely different set of conventions when they sat down to write about war and military service.[35]

James Salter has negotiated the tricky autobiography-memoir distinction by giving the subtitle *Recollections* to his book-length autobiographical narrative *Burning the Days* (1997). As his preface declares:

> This book is more or less the story of a life. Not the complete story which, as in almost any case, is beyond telling—the length would be too great, longer than Proust, not to speak of the repetition. What I have done is to write about people and events that were important to me. . . . I found it difficult, more perhaps than will be apparent, to write about myself. I had, as will be shown in the second chapter, come to believe that self was not the principal thing, and I lived that way for a long time.

Like a memoir, *Burning the Days* claims to focus on other people and events, leaving out more than half the material its author could possibly have included; like an autobiography, it is "more or less the story of a life," requiring of its author wearying self-revelation that halted the writing "for months" and delayed the publication for eight years—though Salter succeeds brilliantly at writing about himself.[36] Scholars of autobiographical writing have long known that "autobiography" and "memoir" are hardly straightforward, simple terms, and this brief case study of personal writing about war and the military has reiterated the larger theoretical conclusion. Before considering other forms of autobiographical texts, however, there is an alternative reading—a gendered reading—of the war memoir–military autobiography split.

In her *Auto/Biographical Discourses: Theory, Criticism, Practice,* Laura Marcus offers a theoretical approach whereby we

> read the memoirs/autobiography, passive/active relationship as more than a convenient way of classifying literary forms; it becomes a statement about the individual's power. . . . The writers of memoirs . . . efface themselves within the histories they observe and record. It is no accident that women have tended to write "memoirs" rather than "autobiographies," and that the memoir-form has been consistently belittled in autobiographical criticism . . . [revealing] the extent to which the autobiography/memoirs distinction is bound up with issues of power and powerlessness.[37]

In other words, autobiographers write their lives, they compose, they assert, they control; historically, they have been for the most part men. Memoirists, on the other hand, merely record, serving in effect as vessels of transmission; historically, as Marcus notes, these vessels have been for the most part women—or rather, women *and soldiers.*

As Philip Caputo succinctly reminds us in his Vietnam memoir *A Rumor of War* (1977), war is about what war does to men as well as what men do in war. To the degree that men perceive "being done to" as passivity, impotence, and dependence, they have historically equated it on some level as emasculating and hence feminizing. This is something of a cliché, of course, the sort of thinking that leads us to conclude that Ernest Hemingway's career of displaying his manhood resulted from his unmanning war wound. As with most clichés, however, it has its merit. Men in uniform have always found themselves subordinated, acted upon, subjected to the results of other's imposed wills—dependent, passive, even domesticated.

Applying Marcus's conceit of the womanly memoirist, then, veterans in the very act of writing memoirs, and even as they try to become the authors of their lives by writing the memoirs, relive their experience not merely through memory but also by literally reinscribing, through the memoir form, their position of relative powerlessness and passivity. Hynes's book carries a telling subtitle: *Bearing Witness to Modern War.* Furthermore, this conceit provides a basis for another speculation as to why the authors of soldier narratives, according to Hynes, divorce this period from their larger sense of themselves—because they must separate or textually enclose that brief moment when the war wrote their lives from the majority of their lives for which they have control, for which they are the "manly" authors. They must lock the madwoman—the shell-shocked, "hysterical" self—in the attic. The widespread practice of male soldier-writers presenting their war experiences in novel form rather than memoir form might also speak to their resistance to their feminized soldiering selves, as novels (at least since World War I) have been considered the more manly art. By transforming their experience into fiction, however superficially, they reassert a degree of artistic control, of autonomy, of power.[38]

Autobiographical Essays

One elementary way of regarding an autobiographical or personal essay is as a short first-person nonfiction narrative—as, in other words, a shorter version of the autobiography-memoir form. As they appear in military history magazines and popular magazines, such pieces are often direct reminiscences, sometimes with political or historiographic commentary. After the Civil War, veterans regularly published such pieces in *The Southern Bivouac;* one of the latest forums to appear is *The Viet Nam Generation Journal,* which debuted in April 2001. Personal essays also, instead of primarily telling a story, frequently follow the tradition of literary-belletristic essays. This form reflects, considers, and wonders, and it dips into memories of war and the military as needed to sustain the contemplative flow. But such a dichotomy of essay types mirrors the traditional distinction between memoir and autobiography; it falls short as a definition for precisely the same reasons. Fussell's essays "My War" and "Thank God for the Atom Bomb" might appear to exemplify the reminiscent and the reflective modes, respectively, but both essays contain some of each. The essays in John Keegan's short *War and Our World* (1998) are historical and philosophic reflections, yet the author's strong presence and voice edges this book toward something more familiar.[39]

Length also seems an insufficient criterion. How many words makes a thing an essay versus an autobiography? Gray's *The Warriors: Reflections on Men in Battle* (1959) is a perfect example of a nonfiction first-person prose book that uses personal memories of war but is organized as an extended, reflective essay rather than an autobiography or memoir. Though the book does have a certain progression, each of Gray's seven chapters can stand alone as an essay on the topic of its title: "Remembering War and Forgetfulness," "The Enduring Appeals of Battle," "Love: War's Ally and Foe," "The Soldier's Relations to Death," "Images of the Enemy," "The Ache of Guilt," and "The Future of War." As essays, these chapters explore their topics and draw conclusions using whatever evidence they can, be it from Gray's own experiences in World War II or his readings in history, literature, and philosophy. Chris Hedges's *War Is a Force That Gives Us Meaning* (2002) similarly incorporates Hedges's personal experience as a war correspondent in what is primarily an essayistic study on war's appeal and meaning.

Other examples include two books by U.S. veterans of the war in Vietnam, Tobias Wolff's *In Pharaoh's Army* (1994) and Pat C. Hoy II's *Instinct for Survival* (1992). Wolff's book, as noted by Lydia Fakundiny in Jolly's *Encyclopedia of Life Writing*, is essentially an essay collection that sustains the spirit of a continuous book-length autobiographical narrative.[40] Hoy's book is both more formally an essay collection and more fully autobiographical in terms of the life covered—from his Arkansas childhood and family legacy, his twenty-year military career, his own family, and his second career as a teacher and writer. Such books might also best be described and classified according to Michel Beajour's idea of the nonnarrative "self-portrait," in contrast to continuous autobiographical narratives.[41]

Finally, essays suffer the same complications as longer narrative forms in terms of status and intention of the authors. William Styron's "A Case of the Great Pox" (1995) recollects an incident in a peacetime army garrison, and Frederick Busch's "My Father's War" (1998) treats the author's relationship with his father, a World War II veteran.[42] A book of previously published war correspondence by a single author—say, Martha Gellhorn—combines features of both journalism and essay collection.

Oral Histories

The oral history is a wonderful tool for capturing the recollections and reflections of people either unable or not inspired to write them down. Christian G. Appy's *Patriots: The Vietnam War Remembered from All Sides* (2003), demonstrates the form's capacity to canvass as many perspectives as possible, from civilian and military leaders to the lowest-ranking soldiers, to affected civilians. Yet the rhetorical situation of oral histories means that we cannot read them the same way we read other forms of personal narratives. Conducted as an interview, with the historian providing prompts, oral histories follow specific conventions, and respondents have varying expectations. Whereas a memoirist might find it appropriate to provide "confessional" details of romantic or sexual relationships before, during, or after the war in question, the oral history respondent might find deeply personal material inappropriate for the occasion. Stanley

Rosenberg's "The Threshold of Thrill: Life Stories in the Skies over Southeast Asia" (1993) contrasts the memoirs of combat pilots from World War II from the oral histories of combat pilots of the American war in Vietnam. Rosenberg finds that women "fade entirely into the background in these [latter] oral histories." In other words, World War II pilot-memoirists relate sexual and romantic adventures, whereas Vietnam era pilot–oral history respondents did not. Though both the memoir and oral history are versions of the autobiographical mode, we cannot ignore the difference in the rhetorical circumstances between a person's authoring a narrative over time utilizing the traditional literary-confessional conventions of the memoir form, and a person's fielding specific questions about his tour of duty during a recorded interview.[43]

The memoirist has time to recall memories, can refer to other resources to refresh the memory, can reconsider and rewrite passages over and over—all options unavailable to the oral history respondent. Yet the oral historian is as much the "author" as the respondent. The historian asks the questions and drives each interview to its conclusion, then edits and assembles the histories. Most available oral histories are published collections, which the historian-editor has selected, excerpted, and arranged—he or she gives it its shape and determines its focus and message. We must be as suspicious of the editor and the ideologies behind oral histories as we are of those of collections of letters.[44]

Diurnal Forms

Letters and diaries (journals) constitute unique subsets of autobiographical narratives with their own attendant theoretical discourses. For Fussell, continuous narrative forms of autobiographical writing—autobiographies and memoirs—cannot escape "the necessity of fiction," because, written after the fact, even if by authors with perfect memory, their very structure is an imposition on the actual events. "The further personal written materials move from the form of the daily dairy," he writes, "the closer they approach the figurative and the fictional."[45] Thus diurnal forms of autobiographical writing promise the most faithful historical record of the individual's experience. The form itself, in certain situations, can also carry immense significance. As Lynn Z. Bloom discusses in "Women's Confinement as Women's Liberation: World War II Civilian Internees in South Pacific Camps," in this volume, the act of composing becomes, for internees for whom keeping a diary was forbidden, an act of resistance and defiance, of extreme risk, of self-assertion and definition. Andrea Peterson's

"War Diaries and Journals" entry in the *Encyclopedia of Life Writing* notes that in World War I, "British privates were forbidden to keep diaries on security grounds," so those who "disobeyed orders and kept diaries or sent diarized letters home" also practiced a form of resistance and self-definition. My own mother's letters to me during the Persian Gulf War are an interesting case as well, because much of their content was devoted to stories of her parents' and grandparents' lives, and of my own childhood; in other words, these letters had little to do with the war and yet would not exist had it not been for the war.

Reading diaries and letters is not without its complications, primarily because any published diary or letter collection undergoes an editing process, and editors have their own agendas. Margaretta Jolly's essay here, "Myths of Unity: Remembering the Second World War through Letters and their Editing," addresses three kinds of collected letters and the interests and ideologies shaping them: collections "presented as military history or war writing aimed for a popular readership"; books "edited by a relative of the letter-writer or the letter-writer themselves"; and collections "that have a scholarly conception . . . aimed at an academic audience and put together by academics for university presses." As she concludes, if the initial letters themselves "construct fantasies of identity and relationship" and are a kind of "creative writing" that can be "highly conventional," edited collections only exacerbate the ideological complexities involved. While published letters and diaries often include helpful clarifying notes (identifying people, locations, battles, objects), the annotating process too cannot escape the note maker's subjectivity. We should be especially wary of personal war accounts published during the early years of a war by or about an earlier war altogether. A Canadian, Conningsby Dawson, published in 1917 a collection of letters to his family, *The Glory of the Trenches*, that is as much a call for the United States to enter the war as it is a record of his experience (his father supposedly compiled and edited the book, complicating our identification of the propagandist).

What happens when a writer uses his or her letters or diary (or both) to assist in creating a memoir or autobiography? The result is perhaps, per Fussell, a product a little less fictional; yet the narrative still has an imposed structure, the diurnal writing was still carefully culled and, if incorporated into the final text, very likely edited. Nevertheless, the use of letters or a diary in this way has the potential to provide direct access to two voices: the one belonging to the self living through the experience, and the one belonging to the self, years later, thinking back. Andrea Peterson's essay "The Female Subject and the First World War: The Case of Vera M. Brittain, VAD London/268, BRCS" demonstrates how Brittain's *Testament of Youth* (1933) accomplished just this double-voicing and in the process demonstrated an understanding of female identity that prefigures today's feminist identity theory.[46]

Online Postings

Theoretical inquiry into the issues and implications of online autobiographical discourses has only just begun. The possible kinds of autobiographical material range from text-only site postings and discussion forum "conversations" to personal Web pages, with their additional possibilities of visual images, audio tracks, and video clips. Even the structure of personal Web sites can reveal identity constructions. Given the emergence of the Internet in the 1990s, most online autobiographies of whatever kind come from veterans of Vietnam and the Persian Gulf and current active-duty military personnel.

A number of Web sites feature personal narratives and invite visitors to post their own story. Two sites for the Vietnam War are *The Virtual Wall* and *Letters from the Heart,* the latter of which is associated with Barbara Sonneborn's 1998 documentary *Regret to Inform.* The History Channel's Web site has a "Veteran's Forum" page featuring eyewitness accounts, interviews with a different veteran each month, an ongoing discussion forum, and space for visitors to submit their stories.[47] Postings to a site or a discussion forum—they are usually short, composed in a single sitting, often in response to another posting and usually with no, or only minor, surface revisions—occupy an odd rhetorical position between private, immediate, diurnal narratives and published, public narratives, as they have a potentially unlimited audience of strangers. Readers of online narratives, like readers of published paperbound accounts, have no easy way to verify the authors' claims; the authenticity of at least one online autobiography, Phill Coleman's *Cannon Fodder,* has been questioned (see Jeff Loeb's "The African American Autobiography of the Viet Nam War," in this volume).

Online postings do have one advantage for veterans and other war survivors over other forms of personal narrative. Because postings usually take place within a virtual community and carry the protection of anonymity, they have a potential therapeutic value. Veterans can bond with others without making themselves vulnerable or uncomfortable. In a personal e-mail, Dan Moeur, a Vietnam veteran and an associate professor of anthropology at Virginia Commonwealth University, told me that his experience as the owner of the NAMVETS-L listserv has led him to conclude that veterans do in fact receive some therapeutic benefit from participating in the listserv.

Visual Forms

Autobiographical scholars in recent years have begun investigating visual presentation of identity and experience through collections of photographs, drawings, and even cartoons produced by an author. Two early military examples of this "form" are Alexander Gardner's *Photographic Sketchbook of the American Civil War 1861–1865* (1866) and Samuel Emery Chamberlain's *My Confession* (1956) a multimedia memoir about the Mexican-American War of the 1840s. Chamberlain made over 150 color paintings of his experience in Mexico, a good number of which accompanied his textual narrative. More modern examples include the photographic testimonies of Lee Miller's *Lee Miller's War* (1992), Robert Capa's *Slightly out of Focus* (1947), Werner Bischof's *After the War* (1997), and Tony Vaccaro's *Entering Germany 1944–1949* (2001). Bischof's book, and much of Vaccaro's, as their titles indicate, are really postwar war memoirs—or, better, postwar photographic war narratives (Vaccaro's covers the 1948 Berlin airlift).[48]

Ordinary Forms

Naval logbooks, incident reports, and other personal statements represent ordinary forms of personal narratives rarely considered by scholars. During Operation Desert Shield, I inscribed in the empty front and back pages of a Bible a number of quotations from the books I had read to fight my boredom. Arguably the sources and content of those quotations, from books like Robert Pirsig's *Zen and the Art of Motorcycle Maintenance*, constituted a form of resistance to (denial of?) my situation. Jennifer Sinor's essay touches on a number of other ordinary forms of non-narrative life writing, including lists, notes, drawings, scrapbooks, school assignments, and even play narratives that are documented or recorded. These texts inscribe a moment in a life; to eliminate them from consideration is to eliminate the very kind of writing those like military children produce.

History

According to Phyllis Lassner, catalogues and bookstores categorize personal narratives of World War II "by soldiers and military and political leaders, usually shelved under World War II; by concentration camp and death camp victims and survivors, listed under the Holocaust; and writing of home front experience, usually by women, under Women's Studies or, more generally, autobiography." Such divisions "create a sense of different wars within this one totality." Holocaust and home-front narratives, Lassner rightly argues, should be considered "not as marginal, but as central to the meanings of the war and its literary heritage"—Winston Churchill's and Charles de Gaulle's accounts of the Second World War provide an "incomplete" historical understanding.[49] Lassner's demand that we consider texts by the little people (the soldier and sailor as well as the spouse, child, and civilian) is not new, nor has it gone unheeded; in fact, as we have noted, the overwhelming majority of criticism on war and military autobiographical writing concerns just such authors. Texts like Churchill's and de Gaulle's rarely appear on the literary scholar's radar screen; critically speaking, theirs are the marginalized voices.

But I do not want to belabor a point made earlier. Instead, I'd like to offer other ways of thinking historically about personal narratives. Two presentations at the 2002 "War Memoirs" conference at Graceland University in Independence, Missouri, mined personal narratives for evidence of general historical attitudes toward a particular subject. Paul Thomas Dean of Washington State University examined World War I doughboy letters to determine the extent to which these soldiers engaged the war rhetoric of President Woodrow Wilson (and found that they did not). James E. Davis of Illinois College interrogated personal narratives by white Union and Confederate soldiers of the American Civil War about their authors' views on blacks and slavery. In addition, we need to consider when the texts were authored. Personal narratives written at some chronological distance from the events suffer distortions from lost memories as well as from gained historical (and cultural) perspectives. Witness-participants writing during a conflict—even if their own participation has concluded—do not know the outcome. Witness-participants writing decades later not only know the outcome but have absorbed any number of interpretations of the events, which doubtless influence their writing. They have absorbed not just interpretations of events, but events themselves. In assembling my own coauthored war memoir, I conducted a fair amount of research about the war and my place in it, with the result that the reader has significantly more strategic and operational knowledge while reading than I ever had while deployed. It's fair to say that this historical information actually fictionalizes the text.

The anthropologist Lawrence Keeley has observed that the myth of a human "pacified past," of a primitive kind of warfare that was merely ritualistic and relatively harmless, "originated in the period immediately following World War II," a period marked by "a pervasive and profound odium for everything connected with warfare."[50] Comparing autobiographical accounts of atrocities in World War II and Vietnam, Cornelius A. Cronin finds less difference in "the nature of the actions" than in the perception of them "by those performing them." World War II American writers tend to dismiss atrocities—namely, the murdering of POWs—as merely part of war, justified within the context of the larger evil the perpetrators found themselves combating. The disturbing ease with which one particular writer dismisses such war crimes makes one wonder how many other such events were never recorded: "Company G committed a war crime," Cronin quotes. "They are going to win the war, however, so I don't suppose it really matters." No details. End of episode. Vietnam veterans who witnessed atrocities and later wrote about them instead call attention to the act and their own moral accountability. Cronin explains the difference in two ways. First, soldiers going to Vietnam, especially in the latter half of the war, questioned everything about the war from the outset, whereas soldiers in the world wars accepted their war much less critically. Second,

> what separates Caputo's Vietnam soldiers from the soldiers of World War II is this doubleness, this clear sense that evil and good are inextricably mixed in war, and that the soldiers must see themselves as individuals capable of acting and therefore capable of performing evil actions. World War I and II soldiers tended to see themselves as passive, as being acted upon by the war and their societies.[51]

The soldiers of the world wars therefore escaped accountability by the nature of their particular wars. It makes sense that memoirs written shortly after World War II shy away from sexual adventures or wartime atrocities by "good guys," whereas those written decades later, after Vietnam, the sexual revolution, and the subsequent liberation of literary material, might not feel such a reluctance. Along with social mores, literary practices also change over the years: Michael Herr's *Dispatches* (1977) and Robert E. Gajdusek's *Resurrection* (1944) could have only been written after the invention and establishment of postmodern narratives.

Propaganda

Journalistic reportage is often referred to as "history's first draft," and it sometimes shares the memoir-as-history's impulse to influence opinion. First-person journalism rarely escapes the propagandist urge, either to celebrate the cause and the heroes or to damn the enterprise altogether. John Steinbeck's literary mission of dramatizing the struggles of the working class in middle and western America takes an unusual turn in *Bombs Away*, his 1942 celebration of the training and skill of ordinary Americans going to war. *Bombs Away* qualifies as book-length journalism, as Steinbeck follows a bomber squad through their training, but its role as propaganda is undeniable. If personal narratives by definition admit their subjectivity, personal narratives serving as propaganda espouse assertions as objective and absolute truth, and slant evidence accordingly—a fact that, for the most cynical critic, qualifies such works as pure fiction. For the less cynical critic, such works verge on the fictional perhaps only slightly more than any other highly subjective personal account. Still, the line between heavily propagandistic nonfiction work and heavily propagandistic fiction can seem so fine that both might more profitably be considered merely propaganda. As one contemporary critic charged, Edith Wharton's novel *A Son at the Front* is "a belated essay in propaganda."[52]

Fictional Renditions

What motivates a writer to present an essentially autobiographical story as fiction? There is actually something of a tradition of dressing up memoirs as fiction in war narratives—Fussell's *The Great War and Modern Memory* discusses both Graves's and Siegfried Sassoon's books in this way, and though Hynes's study avoids "fiction that clearly is fiction" it includes "narratives that are obviously factual but adopt the transparent disguise of invented names" (xv). In 1975, a year before Fussell's seminal study appeared, Peter Aichinger's 1975 *The American Soldier in Fiction, 1880–1963* not only acknowledged this tradition but made a postmodern challenge to readers who think they can clearly distinguish between fiction and nonfiction:

> Furthermore, there is a strong tendency in war literature for memoirs and works of reminiscence to encroach upon the field of pure fiction. It is impossible to clearly separate works like *The Enormous Room* or Robert Graves's *Goodbye to All That*, which are based on factual experiences, from novels such as Leon Uris's *Battle Cry* that are ostensibly fictitious. The whole problem is further complicated by the rise of works of reportage which overlap areas of both memoir and fiction. John Hersey's *Hiroshima* and William Bradford Huie's *The Execution of Private Slovik* are only two of the works that fall into this category. To separate these various works into rigid categories

would be exceedingly difficult and serve no purpose. From this it can be seen that the term "war novel" is a rather loose one; yet it permits a degree of flexibility that is very useful in dealing with war literature as a whole.[53]

What are we to do with Michael Herr's crazy new journalistic *Dispatches* (1977)? Or with Lê Thi Diem Thúy's novel *The Gangster We Are All Looking For* (2003), parts of which previously appeared as nonfiction? Or with T. E. Lawrence's *Seven Pillars of Wisdom* (1935), as Terry Reilly's essay in this volume asks?

In terms of Vietnam texts, the nonfiction status of Tim O'Brien's memoir *If I Die in a Combat Zone, Box Me Up and Ship Me Home* has been critically questioned, and the encyclopedic *War and American Popular Culture* calls Tobias Wolff's *In Pharoah's Army: Memories of the Lost War* "autobiographical fiction," comparing it both to O'Brien's fictional *The Things They Carried* (1990) and Phillip Caputo's memoir *A Rumor of War*.[54] O'Brien insists that *If I Die* is a nonfiction memoir and is gratified that he wrote it before writing any of his novels, doing so having allowed him to get the need to tell his actual story out of his system. Had he not done so, his first novel about Vietnam, *Going After Cacciato*, would have been a different and lesser work, as his mind would not have been free to re-imagine the war. Too many Vietnam war novels fail, he says, because the texts are really memoirs; their authors have failed artistically to transform their experiences into imaginative art. Their imaginations are shackled always to the autobiographical memory.[55]

Veterans who fictionally camouflage their memoirs are perhaps inspired by the lure of money, perhaps by the soldierly distaste for introspective assertions of self in a culture that values action over talk. In 2000 a man sent me a manuscript of a World War II combat novel; he had, he admitted, tried to write it as a memoir but simply could not remember his experience well enough to do so. In this volume, Chris Daley's essay explores the autobiographical dimension of two fictional texts, O'Brien's *The Things They Carried* and Erich Maria Remarque's *All Quiet on the Western Front*, and compares them with Primo Levi's nonfiction *The Drowned and the Saved*. Her essay does not bother sorting the factual from the fictional in O'Brien and Remarque; rather, it treats all three as signifying the authors' personal needs to express their traumatic experience, and their difficulty in doing so. The traumatized patient, as she quotes Freud's observation, "is obliged to repeat the repressed material as a contemporary experience [often though traumatic dreams] instead of . . . remembering it as something belonging to the past." Thus fictional returns to the battlefield might, like dreams, be necessary psychic repetitions—or a means of achieving emotional distance from the things that happened, in effect to pretend they happened to somebody else.[56] Elie Wiesel tells his autobiographical *Night* in the third person, and according to Ted Estess,

> Wiesel has said that the story should be read in view of this state-
> ment: "I swear that every word is true." But there is a difference be-
> tween Eliezer of the book and Elie Wiesel the storyteller. The reader's
> clue to this is the difference in names: the character in the story is
> "Eliezer," while the storyteller uses the name "Elie." The difference
> in names relates to Wiesel's recognition that he cannot adequately
> convey what happened to him and to millions of others. There would
> inevitably be discrepancies between the story he would tell and the
> events he suffered. It is more truthful for him to acknowledge this by
> creating a slight distance between himself and his "character."[57]

Bernat Rosner, another Holocaust survivor and one of the two authors of the dual-narrative memoir *An Uncommon Friendship: From Opposite Sides of the Holocaust* (2001) also writes his story in the third person and in doing so mimics the psychological survival strategy he has used for the past fifty years, pretending that the Holocaust horror he underwent was undergone by somebody else. (The other author, Frederic C. Tubach, is the son of a Nazi German army officer.)

The line between memoirs written in third person and "novels" writ-ten with a changed name is extremely thin. As Hynes has noted, per-sonal war narratives are "something like travel writing, something like autobiography, something like history"—an apt description and one we could easily apply to much war fiction.[58] Postmodern and auto/biographi-cal theory has enjoyed and gained tremendously by deconstructing the constructed division between fiction and nonfiction,[59] and writings about war seem a rich area for such theorizing. Autobiographies do have fictional elements just as fiction has autobiographical elements, and to some ex-tent—for certain critical purposes, and *as long as we acknowledge and ac-count for the author's generic intention*—we are justified in taking Aichinger's strategy of considering both as narratives simply, narratives that can only be treated as such.

But we must tread carefully. *A Farewell to Arms* isn't autobiographi-cal even if it imaginatively incorporates some of Hemingway's experience, and Joseph Heller's *Catch-22* is neither autobiographical nor particularly historical.[60] To assume and posit uncritically that a work of fiction accurately depicts the author's experiences of, or emotional response to, war and the military is to make a rather gross interpretative error.

Poetry

Storm Jameson's 1942 *London Calling: A Salute to America* assembles a number of writers to engage "in deeply personal polemics across the genres —poetry, essay, reminiscences, and stories—to answer the question . . . 'What did you feel when you heard we'd gotten ourselves into the war?'" The nature of Jameson's invitation to his contributors challenges the most fundamental generic divisions, as all of the works—fiction, nonfiction prose, and poetry—are presented as personal and more or less immediate responses to the news. Poetry especially has a reputation as a thoroughly personal, and thus autobiographical, form of expression. In *The Collected Poems of Rupert Brooke: With a Memoir* (1918), Brooke's poems, "only four of which are about the war, are combined with a memoir that includes letters, reminiscences, and biography," so that Brooke's book strongly reinforces the association between the autobiographical and the poetic.

Yet even though many readers "think of poetry as directly autobiographical," Peter Abbs explains,

> such an assumption is dangerous because poets, unless they spell out alternative intentions, have always worked to create a convincing artifact for the imagination. They may well take personal incidents or personal feelings as a staring point but will change and develop these as the poem takes on its distinctive form. . . . In considering the subject of autobiography in poetry, therefore, this essay makes reference only to those poems that are consciously presented to the reader or listener as autobiography—that is to say where the "I" of the poem is seen to relate unambiguously to the actual "I" of the writer.[61]

Yusef Komunyakaa's 1988 *Dien Cai Dau* draws heavily on his firsthand knowledge of the U.S. war in Vietnam, yet few poems in the volume present a clear identification of author with speaker—most in fact involve fictional character and personae. For some theorists there's no such thing as an unambiguous relationship between the "I" of the text and the "I" of the writer. Not only is the textual "I" a discursive construct, an illusory unity, but the writerly "I" is too; when the self is itself ambiguously drawn, what hope has the print edition? But of course this theoretical position applies as well to prose representations of the self; it is also a position beyond the purpose and inclination of the present essay.

Abbs mentions T. S. Eliot's *Four Quartets* as an example of a poem that transforms personal experiences into an object that itself imaginatively transcends its mundane, material sources; as some of those experiences involve World War II, Eliot's poem is appropriately considered here. During the war in Vietnam poets like Denise Levertov and Allen Ginsberg merged the personal with the political in their antiwar poetry, and after the war a fair number of survivors turned to poetry as outlet for their emotions and reflections about the war (for example, W. D. Ehrhart, John Balaban, Walter McDonald, and Bruce Weigel).[62] In this volume, in his essay on eighteenth-century military autobiography, Robert Lawson-Peebles calls attention to Frederick the Great's *L'Art de la guerre* (1760), a long poem that serves as an instruction manual but also, as Lawson-Peebles observes, reflects its author's personal experiences and understanding of war. That poem strikes me as achieving a remarkable degree of generic intermixing.

Literary Criticism

It should perhaps go without saying that when a scholar with significant life experience in or around war or the military turns to analyzing autobiographical narratives about war and the military, a certain personal investment obtains. Much is at stake. Samuel Hynes and Paul Fussell served in combat in World War II and have authored their own narratives of experience as well as two of the essential critical texts or autobiographical war writing. The interpenetration of those projects is inevitable. Pat C. Hoy II's "Once More into the Breach" compares two versions of Fussell's personal essay "My War" and uses this analysis to read *Wartime: Understanding and Behavior in the Second World War,* Fussell's book of cultural criticism on his war. Revisions to "My War" suggest to Hoy how Fussell's sensibility had changed and consequently how *Wartime* "constitutes an act of expiation, an attempt on Fussell's part to assuage that young man's guilt for embracing the great heroic illusions we so often attach to war." Hoy's reading of Fussell cannot but be read itself against Hoy's own war experiences as a Vietnam veteran and a retired U.S. Army colonel, as he confesses:

> [Fussell's] failure has something to do with my own sensibility, one that values complexity as much as his does. Mine too was complicated by war. And so I grow weary in a hurry of an imagination that

turns war and its attendant complexities into unambiguous evil or abject stupidity. . . . [I]mplicit in all that Fussell has written about [war], is simply this: we must never enact it again. We must find some other way to tame our wild, menacing impulses, some other way to overcome those transfixing illusions. Otherwise not a single one of us will live to tell the story of our undoing.

Those final sentences could have easily appeared in one of Hoy's reflective, autobiographical essays; indeed, Hoy refuses to pretend that one can clearly distinguish between literary analysis and familiar essay.[63] His essay in this volume, "War Elegy," also serves as both familiar essay and literary interpretation.

This volume also bespeaks my own ongoing struggle to make sense of my war experience in Desert Shield and Desert Storm. Given Fussell's dismissal of soldiers in his war who did not live though combat day after day, I can imagine his scoffing at my inclusion of works like Susan Griffin's Cold War citizen-warrior's memoir-essay *A Chorus of Stones*. Fussell might see this critical move as compensation for the fact that my war, by his war's standards, was not much of a war at all—and he might be right.

My subconscious compulsions aside, this introductory essay has established solid groundwork for the collective project of studying personal narratives about war, armed conflict, and the military. At the very least, the essay has brought together many of the various strands of the critical conversation. The crossing, blurring, and transgressing of generic boundaries discussed above is inevitable. The different motivations—literary-confessional, historical, military and corporate training, propaganda, and so forth—converge on every veteran-writer and compete for primacy; to use the parlance of current identity and autobiography theory, the resulting texts are multiply determined through the competing discourses. As we segue from the bloodiest century into a century promising to be at least as bloody, making sense of these discourses strikes me as a morally urgent task.

Notes

1. Wayne Karlin, "Those Dying Generations," *Washington Post Book World*, March 9, 1997, 5; Michael D. Mahler, "One Platoon Leader's Catharsis Demeans Those Who 'Gave a Damn,'" *Army* (July 1997): 59–60.

2. Samuel Hynes, *The Soldiers' Tale: Bearing Witness to Modern War* (New York: Penguin, 1997), xiv–xv.

3. Paul Fussell, *Doing Battle: The Making of a Skeptic* (Boston, Mass.: Little, Brown, 1996), 292.

4. Lloyd B. Lewis, *The Tainted War: Culture and Identity in Vietnam War Narratives* (Westport, Conn.: Greenwood, 1985), 13.

5. Fussell, *Doing Battle*, 292.

6. Hynes's limited definition has made him a popular target among scholars who deal with war narratives that fall outside his definition. It's a bit unfortunate, for Hynes had to limit his study somehow, and I seriously doubt he would dismiss other narratives as unworthy of scholarly study.

7. Susan Griffin, *A Chorus of Stones: The Private Life of War* (New York: Anchor Doubleday, 1992), 4, 8, 11, 275.

8. Titles of personal narrative collections from the event of September 11, 2001, include Dean E. Murphy, *September 11: An Oral History* (New York: Doubleday, 2002); Cathy Trost, *Running toward Danger: Stories behind the Breaking News of 9/11* (Lanham, Md.: Rowman and Littlefield, 2002); and CBS News, *What We Saw* (New York: Simon and Schuster, 2002).

9. By the term "literary-confessional" I mean that Augustinian-Rousseauian tradition, which James Olney has demonstrated forms the foundation of Western literary autobiographies. I make this statement fully aware of the problematic notion of literariness and that I am asserting this more-or-less monolithic tradition without considering the complicating presence and influence of more marginalized forms of life writing. Yet for the conventionally educated soldier-memoirist, it is through his sense of this literary-confessional tradition that he writes his own. Such texts are often penned by men and women with literary training and ambition who eventually publish other works; a very short list includes Graves's book, T. E. Lawrence's *Seven Pillars of Wisdom*, Vera Brittain's *Testament of Youth*, even Michael Herr's experimental, new journalistic *Dispatches*.

10. See also: John G. Hubbell, *POW: A Definitive History of the American Prisoner-of-War Experience in Vietnam, 1964–1973* (New York: Reader's Digest, 1976); Richard Van-DerBeets, *The Indian Captivity Narrative: An American Genre* (Lanham, Md.: Univ. Press of America, 1984); Zabelle Derounian-Stodola and James A. Levernier, *Indian Captivity Narrative, 1550–1900* (New York: Twayne, 1993); Elliot Gruner, *Prisoners of Culture: Representing the Vietnam POW* (New Brunswick, N.J.: Rutgers Univ. Press, 1993), a nice bibliography that includes some non–Vietnam era POW sources; Robert C. Doyle, *Voices from Captivity: Interpreting the American POW Narrative* (Lawrence: Univ. Press of Kansas, 1994); Leona Toker, *Return from the Archipelago: Narratives of Gulag Survivors* (Bloomington: Indiana Univ. Press, 2001).

11. See for example: George Mariscal, *Aztlán and Viet Nam: Chicano and Chicana Experiences of the War* (Berkeley: Univ. of California Press, 1999); Leroy TeCube, *Year in Nam: A Native American Soldier's Story* (Lincoln: Univ. of Nebraska Press, 1999).

12. Eric J. Leed, *No Man's Land: Combat and Identity in World War I* (Cambridge, U.K.: Cambridge Univ. Press, 1979), 21.

13. Laura Marcus, *Auto/Biographical Discourses: Theory, Criticism, Practice* (Manchester, U.K.: Manchester Univ. Press, 1994), 9.

14. Edward W. Wood Jr., *On Being Wounded* (Golden, Colo.: Fulcrum, 1991).

15. See Nathaniel Land, *Dispatches from the Front: A History of the American War Correspondent* (1995); Phillip Knightley, *The First Casualty: The War Correspondent as Hero and Myth-Maker from the Crimea to Korea* (New York: Harcourt Brace Jovanovich, 1975, 1982, 2000; updated ed., Baltimore, Md.: Johns Hopkins Univ. Press, 2002); Nancy Caldwell Sorel, *The Women Who Wrote the War* (New York: Arcade, 1999); Ted Bartimus, *War Torn: Stories of War from Women Who Covered Vietnam* (New York: Random, 2002); and the Library of America's volumes *Reporting World War II* (1995) and *Reporting Vietnam* (1998). Harold Evans's essay "Reporting in the Time of Conflict" accompanied the Newseum's 2001 exhibit *War Stories,* appearing both in book and online form at www.newseum.org/warstories.

16. Daniel Hoffman, *Zone of the Interior: A Memoir, 1942–1947* (Baton Rouge: Louisiana State Univ. Press, 2000), 115–16.

17. Milton J. Bates, *The Wars We Took to Vietnam: Cultural Conflict and Storytelling* (Berkeley: Univ. of California Press, 1996), 146–47.

18. A critical study of noncombat male war memoirs could be fascinating. If Cynthia Enloe is correct that women in war are also exposed to the dangers of combat and so "the military has to constantly redefine 'the front' and 'combat' as wherever 'women' are not," then male soldiers serving in places other than these uniquely male spaces might feel insecurity and anxiety about their masculinity. Cynthia Enloe, *Does Khaki Become You? The Militarization of Women's Lives* (London: Pluto, 1983), 15.

19. Of the several books that discuss women soldiers in the Civil War, the most recent is DeAnne Blanton and Lauren M. Cook's *They Fought Like Demons: Women Soldiers in the American Civil War* (Baton Rouge: Louisiana State Univ. Press, 2002).

20. As first-person nonfiction works that record the author's journey to uncover the details of another's life, Palevsky's and Gordon's books are a form of what I call the "biologue" genre. Probably the most famous biologue is A. J. A. Symons, *The Quest for Corvo* (New York: Macmillan, 1934); two examples that explore military figures are Jim W. Corder's *Hunting Lieutenant Chadbourne* (Athens: Univ. of Georgia Press, 1993) and Jonathan Marwil's *Frederic Manning: An Unfinished Life* (Durham, N.C.: Duke Univ. Press, 1988).

21. Hynes, *The Soldiers' Tale,* xiv.

22. Marcus, *Auto/Biographical Discourses,* 3.

23. Fussell, *Doing Battle,* 204, 208.

24. Swofford's book thus suffers a problem analogous to the historical problem of military leaders who struggle to fight a new war using techniques and paradigms from the previous war. *Jarhead* also reveals the anxiety many Gulf War veterans feel at not having fought a "real" war, like Vietnam (an anxiety possibly exacerbated by the unfolding second U.S. war against Iraq).

25. The Franks-Clancy project participates in another trend of the military memoir and of public figures more generally—the use of a ghost-writer or editor, usually identified in the byline after the word *with.* Hynes excludes such books from his study, because "narratives written with the help of another hand—usually some professional writer who wasn't there . . . fail my primary test: they lack an individual voice" (xv). Clancy followed up this title with *Every Man a Tiger,* cowritten with Chuck Horner (2000).

26. "The corpse may have more authority than any other political body. The more corpses, the more authority." Sarah Webster Goodwin and Elisabeth Bronfen, introduction to *Death and Representation* (Baltimore, Md.: Johns Hopkins Univ. Press, 1993).

27. Velma Bourgeois Richmond lists three other books for children, all about World War I: Mrs. Belloc Lowndes's *Told in Gallant Deeds: A Child's History of the War* (London: Nisbet, 1914), Henry Newbolt's *Tales of the Great War* (London: Longmans, Green, and Company, 1916), and Arthur Mee's *The Adventure of the Island: The Story of the Great War Written Down at the Time for the Children of the Future* (no date, in the period 1914–19). Richmond, "World War I," in *Encyclopedia of Life Writing*, ed. Margaretta Jolly (London: Fitzroy Dearborn, 2001), 964.

28. By the time of the two-volume encyclopedia's publication, the "war memoir" entry had disappeared. This fact does not invalidate the following discussion of the problem of generic differentiation.

29. Marcus, *Auto/Biographical Discourses*, 3.

30. Janis E. Haswell, "Review of *The House on Dream Street*," *Viet Nam War Generation Journal* 1, no. 1 (Apr. 2001): 122

31. Other examples: Fred Ottoboni, *Korea between the Wars: A Soldier's Story* (Sparks, Nev.: Vincente, 1997); Carol Barkalow, *In the Men's House: An Inside Account of Life in the Army by One of West Point's First Female Graduates* (New York: Poseidon, 1990). Other examples from the U.S. Military Academy: H. Irving Hancock, *Life at West Point: The Making of an American Army Officer: His Studies, Discipline, and Amusements* (New York: Putnam's, 1902); Jaime Mardis, *Memos of a West Point Cadet* (New York: McKay, 1976); Tully McCrea, *Dear Belle: Letters from a Cadet and Officer to His Sweetheart, 1858– 1865* (Middletown, Conn.: Wesleyan Univ. Press, 1965); Donna Peterson, *Dress Gray: A Woman at West Point* (Austin, Tex.: Eakin, 1990).

32. Alex Vernon, "Military Autobiography," in *Encyclopedia of Life Writing*, ed. Jolly, 603. See also the other relevant entries in the encyclopedia: "American Civil War Writings"; "Holocaust Writings"; "Vietnam War Writings"; "War Diaries and Journals"; "War Letters"; "World War I Writings"; "World War II Writings"; and the individual authors noted in the encyclopedia's thematic list of entries under "War" (xxxi).

33. Edward F. Palm, "Ehrhart, W. D. (1948–)," in *Encyclopedia of American War Literature*, ed. Philip K. Jason and Mark A. Graves (Westport, Conn.: Greenwood, 2001), 105.

34. "Memoirs," in *Encyclopedia*, ed. Jolly, 595–96. Arguably the historical spirit of the leader's military memoir still strongly influences contemporary first-person texts by generals, politicians, and the like.

35. See also the opening chapters in Marcus, *Auto/Biographical Discourses*.

36. James Salter, *Burning the Days: Recollections* (New York: Random House, 1997), ix–x. On publication due date and delay see also William Dowie, *James Salter* (New York: Twayne, 1998), 13.

37. Marcus, *Auto/Biographical Discourses*, 151.

38. I recognize the historical and pragmatic reasons for soldiers' restricting their narratives to the war experience, which is why I hesitate to make anything beyond a speculative case for such a gendered reading. Still, I believe we can at least safely conclude that the memoir form for soldier-memoirists occupies a troubling gendered genre position.

39. Keegan's *Fields of Battle: The Wars for North America* (New York: Knopf, 1996) is an interesting mingling of first-person travel memoir and military history, as Keegan recounts his several visits to the United States and Canada and in the process reflects upon how the landscape shaped the battles that in turn shaped history.

40. Lydia Fakundiny, "Autobiography and the Essay," in *Encyclopedia of Life Writing*, ed. Jolly, 80.

41. See Beajour's *The Poetics of the Literary Self-Portrait* (New York: New York Univ. Press, 1980; originally published as *Miroirs d'encre*).

42. Styron, *The New Yorker*, September 18, 1995; Busch, in *A Dangerous Profession: A Book about the Writing Life* (New York: St. Martin's, 1998).

43. Rosenberg sees a corresponding "bifurcation" between the World War II pilots and the Vietnam pilots in terms of their expressions of the erotic—the latter eroticize their military lives (and their aircraft) in a way the former did not. But contrary evidence exists; *The Love and Fear of Flying* (New York: International Universities Press, 1952) by Douglas D. Bond, professor of psychiatry and the department head at the Western Reserve University's Medical School, draws on the author's experience examining (i.e., interviewing) and treating combat flyers in World War II as well as from reading memoirs. Bond finds that World War II pilots eroticized their relationship with their planes—and with the other pilots—just as much as later pilots. "The aircraft itself," writes Bond, "becomes an object of erotic love. . . . The climactic quality of flight and the relief that flying brings have their counterparts in direct sexual expression" (23). Perhaps the Vietnam oral interview respondents transferred their need for erotic expression onto their flying, because they did not have the opportunity to otherwise "write" about their erotic life; perhaps Bond's Freudian brand of psychology influenced his interrogations and interpretations to an extreme. Whatever the case, the point stands—scholars must consider going beyond a text's words and examine the producing circumstances.

44. Documentary films, to the degree that they rely on "talking head" testimonials, have very much brought oral history to the visual medium. The foundation of Barbara Sonneborn's *Regret to Inform* (New York: Sun Fountain Productions, 1998), for example, is a series of filmed interviews with U.S. and Vietnamese widows of dead soldiers from that war.

45. Fussell, *Doing Battle*, 310–11.

46. See "War Diaries and Journals," "War Letters," "Diaries and Journals: General Survey," "Women's Diaries and Journals," and "Letters: General Survey," in *Encyclopedia of Life Writing*, ed. Jolly.

47. "The Virtual Wall," at www.virtualwall.org; "Letters from the Heart" www.pbs .org/pov/pov1999/regrettoinform/memorial.html; The History Channel's "Veteran's Forum," at veterans.historychannel.com/default.asp (all accessed June 9, 2004.)

48. On *Lee Miller's War*, see Jean Gallagher, *The World Wars through the Female Gaze* (Carbondale: Southern Illinois Univ. Press, 1998), 68–93. Documentary films can be understood as combining the visual form with the oral history. Two famous examples are Peter Davis's *Hearts and Minds* (Beverly Hills, Calif.: Touchstone for BBS Productions, 1974) and *Dear America: Letters Home from Vietnam* (New York: HBO Video, 1988),

in which professional actors play the authors of the letters from Bernard Edelman's book of the same name. In June 2001 the music video television channel VH1 launched a series called *Military Diaries*. Dozens of U.S. military personnel provided daily video diary entries over a three-week period, from which VH1 editors produced several thematic episodes (the subjects' musical tastes figure prominently).

49. Phyllis Lassner, "World War II," in *Encyclopedia of Life Writing*, ed. Jolly, 965.

50. Lawrence H. Keeley, *War before Civilization* (New York: Oxford Univ. Press, 1996), 164.

51. Cornelius A. Cronin, "Lines of Departure: The Atrocity in Vietnam War Literature," in *Fourteen Landing Zones*, ed. Philip K. Jason (Iowa City: Univ. of Iowa Press, 1991), 211, 207, 215. Joanna Bourke has drawn similar conclusions about Vietnam and offers three reasons why it has been imagined as "unusually bloodthirsty" even though atrocities "have a long history" in twentieth-century wars. First, combatants in Vietnam "were more willing to admit to atrocities, whether boastfully or humbly"; second, they could not justify such actions in the contest of a good and "just" war; and third, "many groups and institutions within [American] society," including the armed forces, veterans, and various public groups and interests, "had a political and moral agenda which could be furthered by portraying the Vietnam War as particularly gruesome.... For all commentators, 'the problem' became 'Vietnam' rather than themselves" (169). Literary criticism has only fostered the misperception for its own purposes. Joanna Bourke, *An Intimate History of Killing: Face-to-Face Killing in Twentieth-Century Warfare* (London: Granata, 1999), 169.

52. Cynthia Watchtell, "Wharton, Edith (1862–1937)," in *Encyclopedia of American War Literature*, ed. Jason and Grave, 363. See also the section "Propaganda vs. Professionalism" in Evans's "Reporting in the Time of Conflict."

53. Peter Aichinger, *The American Soldier in Fiction, 1880–1963: A History of Attitudes toward Warfare and the Military Establishment* (Ames: Iowa State Univ. Press, 1975), x–xi.

54. Although I have yet to determine the rationale for this characterization of Wolff's book.

55. In Eric James Schroeder, "Two Interviews: Talks with Tim O'Brien and Robert Stone," *Modern Fiction Studies* 20, no. 1 (Spring 1984): 147–48.

56. Mark A. Heberle has argued as much about the Tim O'Brien canon in *A Trauma Artist: Tim O'Brien and the Fiction of Vietnam* (Iowa City: Univ. of Iowa Press, 2001).

57. Ted Estess, *Elie Wiesel* (New York: F. Ungar, 1980), 17–18.

58. Michael S. Reynolds's *Hemingway's First War: The Making of* A Farewell to Arms (Princeton, N.J.: Princeton Univ. Press, 1976) discusses *A Farewell to Arms* in terms of travel literature and of its historical accuracy (despite the fact that Hemingway did not witness much of the history he depicts).

59. Though there is a movement to reestablish the line. See Dorritt Cohn, *The Distinction of Fiction* (Baltimore, Md.: Johns Hopkins Univ. Press, 2000).

60. Heller in James H. Meredith, *Understanding the Literature of World War II: A Student Casebook to Issues, Sources, and Historical Documents* (Westport, Conn.: Greenwood, 1999), 52.

61. On Jameson in Phyllis Lassner, "World War II," in *Encyclopedia of Life Writing,* ed. Jolly, 966; on Brooke in Velma Bourgeois Richmond, "World War I," ibid., 964; Peter Abbs, "Autobiography and Poetry," ibid., 81.

62. See Roopa Chauhan, "Vietnam War," in *Encyclopedia of Life Writing,* ed. Jolly, 915–16. Chauhan singles out the poems in Lynda Van Devanter and Joan A. Furey's *Visions of War, Dreams of Peace: Writings of Women in the Vietnam War* (New York: Warner, 1991).

63. Pat C. Hoy II, "Once More into the Breach," *Sewanee Review* 98, no. 2 (Spring 1990): 292, 288, 296. In this "refusal to pretend," Hoy seems to be calling Fussell to task for such pretense. "Familiar essay" is the term Hoy prefers, as for him personal essay suggests a confessional mode in which not all first-person reflective essays participate. Thus "familiar essay" suggests a broader range of authorial voice and purpose.

One

Xenophon's *Anabasis* and the Origins of Military Autobiography

JOHN W. I. LEE

In the fourth century BC, Xenophon, a wealthy, aristocratic Athenian and sometime associate of the philosopher Socrates, wrote the first soldier's memoir in world literature: the *Anabasis*.[1]

The *Anabasis* is a prose account, written in the third person, some ten thousand words long. In it Xenophon tells the story of the Cyreans, mercenaries recruited by the Achaemenid prince Cyrus for his abortive attempt to usurp the throne of the Persian empire. The text begins rather abruptly in 402 BC with the immediate background to Cyrus' expedition. From there Xenophon traces the march of Cyrus and his troops toward the Persian capital of Babylon, recounts Cyrus's death at the battle of Cunaxa in 401, and follows the Cyreans as they make an arduous escape north from Mesopotamia to the Black Sea. The account ends, even more abruptly than it began, with the surviving mercenaries joining a Spartan army in March 399. Along with a detailed, day-by-day narrative of the Cyrean march, Xenophon includes speeches in direct address, ethnographic and geographic observations, and tactical advice. Unique among ancient Greek authors, he records the experiences and reactions of common soldiers at war. Indeed, the *Anabasis* has been called "the only work that throws light upon the facts of military life" in classical Greece.[2] For these reasons, the *Anabasis* is today read most often by scholars of ancient history, who find in it invaluable information on Greek warfare, politics, and culture in the fifth and fourth centuries BC.

This essay, however, is not written from a historical point of view but rather takes a different, more literary approach to the *Anabasis*. It begins by looking at when and why Xenophon composed the *Anabasis*. Then it employs perspectives from Samuel Hynes's work on personal narratives of

41

war to find what, if anything, Xenophon finds in common with modern writers of the soldiers' tale. Finally, Xenophon's influence on subsequent military life writing merits recognition as the progenitor of the military autobiographical tradition.

Historical Background

Greece at the end of the fifth century BC was an unsettled, uncertain place, its *poleis* (city-states) still sorting through the aftermath of the agonizing Peloponnesian War (431–404). The once-mighty Athenians, shorn of their maritime empire, had seen their city walls demolished to the music of flute girls. For a time even Athens's famed democracy had disappeared, replaced by a murderous aristocratic junta. The victorious Spartans faced challenges of their own. Wartime allies and former Athenian subjects chafed under Sparta's overbearing hegemony; while Sparta had gone to war under the banner of Greek freedom it now began to seem a tyrant. And across the Aegean Sea loomed the immensity of Achaemenid Persia, chastened by the Greeks at the battles of Marathon and Salamis nearly a century before but still the mightiest empire the world had yet known.

In the years following the Peloponnesian War, thousands of Greeks sought escape from the economic and political difficulties of their homeland by taking up arms for perhaps the most unexpected of paymasters: the Persians. Mercenary service was nothing new to the Mediterranean—already in the early seventh century BC Greek soldiers of fortune in Egypt were chopping graffiti into pharaohs' basalt statues—but by the end of the fifth century unprecedented numbers of Greeks had entered Persian employment.[3] Many became garrison troops for the Persian-controlled Greek cities of Ionia, in western Asia Minor. It would have raised no eyebrows, therefore, when in late 402 BC a twenty-three-year-old Persian prince named Cyrus dispatched orders to his Ionian garrison commanders instructing them to "enlist as many . . . soldiers of the best sort as they could" (*Anab.* 1.1.6).[4] Unbeknown to his commanders, however, the prince was plotting to usurp the throne of his older brother Artaxerxes II, great king of Achaemenid Persia.[5] Having gathered some twelve thousand mercenary foot soldiers along with an uncertain number of Persian levies, Cyrus set out in March 401 from his provincial capital of Sardis (modern Sart, in western Turkey). The young prince at first proffered a succession of flimsy pretexts for the expedition, but as his force marched across Anatolia and into the heart of Mesopotamia, the mercenaries finally discovered Cyrus's true purpose. A few deserted, but for the majority it was too late to back out.

In September the armies of Cyrus and Artaxerxes met near Cunaxa, a hamlet just north of Babylon. Cyrus's heavily armed mercenaries won him the battle, but the prince himself was killed in the fighting. His native troops quickly fled or switched their loyalties to Artaxerxes, leaving the mercenaries stranded in unfamiliar and hostile territory. Their commanders attempted to negotiate a way out of the predicament but were lured into Artaxerxes' camp under a deceptive truce and then massacred. Rather than surrendering or dispersing after this calamity, however, the former mercenaries chose new leaders from their ranks and embarked on an arduous trek out of Persian territory. Unable to return the way they came, the troops slogged north up the Tigris valley, then across the rugged mountains of what is today eastern Turkey, finally reaching the Black Sea at Trapezus (Trabzon) in February 400. From there they marched west along the water, plundering coastal settlements as they went. Arriving at Byzantium (Istanbul) that October, the soldiers then spent the winter as employees of the dynast Seuthes in European Thrace.

Finally, in March 399 the survivors were incorporated into a Spartan army assembling in western Asia Minor under the general Thibron. In two years of marching and fighting, the Cyreans had covered some two thousand miles—a journey roughly equivalent to walking from Los Angeles, California, to Chicago, Illinois.[6] Of the twelve thousand Cyreans who set out from Sardis in March 401, approximately six thousand remained under arms in March 399. At least a thousand had deserted along the way; the others had succumbed to wounds, frostbite, hunger, or disease.

Xenophon's Life and Works

Xenophon the son of Gryllus was born about 427 BC into a wealthy, aristocratic family from the deme (district) of Erchia in rural Attica some ten miles east of Athens proper.[7] "He was modest and superlatively handsome," opines a much later biographer.[8] Xenophon spent his early years in a city at war. As a teenager, he probably rode with the Athenian cavalry helping defend Attic farmland against Spartan incursions. He also found time to join the circle of highborn young men who clustered admiringly around Socrates. In 401, at the invitation of his old friend Proxenus, a twenty-something Xenophon joined the army of Cyrus. Proxenus, from Boeotia in central Greece, had recruited a mercenary contingent for Cyrus and held a general's rank in the army. For his part, Xenophon came along as a sort of observer, being "neither general nor captain nor common soldier" (*Anab.* 3.1.4). When the Cyrean commanders, Proxenus among them, were massacred after Cunaxa, Xenophon stepped forward in his friend's place. He became a general and helped lead the Cyreans on their retreat from Cunaxa to the sea and thence to Byzantium.

It would be decades, though, before Xenophon could set this story down on papyrus. He did not go home to Athens in March 399 because the Athenians had sentenced him to exile during or shortly after the conclusion of the Cyrean march.[9] Instead, from 399 to 394 Xenophon remained in Asia Minor with the Cyreans. Although he clashed with Thibron, he got along famously with the Spartan king Agesilaus II (c. 445–359), who took over from Thibron in 396.[10] Agesilaus was supposed to be waging a panhellenic crusade against the "barbarian" Persians, but in 395 Sparta's erstwhile Greek allies rebelled, forcing Agesilaus's army back to mainland Hellas. Xenophon traveled with Agesilaus, allegedly even fighting on the Spartan side at the battle of Coronea in 394, against a Greek force that included Athenians. Unable to return to Athens, Xenophon turned to Agesilaus and other Spartan friends, who in 387 granted him a country estate at Scillus, near Olympia, in the Peloponnesus. There Xenophon settled until at least 371. He married and had children, sending his two sons to be educated at Sparta. The collapse of Spartan hegemony in the early 360s seems to have compelled Xenophon and his family to leave Scillus for Corinth, but a way home finally opened when, perhaps in 365, the Athenians rescinded their decree of exile. Xenophon divided the final years of his life between Corinth and Athens. His sons served in the Athenian cavalry, helping to redeem their father's reputation; one of them, Gryllus, fell in battle for Athens in 362. Exactly where Xenophon himself died, sometime around 355, remains uncertain; it may have been at Corinth, although five centuries later the locals at Scillus were fond of showing Roman tourists "the tomb of Xenophon."[11]

Wherever he died, it was at Scillus that Xenophon probably began writing in earnest. He wrote prodigiously, eventually producing some fourteen separate titles on a striking variety of subjects. His corpus includes philosophical dialogues, featuring Socrates; technical treatises on cavalry tactics, economics, horsemanship, hunting, and household management; a primer on Spartan government; a posthumous encomium of Agesilaus; a history of fourth-century Greece, a fictionalized biography of Cyrus the Great (founder of the Persian Empire); and the *Anabasis*.

Xenophon might have penned an early draft of the *Anabasis* while at Scillus, but the chronology of its composition remains a matter of contention.[12] Like several of his other works, it may have been set down in sec-

tions rather than as a unitary whole. There are some plausible grounds for
a later date. For example, at one point in the text Xenophon seems to describe his Peloponnesian estate as a thing of the past. He reminds whoever
holds and enjoys the place to offer the proper sacrifices to Artemis, lest
they displease the goddess.[13] The tone suggests that he was writing after
his removal from Scillus, his second home. Given this, it is not unreasonable to suggest that the *Anabasis* in the form we possess today was published perhaps in the early 360s, after Xenophon left Scillus but before he
was able to return to Athens. Ultimately though, "all that can be said with
confidence is that [it] was written late in Xenophon's life, not earlier."[14]

Consider, then, the circumstances under which Xenophon came to
write the *Anabasis*. Having spent a decade campaigning with the Cyreans
and then with the Spartans, he found himself an exile twice over, from Athens and then Scillus. He may have had some written records of the march—
possibly lists of distances and routes traveled—but almost certainly no daily
journal to spark his memory.[15] A full plate of other literary endeavors, from
history to Socratic dialogues, demanded his attention. Moreover, Greece
itself was in turmoil, because by the 360s the Thebans had defeated the
heretofore invincible Spartans in battle and embarked on a short-lived he-
gemonic venture of their own. Why bother with the *Anabasis*?

The *Anabasis* as Apologia

There are certainly elements of the *Anabasis* that address the troubled times
of its composition. For instance, Xenophon includes numerous passages
of practical military advice, not just for battle in open country but also for
maneuvering in rugged terrain against irregular foes. Such tactical lessons would have found a ready audience in war-wracked fourth century
Greece. Moreover, the *Anabasis* bears a subtle but clear panhellenist message: if only the Greeks would stop wrangling amongst themselves for
hegemony at home and unite against Persia, they could easily destroy
the Achaemenid empire.[16] Xenophon emphasizes the weakness and cowardice of Persian troops in contrast to the manly, courageous Cyreans.
Persian power, he implicitly asserts, is a Potemkin village; if the Cyreans
marched their way in and out of Persian territory, surely another Greek
force could do the same. Indeed, the account of Cyrus's advance to Cunaxa
essentially furnishes a road map—complete with descriptions of provisioning places, river crossings, and waterless stretches—for anyone planning to invade Mesopotamia.[17]

The predominant answer to the question of why Xenophon wrote, however, remains the one by Félix Dürrbach more than a century ago: the *Anabasis* is an apologia, a self-defense intended to justify or even exaggerate its author's actions during the march.[18] Those who accept this explanation note that Xenophon was neither the first nor the only writer to narrate the story of the Cyreans. In particular, at least one other general, Sophaenetus of Stymphalus, apparently produced his own *Anabasis*, of which only the barest scraps survive.[19] It is impossible to reconstruct how Sophaenetus portrayed Xenophon, but some speculate that Xenophon wrote at least in part to publicize his own achievements, which he felt Sophaenetus had slighted. On this view, Xenophon adopted a third-person perspective to create an impression of greater objectivity, in essence to seduce the reader into believing Xenophon's version of events.

Reading the *Anabasis* as apologia has its attractions because Xenophon sometimes comes off as implausibly competent for a relatively inexperienced young man surrounded by seasoned, mostly older mercenaries. After the massacre of the generals, for instance, the Cyreans lie about in despair until Xenophon, prompted by a vision from Zeus, induces them to take heart and appoint new officers. His military recommendations, whether they involve preparing the army for the retreat, assaulting fortified enemy positions, or obtaining provisions, are almost invariably accepted, and they always turn out to be the right ones. He is strong and brave when others falter. In the mountains of Armenia, for example, with other men going snow-blind or freezing to death, Xenophon runs tirelessly back and forth along the army's marching column, distributing food and motivating stragglers.[20] Not even in wars of words does Xenophon come off poorly. Those who stand up against him in officers' councils or the army assembly often end up humiliated or tongue-tied; Xenophon usually remains eloquent and persuasive.[21]

Yet even the most cynical reader cannot find Xenophon an insufferable apologist because he recounts his follies along with his successes. Like other Cyreans, Xenophon, when he realizes the true goal of the expedition, follows Cyrus more from fear of seeming cowardly than from anything else. He repeatedly stresses his youth, admittedly sometimes to underline his precocious ability, but at other times to highlight his shortcomings.[22] In Thrace with Seuthes he drinks too much and delivers an impromptu, too-flowery speech. Nor does he omit his ill-advised and unsuccessful attempt to found a colony on the Black Sea coast, an incident that fueled much dissension amongst the Cyreans.[23] Xenophon may dwell on his achievements, but he tempers these with humor. At Cerasus on the Black

Sea, for example, he tells his troops to "take note that now, by the blessing of the gods, I am more confident than I was [before] and that I am bolder now than then and drink more wine" (*Anab.* 5.8.19). It is an appealing mix of boast and self-deprecation.

So the *Anabasis* reveals a Xenophon who is not omnicompetent but sometimes callow, drunk, and foolish. Moreover, the narrative incorporates much that seems to have no place in an organized, intentional apologia. William Higgins makes the point forcefully:

> Why must Xenophon have necessarily have had an immediately practical purpose in mind when writing the *Anabasis* . . . ? Even if . . . he could have blown the dust off issues and events long past, why . . . spend so much time [on] so many things unrelated to apologia, like . . . the different kinds of native dances, descriptions of foreign food and foreign customs, strategic devices like winter leggings, various kinds of bows, and ways to cut glare from the sunlit snow? What has apologia got to do with men chasing ostriches and wild donkeys or getting sick on honey?

The *Anabasis*, Higgins continues, features Xenophon so prominently because it was intended as his idiosyncratic vision of the Cyrean march, not as a response to attacks by others; the work is "avowedly, not deceitfully or apologetically, one-sided."[24] Those who would censure Xenophon for his inaccuracies would, in any case, do well to remember Tim O'Brien's comment, "In war you lose your sense of the definite, hence your sense of truth itself, and therefore it's safe to say that in a true war story nothing is ever absolutely true."[25] Certainly the *Anabasis* constitutes to some degree tactical manual, panhellenist tract, even retrospective self-defense, but to focus on these aspects exclusively is unsatisfying because it obscures the defining character of the text: Xenophon himself.

A Personal Journey

The title *Anabasis* derives from the Greek verb *anabainô*, "go up" or "go inland," hence its usual translation as *The March Upcountry*. In strictly geographical terms, as Leo Strauss noted, this describes only the first part of Xenophon's story, the advance from Sardis to Cunaxa; others divide the remainder of the narrative into *katabasis* ("march downcountry," from Cunaxa to the sea) and *parabasis* ("march alongside," on the Black Sea coast to Byzantium).[26] Yet such a literal interpretation seems misleading, as

Diogenes Laertius intimated centuries ago. Xenophon, asserts Diogenes, "did not march into Persia just for Cyrus; he was seeking a way up to Zeus, whatever it might be."[27] The title *Anabasis*, then, need not refer so much to the physical path of Cyrus's army as to Xenophon's own metaphorical ascent, his journey from being "neither general nor captain nor private soldier" to being leader of the Cyreans.

Xenophon's ascent begins in innocence. Neither he nor Proxenus—nor any of the mercenaries for that matter—realize what lies ahead.[28] Indeed, his preparations for the journey reveal a youthful impetuosity. Receiving the invitation from Proxenus, Xenophon asks the advice of Socrates, who tells him to consult the oracle of Apollo at Delphi. This Xenophon does, although Socrates afterwards chides him "because he did not first put the question whether it were better for him to go or stay, but decided for himself that he was to go and then asked the god as to the best way of going" (*Anab.* 3.1.7). Socrates had reason to be cautious because associating with a Persian prince was a good way for an aristocratic young man to get bad marks from the democratic Athenian government. Yet Xenophon, unaware that he will never see Socrates again, happily sets off for Sardis and Cyrus. Before Cunaxa, Xenophon presents himself as awake but unaware, knowing where the expedition is headed but too ashamed to drop out. After Cunaxa and the massacre of the generals, though, Xenophon's ascent, his spiritual "journey up," accelerates abruptly. Inspired by Zeus, he awakens from despondency, rallies the dispirited Cyreans, becomes a general, and reorganizes the army for retreat. The remainder of the *Anabasis* demonstrates the possibilities and limitations for Xenophon of his new self-awareness. The march to the sea, for instance, is all about possibilities. There are hostile tribesmen to be overcome, mountain passes and rivers to be crossed, soldiers to be inspired and commanded. The Cyreans surpass one obstacle after another, and with each step Xenophon accomplishes more, sees more, learns more.

Along the Black Sea shore, however, the lessons are different. Despite all that Xenophon now knows, he fails in his colonizing venture, provokes division amongst the Cyreans, and finds his authority challenged by rival officers. Coastal settlements refuse to provide provisions, soldiers desert or mutiny, and the army splits temporarily into three factions. By its final chapters, Xenophon's narrative betrays a certain weariness as one battle blurs into the next. Xenophon would like to go home, but he is repeatedly prevented from relinquishing command of the Cyreans. At last, he writes, "Thibron arrived and took over the army, and uniting it with the rest of his Greek forces, proceeded to wage war" on the Persians (*Anab.* 7.8.24). Yet even this final sentence carries no promise of closure. Xenophon has made the journey from innocence to experience; his *Anabasis* is over, but his wandering life has only just begun.

Questions of Genre: Ancient and Modern

If the *Anabasis* represents a personal vision of Xenophon's ascent to experience, where does it fit into the currents of ancient Greek literature? Paul Cartledge names the *Anabasis* "the earliest example of the genre of reflective autobiographical travelogue."[29] This is quite a mouthful and only reflects the difficulty of neatly categorizing such an innovative work. Xenophon clearly borrowed from a range of established classical genres, including travel writing, history, and rhetoric.[30] For instance, the *Anabasis* constitutes in some sense a historical account of Cyrus's expedition and its aftermath, one in which "possibly for the first time in Greek historiography, the presentation of the individual and his activities are the primary means by which the historian communicates information about the past."[31] At another level, it represents a pioneer experiment in autobiography, a term for which fourth-century Greeks possessed no real equivalent.[32] Or it can be seen as a prototype of the technical military-campaign commentary, of which Caesar's writings are probably the best-known examples. Yet pigeonholing the *Anabasis* into any single genre is as unsatisfying as reading its title literally. Much ancient literature did not hew to rigid boundaries; autobiographical writing in particular comprehended a range of overlapping traditions, lengths, forms, and styles. Xenophon likewise mixes history, autobiography, and didactic commentary, but his personal vision shapes the *Anabasis* into something altogether new.

Although its form was unprecedented in antiquity, the *Anabasis* shares much in common with what Samuel Hynes calls the "personal narrative" genre of modern military writing, "first-person writings in prose by participants in the events recorded." For Hynes, post-facto memoirs are the "more complex kind of personal narrative: reflective, selective, more self-consciously constructed than the immediate reports, an old self looking back—sometimes across half a century—at what the young self did, what happened to him, what changed him." Such memoirs are neither history, nor travel writing, nor autobiography, but stories, attempts to explain the unexplainable sensations of war. And, Hynes asserts, there is "always one story—the individual's journey from innocence into experience, the serial discovery of what had before been unimaginable, the reality of war."[33]

The congruence between the *Anabasis* and Hynes's conception of the memoir as a journey into experience is evident. There are other congruencies. Modern memoirists, for instance, tend to report their wars plainly and without metaphor, adopting a style that comes "as close as language can to rendering the things of the material world as they are."[34] Some of them unconsciously, others deliberately, these memoirists focus on seeing, smelling, feeling the realities of war. Xenophon likewise appeals to physicality, to the language of the senses. Here is how he recounts part of the Cyrean ordeal in the mountains of Armenia (*Anab.* 4.4.11–13):

> There came such a terrible snowfall . . . that it completely covered both arms and men as they slept . . . and everybody was very reluctant to get up, for as the men lay there the snow that had fallen upon them . . . was a source of warmth. But once Xenophon had mustered the courage to get up without his cloak and set about splitting wood, another man also speedily got up, took the axe away from him, and went on with the splitting. Thereupon the rest got up and proceeded to build fires and anoint themselves; for they found ointment there in abundance which they used in place of olive oil—made of pork fat, sesame, bitter almonds, or turpentine. They also found a fragrant oil made out of these same ingredients.

Even in its original Greek, this passage is straightforward and unadorned, no complex verb constructions or fancy word order. Notice in particular the specificity with which Xenophon names the ointment and oil his men find, how his description highlights the smell and feel of the moment. Indeed, he is always exacting in his choice of vocabulary. Like World War I soldiers who write "five-nines"—German 5.9 centimeter guns—rather than generic "artillery," Xenophon pays special attention to the vocabulary of destruction. When a weapon appears in the *Anabasis,* it is not just a "sword," but a *machaira,* a particular type of machete-like slashing blade, or an *encheiridion,* a knife small enough to be concealed in the hand.[35]

In fact, Xenophon goes a step beyond the bounds Hynes sets. By using a third-person perspective, he essentially creates another Xenophon, a younger self. The reader becomes Xenophon's older self, looking back across three decades at the brash youth who asked Apollo not whether he ought to join Cyrus but to which gods he should sacrifice before going. Like modern soldiers looking back at their wartime experiences, Xenophon confronts the challenges of fading memory and confined vision. He succeeds in bearing witness to how things felt, to what it was like to be there, not because he sought to deceive but because he wanted to remember.

Soldier Narrative and Commander Narrative

Italo Calvino once compared reading the *Anabasis*, with its flickering images of men struggling against enemies and weather, to watching an old war documentary on late-night television.[36] Yet the *Anabasis* is not just a modern soldiers' tale dressed up with spears and bronze helmets. For one thing, Xenophon is no common soldier but a general. Hynes excludes the lives of generals, noting that "in modern wars, commanders don't usually do the fighting, or live with their troops, or get themselves shot at."[37] Xenophon does all three, simply because his army travels in a different technological world. In the twentieth and twenty-first centuries, commander narratives and personal soldier narratives are inevitably separate affairs. Generals use radio or telephone to direct their troops, who of necessity spread out across the landscape seeking cover and concealment. Artillery or air strikes can be summoned from miles away. The modern general is a battle manager, not a frontline fighter.

This separation was impossible in antiquity, where long range on the battlefield meant no more than the two hundred yards or so that a skilled slinger could cast his lead bullet.[38] Battles in the ancient Greek world were decided by men wielding shield and spear in close-order formation, their leaders fighting alongside them rather than directing from the rear. The conditions of the Cyrean march, in addition, meant that Xenophon could never withdraw to a comfortable headquarters behind the lines. The entire army was a front line, and so Xenophon marched, cooked, ate, and slept alongside his men, night and day, for two years. For him there was no dividing line between commander narrative and soldier narrative.

Of course, in modern warfare before the twentieth century, commanders often shared the dangers of battle and the hardships of campaign life with their troops. Even in nonmechanized armies, however, the distance between commander and fighter persists, psychologically if not physically. Officers in eighteenth- and nineteenth-century European armies, for instance, for the most part were of a socioeconomic class distinctly different from that of the men they commanded. Moreover, officer status tended to carry with it powerful social and legal privilege. The situation was entirely different for Xenophon. Among the Cyreans, officers could be elected, and soldiers could voice their opinions in an army assembly. Corporal punishment, a disciplinary standard in European armies, was generally unacceptable to the Cyreans; Xenophon in fact found himself at one point accused in the assembly for having unjustly struck a soldier.[39] In the *Anabasis*, in other words, not just the physical but also the psychological distance between officers and men was minimal.

Representations of Injury and Death

The *Anabasis* also diverges from modern war memoirs in its representation of injury and death. Here again technological mediation has a decisive effect. Explosives, napalm, and high-velocity bullets, the staples of twentieth- and twenty-first-century war, disfigure and destroy as they kill. As Hynes notes, modern warfare turns even human bodies into grotesque, broken rubbish, hence the nauseating depictions of battlefield death that form a cornerstone of modern war memoirs.[40] Things were different in antiquity. True, spears and swords could inflict horrible injuries—after the massacre of the generals, Xenophon records, "Nikarchos the Arkadian reached the camp in flight, wounded in his belly and holding his intestines in his hands" (*Anab.* 2.5.33). Still, no ancient technology could wholly obliterate human bodies as a Japanese eight-inch shell did William Manchester's buddies one morning on Okinawa.[41] The dead of the *Anabasis*, even horribly mutilated, remain recognizable as human forms. Nor did Xenophon regularly face death in the industrial quantities produced by machine guns, artillery, and poison gas. True, there appear on occasion heaps of corpses for the Cyreans to deal with but never so many and not so often as in modern war. Death in the *Anabasis* appears fleetingly and quietly and in less overwhelming doses than in modern war narratives.

Xenophon rarely depicts individual death, and when he does it is with restraint. In the mountains of Kardouchia, for example, his rearguard was forced to move so quickly that its progress "became more like a flight than a march. Then it was that a brave man was killed, Kleonymos the Lakonian, who was pierced in the side by an arrow that went through his shield and jerkin; also Basias the Arkadian, who was shot clean through the head" (*Anab.* 4.1.18). Some liken this passage to the combat scenes of the *Iliad* and see Xenophon adopting a Homeric, epic style here. Yet Homer's battle deaths are graphic if not lurid, full of splattering blood and improbably dismembered bodies. Xenophon in contrast gives Kleonymos and Basias swift, quiet deaths. Later, he reproaches Cheirisophus, commander of the army's advance guard: "And now two good and brave men are dead, and we weren't able to retrieve their bodies or bury them" (*Anab.* 4.1.19). There were tactical reasons for hurrying, Cheirisophus explains, but Xenophon makes his point: brave men deserve proper burial.

Xenophon's reproach to his fellow general introduces another divergence between the *Anabasis* and modern war memoirs. Whenever possible, the Cyreans gave proper ritual attention to their own dead, if not immediately then soon after battle. On the Black Sea coast, for instance, the army mounted a special expedition to collect and bury several hundred men who had been killed the previous day on an abortive foraging expedition.[42] Elsewhere, the soldiers make time to honor a number of Arkadians who had fallen in an ambush (*Anab.* 6.4.9):

> They buried the greater part of the dead just where they each had fallen; for they had already lain unburied five days, and it was not now possible to carry away the bodies; some that lay upon the roads, however, they did gather together and honor with as fine a burial as their means allowed, while for those they could not find, they erected a great cenotaph, and placed wreaths upon it.

Leaving Kleonymos and Basias unburied, then, was unusual. Normally the Cyreans found time to mourn their dead properly. Modern armies in contrast often treat human bodies, if they can be retrieved at all, as simply another industrial byproduct. Jonathan Shay, in fact, counts the indifference or disrespect of Graves Registration personnel and the hasty, anonymous removal of the dead from the battlefield among the great failings of the American army in Vietnam.[43] For twentieth-century memoirists, the unburied dead represent "materials of the earth, to be walked over or around, and even used, when necessary, in the construction projects of war."[44] The dead of the *Anabasis* retain their humanity. In the modern soldiers' tale they too often become objects.[45]

A Community on the March

There are further cultural differences to consider. Modern armies are formal, contained units; noncombatants such as family members and prostitutes are, at least in theory, kept out of and away from the fighting units. The comforts of home and sex are supposed to exist somewhere else, subjects for nostalgia or fantasy. In truth, soldiers in virtually all times and places have had recourse to sex, both heterosexual and homosexual. According to Hynes, not until Vietnam did brothels and drunkenness figure much in modern narratives of war as memoirs of the two world wars scarcely mention soldiers' sexuality.[46] Xenophon, in contrast, makes no secret of the fact that the Cyreans were at various times accompanied by large numbers of both female and male noncombatants. Indeed, at one point the army accumulated so many captives that the generals felt compelled to sort them out and expel them. Even so, the soldiers smuggled through a number of beautiful boys and women, who then marched with the army all the way to Byzantium. These captives soon formed lasting sexual and emotional liaisons with the soldiers, which Xenophon recounts as part of the everyday routine of the army.[47] He does not foreground these noncombatants, but their presence transforms the *Anabasis* into a narrative not just of war but also of community life.

Comradeship and Small-Group Bonds

There was, however, no formal logistical structure in the *Anabasis* army: no chow line, no supply sergeants, no post exchange. Cyreans had to fend for themselves, forming into small groups of *suskênoi* ("tent-mates") to obtain the necessities of life. The perils of this nonsystem appear vividly in Xenophon's account (*Anab.* 4.5.5):

> They got through that night by keeping up fires, for there was wood in abundance at the stopping place; those who came up late, however, had none, and consequently the men who had arrived early and were keeping a fire would not allow the late comers to get near it unless they gave them a share of their wheat or anything else they had that was edible.

Comradeship and intense primary group fidelity are, undeniably, central to the modern soldiers' tale.[48] Indeed, Spielberg's *Saving Private Ryan*, by highlighting a theme prominent in a number of World War II narratives, succeeded in making "group bonding" something of a cliché. The *Anabasis* and modern memoirs share an emphasis on the importance of comradeship in small units, but for the Cyreans comradeship was far more pervasive. In the *Anabasis* soldiers rely utterly on each other not just during battle but also during every moment of the march. A man without *suskênoi* was left behind in the snow to die. Few modern narratives, with the exception perhaps of World War II Axis memoirs of winter retreat in Russia, portray comradeship with such intensity.[49]

Technological and cultural differences make the *Anabasis* unlike the modern soldiers' tale in several key respects. Still, there are congruencies between Xenophon and more recent memoirists, made more striking by the millennia separating him from the soldiers Hynes investigates. It is worth examining Xenophon's influence on subsequent military life writing.

Influences on Subsequent War Writing

In antiquity Xenophon earned praise as "the Attic bee" for his sweet, pure prose.[50] The *Anabasis* was widely read and referenced, in particular by the Roman Imperial writer Arrian (Lucius Flavius Arrianus, ca. AD 80–160), who styled himself the New Xenophon and systematically imitated some of Xenophon's writing.[51] Like Xenophon, Arrian was a military man and versatile writer who had seen his share of combat. Yet his *Anabasis Alexandri* is no personal journey into experience but rather a heroic history of Alexander the Great's campaign against Persia. Indeed, Arrian's account of his own battle experiences, the *Order of Battle against the Alans*, reads more like a parade-ground handbook than a memoir.

Republican Romans also read Xenophon; Cicero in fact grumbled that his contemporaries were brought up on stories from Xenophon and other Greek writers rather than having learned the deeds of famous Romans.[52] The military commentaries of the most famous of Cicero's contemporaries, Julius Caesar, reveal an apparent similarity with the *Anabasis* in that Caesar too uses a third-person narrative. Caesar, however, used this technique for entirely different purposes than did Xenophon. He was not writing decades after the fact and for personal reasons but was producing what might be termed a collection of official communiqués, straight from the battlefields of Gaul and Greece, intended to celebrate his own glory as leader and commander. None of the reflection, the looking back at a younger self, that appears so strongly in the *Anabasis* is displayed in Caesar's commentaries.

Arrian and Caesar, it would seem, started a trend. Ancient or modern, authors who reference the *Anabasis* tend to pick up its surface characteristics, not Xenophon's personal vision.[53] For many the *Anabasis* represents the original long march. R. E. Dupuy, for instance, describes the Czech Legion's 1918–20 trek across Russia as "the most remarkable Anabasis and Katabasis since the days of Xenophon and the Ten Thousand."[54] When seven thousand Zulu workers made a two-week, four-hundred-kilometer escape across the South African veldt at the outbreak of the Boer War,

London newspapers readily drew analogies to Xenophon.[55] Similarly, American journalists thrilled in comparing the *Anabasis* to the 1846–47 exploits of Colonel Alexander Doniphan, who led an army contingent from New Orleans across the Santa Fe Trail and south into Mexico.[56] "Xenophon and Doniphan," crowed William Cullen Bryant, "these are the names of two military commanders who have made the most extraordinary marches known in the annals of warfare. . . . These two men, whose names are in sound so similar, have each performed the most wonderful march."[57]

Relatively few personal narratives, however, explicitly trace their lineage to the Cyreans. Jaroslav Hasek, in a picaresque novel drawing from his World War I experiences, makes his "good soldier" Svejk recall the *Anabasis*.[58] Italo Calvino comments that Xenophon finds echoes in the stories of Italian Alpini troops on their retreat from Russia; one of them even dubbed his memoir "a little *Anabasis* in dialect."[59] Eugenio Corti, another Italian veteran, displays classical erudition by comparing his Russian ordeal to the Athenian retreat from Syracuse in 413 BC rather than to the march of the Cyreans.[60] References to Xenophon, it seems, come more often from later commentators than from the memoirists themselves.[61]

There is another factor to consider: Xenophon's place in the canon of modern classical education. Xenophon was widely read in seventeenth- and eighteenth-century Europe but fell out of favor by the nineteenth century.[62] The same purity of style and language that drew Arrian to him led many nineteenth- and, eventually, twentieth-century classicists to disdain Xenophon. He seemed too simple, too credulous, to be worthy of study or imitation.[63] The best-known of classically educated war writers, the British authors and poets of the Great War, preferred more erudite authors like Homer or the poets of the Greek Anthology.[64] The vast majority of modern soldiers who did not enjoy the luxury of a classical Greek and Latin education were, it seems fair to say, even less likely to be exposed to Xenophon.

But perhaps to look for explicit traces of Xenophon in later military lifewriting is misguided, for as Hynes observes, most war narratives display "nothing to suggest that the author is aware of any previous example."[65] Even those soldiers who did read him, then, need not have taken Xenophon as their model. So it may well be that Xenophon stands in the peculiar position of being the first author to write in a genre without a tradition, insofar as we can reasonably speak of a single unified genre of war writing extending across three millennia. Between him and the other writers examined in this volume lie centuries of cultural, technological, and literary change. Probably no more than a handful of these writers ever heard of, much less read, Xenophon's memoir. The *Anabasis* remains in some respect most noteworthy for the ways in which it diverges from rather than conforms to modern concepts of military autobiography. Yet for all this difference, Xenophon shares an intimate link with the men and women whose stories appear in the following pages. Like them, he conveys a particular, personal vision of military life. Like them, he mourns the death of comrades and exults in friendship and in the pleasures of small respites from the bleakness of combat. Like them, he attempts to describe the indescribable sensations of war: fear, hunger, sickness, exhaustion. Whether or not they realize it, anyone who writes of arms and the self marches with Xenophon.

Notes

1. All quotations from Xenophon's *Anabasis* are drawn, with some slight modifications, from the readily available Loeb Classical Library translation by C. L. Brownson and edited by John Dillery, *Xenophon:* Anabasis (Cambridge, Mass.: Harvard Univ. Press, 1998), and are used by permission of the publishers and trustees of the Loeb Classical Library, copyright © 1998 by the president and fellows of Harvard College. In accordance with the conventions of classical studies, references to the *Anabasis* (abbreviated "*Anab.*") are by book, chapter, and section number. Translations from ancient authors besides Xenophon are my own except where otherwise indicated. In order to serve a broad audience, I have kept secondary source citations to a minimum and indicated works accessible to nonspecialists.

2. Ernst Badian, "Alexander's Mules," *New York Review of Books* (Dec. 20, 1979): 54–56.

3. The standard history of Greek mercenary service remains H. W. Parke, *Greek Mercenary Soldiers from the Earliest Times to the Battle of Ipsus* (Oxford, U.K.: Clarendon, 1933).

4. Cyrus specifically mentions Peloponnesians, who were renowned for their military prowess.

5. The expedition of Cyrus has generated a sizeable bibliography, much of it usefully collected in Otto Lendle, *Kommentar zu Xenophons* Anabasis *(Bücher 1–7)* (Darmstadt, Ger.: Wissenschaftliche Buchgesellschaft, 1995), and Jan P. Stronk, *The Ten Thousand in Thrace: An Archaeological and Historical Commentary on Xenophon's Anabasis, Books VI.iii–vi–VII* (Amsterdam, Neth.: Gieben, 1995). Nonspecialists may find Dillery, *Xenophon*, 1–40, of most use.

6. For detailed itineraries see Arthur Boucher, *L'Anabase de Xénophon (Retraite des Dix Mille) avec un commentaire historique et militaire* (Paris: Berger-Levrault, 1913); and H. R. Breitenbach, "Xenophon von Athen," in *Paulys Realencyclopädie der classischen Altertumswissenschaft* 9.A.2, 1569–1928 (1967). For maps, consult Lendle, *Kommentar zu Xenophons Anabasis*, and Valerio Manfredi, *La Strada dei Diecimila: Topografia e Geografia dell'Oriente di Senofonte* (Milan, Ital.: JACA, 1986).

7. On Xenophon's life and writings see Breitenbach, "Xenophon von Athen"; J. K. Anderson, *Xenophon* (New York: Scribner's, 1974); Édouard Delebecque, *Essai sur la vie de Xénophon*, (Paris: Librairie C. Klincksieck, 1957); W. E. Higgins, *Xenophon the Athenian: The Problem of the Individual and the Society of the Polis* (Albany: State Univ. of New York Press, 1977). For insightful short treatments, see Peter Krentz, *Xenophon: Hellenika II.3.11-IV.2.8.* (Warminster, U.K.: Aris and Phillips, 1995), 1–11; Sarah Pomeroy, *Xenophon, Oeconomicus: A Social and Historical Commentary* (Oxford, U.K.: Clarendon, 1994), 1–5; and Christopher Tuplin, s.v."Xenophon (1)," *The Oxford Classical Dictionary*, 3d ed. (1996), 1628–1631.

8. Diogenes Laertius 2.48 (trans. Anderson); Diogenes wrote in the third century AD.

9. It remains uncertain whether Xenophon was exiled in 399 (on account of his friendship with Socrates, who was executed that same year) or in 394 (for being pro-Spartan).

10. On Xenophon and Agesilaus, see Paul Cartledge, *Agesilaus and the Crisis of Sparta* (London: Duckworth, 1987).

11. See *Anab.* 5.3.7–13 (Xenophon's description of Scillus) and Pausanias 5.6.6 ("the tomb of Xenophon").

12. Dillery, *Xenophon*, 8–9; Stronk, *The Ten Thousand in Thrace*, 8–10.

13. *Anab.* 5.3.13 (proper sacrifices to Artemis).

14. Dillery, *Xenophon*, 9.

15. James Roy, "Xenophon's *Anabasis:* The Command of the Rearguard in Books 3 and 4," *Phoenix* 22, no. 2 (1968), 158–59; James Roy, "Xenophon's Evidence for the *Anabasis*," *Athenaeum: Studi Periodici di Letteratura e Storia dell'Antichità* New Series 46 Fasc. I-II (1968), 37–46. See also Breitenbach, "Xenophon von Athen," 1649–50.

16. For a different perspective, see Higgins, *Xenophon the Athenian*, 97–98.

17. Scholars who have walked the Cyrean route for themselves confirm the accuracy of Xenophon's topography; see for example Frank Williams, "Xenophon's Dana and the Passage of Cyrus' Army over the Taurus Mountains," *Historia* 45, no. 3 (1996), 284–314.

18. Félix Dürrbach, "L'apologie de Xénophon dans l'*Anabase*," *Revue des Études Grecques* 6 (1893), 343. See also Anderson, *Xenophon*, 80–84; and Dillery, *Xenophon*, 6–8.

19. Fragments of Sophaenetus' writing survive only as brief quotations in the work of the grammarian Stephanus of Byzantium (sixth century AD).

20. *Anab.* 3.1.11–25 (Xenophon rallies the Cyreans); *Anab.* 3.2.27–33 (preparations for retreat); 4.8.10–14 (assault); 5.1.5–13 (provisioning); 4.5.7–9 (in the mountains of Armenia).

21. See, for example, *Anab.* 3.1.26–32 (a company commander is ridiculed and driven away for contradicting Xenophon); 5.8.1–26 (Cyreans who accuse Xenophon of too-harsh discipline end up admitting it was all for their own good).

22. *Anab.* 3.1.10 (fear of seeming cowardly). Stress on youth: see, for example, *Anab.* 3.2.37 (older generals should take the lead) and 3.4.42 (an older general should stay in command of the army).

23. *Anab.* 7.3.26–33 (in Thrace with Seuthes) and 6.5.15–20 (Black Sea colony).

24. Higgins, *Xenophon the Athenian*, 93–94, 95–96; against this view see Arnold Momigliano, *The Development of Greek Biography*, exp. ed. (Cambridge, Mass.: Harvard Univ. Press, 1993), 57.

25. Tim O'Brien, *The Things They Carried* (New York: Broadway, 1990), 82.

26. Leo Strauss, "Xenophon's *Anabasis*," *Interpretation: A Journal of Political Philosophy* 4:3 (1975), 117. See also Dillery, *Xenophon*, 8, and Stronk, *The Ten Thousand in Thrace*, 7.

27. Diogenes Laertius 2.58.

28. *Anab.* 3.1.4–10.

29. Paul Cartledge, *The Greeks: A Portrait of Self and Others* (Cambridge, U.K.: Cambridge Univ. Press, 1993), 44.

30. Momigliano, *The Development of Greek Biography*, 14–15 and 45–57.

31. Dillery, *Xenophon*, 71.

32. Momigliano, *The Development of Greek Biography*, 14 and 47. Greeks spoke of *hupomnêmata* or "memoirs" but not of autobiography per se. Xenophon's obituaries of Cyrus (*Anab.* 1.9.1–31) and the murdered Cyrean generals (2.6.1–30), including Proxenus (2.6.16–20), stand out as the first biographical epilogues in Greek literature.

33. Samuel Hynes, *The Soldiers' Tale: Bearing Witness to Modern War* (New York: Penguin, 1997), xiv, 1–16, 17.

34. Hynes, *The Soldiers' Tale*, 25–26.

35. *Anab.* 4.3.12 (*encheiridion*); *Anab.* 1.8.7 (*machaira*). On Xenophon's specificity of language see Higgins, *Xenophon the Athenian*, 2–7.

36. Italo Calvino, *Why Read the Classics?* trans. Jonathan Cape (New York: Pantheon, 1999), 19.

37. Hynes, *The Soldiers' Tale*, xv.

38. That slingers using lead bullets could shoot this distance, outranging even archers, is but one of the tiny but telling details Xenophon provides; see *Anab.* 3.3.16–18.

39. *Anab.* 5.8.1–26.

40. Hynes, *The Soldiers' Tale*, 7–8.

41. William Manchester, *Goodbye, Darkness: A Memoir of the Pacific War* (Boston: Little, Brown, 1979), 384.

42. *Anab.* 6.5.5–6. See also Pamela Vaughn, "The Identification and Retrieval of the Hoplite Battle-Dead," in *Hoplites: The Classical Greek Battle Experience*, ed. Victor Davis Hanson (London: Routledge, 1991), 38–62.

43. Jonathan Shay, *Achilles in Vietnam: Combat Trauma and the Undoing of Character* (New York: Simon and Schuster, 1994), 57–62.

44. Hynes, *The Soldiers' Tale*, 69.

45. This is not to say modern soldiers never treat their dead with reverence. Perhaps the difference lies in time constraints: usually the Cyreans had time to look after their dead, in between episodes of battle; the continuous operations of modern warfare, in contrast, offer less opportunity for such rituals.

46. Hynes, *The Soldiers' Tale*, 186.

47. *Anab.* 4.1.12–14 (some captives expelled, others smuggled through). For relationships between captives and soldiers, see especially *Anab.* 4.3.19, 4.6.1–3 and 7.4.7–11.

48. Hynes, *The Soldiers' Tale*, 9–10.

49. See for instance Eugenio Corti, *Few Returned: Twenty-eight Days on the Russian Front, Winter 1942–1943* (Columbia: Univ. of Missouri Press, 1997); Guy Sajer, *The Forgotten Soldier* (New York: Harper and Row, 1971).

50. Pomeroy, *Xenophon, Oeconomicus*, 11–15.

51. A. B. Bosworth, *A Historical Commentary on Arrian's* History of Alexander (Oxford, U.K.: Clarendon, 1980).

52. Anderson, *Xenophon*, 2.

53. Anderson, *Xenophon*, 1–8, reviews European attitudes to Xenophon from the sixteenth to nineteenth centuries.

54. R. Ernest Dupuy, *Perish by the Sword: The Czechoslovakian Anabasis and Our Supporting Campaigns in North Russia and Siberia, 1918–1920.* (Harrisburg, Pa.: Military Service, 1939), 54; see also Edgar Chen and Emily Van Buskirk (2001). "The Czech Legion's Long Journey Home," *Military History Quarterly* 13, no. 2 (2001), 42–53.

55. Elsabé Brink, *1899, The Long March Home: A Little-known Incident in the Anglo-Boer War* (Cape Town, South Africa: Kwela, 1999), 99–101.

56. Joseph G. Dawson III, *Doniphan's Epic March: The 1st Missouri Volunteers in the Mexican War* (Lawrence: Univ. Press of Kansas, 1999), 191–202.

57. Dawson, *Doniphan's Epic March*, 198.

58. Jaroslav Hasek, *The Good Soldier Svejk and His Fortunes in the World War*, trans. Cecil Parrott (New York: Penguin, 1985).

59. Elio Vittorini, *Il sergente nella neve*, qtd. in Calvino, *Why Read the Classics?* 22.

60. Corti, *Few Returned*, 245; Thucydides briefly describes the Athenian retreat in book seven of his history of the Peloponnesian War.

61. Echoes of the *Anabasis* appear in one scene of T. E. Lawrence's *Seven Pillars of Wisdom*; see Jeffrey Meyers, *The Wounded Spirit: T. E. Lawrence's Seven Pillars of Wisdom* (New York: St. Martin's, 1989), 22–23. For more on Lawrence's literary inheritances, see Terry Reilly, "T. E. Lawrence, Modernism, and Cultural Poetics," in this volume.

62. Anderson, *Xenophon*, 4–8.

63. Xenophon's works, particularly the *Anabasis*, were widely used for beginning Greek instruction in the nineteenth and twentieth centuries. This, paradoxically, may have put later writers off Xenophon—as they looked for literary models, they sought to avoid the bad memories of their early struggles with Greek grammar and syntax.

64. Paul Fussell, *The Great War and Modern Memory* (Oxford, U.K.: Oxford Univ. Press, 1975), 161, 180–181.

65. Hynes, *The Soldiers' Tale*, 4.

Two

Style Wars

The Problems of Writing Military
Autobiography in the Eighteenth
Century

ROBERT LAWSON-PEEBLES

The Lack of Precedent

The difficulties confronting eighteenth-century writers of personal military narratives can perhaps best be understood by approaching them through twentieth-century military autobiographies. The account of his life by one of the most famous soldiers of the twentieth century begins:

> I was born in London, in St. Mark's Vicarage, Kennington Oval, on 17th November 1887.
> Sir Winston Churchill in the first volume of *Marlborough, His Life and Times* wrote thus about the unhappy childhood of some men:
> "The stern compression of circumstances, the twinges of adversity, the spur of slights and taunts in early years, are needed to evoke that ruthless fixity of purpose and tenacious mother-wit without which great actions are seldom accomplished."
> Certainly I can say that my own childhood was unhappy. This was due to a clash of wills between my mother and myself. My early life was a series of fierce battles, from which my mother invariably emerged the victor. If I could not be seen anywhere, she would say— "Go out and find what Bernard is doing and tell him to stop it."

Field Marshal the Viscount Montgomery of Alamein suggests that his autobiography might lack "literary style," but it is among the most assured. It pays due homage to chronology; makes claims to truth; discusses at length both the battles that made him famous and his dealings with the others in the ranks of the great and (mostly) good; reflects upon a life that he treats as a unity; and hopes to be exemplary. He therefore starts with the facts of his origin and continues to pepper his text with such details as times of day, documents, photographs, and maps. The second sentence begins with the initial reference to the man who will figure large in the story and whom he regarded in 1958 (the year of the book's publication) as "chief among all my friends."[1] Montgomery's account of his relations with his mother operates simultaneously as the opening gambit in the claim to unity—describing his relations with her in terms of a military metaphor—and as a joke. His confident knowledge of the outcome of his life allows him to laugh about his childhood adversities; he knows, and we will find out, that in mature life he has usually won the battles he has fought. The lesson for Montgomery's readers is that he succeeded because he would not stop what he was doing, and as he begins his story, he emphasizes the lesson by reference to that illustrious forbear of his chief of friends, the first Duke of Marlborough, one of the most famous soldiers of the early eighteenth century.

It is not because of any uncertainty over genre that Montgomery calls his autobiography *The Memoirs*. The most senior army officers over the last two centuries tended to give their texts that title, or their heirs and translators did. Thus we have *The Memoirs and Correspondence of Field-Marshal Viscount Combermere* (1866), *The Memoirs of Field Marshal Lord Gren-fell* (1925), and Michael Carver's *Out of Step: Memoirs of a Field Marshal* (1989). English translators have forced German officers to march in step with the English counterparts. Albert Kesselring's 1953 autobiography *Soldat bis zum letzten Tag*, which could have been modestly and accurately translated as *A Soldier until My Dying Day*, appeared in English as *The Memoirs of Field-Marshal Kesselring* (1988). A similar fate, if for different reasons, awaited the translation of Wilhelm Keitel's writings. Keitel was notorious for the *Nacht und Nebel* (night and fog) order, condemning citizens of occupied countries to death as surrogates for those who offended the Reich. His papers were gathered fifteen years after his execution in 1946 as *Generalfeldmarschall Keitel, Verbrecher oder Offizier?* (criminal or officer?). When David Irving published his translation in 1965 he removed the question, and the text became *The Memoirs of Field-Marshal Keitel*.

In contrast, literary critics have reserved that term for the less unified, more anecdotal form of autobiography. Frank Kermode's witty *Not En-titled: A Memoir* (1996), its dubiety increased by the indefinite article, describes that Manxman's career as a Royal Navy officer in World War II as part of a life conceived ironically, if inaccurately, as that of one of the disenfranchised, a resident alien like T. S. Eliot. Initially Kermode finds himself "fighting for freedom by proxy" in Reykjavik. A few days after he is invited to lunch in the HMS *Hood*, the ship is sunk by the *Bismarck*. When at last he is transferred to an escort carrier, it is disabled near Lowestoft by a mine, presumably British. By the time the ship is repaired the sea war in the West is almost over, and it is sent to the Pacific. "For the first time," Kermode writes, "I was employed in a genuine warship and about to take part in a real war." But when the action starts he depicts himself "like Stendhal's hero at Waterloo," having "very little idea of what was happening, or even of where the battle was." He provides a stark contrast to Montgomery's facts and maps.

Yet for all their differences, Montgomery and Kermode are united in being licensed to write their memoirs by the existence of a preceding textual network. In Montgomery's case it was the large number of biographies and autobiographies, military or otherwise, published before 1958. His authorship, as it were, receives its authority from, among others, Churchill's biography, quoted in the second sentence. In Kermode's case it is an enormous range of literary texts, present on every page as a barely submerged net of allusion. His first sentence, appropriately, begins with an allusion to Eliot's "Hollow Men": "Between these origins and that ending is where the weather is, fair or foul: the climate of a life." Kermode describes the battle for Okinawa in terms of *The Charterhouse of Parma* (1839), which means that for him World War II ends with a whimper rather than a bang.[2]

There is, no doubt, an overlap between the nets on which the two texts rest—the community of canonical readings that would have directed the education, formal and informal, of both men. That community would have included, for instance, *Robinson Crusoe* (1719), the first sentence of which is reshaped by Montgomery to open his own life. However, even though they are likely to have read Defoe's novel, many eighteenth-century military men would not have regarded this work of fiction as an appropriate model. From Defoe to Austen, the eighteenth century was marked not only by a conspicuous development in the techniques of prose fiction but by a concern over its relation to the lived experience. Thomas Jefferson can act as a barometer of taste. In a 1771 letter to Robert Skipwith he recommended Sterne's *A Sentimental Journey*, for instance, because "considering history as a moral exercise, her lessons would be too infrequent if confined to real life." By 1818 he had modified his view. In a letter to Nathaniel

Burwell he asserted that "the inordinate passion prevalent for novels" had led to "a bloated imagination, sickly judgment, and disgust towards all the real businesses of life."

Those who contemplated writing about the self, therefore, had to disown any hint of fictionality. For instance, *An Account of the Remarkable Occurrences in the Life and Travels of James Smith* was not published by its author until 1799, forty years after the events it describes, because he feared that "a great part of it would be viewed as fable or romance." Similarly, Edward Gibbon asserted in his autobiography that "naked unblushing truth" was its "sole recommendation," a sentiment echoed by Montgomery, if not by the more knowing Kermode.[3] Gibbon sought the truth through six drafts, and his text, *Memoirs of His Life and Writings*, was only published by his friend Lord Sheffield in 1796, two years after Gibbon's death. The experience of writing an autobiography in the eighteenth and early nineteenth centuries was problematic because, among other reasons, it was morally suspect as a product of vanity and egotism—serious figures, public men, should be thinking about things other and greater than their petty selves.[4] The climate of a writing life for Gibbon and his predecessors was very different from that of Montgomery and Kermode.

Indeed, it was not until 1809 that Robert Southey used the term "autobiography" in its present-day sense, closing a review of *The Memoirs of the Life and Writings of Percival Stockdale*. He complained that "if the populace of writers become thus querulous after fame, (to which they have no pretensions) we shall see an epidemical rage for auto-biography break out" that would be both widespread and pernicious. Southey's view here suggests that fame should be achieved by means other than merely writing about oneself. A similar hesitancy surrounded the term "memoir." It emerged, long before Southey's neologism, from the Latin *memoria*. In the eighteenth century it often denoted, anticipating the later literary-critical use, an inferior form of history. Robert Beatson's six-volume *Naval and Military Memoirs of Great Britain, from the Year 1727, to the Present Time* (1804) is a chronological narrative that nevertheless refuses to assume the mantle of "history" because, says Beatson, "he is diffident of his own abilities." Autobiographers in the eighteenth century did not therefore have secure access to either of the titles normally used today to denote this genre.[5]

It follows that this form of writing was characterized by uncertainty, subject to shifting concepts and styles of presenting the self. Thomas Jefferson's "Autobiography," for instance, was written, he said, only "for my more ready reference & for the information of my family." It was not published until long after his death. Many critics would argue that such uncertainty is in a dynamic relation with an instable self—you are what you write. Benjamin Franklin's "Recollection" (as he put it in his opening paragraph) is a good example of these conjoint instabilities in the second half of the eighteenth century. As Bonnie J. Gunzenhauser writes about the genre in general, "the evolution of autobiography . . . has shown a unique capacity for registering changing cultural conceptions of the self."[6] Ever since Lawrence's *Studies in Classic American Literature,* Franklin's *Autobiography* has been recognized as a key text in American cultural history. Yet it was not given that now-customary title until 1849, when Jared Sparks, the first professor of history at an American university, published three of its four extant fragments as part of his edition of Franklin's *Works.* Each fragment seems to present a different Franklin, to the extent that Franklin has sometimes been portrayed as an early instance of the American confidence trickster. The textual Franklin that figures so prominently in American culture is a posthumous imposition upon a complex, changing man reacting to complex, changing times.

This is not to say that military men were completely deterred from writing about themselves in the eighteenth century. They certainly did not write in the form that Montgomery used. Neither did they write as profusely as their successors. Unlike those modern field marshals, some of the most famous did not write autobiographies at all. When William Thomson mustered the *Military Memoirs, Relating to Campaigns, Battles, and Stratagems of War, Antient and Modern; Extracted from the Best Authorities* (1804), he was often forced to draw his authority from secondary sources. Thomson regretted that Marlborough had left no personal narrative of his campaigns; he drew his account of the battles of Frederick of Prussia from Count Philippe de Grimoard's *Tableau historique et militaire de la vie et du regne de Frederic le Grand* (1788). Henry Lloyd, who had served as a general in the Austrian army, begins *The History of the Late War in Germany* (1764) by complaining that "the moderns, who have undertaken to write the history of different wars, and of some renowned Commanders, being chiefly men of learning only, and utterly unacquainted with the nature of military operations, have given us agreeable, but useless productions."[7] The problem identified by Lloyd was still apparent forty years later. William Thomson was a lawyer, while Robert Beatson was what used to be called a "miscellaneous writer," publishing among other things *A Political Index to the Histories of Great Britain and Ireland* (1786) and *An Essay on the Comparative Advantages of Vertical and Horizontal Wind Mills* (1798).

Military writers were confronted with a paucity of suitable precedents. The problem is most easily summed up by a brief discussion of the form temporally and stylistically closest to military autobiography, the captivity narrative. In February 1676 a group of American Indians from the Narragansett tribe attacked Lancaster, Massachusetts, and took some hostages, including Mary Rowlandson, who was held for nearly twelve weeks before she was ransomed. Six years later she published an account of her experience: *The Soveraignty and Goodness of God, Together with the Faithfulness of His Promises Displayed; Being a Narrative of the Captivity and Restauration of Mrs. Mary Rowlandson.* There are accounts of captivity that long predate Rowlandson, such as Cabeza de Vaca's *La Relacion* (1542) and John Smith's *A True Relation* (1608). Rowlandson's text, however, is probably the first instance in which warfare provided a focus for a thorough examination of the self. Variously titled, it has reappeared in a large number of editions and anthologies; it owes its success to the ways in which it unites four earlier forms.

Three of them are deeply embedded in the Puritan experience. One is the sermon, with its didacticism and care with biblical precedent. Another is the jeremiad, the lament over backsliding. The third is spiritual autobiography, which can be traced back to the *Confessions* of St. Augustine (AD 354–430), the bishop of Hippo (in North Africa), whose account of his sins and conversion to Christianity was adopted by the Protestant theocracy as a model for the self-scrutiny and successful outcome.[8] The fourth source, adding much-needed spice to the other three, was the atrocity story. Rowlandson's narrative begins with an account of the Narragansett attack at dawn:

> Hearing the noise of some guns, we looked out; several houses were burning and the smoke ascending to heaven. There were five persons taken in one house. . . . Another there was who running along was shot and wounded and fell down; he begged of them his life, promising them money (as they told me), but they would not hearken to him but knocked him in [the] head, stripped him naked, and split open his bowels. . . . Now is that dreadful hour come that I have often heard of (in time of war as it was the case of others), but now mine eyes see it. . . . The bullets flying thick, one went through my side, and the same (as would seem) through the bowels and hand of my dear child in my arms. One of my elder sister's children, named William, had then his leg broken, which the Indians perceiving, they knocked him on the head. Thus were we butchered by those merciless heathen, standing amazed, with the blood running down to our heels.

The realism of the account is sustained by its detail and by the use of first person, singular and plural. The aborigines are established as representatives of evil, the inhabitants of "the vast and desolate wilderness" into which Rowlandson is then forced to travel. They present her with a series of trials that she must undergo before, in "a remarkable change of providence," she is released. Native duplicity is contrasted with the narrative style, which, in addition to claiming to tell the truth, provides a series of confessions underpinned by biblical reference.[9]

The captivity narrative was a much-read public form until the later nineteenth century. In some ways it presents a useful model for military autobiographers in its claim to tell the truth, its ability to detail the unpleasant elements of war, and for some its belief in divine intervention. But in more important ways the form is unsuitable. It is rooted in the ideology of domesticity and usually presents the narrator as a passive supplicant. Its division of the participants between the representatives of good and evil is at odds with the belief in order and the ideal of gentility, which informed much if not all eighteenth-century combat. *The Military Mentor*, for instance, one of the most widely read army conduct manuals of the early nineteenth century, is subtitled *Comprising a Course of Elegant Instruction, Calculated to Unite the Characters and Accomplishments of the Gentleman and the Soldier*. In the preface the writer says he will "illustrate his positions by the examples of the most celebrated heroes who have graced the pages of history." They include some of the soldiers to be discussed shortly, particularly Frederick the Great (1712–86).

The conditions in which such men operated were far removed from the chaos of the American frontier that gave rise to the captivity narrative. There are, to be sure, a number of male captivity narratives—for example, the Reverend John Norton's *The Redeemed Captive* (1748)—but a search through the major bibliographies for the eighteenth-century produced only three well-distributed texts that at first sight could qualify as military captivity narratives. One has already been mentioned, James Smith's *Account*. Smith (1737–1812) was captured when he was eighteen; the experience informed his later work as a lieutenant in Henry Bouquet's 1764 campaign and as a colonel in George Washington's army. It mixes ethnography with advice on the use of native methods of warfare against European armies. The second was published in 1736 by Captain John Gyles, described as "commander of the garrison on St. George's River," in what is now Maine. It is an account of his captivity in 1689 during King William's War, when he was a child. The third is Captain Jonathan Carver's *Travels*, published in 1778, a decade after his westward journeys and two after he had apparently been captured during the massacre at Fort William Henry (1757).[10] It was extremely popular at the time for its account of American Indians. Its subject is neither war nor the self but rather ethnography combined with traveler's tales, some of them borrowed and some of them tall.

The Search for a Form

One eighteenth-century military autobiography, the 1765 *Journals* of Major Robert Rogers, commander of the First Battalion of the Royal Americans, shows an awareness of the captivity narrative while also pointing the way forward to the more modern form of military autobiography. Other than Rogers's text (discussed at the end of this essay), military autobiographies of the period can be organized into three kinds: "indirect," "purposive," and "mundane."

The most famous soldier who wrote *indirect* autobiography is Frederick the Great. As the thirty-three-volume Preuss edition of his works bears witness, Frederick was a prolific writer, from around the age of eighteen until his death, and a writer who tried whenever possible to combine truthtelling with objectivity by excluding himself from his work. In the preface to his *History of My Own Times* (1746) he declared, "I shall paint princes as they are, without prejudice in favour of my allies, or hatred for my enemies; I shall mention myself only when obliged by necessity, and must be permitted, after the example of Caesar, to speak of what relates to myself in the third person, to avoid the disagreeable effects of egotism."

The preface to his *The History of the Seven Years War*, published posthumously in 1788, suggests that only another great war could have dragged him into another quill-driving dalliance with his times: "I have before written a narrative of the two wars which Prussia made on Silesia and Bohemia. This narrative was the work of a young man, and the consequence of that frenzy for writing which, in Europe, is become a kind of epidemic disease. After the peace of 1746 I renounced history. . . . The war which happened in 1756 occasioned me to change my opinion."[11] Like many of the most senior officers of the time, Frederick is concerned that writing is susceptible to self-indulgence and hence a lack of control. Vestiges of the concern about self-indulgence may still be seen in the British military use of "one" as a pronoun.

Some time before Southey, Frederick used a medical metaphor to describe autobiography and worried about it accordingly. Frederick's personal reflections about his success in warfare therefore had to be deduced from his nonnarrative work. He usually wrote in French, but British officers translated some of his works into English, for they were keen to learn how Frederick had succeeded in shaping the Prussian army. For instance, one officer, concerned that "our language does not abound with books on the art of war," gave Frederick's 1747 *Instruction pour les generaux* an autobiographical gloss when in 1762 he translated the text as *Military Instructions . . . for the Generals of his Army, Being His Majesty's Own Commentaries on His Former Campaigns.* His readers learned very quickly that discipline, for which the Prussian army was famous, was the result of drill: "Armies are composed chiefly of indolent people: if the Commander is not constantly attentive to the duty of every individual, the machine, which being artificial cannot be perfect, will soon be dislocated, and in a little time you will have an army disciplined only in idea."

An army may be a machine, but the machine is run by men. Officers learned to combine discipline with solicitude from Frederick's long poem *L'Art de la guerre* (1760), published in English in 1782. *The Art of War* was dedicated to Lieutenant General William Keppel and was "translated by an Officer at his leisure Hours while encamped under his command at Coxheath," near Maidstone in Kent. The translator clearly also spent some of his leisure reading Pope:

> When train'd for fight th'embattled cohorts stand,
> The meanest soldier helps to form the band;
> These are the limbs, and discipline the soul,
> Pervades, informs, and regulates the whole. . . .
>
> No! with parental care your army lead,
> Behold with grief the meanest soldier bleed,
> They love their leaders, but their tyrants hate,
> We owe their lives and welfare to the state.[12]

It was as an exemplar text that Lieutenant General Adam Williamson (1676?–1747), Deputy-Lieutenant of the Tower of London, translated the *Military Memoirs and Maxims of Marshal Turenne,* otherwise known as Henri de la Tour d'Auvergne (1611–75), the commander of the French army during the Thirty Years' War and the wars of the Fronde. In his preface, Williamson suggested that his book "will take little more room than a snuff-box, and if as often look'd into, will be of greater use." Also intended to be more useful than a snuffbox was *General Wolfe's Instructions to Young Officers,* a compilation published in 1768, nine years after he had been killed on the Plains of Abraham. The text, which began with the House of Commons' motion to erect a monument to the hero, was a homily on discipline constructed at Wolfe's bequest to the British army. The original owner of the British Library's copy treated it that way, for at the end of the text he wrote a version of Wolfe's last order, issued the night before he died: "The officers and men will remember what their country expects from them, and what a determined body of soldiers are capable of doing against five weak batallions [sic], mingled with a disorderly peasantry."[13]

The second kind of eighteenth-century military autobiography might be called *purposive narrative*, because it is aimed at explaining conduct or achieving a specific objective. Four such narratives can be cited to illustrate the range. One is James Smith's *Account*, which ends by suggesting that if "our men" were taught "the Indian art of war . . . no European power, after trial, would venture to shew its head in the American woods." One of the Europeans who had experience of the American woods was Sir Henry Clinton (1738?–95), who returned to England in 1782 after seven years' service in America. His courageous action had resulted in the British success at Bunker Hill, and from 1778 until 1782 he had been commander in chief of British forces in America. But Clinton suffered from bad luck; he found that in his absence from Britain he had been scapegoated for the defeat at Yorktown. In response he published a *Narrative . . . Relative to his Conduct . . . in North America*. In it Clinton accused Charles Cornwallis of insubordination and of errors during the Virginia campaign that led to his becoming trapped at Yorktown. Clinton concluded: "Upon the whole I am persuaded, that had I been left to my own plans, and a proper confidence had been earlier reposed in me, the campaign of 1781 would not probably have ended unfortunately." Like many generals since, he had asked for more troops to reverse the failures. But the *Narrative* itself was another example of Clinton's bad luck. As it was being published, the American commissioners John Adams, Benjamin Franklin, and John Jay were in Paris negotiating with the British plenipotentiary, David Hartley, negotiations that concluded on September 3, 1783, with British recognition of American independence.[14]

A quite different purpose was served by the *Military Memoirs of Mr. George Thomas* (1803). Thomas was lucky. The title that he was given by the text, "Mr.," confirms that he was "an obscure individual," but he rose, as the subtitle put it, *to the Rank of a General, in the Service of the Native Powers in the North West of India*. William Francklin, who "compiled and arranged" Thomas's documents, noted that "his adventures, his talents, his successes, and his misfortunes, detailed in the following sheets [may] afford some useful instruction to the reader." Thomas's text might be regarded as a supplement to the *Autobiography of Benjamin Franklin*, the first fragment of which appeared in an English edition in London in 1793. It shows that at another margin, far away from the patronage and purchase systems that governed the British officer corps, it was possible for ordinary men to apply their talents and emerge, in Benjamin Franklin's words, from "Poverty & Obscurity . . . to a State of Affluence & some Degree of Reputation in the World." Thomas's *Memoirs* anticipates the famous advice that Horace Greeley would give, though suggesting that young men should go east rather than west.

The last example of a purposive narrative is better known than Smith's *Account*, Clinton's *Narrative*, or Thomas's *Memoirs*, if only because it was used as the basis of a Herman Melville novel. *The Life and Remarkable Adventures of Israel R. Potter* begins like *Robinson Crusoe*: "I was born of reputable parents in the town of Cranston, State of Rhode Island, August 1st 1744." Potter ran away and after a number of seaborne adventures joined the Continental Army in time to fight the battles of Lexington and Bunker Hill. Returning to sea, he was captured by the Royal Navy and transported to Britain, where he had many more adventures. Eventually he returned, a broken man, to the United States, where he published his picaresque narrative, aiming it at Congress with a plea for a pension. If Melville was later moved by this story, Congress was not, and Potter ended his days in poverty.[15]

Mundane military autobiographies have their origin, as the name suggests, in diaries and journals. Because they are shaped by the desire to make a daily record, they are sometimes mundane in the less happy sense of the term. Here, for instance, is the entry by John Millner, a sergeant in the Royal Regiment of Foot of Ireland, for May 17, 1707:

> Our whole Army, by break of Day, decamp'd at *Soignes*, and all went to Prayers; after which, we advanced out a little in the Front of where we had encamp'd, in order and full design to attack or force the Enemy to Battle: But a very heavy Fog having fallen, that we could scarcely see what we were about, or from the Right to the Left of each Regiment, for the Space of three Hours that we stood at Arms; which baulk'd the Duke's Design, but proved very beneficial to the Enemy, who embraced the Opportunity theoreof; that instead of giving us Battle, they made off another Way.

The reader might agree with Millner when he notes in his preface that the journal filled his "vacant Hours, both in Camp and Garrison, the which might have been better employed." The reason for the text's publication in 1733, twenty-one years after the completion of the journal, is almost certainly its praise, which first appears in the preface, of the "judicious Care, good conduct, and undaunted Courage of our excellent prudent General and warlike Hero, the Duke of Marlborough."[16]

Military diaries and journals were usually published long after they were written and therefore for purposes other than those for which they were originally composed. The accounts of the Flanders campaigns by General Richard Kane (1661–1736), first published in 1745, and Captain Robert Parker, published by his son in Dublin in 1746 some while after Parker's death, joined Millner's in praising Marlborough, presenting him alongside William of Orange as a Protestant military hero. Here, for instance, is Parker's portrait of Marlborough during the siege of Bouchain on August 9, 1711:

> Our British grenadiers were ordered to march up to the top of the hill on the left of their works, in order to begin the attack on that side. Here we were posted in a large high grown field of wheat, about seventy or eighty paces from their works, expecting every moment, when the signal should be given to fall on.
>
> I must confess I did not like the aspect of the thing. We plainly saw that their entrenchment was a perfect bulwark, strong and lofty, and crowded with men and cannon pointed directed at us. . . . But while I was musing, the Duke of Marlborough (ever watchful, ever right) rode up quite unattended and alone, and posted himself a little on the right of my company of grenadiers, from whence he had a fair view of the greater part of the enemy's works. It is quite impossible for me to express the joy which the sight of this man gave me at this very critical moment. I was now well satisfied, that he would not push the thing, unless he saw a strong probability of success.

Churchill included this extract in his biography of Marlborough, published in 1933. Perhaps Montgomery had read it before he embarked on the battle of Alamein. Kane and Parker, or their editors, constructed their accounts as melodramas in which the hero Marlborough is counterpointed against a villain—the Duke of Ormonde, known to Parker from boyhood, and characterized by Kane as "a good-natur'd, but a weak and ambitious Man, fit to be made a Tool by a Set of crafty Knaves." Ormonde replaced

Marlborough as Captain-General of the army in 1712 but was impeached in 1715, dying as a Jacobite in Spain in 1745. Clearly, it was the Second Jacobite Rebellion of 1745 that had inspired the publication of the two books. As Parker's son noted, his father's *Memoirs* "were not wrote [sic] with a view to making them publick," but their "faithful and true relation . . . is particularly seasonable at this time, when we are engaged in a War with *France*."[17]

There are more complex reasons for the publication of *Select Passages from the Diary and Letters of the Late John Blackader, Esq*, a lieutenant colonel of the Cameronians during Marlborough's campaigns. Blackader's first editor, Rev. John Newton, rector of St. Mary Woolnoth in London, claimed that his manuscripts had been "sold a few years ago as waste paper." Fortuitously, Newton came across them and published them in 1806, during the Napoleonic Wars. Newton's preface compares Blackader with Colonel James Gardiner, who had been killed at the battle of Prestonpans on 21 September 1745. Gardiner had left no memoirs, but the nonconformist minister Philip Doddridge published his biography in 1747. *Some Remarkable Passages in the Life of the Honourable Colonel James Gardiner* was extremely popular and was frequently reprinted in the next eighty years. Doddridge constructed his biography on the model of St. Augustine's *Confessions*, portraying Gardiner as a reformed sinner. Blackader's Christianity was more constant and doom laden. After walking across a field strewn with dead bodies he called on God to make him "humble and thankful." When he was complimented on the drill of the Cameronians, he reflected that "all this is the goodness of God alone." Blackader's all-pervasive Protestantism was manna for Newton, who preached: "Thanks be to God, we have had, and still have, both officers and privates, in the navy and the army, whose courage is animated by Christian principles." They were "the true patriots."[18]

Newton left no record of his attitude toward George Hamilton, surgeon on HMS *Pandora*. The frigate had been sent in 1790 to capture the officers and seamen who had mutinied against Captain William Bligh of the *Bounty*. Hamilton's record of the ship's circumnavigation was, for once, promptly published (in 1793), no doubt because the mutiny had been a cause célèbre, but also because the official publication of Captain James Cook's journals, to which Hamilton makes frequent reference, had been a great success. The text reflects, as Cook's had, the scientific influence of Sir Joseph Banks, but it also devotes much space to the less scientific activities of the Polynesian women, described with an amused detail that would have horrified Newton. Hamilton freely admitted that he did not maintain a prophylactic distance from the amatory activities of the crew. A Tahitian king, Matuara, expected Hamilton to pay him "a compliment, by cherishing his wife." Hamilton was uneasy because the lady, "named Peggy Ottoo," was of a high rank and had been the model for "the right hand dancing figure so elegantly delineated in Cook's Voyages." Then he recollected that since modeling for Cook "Peggy had seen much service, and bore away many honourable scars in the fields of Venus." Reassured by these military metaphors, he decided "his Majesty's service must be done." A few days after undertaking this onerous service he discovered, like his other loyal shipmates, "that the ladies of Otheite had left us many warm tokens of their affection." He did not provide details of the cure.[19]

Many mundane military autobiographies have been published in the interests of historical or antiquarian record. Caroline Scott was the commander of Fort William during its siege by the Jacobite army in 1746. His *Diary of the Siege of Fort William* was published in 1900 by the local newspaper. Lieutenant General Adam Williamson, who was so keen to publish the memoirs of Marshal Turenne, did not have his own *Official Diary* published until 1912 by the Royal Historical Society. The brothers Jeffrey and William Amherst both kept journals of the 1758 expedition to Nova Scotia; they were published in 1928 and 1931. William Amherst (1732?–81) kept a vivid record of the attack on Louisbourg, showing that although the technology had improved, tactics for the 1944 Normandy landings had changed only slightly:

> The Grenadiers landed & after, the Light Infantry, Irregulars & High-landers, and this was done at a place which appeared almost inaccessible, from the violence of the surf, under a very brisk fire of cannon and small arms, from intrenchments [sic] all round the Cove. The Light Infantry were very alert, flanked the intrenchments, & forced the enemy to retire. We seized their batteries, took & drove some skulkers out of the woods, & pursued their main body, who ran hard for it towards the town. The men behaved with a great deal of spirit.

Augustus John Hervey, third Earl of Bristol and Vice Admiral of the Blue (1724–79), behaved with spirit in several fields. He kept from 1746 to 1759 a journal that was not published until 1953, at the behest of Theodora, Marchioness of Bristol. It spends much time detailing his foreign sexual conquests, as well as his home life and combat at sea.[20]

Numbers of diaries of soldiers on both sides of the War of American Independence have been published, particularly in the years after the bicentennial. The diary of Jeremiah Greenman, published in 1978, records, for instance, the tedium of being a captive of the British on Long Island: "Continuing in Graves End at my Quaters [sic] very sedentary. . . . Nothing worthy [of] remark happened." The journal of Colonel Johann Friedrich Specht, published in 1995, records the service of the Braunschweig Regiment during General John Burgoyne's disastrous invasion of New York, ending in the surrender on October 17, 1777, at Saratoga, when Specht went into captivity until he was exchanged in 1780. John Peebles, a captain in the Black Watch whose diary was published in 1998 by the Army Records Society, reveals a range of experience that was remarkably wide for a relatively junior officer. His diary closes on March 2, 1782, with an account of a meeting in New York with Sir Henry Clinton, hearing Clinton's complaints about Cornwallis that would soon appear in Clinton's *Narrative*. In February 1777 Peebles recorded a very different experience. When he led a foraging party of twenty men out of Amboy, New Jersey, his unit was persistently attacked by Continental troops operating from the cover of woods, leaving him the only person unscathed. He grew to respect the people he called "Rebels"; they might be a "ragged dirty looking set of people," but they operated with "discipline."[21]

The First Modern Military Autobiography

The Continental troops, disciplined by such officers as James Smith, learned their tactics from the Royal American Regiment, formed in response to General Edward Braddock's defeat in July 1755 by a smaller force of French and Indians at the battle of the Monongahela. According to Benjamin Franklin's *Autobiography*, Braddock muttered, "*We shall better know how to deal with them another time;* and dy'd a few Minutes after." The Royal Americans did know better. Their training is reflected in the *Journals* of Major Robert Rogers, published in 1765. His biographer, John R. Cuneo, claims that the *Journals* was the first written manual of warfare in the New World (it predates Smith's *Account* by thirty-four years). As a training manual, a depiction of warfare in the New World, and as a published journal, Rogers's work participates in all three of the eighteenth century's military narrative traditions: the indirect, the purposive, and the mundane. Yet in its insistence on communicating personal experience, it is very likely that Rogers's *Journal* is the first modern military autobiography.

Rogers answers Henry Lloyd's complaint about authors "unacquainted with the nature of military operations," made the year before, by remarking in his introduction that "it is the soldier, not the scholar, that writes." While, like Frederick's *History of My Own Times*, the *Journals* claims "the merit of impartially relating matters of fact," it also discloses a strong autobiographical impulse. Rogers does not go as far as Montgomery, refusing to "gratify the curious [with] a particular account of my life, preceding the war." His text, rather, is indebted to the captivity narrative, for it uses warfare as a focus for reflecting on the self. Like the captivity narrative, Rogers freely employs the first person singular, even to the extent of confessing errors, yet he moves away from the limited biblical drama of the white protagonist-victim, giving voice instead to a point of view not unlike that of the American Indian opponents. Rogers provides a good example of this near the beginning of his text, when he describes an incident of October 21, 1755. He had led a small unit to the western side of Lake George with orders to capture a prisoner for interrogation:

> My men lay concealed in a thicket of willows, while I crept something nearer, to a large pine-log, where I concealed myself by holding bushes in my hand. . . . About ten o'clock a single man marched out directly towards our ambush. When I perceived him within ten yards of me, I sprung over the log, and met him, and offered him quarters, which he refused, and made a pass at me with a dirk, which I avoided, and presented my fusee to his breast; but notwithstanding, he still pushed on with resolution, and obliged me to dispatch him. This gave an alarm to the enemy, and made it necessary for us to hasten to the mountain.[22]

If the mission was a failure, Rogers's account of it is a success. The thickly detailed fabric of the narrative, particularly in the piled-up clauses of the longer sentences, conveys an air of realism and makes the text here resemble a debriefing. The reflective tone is one of a learning experience, not in the ways of the Lord but in the methods of New World warfare. The normal European procedure of offering "quarter" (mercy) to an enemy, drawing on long-established rules for the conduct of war, does not work in the woods of North America.

As Captain Peebles discovered twenty-two years later, European military methods, in fact, often seemed out of place. Rogers is the first officer in a British regiment to write about what he had learned from American Indians. For instance, Jonathan Carver's *Travels* noted that "the

Indians think there is little glory to be acquired from attacking their enemies openly in the field."[23] When Rogers set out his "Rules of Discipline," he applied native methods; hence rule "VII If you are obliged to
receive the enemy's fire, fall, or squat down, till it is over, then rise and
discharge at them." At times, indeed, he suggested that it was necessary
to abandon all rules, "in which case every man's reason and judgment
must be his guide, according to the particular situation and nature of
things." Rogers illustrated his methods by recounting some of the exploits of the unit that came to be known as "Rogers's Rangers." They give
a vivid impression of irregular warfare, quite different from the formal,
drilled maneuvers of massed troops on contemporary European fields.
When Rogers led the attack on the fort at St. d'Estresse on May 15, 1760,
he "observed two large store-houses in the inside, and that the enemy
were carting hay into the fort. I waited for an opportunity when the cart
had just entered the gate-way, run [sic] forward, and got into the fort before they could clear the way for shutting the gate. . . . We took in the fort
twenty-four soldiers . . . my best way was to burn the fort and village,
which I did."[24] Irregular warfare demanded an individual approach. It
would be an approach adopted by many later individualistic—and often
deliberately unkempt—warriors, such as the Long Range Desert Group,
used by Montgomery for reconnaissance and raiding.

Although, as the use of the Spanish term suggests, guerilla activity
became well known during the Peninsular War (1808–14), its methods
had existed for centuries, long before the exploits of Rogers's Rangers.
The novelty of Rogers's *Journals* was that the drive to write about New
World warfare had prompted him into using the first person singular.
Indeed, Rogers's account of the attack on St. d'Estresse suggests that he
fought almost alone. The first person singular reflected the individual,
often lonely nature of warfare in the American woods. Despite Rogers's
claim to impartiality, his use of the pronoun had driven him into "the
disagreeable effects of egotism" detested by Frederick the Great and by
Caesar before him. One consequence of such subjectivity, however, was
recognition of the psychological costs of warfare. In his introduction Rogers
remarked that his work had been written "amidst the hurries, disorders,
and noise of war, and under that depression of spirit, which is the natural
consequence of exhausting fatigue." The first person singular also allowed
Rogers to produce a shaped text, conveying a sense of a military life unified by planning, action, and reflection, and consequently rewarded by
growing success. The *Journals* opens with an entry for September 24, 1755,
reminiscent of the leaden Sergeant Millner: "Pursuant to orders of this

date from Major-General Johnson . . . I embarked with four men upon Lake George." Yet within one page Rogers describes spying on a fort at Crown Point, the initial intelligence-gathering that would lead by stages to the success of British arms, and summarizes its significance:

> Thus, at length, at the end of the fifth campaign, Montreal and the whole country of Canada was given up, and became subject to the King of Great Britain; a conquest perhaps of the greatest importance that is to be met with in the British annals, whether we consider the prodigious extent of country we are hereby made masters of, the vast addition it must make to trade and navigation, or the security it must afford to the Northern provinces of America . . . and the importance it must give the British crown among the several states of Europe.[25]

Rogers's triumph was short-lived. In twenty-one years many of those provinces would be lost to Britain, and Rogers's later life would be marked by failure and poverty. His *Journals*, however, marked a new style of autobiography available to men and women of arms who followed.

Notes

1. Bernard Law Montgomery, *The Memoirs of Field-Marshal the Viscount Montgomery of Alamein* (London: Collins, 1958), 16–17, 68.

2. Frank Kermode, *Not Entitled: A Memoir* (London: HarperCollins, 1996), 3, 112, 148.

3. Thomas Jefferson, letters August 3, 1771, and March 14, 1818, in Thomas Jefferson, *Writings*, ed. Merrill D. Peterson (New York: Library of America, 1984), 741–42, 1411; James Smith, *An Account of the Remarkable Occurrences in the Life and Travels of James Smith* (1799; repr. Cincinnati, Ohio: Robert Clarke, 1870), n.p.; Edward Gibbon, *Memoirs of My Life* (1796; repr. Harmondsworth, U.K.: Penguin, 1984), 39.

4. See the introduction and first chapter of Laura Marcus's *Auto/Biographical Discourses: Theory, Criticism, Practice* (Manchester, U.K.: Manchester Univ. Press, 1994).

5. Robert Southey, review of *The Memoirs of the Life and Writings of Percival Stockdale*, *Quarterly Review* 1, no. 2 (May 1809): 386; Robert Beatson, *Naval and Military Memoirs of Great Britain, from the Year 1727, to the Present Time*, 6 vols. (London: Longman, 1804), 1: vii.

6. Bonnie J. Gunzenhauser, "Autobiography: General Survey," in *Encyclopedia of Life Writing*, ed. Margaretta Jolly (London: Fitzroy Dearborn, 2001), 76; Jefferson, *Writings*, 3.

7. William Thomson, *Military Memoirs: Relating to Campaigns, Battles, and Stratagems of War, Antient and Modern; Extracted from the Best Authorities* (London: J. Johnson, 1804), 396, 400; [Henry Lloyd,] *The History of the Late War in Germany; with Occasional Remarks* (London: printed for the author, 1766), [fo.B^r].

8. Examples of spiritual autobiography are John Bunyan's *Grace Abounding to the Chief of Sinners*, written while he was in prison and published in 1666, while *The Autobiography of Thomas Shepard*, who died in 1649, was probably the first American autobiography, treating the transatlantic crossing as the conversion experience.

9. Rowlandson, "The Sovereignty and Goodness of God", in *Puritans Among the Indians: Accounts of Captivity and Redemption, 1676–1724*, ed. Alden T. Vaughan and Edward W. Clark (Cambridge, Mass.: Harvard Univ. Press, 1981), 33–34, 37, 70.

10. *The Military Mentor. Being a Series of Letters Recently Written by a General Officer to His Son, on His Entering the Army*, 2 vols. (London: Richard Phillips, 1804), 1:iii; John Gyles, *Memoirs of Odd Adventures, Strange Deliverances, &c. in the Captivity of John Gyles, Esq.* (Boston, Mass.: S. Kneeland and T. Green, 1736); Jonathan Carver, *Three Years' Travels throughout the Interior Parts of North America, in the Years 1766, 1767, and 1768* (1778; repr. Charlestown, Mass.: West and Greenleaf, 1802).

11. *Posthumous Works of Frederic II, King of Prussia*, 6 vols., trans. Thomas Holcroft (London: G. G. J. and J. Robinson, 1789) 1:xv, 2:vii.

12. Frederick II, *Military Instructions . . . for the Generals of His Army, Being His Majesty's Own Commentaries on His Former Campaigns* (London: T. Becket and P. A. De Hondt, 1762), 6; Frederick II, *The Art of War* (London: G. Riley, 1782), 5, 54.

13. Adam Williamson, *Military Memoirs and Maxims of Marshal Turenne* (London: J. and P. Knapton, 1740), iii–iv; *General Wolfe's Instructions to Young Officers* (London: J. Millan, 1768), 1, 104–5.

14. Smith, *An Account*, 160–61; Clinton, *Narrative of Sir Henry Clinton, K. B., Relative to His Conduct during Part of His Command of the King's Troops in North-America* (New York: Sower, Morton and Horner, 1783), 12.

15. *Military Memoirs of Mr. George Thomas*, ed. William Francklin (Calcutta, India: [W. Francklin], 1803), 1; Benjamin Franklin, *Autobiography and Other Writings*, ed. Ormond Seavey (Oxford, U.K.: Oxford Univ. Press, 1993), 3; *The Life and Remarkable Adventures of Israel R. Potter (a Native of Cranston, Rhode Island)* (Providence, R.I.: printed for I. R. Potter, 1824), 5.

16. John Millner, *A Compendious Journal of all the Marches, Battles, Sieges and Other . . . Actions of the Allies in Their . . . War against . . . France* (London: n.p., 1733), 197, x.

17. *Military Memoirs of Marlborough's Campaigns, 1702–1712, by Captain Robert Parker . . . and the Count de Merode-Westerloo*, ed. David Chandler (London: Greenhill, 1998), 108; Winston S. Churchill, *Marlborough: His Life and Times*, 4 vols. (repr. London: Sphere, 1967), 4: 69–70; Richard Kane, *Campaigns of King William and the Duke of Marlborough*, 2d ed. (London: J. Millan, 1747), 102; Publisher's preface to Robert Parker, *Memoirs of the Most Remarkable Military Transactions from the Year 1683 to 1718* (Dublin, Ire.: G. and A. Ewing, 1746), n.p.

18. *Select Passages from the Diary and Letters of the Late John Blackader, Esq.* ed. John Newton (Edinburgh, Scot.: John Ritchie, 1806), 19, 57, and preface.

19. George Hamilton, *A Voyage Round the World, in His Majesty's Frigate* Pandora (1793; repr. Sydney, Australia: Hordern House, 1998), 39–40, 66.

20. Caroline F. Scott, *Diary of the Siege of Fort William*, ed. D. M. Rose (Oban: reprinted from the *Oban Times*, 1900); *The Official Diary of Lieutenant-General Adam Williamson*, ed.

John Charles Fox (London: Royal Historical Society, 1912); *Journal of William Amherst in America, 1758–1760*, ed. John Clarence Webster (London: Butler and Tanner, 1928), 14; *The Journal of Jeffrey Amherst, Recording the Military Career of General Amherst in America from 1758 to 1763*, ed. John Clarence Webster (Toronto, Ont.: Ryerson, 1931); *Augustus Hervey's Journal: Being the Intimate Account of the Life of a Captain in the Royal Navy Ashore and Afloat, 1746–1759*, ed. David Erskine (London: William Kimber, 1953).

21. *Diary of a Common Soldier in the American Revolution, 1775–1783: An Annotated Edition of the Military Journal of Jeremiah Greenman*, ed. Robert Bray and Paul Bushnell (De Kalb: Northern Illinois Univ. Press, 1978), 217; *The Specht Journal: A Military Journal of the Burgoyne Campaign*, trans. Helga Doblin, ed. Mary C. Lynn (Westport, Conn.: Greenwood, 1995); *John Peebles' American War: The Diary of a Scottish Grenadier, 1776–1782*, ed. Ira D. Gruber (Stroud, U.K.: Sutton for the Army Records Society, 1997), 97, 372, 510–11.

22. Franklin, *Autobiography and Other Writings*, 148; John R. Cuneo, *Robert Rogers of the Rangers* (New York: Oxford Univ. Press, 1959), 55; Rogers, *Journals of Major Robert Rogers Containing an Account of the Several Excursions He Made . . . during the Late War* (London: J. Millan, 1765), v–vi, 5.

23. Jonathan Carver, *Travels through America, 1766–1768*, ed. Norman Gelb (New York: John Wiley and Sons, 1993), 158. This, the only recent edition of the *Travels*, omits Carver's account of the massacre at Fort William Henry.

24. Rogers, *Journals*, 60, 62, 70, 183–85.

25. Ibid., vi, 1, 196.

Three

T. E. Lawrence

Writing the Military Life from Homer to High Modernism

TERRY REILLY

I thought out my problems mainly in terms of Hejaz, illustrated by what I knew of its men and its geography. These would have been too long if written down; and the argument has been compressed into an abstract form in which it smells more of the lamp than of the field. All military writing does, worse luck.

—T. E. Lawrence, *Seven Pillars of Wisdom*

Considering their scope and diversity, the writings of T. E. Lawrence, also known as Lawrence of Arabia, have received relatively little critical attention. Most commentators have tended to focus either on Lawrence personally or on *Seven Pillars of Wisdom*,[1] the semiautobiographical account of the Arab campaign he helped lead against the Turks during World War I. In *The Golden Warrior: The Life and Legend of Lawrence of Arabia*, Lawrence James synopsizes the history of criticism about Lawrence from his death in 1935 until the early 1990s. James finds that after a twenty-year period of hero worship culminating in David Lean's 1955 film *Lawrence of Arabia*, Lawrence, as well as many of the values he represented, came under attack, remaining so from the late 1950s to the late 1960s. Several books that appeared in the late 1970s sought to rehabilitate Lawrence's reputation; however, since then, book-length studies about Lawrence have become increasingly rare, with Lawrence James's biography and M. D. Allen's *The Medievalism of Lawrence of Arabia* emerging as the most significant critical works in the 1990s.[2]

Paul Fussell's *The Great War and Modern Memory*, unquestionably one of the seminal works about memoirs of World War I, is conspicuously absent from the list of critical works listed above. Fussell mentions Lawrence only once, and that in a disparaging footnote attributed to Robert Graves. Fussell accounts for this, in part, in his introduction: "This book is about the British experience on the Western Front from 1914 to 1918 and some of the literary means by which it was remembered, conventionalized, and mythologized . . . [thus] largely disregarding events in Mesopotamia, Turkey, Africa, and Ireland."[3] Fussell's introduction thus privileges the narratives of Siegfried Sassoon, Robert Graves, Edmund Blunden, and other works by soldier-authors who served in France (including himself in the next world war) while marginalizing or disregarding memoirs like Lawrence's *Seven Pillars of Wisdom*. Nevertheless, Fussell's interpretive rubric works particularly well as a means to discuss Lawrence's writing, and the essay that follows frequently draws parallels between Lawrence's writing and Fussell's interpretations of features particular to World War I military writing. In other words, while the main argument here is that Lawrence's oeuvre collectively represents a distinguishable pattern of autobiographical military writing, the intention is also to call attention to ways that Lawrence's writings can be included within the locus of Fussell's critical perspectives about Great War narratives.

The concept of looking at Lawrence's work from within the context of military life writing provides an interesting new perspective from which to revisit not only Lawrence's life and *Seven Pillars of Wisdom* but also his other works, which cover a wide range of different genres, including a rather large corpus of over a thousand extant letters. Two things will become quite clear as Lawrence's collected works within this context are considered and discussed. The first is that each of Lawrence's works emanates from a military perspective, although these perspectives shift according to the genre and subject matter of the piece. Examples from three of Lawrence's works illustrate what is meant by this. In an encyclopedic narrative such as *Seven Pillars*, Lawrence plays a number of roles—clerk, Arab chieftain, English officer, civilian diplomat, guerilla leader, terrorist—and for each persona he develops a distinct style and voice. In *The Mint*, however, the short choppy prose and minimalist vocabulary reproduces the perspective of an enlisted man in the post–World War I English army. In *A Handbook to the 37-1/2 Foot Motor Boats of the 200 Class*, he assumes the voice of the anonymous military technical writer.

The second point is that, when considered collectively within the contexts of literary and military history, Lawrence's works reveal his talents both as a master of literary impersonation and as a military historian. When a scene or situation is Homeric (as in the feast of the lamb in chapter

46 of *Seven Pillars*), for example, he writes in an Homeric style; when something reminds him of Malory (such as his description of Auda, an Arab chieftain, "as fantastic as the hills of Rumm, old as Malory"),[4] he not only directly refers to Malory but describes the scene in Malory's style and language. Lawrence sums up his knowledge of and approach to military history quite clearly in this long passage from chapter 33 of *Seven Pillars:*

> In military theory I was tolerably read, my Oxford curiosity having taken me past Napoleon to Clausewitz and his school, to Caemmerer and Moltke, and the recent Frenchmen. They had all seemed to be one-sided; and after looking at Jomini and Willisen, I had found broader principles in Saxe and Guibert and the eighteenth century. However, Clausewitz was intellectually so much the master of them, and his book so logical and fascinating, that unconsciously I accepted his finality, until a comparison of Kuhne and Foch disgusted me with soldiers, wearied me of their officious glory, making me critical of all their light. In any case, my interest had been abstract, concerned with the theory and philosophy of warfare especially from the metaphysical side.
>
> Now, in the field everything had been concrete, particularly the tiresome problem of Medina; and to distract myself from that I began to recall suitable maxims on the conduct of modern, scientific war. But they would not fit, and it worried me.[5]

In the ensuing pages, Lawrence, stricken with fever and dysentery, lies in his tent in the desert for eight days, formulating his own theory of guerilla warfare. During this period, Lawrence says, he envisioned the entire military plan for the Arabian campaign, a plan that entailed, paradoxically, avoiding battles and casualties when possible. Lawrence suggests that his clearly articulated though complex theory of guerilla warfare was the result of hallucinations reminiscent of a vision quest or early Christian epiphany resulting from mortification of the flesh, thus bringing together autobiography, military theory, and medieval literary constructs in a complex hybrid form. This remarkable chapter ends with this essay's epigraph, in which Lawrence reflects on the possibilities and limitations of military, and thus his own, writing.

As we shall see, Lawrence's voracious reading and remarkable memory helped him to create in his writing a literary multivoicedness that critics have found difficult to categorize. However, Stephen Ely Tabachnick has argued convincingly that in *Seven Pillars,*

Lawrence reveals to us the difficulty of waging heroic war in the modern world, clad only in the armor of Homeric ideals and a fin-de-siecle world-weary longing for death. Like Joseph Conrad and Stephen Crane, who straddle the transition from romanticism's last gasp, the "Death in Venice" of a tradition which sees dying bravely as something good, to the new age of Hemingway's antiheroism, Lawrence finds himself facing a new situation with outmoded philosophical tools. The result is that romantic and anti-romantic views of death, among other things, exist side by side in *Seven Pillars of Wisdom* in discordance.[6]

Considered within the context of literary history and the genre of military writing, Lawrence's works collectively articulate, perhaps more clearly than any other twentieth-century writer, literary and sociological transitions from Victorianism to high modernism in English culture. Tabachnick says that Lawrence's work expresses "why it is hard to be a hero in the modern world," while Fussell notes that the "special quality" of memoirs of the Great War is that "the passage of these literary characters from prewar freedom to wartime bondage, frustration and absurdity signals . . . the passage of modern writing from one mode to another, from the low mimetic of the plausible and the social to the ironic of the outrageous, the ridiculous, and the murderous." Moreover, Fussell argues that despite their blunt violence, these memoirs are "delicately transitional, pointing at once in two opposite directions—back to the low mimetic, forward to the ironic." Lawrence's writing shows us how difficult it is to find literary language to express such an important cultural transition, a point that Fussell underscores: "One of the cruxes of the war, of course, is the collision between events and the language available—or thought appropriate—to describe them. To put it more accurately, the collision was one between events and the public language used for over a century to celebrate the idea of progress."[7]

In sum, as the epigraph from *Seven Pillars* indicates, Lawrence was not only thoroughly versed in the history and stylistic elements of classical literature and military writing but acutely aware of these genres' strengths and weaknesses. Moreover, since virtually all of Lawrence's writing took shape within the broad, richly textured genre known as "military writing," such a focus shifts the perspective on Lawrence's writing from one concerned with interrelationships between the man and his work or between autobiography and history, to one that first explores the roles of writer as soldier and soldier as writer, in order to consider ways that a mature, educated, articulate modern soldier is able to write about himself and his own historical sense of place.[8]

Biography and Literary Chronology

Before discussing stylistics and Lawrence's art of literary impersonation in detail, let us first examine an overview of his works and their respective generic concerns.[9] In *Crusader Castles*, Lawrence's undergraduate thesis completed in 1910 for a bachelor of arts at Oxford, he uses the highly stylized languages of heraldry and medieval militarism to consider plans of both attack and defense as they relate to the construction of various castles on the Crusaders' route to Jerusalem. Often, he shapes these descriptions as types of eyewitness accounts, as he does in this description of the castle at Safita:

> The roof on the other hand is flat and unencumbered with fittings, and on the top of each merlon is a recessed socket, for the swinging bar of the shutter that closed the crenellations: this shows that some use was made of it in attacks, but even so the keep of Safita can never have been a very efficient stronghold. It would be crowded with a garrison of 200 men and the necessary stores, which must have included water, for the upper floor (evidently meant, by its barred door, as a last resort) has no means of access to the cistern of the foundations.[10]

Similarly, in one of his last works, a prose translation of Homer's *Odyssey*, Lawrence creates through detail and modern language a sense of immediacy and presence that brings the text to life. Perhaps the clearest example of this can be seen not in the translation of the *Odyssey* itself but in one of Lawrence's letters to publisher Bruce Rogers, in response to a reader's criticism of Lawrence's translation:

> You may have thought me cavalier in preferring my own way to W.'s professional suggestions, sometimes: not his verbal suggestions, but his archeology. Yet, actually, I'm in as strong a position vis-à-vis Homer as most of his translators. For years, we were digging up a city of roughly the Odysseus period. I have handled the weapons, armour, utensils of those times, explored their houses, planned their

cities. I have hunted wild boars and watched wild lions, sailed the Aegean (and sailed ships), bent bows, lived with pastoral peoples, woven textiles, built boats and killed many men. So I have odd knowledges that qualify me to understand the *Odyssey*, and odd experiences that interpret it to me. Therefore a certain heartiness in rejecting help.[11]

In this remarkable passage, Lawrence stops short of asserting that he is indeed either the heir to or the reincarnation of Odysseus, but his references to "odd knowledges" and "odd experiences" clearly invoke the idea that during certain periods of his life he regarded himself as a "type" of Odysseus, in the sense of mythological or biblical typology. On one level, Lawrence sees the act of translating the *Odyssey* as what we may describe as shared autobiography, of shouldering Homer aside and telling Odysseus' story as if it were at least partially his own. On another level, in Lawrence's translation of the *Odyssey*, it is not difficult to see Odysseus in much the same position as Lawrence and thousands of other Europeans and Americans at the time—as simply a wandering soldier "demobbed" after surviving a long and dreadful war.

In addition to *Seven Pillars*, *Crusader Castles*, and the translation of the *Odyssey*, Lawrence wrote a number of other texts, including an archeological report, "Carchemish: Report on the Excavation at Djerabis on Behalf of the British Museum" (1914), and *The Wilderness of Zin* (1915), cowritten with Leonard Woolley. This latter work, as Stanley and Rodelle Weintraub note, was presented as a scientific trip through the Suez, but this explanation served "as camouflage for a map making reconnaissance from Gaza to Aqaba destined to be of strategic value even sooner than anticipated."[12] From 1916 to 1918, Lawrence wrote a number of entries for the *Arab Bulletin*, an intelligence-gathering journal dedicated to collecting information about the Arab revolt. Lawrence worked on the several editions of *Seven Pillars* from 1919 to 1922, and then from 1922 to 1928 he wrote *The Mint*, a story of his experiences as an enlisted man in the Royal Air Force (RAF). Thomas O'Donnell sees *The Mint* as a Romantic confessional journal in the tradition of St. Augustine, while the Weintraubs describe it as a "sharply etched service chronicle"; Tabachnick regards the style as "austere" and notes "the linear, introspective aspects of a modern novel."[13] Such diverse judgments, taken together, describe *The Mint* as a combination of medieval and high modernist elements presented in autobiographical, journalistic form. Such a combination, within an overarching military framework, is characteristic of much of Lawrence's work, including *Seven Pillars*.

In 1927 Lawrence published *Revolt in the Desert,* a revision of *Seven Pillars* that Jeffrey Meyers unflatteringly characterizes as follows: "*Revolt* is purely military history with and emphasis on action and with no digressions. Some of the dullest and least important chapters are included, while all the personal and subjective, the cruel and horrible, the intellectual and philosophical chapters, are deleted."[14] While Lawrence's motives for writing *Revolt in the Desert* were primarily financial,[15] perhaps a more important point here is that as Lawrence takes himself out of *Revolt in the Desert* and writes what we might refer to as "straight" military history, he not only demonstrates his ability to write effectively and well in that genre but indicates that *Seven Pillars* was meant to be something different—something more personal, more richly textured and perhaps more controversial and confrontational—than a simple autobiography or military history. Moreover, the "literary" content and style of *Seven Pillars* clearly emerges when compared head to head with *Revolt in the Desert.*

Also in 1927 Lawrence wrote several pieces of literary criticism for the *Spectator* under the assumed nom de plume of "C. D." Characteristically, an overarching military perspective informs Lawrence's literary criticism. In the September 10, 1927, issue, for example, his article is titled "Hakluyt—the First Naval Propagandist," and in the following passage from another essay for the *Spectator,* he criticizes D. H. Lawrence and E. M. Forster for not writing more about the war:

> In those early days before the War, readers' hopes lay in Lawrence and Forster. These two heirs, through the Victorians, of the great tradition of the English novel were fortunate to have made good their footing before war came. Its bursting jarred their stride, indeed. [D. H.] Lawrence glances at the War twice or thrice, and wrote a haunting poem about a train journey in uniform but no more. Each man had tired of politics and action, and plunged into the dim forest of character in time to save himself from chaos.[16]

T. E. Lawrence, of course, was not able to turn away from the war or to save himself from the emotional and psychological chaos that resulted in his own personal life. As Phillip Knightly and Colin Simpson point out, Lawrence was in "a deeply disturbed emotional state . . . a condition near to madness" when he returned to England after the war, and the possibility of severe post-traumatic stress has not been afforded a proper role when assessing Lawrence's reconstruction of events while writing *Seven Pillars* from 1919 to 1922.[17]

As mentioned above, Lawrence translated Homer's *Odyssey* from 1928 to 1931 while serving in India with the Royal Air Force under the name "T. E. Shaw," and in 1933 he anonymously authored the technical journal *A Handbook to the 37-1/2 Foot Motor Boats of the 200 Class*. After his death in a motorcycle crash in May 1935, partially completed fragments of a manuscript about life in the RAF, *Leaves in the Wind*—speculatively identified as either a sequel to or continuation of *The Mint*—was found in Lawrence's cottage in Dorset. The Weintraubs note that the style of the fragments continues that of *The Mint*, with short, choppy sentences and a dearth of descriptive or colorful adjectives, but the content is often unpleasantly scatological to the point of offensiveness.[18] *Leaves in the Wind* may be described as postmodern, with minimalist prose and conscious flattening of affect, but more important it suggests that Lawrence was experimenting with yet another style and literary persona at the time of his death.

The many voices in Lawrence's writing may be attributed in part to his own protean sense of self. During his lifetime, Lawrence changed his identity and name several times to fit his professional or literary circumstances. Thomas Edward Lawrence, "Ned" to his friends and family, was the second of five illegitimate sons born to Thomas Chapman, the grandson of an Irish baronet, and Sarah Junner, the nanny for Chapman's daughters. Unable to secure a divorce from his wife, Chapman simply changed his name to Lawrence and moved with Junner to England, where they presented themselves as man and wife.[19] His father's actions may have contributed to Lawrence's own shifting sense of identity and his various names: born to a father named Chapman, he grew up as "Ned" Lawrence; in the Middle East, he was known to the Arabs and Turks as "Aurens" and, later, to the rest of the world as "Lawrence of Arabia." In 1922, he enlisted in the RAF as a private under the name "John Hume Ross" and was discharged when his identity was discovered. In 1923 he joined the Royal Tank Corps as T. E. Shaw, a name derived in part from his friendship with George Bernard Shaw. After threatening to commit suicide, he was allowed to reenlist in the RAF in 1925 as Airman T. E. Shaw.[20]

Lawrence's shifting sense of identity may be regarded both as signs of a complex, conflicted psyche and as a series of conscious writerly decisions. When he was writing literary criticism for the *Spectator*, for example, Lawrence first insisted on anonymity and used "C. D." as his byline, but later he gave instructions to editor Francis Yeats-Brown gradually to reveal his identity to the public. Curiously, while C. D. apparently referred to a person named Colin Dale, it was, in fact, a transformation of "Colindale," the London underground station nearest to Hendon Aerodrome, where

Lawrence was then living as Airman Shaw.[21] Such conscious multileveled deception, offset by Lawrence's intention that the ruse should gradually be exposed, illuminates a pattern that recurs in much of Lawrence's autobiographical writing.

Tabachnick, for example, notes that early in *Seven Pillars* Lawrence simply imitated the Arabs but that he eventually felt that he was doing too good a job; as he notes in chapter 1, a man following his model among the Arabs "may imitate them so well that they spuriously imitate him back again."[22] This complex form of imitation, where Arab behavior becomes based on a simulacrum, or impersonation of a perception of Arab behavior by a European Other, endlessly repeats itself, echoing until eventually it becomes a type of psychological hall of mirrors that reduces any sense of self to mere fragments. Tabachnick centers this issue around the problems Lawrence has using the word "we" in *Seven Pillars*: sometimes it refers to the Arabs, at others to the British, and later to Lawrence and his select band of bodyguards.[23] The question, "who are 'we'?" of course, eventually resonates outward to include the question, "whose autobiography is Lawrence writing?" Or perhaps more broadly, what happens to the genre of autobiography when the writer does not have a clear or fixed sense of self, or when the writer describes himself in the language of others? We can begin to answer this last question by looking at two issues frequently discussed in Lawrence's works—his sources and his style.

Sources

Paul Fussell notes that "by 1914, it was possible for soldiers to be not merely literate but vigorously literary. . . . The belief in the educative powers of classical and English literature," Fussell adds, caused the memoirs of the Great War to be full of literary allusions, references, and earnestness. Similarly, several critics have traced parts of *Seven Pillars of Wisdom* to a number of literary sources, including military history, travel narratives, Romantic poetry, and fiction from Malory to Joyce. Jeffrey Meyers, for example, notes that Lawrence's description of the Aqaba campaign is based on Homer and the final bathing in the sea on Xenophon's *Anabasis*. The Weintraubs call attention to the presence of Caesar's *Commentaries* among his sources, and Tabachnick finds that Lawrence borrowed from Thucydides' *Peloponnesian Wars* and Herodotus' *Histories*. The Weintraubs, in fact, argue that while Shaw hoped *Seven Pillars* would be history on the Thucydidean model, they see it as "Iliad history—full of inaccuracies, extravagances, diffuseness, artificiality, and a sustained genius for language."[24]

A number of critics have also argued that *Seven Pillars* is heavily informed by various travel narratives, or what Tabachnick calls "autobiographies of travel," including Charles Doughty's *Travels in Arabia Deserta*, Alexander Kinglake's *Eothen*, and W. H. Hudson's *Idle Days in Patagonia*, *The Purple Land*, and *Green Mansions*.[25] Commentators have likewise traced a number of literary allusions in the text. Meyers, for example, says that the dedicatory poem is not a very good one and one that "imitates the long loose line and misty fin de siecle sentiment of Ernest Dowson's 'Impenitentia Ultima,' which [Lawrence] quotes in Chapter 53." Meyers argues that Tolstoy and Nietzsche influenced Lawrence strongly in later chapters, while the Weintraubs assert that Lawrence frequently compared *Seven Pillars* to *Moby-Dick*. Moreover, they find a "striking similarity in how [Lawrence and Melville] put their books together. In each case—whether the book is fiction or fact embroidered and used fictionally—the quest of the protagonist is interleaved with documentary chapters." Although the Weintraubs may push this connection too far, on one level it is safe to say that *Seven Pillars of Wisdom* is "about" the Arab Revolt in much the same way that *Moby-Dick* is "about" whaling.[26]

In a more modern sense the Weintraubs also argue that Lawrence "was reading Conrad's *Lord Jim* at about the time he was writing *Seven Pillars*,"[27] and Tabachnick notes that Lawrence was a close correspondent of Conrad's and read most of his books.[28] Moreover, it is evident from Lawrence's letters that he was very familiar with the works of Eliot, Joyce, Pound, and other modernists, as well as of Thomas Hardy, Shaw, and Graves, all relatively close personal friends. That several critics have identified numerous examples of derivative styles and passages suggests that Lawrence's impersonatory writing style may be more akin to that of Joyce in the "Oxen of the Sun" chapter of *Ulysses* than to more conventional historical narratives. Like Joyce as well, Lawrence's allusive use of sources often produces a symbolic system that points in several directions at once. For example, Tabachnick argues that the title may have come from several sources. One may be from Proverbs 9:1: "Wisdom hath builded her house, she hath hewn out her seven pillars." Alternatively, it may be that the figure seven implies completeness in Semitic languages, or that it is a reference to the seven biblical lands that must be governed morally. Allen asserts that the title is from Ruskin's *The Seven Lamps of Architecture*, but Tabachnick argues that the title "refers first and foremost to the military architecture of the revolt. A manuscript notebook (M.S. Eng 1252, 355) in the Houghton Library makes this clear and demonstrates the fundamental importance of the military plot to Lawrence's conception of the book's structure." Tabachnick's comment foregrounds the idea that *Seven Pillars of Wisdom* is first and foremost a type of military writing, thus reinforcing the view that Lawrence regarded military concepts and his dual position as author and soldier as paradigmatic structures that gave shape to his narratives.[29]

The uncertain origin or multiple sources of the title is offset by the subtitle of *Seven Pillars of Wisdom*, "A Triumph," which most critics regard as Lawrence's darkly ironic and tragic personal comment, given the hollowness of his victory and the subsequent betrayal of the Arabs by the British in Damascus and at the Paris peace talks. Finally, the inscription in Arabic on the cover of the first public editions, which reads "The sword also means cleanness and death," is also polysemous, given that Feisal's name in Arabic literally means "the sword flashing downward in the stroke." "Feisal" thus brings life to the Arab cause, just as "Feisal" also brings death.[30]

Style and Historical Location

The complex representations of both Arabic and English metaphors in *Seven Pillars of Wisdom* provide an interesting insight into the ways in which Lawrence's writing style changed over the years. For example, on May 5, 1927, while he was working on the book, Lawrence wrote a letter to William Rothenstein describing his style: "My style is a made-up thing, very thickly encrusted with what seemed to me the tit-bits and clever wheezes of established authors. So, for book-learned people, threading it constantly, but not too sharply, [it] tickles their literary memory, by half-reminding them of half forgotten pleasures. There isn't any good, or permanence, in such a derivative effort."[31] Lawrence's clear characterization of his allusive style of writing is reminiscent of the styles employed by Joyce, Eliot, Woolf, Pound, and others often described as "high modernists."

In a footnote to his memoir *Orientations*, Ronald Storrs, who made several trips with Lawrence, provides another insight into Lawrence's style at the time of *Seven Pillars*. Discussing what Lawrence may have meant when he told Shaw that the book was an attempt at "dramatizing reality," Storrs argues that "Lawrence's account of the voyage, particularly the conversations, is heightened by the use of what *The Thousand Nights and a Night* calls *Lisan al-hal*, the 'tongue, of the state or occasion'; i.e., the language deemed appropriate to the characters or circumstances." Such a comment points to Lawrence's awareness and use of generic Arabic conventions and the Arab practice of using different literary styles and voices for different occasions. Tabachnick notes that Thucydides uses a similar technique in *The Peloponnesian War*. *Lisan al-hal* helps to explain why the Homeric episodes in *Seven Pillars* are rendered in archaic, highly styled Homeric language and also why, as Meyers points out, Lawrence characterizes General Edmund Allenby with references either to Julius Caesar or the language of Caesar's *Commentaries*.[32]

The Weintraubs and Tabachnick provide yet another interesting insight into how Lawrence wrote. The Weintraubs believe

> Lawrence forced himself into what might now be called a "mind-expanding state," exciting his imagination "with hunger and cold and sleeplessness," he thought, "more than de Quincey with his opium." Explaining his method (but ignoring the considerable mass of preliminary material he had as foundation) he wrote, "I tie myself into knots trying to reenact everything, as I write it out. It's like writing in front of a looking-glass and never looking at the paper but always at the imaginary scene."[33]

Tabachnick argues that in Lawrence's letters his "most interesting and detailed comments relate to the art of style": "His method of styling his work was first to write down his sentences quickly and spontaneously. . . . Then he would return over the sentences again and again, making sure that each captured his individuality. So Lawrence's style has both a romantic spontaneity, a very deep expression of his feelings at the moment of writing, and a very deliberate and conscious polish." The result of Lawrence's polishing, for Tabachnick, is a highly complex, sophisticated, artificial prose (unlike normal speech); "his own complex style grew naturally out of his own personality and experiences and thus suited the post–World War I age even as it appeared both to be a throwback to the nineteenth century."[34] For anyone who has studied Joyce and seen the Rosenbach manuscript of *Ulysses*, Tabachnick's description is remarkably similar to Joyce's allusive style and multidraft composition techniques.

Lawrence's obsession with stylistic concerns can be seen in his letters, in several instances in *Seven Pillars*, and in the complicated publication history of the book. The Weintraubs note that a major portion of Lawrence's postwar correspondence was directed to creative writers and critics, about other writers and critics. Most of these letters contain comments or critiques about style, such as the following concerning Charles

Doughty's *Arabia Deserta:* "It is a book which begins powerfully, written in a style which apparently has neither father nor son, so closely wrought, so tense, so just in its words and phrases, that it demands a hard reader." In this and other letters, Lawrence's interest in evaluating other writers' styles points to his increasing ability to impersonate those styles.[35]

In chapter 48 of *Seven Pillars,* Lawrence tells a long digressive tale, a "close parody of Auda's epic style," that produces waves of laughter among the Arabs, who "recognized the original, but for whom parody was a new art form. . . . Auda laughed the loudest and longest, for he loved a jest upon himself; and the fatuousness of my epic had shown him his own sure mastery of descriptive action."[36] Later, after massacring the Turks on the road to Kerak but failing to pursue them because of a snowstorm, Lawrence writes:

> We should have pushed past Kerak on the heels of victory, frighting the Turks to Amman with our rumour: as it was, nothing came of all the loss and effort, except a report which I sent over to the British headquarters in Palestine for the Staff's consumption. It was meanly written for effect, full of quaint similes ["smiles" in the 1937 edition] and mock simplicities; and made them think me a modest amateur, doing his best after the great models; not a clown, leering after them where they with Foch, bandmaster, at their head went drumming down the old road of effusion of blood into the house of Clausewitz. Like the battle, it was a nearly proof parody of regulation use. Headquarters loved it, and innocently, to crown the jest, offered me a decoration on the strength of it. We should have more bright breasts in the Army if each man was able, without witnesses, to write out his own dispatch.[37]

In each instance, Lawrence shapes his words into a parodic form designed both to illuminate the situation and to foreground his own involvement. In the case of the parody of Auda's tale-telling, his mock epic strengthens his relationship with the Arabs, although he knows even then that his mission will require him ultimately to deceive them. After the battle at Kerak, his parodic report becomes a scathing satire on the English army, although his report ironically results in his receiving a medal.

Lawrence's desire to shape parts of his narrative into clearly identifiable generic forms was accompanied by an unusual aesthetic obsession with the form of the overall book. As the Weintraubs note,

His specification included a page of a uniform thirty-seven lines, each page beginning with a new paragraph. Most pages had to begin with an ornamental capital so that when the book lay open its two pages would balance in appearance. The last line of each page had to be solid, with the last lines of other paragraphs running beyond the middle of the line, again to avoid blocks of white space. Words were not to be split at the ends of lines, and every chapter had to end at the bottom righthand corner.[38]

Moreover, as Meyers notes, "each letter was to be used as an engraved capital to open a paragraph at least once, and he starts new chapters with all but three letters." Critical responses to these esoteric demands have been characteristically mixed. Meyers argues that the fastidious aesthetic efforts often resulted in a "strained, awkward, and artificial style," while the Weintraubs assert that because of Lawrence's "amazing command of word and phrase . . . the most careful reader of the later popular edition, where all of this typographical precision is dropped, would never suspect that the text had been so forced."[39]

Such divergent opinions carry over to the commentary regarding the appeal of *Seven Pillars* to readers. Tabachnick asserts that "written as it was in the 1920s, when the period of personalized prose was already past, *Seven Pillars of Wisdom* appeared as a throwback in style as well as heroic content, and found its greatest acceptance among older writers, like H. G. Wells and Arnold Bennett, who were able to appreciate its virtues independently of current fashions."[40]

On the one hand, Tabachnick's comment seems well founded, considering that H. G. Wells called Lawrence's book "the finest piece of prose that has been written in the English language for 150 years."[41] Winston Churchill's comments were even more glowing: "As a narrative of war and adventure, as a presentation of all that the Arabs mean to the world, the *Seven Pillars* is unsurpassable. It ranks with the greatest books ever written in the English language."[42] On the other hand, a few critics have regarded *Seven Pillars* as a modern text for its time, one that prefigured literary developments to come. French critic Jean Beraud Villars, for example, writes that

the combination of profound introspection and naked confession in *Seven Pillars* . . . reminds one of Proust or Gide . . . [and] Lawrence's balance between romanticism and naturalism was the essence of a new form of literature to be seized upon by a generation of writers who were reacting to an upbringing pervaded by naturalism yet unable to withstand its attractions. Lawrence, by combining romanticism with naturalism, gave new dignity to horror.[43]

Moreover, according to Villars,

Into the *Seven Pillars* he dragged in the musty smells of homosexuality, of cruelty, and of death. A certain sadism that had been carefully expurgated from the accounts of other war writers, who by tacit consent presented themselves as martyrs and paladins that were not supposed to have such troubled sensations.

Lawrence proved to be the forerunner. Before Malraux, Koestler, Kafka and Jean-Paul Sartre, before the writers of the Resistance and those who described Nazi and Soviet atrocities . . . he invented a style which was to be largely exploited by a whole generation of writers.[44]

That Jeffrey Meyers also sees *Seven Pillars* as a modernist text is evident in his comparison of it with Doughty's *Arabia Deserta:*

Though [both] are spiritual autobiographies, the emphasis, attitudes, and ideas in the books are often very different. Lawrence says that Doughty was keen only on life and death, and that he stressed politics and psychology. *Arabia Deserta* is a Victorian and an Christian book, self-possessed and full of certainty; *Seven Pillars* is a modern and a secular work, introspective, uneasy and morbid. Where Doughty is rooted and definitive, Lawrence is unstable and ambiguous.[45]

Meyers's synopsis makes a good, clear distinction between Victorian and modernist poetics, ethics, and stylistics.

Another way to reconcile these very different views of the text—either as a throwback to the Victorian period or as a novel and innovative text in the age of high modernism—is to look closely at chapter 80, undoubtedly one of the most important in the book. In it Lawrence describes the most decisive moment in his life: his capture and the agonizing torture and rape that he suffered at Deraa. In a letter to Edward Garnett on August 22, 1922, he writes of chapter 80: "I put it into print very reluctantly, last of all the pages I sent to press. For weeks I wanted to burn it in the manuscript: because I could not tell the story face to face with anyone." Lawrence describes the events of his capture in painful, graphic detail and concludes the chapter with two realizations. First, he sardonically observes, "Not that my maimed will now cared a hoot about the Arab Revolt (or about anything but mending myself): yet, since the war had been a hobby of mine, for custom's sake I would force myself to push it through." Finally, the friendliness of the local Arabic tribesmen "momentarily stayed me to carry the burden, whose certainty the passing days confirmed: how in Deraa that night the citadel of my integrity had been irrevocably lost."[46]

A number of critics have challenged the accuracy and historicity of Lawrence's account of the events in this chapter, in part, as Jeffrey Meyers notes, because Lawrence tells us that although he went into Deraa with two Arabs, he alone was captured; in any case, there is no way to verify his story. Moreover, argues Meyers, "in the course of his revisions, much of the factual documentation of the Revolt was either lost or destroyed, so that with each version of *Seven Pillars of Wisdom*, Lawrence moved farther from actual history and closer to an imaginative re-creation of it." Meyers's skepticism stems from Lawrence's letters, in which he often takes contradictory approaches to historical accuracy. In a letter to Shaw in 1928 he writes that *Seven Pillars* "was an effort to make history an imaginative thing." In another letter dated December 1, 1927, he tells Edward Garnett, "The thing follows an exact diary sequence, and is literally true throughout." Later, although he told Robert Graves, "I have tried not to be inaccurate throughout," he adds, "I was on thin ice when I wrote the Damascus chapter and anyone who copies me will be through it, if he is not careful. *Seven Pillars of Wisdom* is full of half-truth: here." Finally, in a letter to H. S. Ede, Lawrence writes that "the interests of truth and form often differ."[47]

As a soldier and officer in the midst of a war, Lawrence's historical accuracy is questionable, in part, because he could not keep a detailed diary due to the risk of capture. His extant diaries include cryptic entries often consisting of sentence fragments or isolated words designed to trigger his memory. He also used a number of his own photographs in helping to reconstruct the narrative, many of which are included in *Lawrence of Arabia and His World* (New York: Scribner, 1976) by Richard Perceval Graves. Once again, Tabachnick is helpful here, as he sees Lawrence as an "autobiographical artist" rather than an "objective historian" who "worked always toward heightened literary effectiveness within the framework of a basic fidelity to fact."[48]

Despite these questions of accuracy, Lawrence's re-creation of the events in Deraa in chapter 80 marks an important transition. After this chapter, the book's tone becomes much darker, and the idea of chivalric and heroic warfare conveyed earlier in the text gives way to horrific encounters, such as the ferocious massacre of civilians by the Turks in Tafas and the subsequent slaughter of the Turkish police battalion in chapter 117, as well as the graphic description in chapter 121 of the appalling conditions in the Turkish hospital in Damascus. As "honorable" warfare between combatants gives way to the killing of civilians and indiscriminate slaughter, Lawrence's style changes noticeably. In the early chapters, by contrast, the style is often loose, flowing, and colorful, as we see in this rather pastoral passage from chapter 11:

> Tafas [el Raashid] haltered the camels, loosed their girths, and strewed before them green fodder from a fragrant pile before the gate. Then he led me into the guest room of the house, a dark clean little mud-brick place roofed with half palm-logs under hammered earth. We sat down on the palm leaf mat which ran along the dais. The day in this stifling valley had grown very hot; and gradually we lay back side by side. Then the hum of the bees in the gardens without, and of the flies hovering over our veiled faces within, lulled us to sleep.[49]

In the later chapters, the sentences, often fragments, are stark, brutal, and colorless, as we see in this long passage from chapter 117:

> In a madness born of the horror of [the village of] Tafas we killed and killed, even blowing in the heads of the fallen and of the animals; as though their death and running blood could slake our agony.
>
> Just one group of Arabs, who had not heard our news, took prisoner the last two hundred men of the central section. Their respite was short. I had gone up to learn why it was, not unwilling that this remnant be let live as witnesses of [Sheik] Tallal's price; but a man on the ground behind them screamed something to the Arabs, who with pale faces led me across to see. It was one of us—his thigh shattered. The blood had rushed out over the red soil, and left him dying; but even so, he had not been spared. In the fashion of to-day's battle he had been further tormented by bayonets hammered through his shoulder and other leg into the ground, pinning him out like a collected insect.
>
> He was fully conscious. When we said, "Hassan, who did it?" he dropped his eyes towards the prisoners, huddling together so hopelessly broken. They said nothing the moments before we opened fire. At last, their heap ceased moving; and Hassan was dead; and we mounted again and road home slowly.[50]

Here, as in many other instances, Lawrence's stylistic transitions call attention to the limits of language and literary style in conveying his story. Tabachnick says of this section that "Lawrence assumes the Homeric tone, but . . . he can find no flicker of grandeur, and his soft modernity betrays the epic pose."[51]

According to Fussell, many Great War chroniclers faced a similar dilemma: "Very often the new reality had no resemblance whatever to the familiar, and the absence of a plausible [traditional] style placed some writers in what they thought was an impossible position." Tabachnick sees these later chapters as iterating ideas similar to those of Crane, Hemingway, and Conrad; in them Lawrence explains why it is hard to be a hero in the modern world. Moreover, he notes, "As the product of a modern outsider in an alien and primitive environment that ultimately destroys him as a complete Englishman as well, *Seven Pillars of Wisdom* carries a message strikingly similar to Conrad's *Heart of Darkness*, Forster's *A Passage to India*, Orwell's *Burmese Days*, Cary's *Mister Johnson*, and other British colonial literature of our century." The primary difference, of course, is that while the examples Tabachnick provides are fictional, Lawrence lived the events he describes. Thus, while the smooth stylistic flow of fiction often conveys a sense of reality, the closeness and immediacy of Lawrence's experiences often imbue the prose with a stylistic unevenness that paradoxically conveys a sense of artificiality. In *Seven Pillars*, Tabachnick concludes, it is "as if Kurtz himself were to try to describe his own descent into savagery without the benefit of an objective, intermediary narrator like Marlow." Such a process in autobiography customarily requires a great distancing in time, but because Lawrence wrote *Seven Pillars* shortly after the horrific scenes he had experienced, his representations are necessarily a maze of conflicting emotions that he is unable to articulate fully or clearly.[52]

After completing *Seven Pillars of Wisdom*, Lawrence went on to write *The Mint*, and his approach to style became radically different. In a letter to Edward Garnett on October 4, 1923, he writes: "Do you know that lately I have been finding my deepest satisfaction in the collocation of words so ordinary and plain that they cannot mean anything to a book-jaded mind: and out of some of such I can draw deep stuff. Is it perhaps that certain sequences of vowels or consonants imply more than others: that writing of this sort has music in it?" Tabachnick argues that by the time he finished *Seven Pillars*, Lawrence had retreated into "the exotic land of an art-prose all his own. . . . His concern with alliteration and assonance, with the rise and fall of his paragraphs, with keeping in tune with his subject matter, appears more in line with the poetry of Keats and Swinburne and the prose of Sir Thomas Browne and Thomas Traherne than with the art of his own century."[53]

In his later publications Lawrence evidences an increasing desire for anonymity, despite, or perhaps because of, his enormous popularity around the world. He writes *The Mint* under the pen name of "John Hume Ross," but the book was not published until after his death, and then under his real name; he translates the *Odyssey* under the name "T. E. Shaw"; he writes literary criticism under the initials "C. D"; and in his last work—*A Handbook to the 37-1/2 Foot Motor Boats of the 200 Class*—he is the anonymous author of a military technical journal. Of this last work Lawrence wrote, "I pride myself that every sentence in it is understandable to a fitter."[54] In short, as Lawrence had become Anonymous writing for Everyman, he was also No One writing for Everyone.

Conclusion

Lawrence's retreat into anonymity may be explained, in part, by both the critical reception of *Seven Pillars of Wisdom* and his own self-abnegation. Writing about *Seven Pillars*, Forster sees Lawrence as recording "what is probably the last of the picturesque wars. Camels, pennants, the blowing up of little railway trains by little charges of dynamite in the desert—it is unlikely to recur."[55] As Forster's comments indicate, many Englishmen saw Lawrence's exploits as little more than fabricated knight-errantry; they argued, like Fussell, that the "real war" took place in Europe. It is not coincidental that Lawrence's two sharpest critics, Richard Aldington and Herbert Read, both fought in the trenches in France during World War I. Moreover, two of Lawrence's four brothers, Frank and Will, were killed in action in France in 1915, and these deaths produced a burden of self-imposed guilt he was to carry with him the rest of his life.[56]

The paradox then is clear. Lawrence was fighting a war the way war was supposed to be fought from the medieval through the late Victorian period—with gallantry, chivalry, panache, and above all, honor—but the circumstances of modern war made these former virtues obsolete and thus subject to question and ridicule. Lawrence wrote the book, and we read it because he was successful and because he lived through the war; if he had failed or died, either his story would have been lost or he would have joined the ranks of Rupert Brooke, Wilfred Owen, Edward Thomas, Isaac Rosenberg, and the other young writers who died during the war and have become known simply as "the World War I Poets." Instead, he lived through the war and became subjected to the same sort of negative criticism leveled at such English veterans of World War I as Siegfried Sassoon, Ivor Gurney, David Jones, and Robert Graves.

Graves, one of Lawrence's closest friends, was able to put the war behind him by writing his autobiography, *Good-bye to All That*, in 1929 at the age of thirty-four. Graves's book is a type of ritualistic writerly suicide, a way to kill his former identity and move on (in his case, to ancient mythology). Lawrence, unfortunately, was never able to make such a break, and in many letters written in his last two years of life he sees himself and his writing as relics that have outlived their time: "It's odd, you know, to be reading these [T. S. Eliot's] poems, so full of the future, so far ahead of our time; and then to turn back to my book, whose prose stinks of coffins and ancestors and armorial hatchments. Yet people have the nerve to tell me it's 'a good book.' It would have been, if written a hundred years ago: but to bring it out after *Ulysses* is an insult to modern letters."[57]

Although Lawrence here sees *Seven Pillars of Wisdom* as a vestigial throwback to an earlier time, given the distance and hindsight of almost eighty years, his work has emerged as a vital document that is both produced by and reproduces the cultural ethos not only of the distant literary past and the modernist period of English literature but of both the Great War in the Middle East and the current situation in that region of the world.

In 1934 Lawrence wrote to John Buchan that he was resigning from the RAF because of his age, "but if I could have remained perpetually young, nothing would have pleased me better" than to remain in military service.[58] Lawrence, as "T. E. Shaw," left the RAF in March 1935 and died two months later in a motorcycle accident. Tabachnick notes that Lawrence's sincerity about his commitment to the military has been called into question, mainly by critics who have not themselves been in the armed forces and who are therefore skeptical about the positive aspects of military experience about which Lawrence writes so simply and truly. Military service can in fact offer the kind of comradeship and satisfaction that would be available in no other way to an intellectual like Lawrence.[59] It may also provide insights into his writing that have heretofore gone unacknowledged.

Notes

1. T. E. Lawrence, *Seven Pillars of Wisdom* (New York: Doubleday, Doran, 1937). The publication history of *Seven Pillars of Wisdom* is extremely complex, mainly because Lawrence wrote at least four significantly different versions of the text. The ongoing debate concerning the importance of these textual variations is tangentially related to my

topic, but to engage in the debate effectively here is not possible, given the length of the article. Rather, here I use the 1937 Doubleday, Doran edition of *Seven Pillars of Wisdom;* all citations from *Seven Pillars of Wisdom,* unless otherwise noted, are from this edition.

2. For works written in the late 1950s and 1960s critical of Lawrence, see Richard Aldington, *Selected Critical Writings, 1928–1960,* ed. Alister Kershaw (Carbondale: Univ. of Illinois Press, 1970); Herbert Read, *A Coat of Many Colors* (London: Routledge, 1945); Suleiman Mousa, *T. E. Lawrence: An Arab View* (Oxford, U.K.: Oxford Univ. Press, 1966); and Phillip Knightly and Colin Simpson, *The Secret Lives of Lawrence of Arabia* (New York: McGraw-Hill, 1970). Books appearing in the middle to late 1970s include Stephen Ely Tabachnick, *T. E. Lawrence* (Boston: Twayne, 1978); Stanley Weintraub and Rodelle Weintraub, *Lawrence of Arabia: The Literary Impulse* (Baton Rouge: Louisiana State Univ. Press, 1975); Jeffrey Meyers, *The Wounded Spirit: T .E. Lawrence's* Seven Pillars of Wisdom (New York: St. Martin's, 1989); Thomas J. O'Donnell, *The Confessions of T. E. Lawrence: The Romantic Hero's Presentation of Self* (Athens: Ohio Univ. Press, 1979); and John E. Mack, *A Prince of Our Disorder: The Life of T. E. Lawrence* (Boston, Mass.: Little, Brown, 1976).

3. Paul Fussell, *The Great War and Modern Memory* (Oxford, U.K.: Oxford Univ. Press, 1975). Fussell's only mention of Lawrence occurs in Graves's sardonic advice on "the obligatory ingredients of a popular memoir" (204). In addition to including references to food and drink and to kings and ghosts, Graves notes, "People also like reading about other people's mothers. . . . And they like hearing about T. E. Lawrence, because he is supposed to be a mystery man. . . . And, of course, the Prince of Wales" (204–5). For Fussell on the book's western-front focus, see page ix.

4. T. E. Lawrence, *Seven Pillars of Wisdom,* 549.

5. Ibid., 188.

6. Tabachnick, *T. E. Lawrence,* 46.

7. Ibid., 60; Fussell, *The Great War and Modern Memory,* 169, 312.

8. To say all of Lawrence's published works have a military emphasis is a slight exaggeration. Under the name J. H. Ross, Lawrence translated from French to English a book on redwood trees. Adrien Le Corbeau, *The Forest Giant* (London: Jonathan Cape, 1924), and he put together an anthology of poetry, *Minorities,* ed. J. M. Wilson (London: Jonathan Cape, 1971). Also, many of his collected letters do not include a military perspective.

9. The chronology I provide here is based on when Lawrence wrote the works, not when they were published, since several were published posthumously. *Crusader Castles,* for example, was written in 1910 but was not published until 1936. *The Mint,* although written from 1922 to 1928, was not published until 1955.

10. T. E. Lawrence, *The Essential T. E. Lawrence,* ed. David Garnett (New York: Viking, 1963), 39–40.

11. Ibid., 298.

12. Weintraub and Weintraub, *Lawrence of Arabia,* 4.

13. O'Donnell, *The Confessions of T. E. Lawrence,* 13–20; Weintraub and Weintraub, *Lawrence of Arabia,* xiii; Tabachnick, *T. E. Lawrence,* 19.

14. Meyers, *The Wounded Spirit,* 66.

15. The Weintraubs note that Lawrence wanted to sell thirty thousand copies to pay off debts incurred for the private edition and then withdraw the book. Forty thousand copies were sold in the first three weeks, and by the time Lawrence—stationed in India with the RAF—was able to withdraw the book in June, more than ninety thousand copies had been sold. Lawrence gave his royalties to a charitable trust he set up for the welfare of RAF families (Weintraub and Weintraub, *Lawrence of Arabia*, 44–45n).

16. "D. H. Lawrence's Novels," *Spectator* (Aug. 6, 1927): 223.

17. Knightly and Simpson, *The Secret Lives of Lawrence of Arabia*, 175–82.

18. Weintraub and Weintraub, *Lawrence of Arabia*, 120–21.

19. Lawrence James, *The Golden Warrior: The Life and Legend of Lawrence of Arabia* (New York: Paragon House, 1993), 3–5.

20. For this and more biographical information, see James, *The Golden Warrior;* Knightly and Simpson, *The Secret Lives of Lawrence of Arabia;* and Mack, *A Prince of Our Disorder.*

21. Weintraub and Weintraub, *Lawrence of Arabia*, 101–2.

22. T. E. Lawrence, *Seven Pillars of Wisdom*, 31.

23. Tabachnick, *T. E. Lawrence*, 100–104.

24. Fussell, *The Great War and Modern Memory*, 157; Meyers, *The Wounded Spirit*, 22–23; Weintraub and Weintraub, *Lawrence of Arabia*, 51, 62; Tabachnick, *T. E. Lawrence*, 67.

25. Samuel Hynes's study of twentieth-century war memoirs characterizes these narratives as "something like travel writing, something like autobiography, something like history" (5)—and *Seven Pillars* qualifies as all of these. War novels too frequently become like travel writing and like history; one good example of this genre blending is Ernest Hemingway's *A Farewell to Arms* (see Michael Reynolds, *Hemingway's First War* (Princeton, N.J.: Princeton Univ. Press, 1976).

26. Tabachnick, *T. E. Lawrence*, 28–46; Meyers, *The Wounded Spirit*, 68; Weintraub and Weintraub, *Lawrence of Arabia*, 49. Of Lawrence's literary friends, the Weintraubs argue, only E. M. Forster identified the *Moby-Dick* aspect of Seven Pillars, observing in a review of the posthumous trade edition that it was "a *Moby-Dick* of a book." Melville's masterpiece was ostensibly about catching a whale, and "round this tent pole of a military chronicle, T. E. has hung an unexampled fabric of portraits, descriptions, philosophies, emotions, adventures, dreams" (in Weintraub and Weintraub, *Lawrence of Arabia*, 50).

27. Weintraub and Weintraub, *Lawrence of Arabia*, 54.

28. Tabachnick, *T. E. Lawrence*, 103.

29. Weintraub and Weintraub, *Lawrence of Arabia*, 54; Tabachnick, *T. E. Lawrence*, 103, 119; M. D. Allen, *The Medievalism of Lawrence of Arabia*, 28.

30. Meyers, *The Wounded Spirit*, 72–73.

31. Qtd. in Weintraub and Weintraub, *Lawrence of Arabia*, 46.

32. Storrs in Tabachnick, *T. E. Lawrence*, 67–68; Meyers, *The Wounded Spirit*, 35.

33. Qtd. in Weintraub and Weintraub, *Lawrence of Arabia*, 20.

34. Tabachnick, *T. E. Lawrence*, 125–26.

35. Weintraub and Weintraub, *Lawrence of Arabia*, 98; letter in Tabachnick, *T. E. Lawrence*, 41.

36. T. E. Lawrence, *Seven Pillars of Wisdom*, 278–79.

37. Ibid., 483.

38. Weintraub and Weintraub, *Lawrence of Arabia*, 33–34

39. Ibid.; Meyers, *The Wounded Spirit*, 65.

40. Tabachnick, *T. E. Lawrence*, 125.

41.; H. G. Wells, qtd. in Arnold Walter Lawrence, ed., *T. E. Lawrence by His Friends*, (New York: McGraw-Hill, 1963), 131.

42. Winston Churchill, qtd. in Arnold Walter Lawrence, ed., *T. E. Lawrence by His Friends*, 191.

43. Jean Beraud Villars, qtd. in Weintraub and Weintraub, *Lawrence of Arabia*, 57.

44. Villars, *T. E. Lawrence, or the Search for the Absolute*, trans. Peter Dawnay (London: Jonathan Cape, 1958), 296–97.

45. Meyers, *The Wounded Spirit*, 82.

46. T. E. Lawrence, *The Letters of T. E. Lawrence*, ed. David Garnett (London: Jonathan Cape, 1938), 358, 447.

47. Meyers, *The Wounded Spirit*, 60; letter to Shaw in Tabachnick, *T. E. Lawrence*, 67; letter to Garnett in *Letters of T. E. Lawrence*, 258; comment to Graves in *T. E. Lawrence to His Biographer, Robert Graves* 1:104, 118; letter to Ede in Tabachnick, *T. E. Lawrence*, 83.

48. Tabachnick, *T. E. Lawrence*, 68.

49. Lawrence, *Seven Pillars of Wisdom*, 88.

50. Ibid., 633.

51. Tabachnick, *T. E. Lawrence*, 57.

52. Fussell, *The Great War and Modern Memory*, 174; Tabachnick, *T. E. Lawrence*, 76–77, 85.

53. Garnett in Weintraub and Weintraub, *Lawrence of Arabia*, 110–11; Tabachnick, *T. E. Lawrence*, 128.

54. Qtd. in Weintraub and Weintraub, *Lawrence of Arabia*, 124.

55. E. M. Forster, *Abinger Harvest* (New York: Doubleday, Doran, 1936), 146.

56. Weintraub and Weintraub, *Lawrence of Arabia*, 5, 59.

57. Qtd. in Tabachnick, *T. E. Lawrence*, 50.

58. Qtd. ibid., 154.

59. Ibid., 142.

Four

The Female Subject
and the First World War

The Case of Vera M. Brittain, VAD
London/268, BRCS

ANDREA PETERSON

Vera Brittain is best known for *Testament of Youth*, a 1933 account of her wartime experiences as a Voluntary Aid Detachment nurse, and this chapter will focus on that text. However, it should be noted that Brittain had already drawn on these experiences for a volume of poetry, *Verses of a VAD and Other War Poems* (1918), and two novels, *The Dark Tide* (1923) and *Not without Honour* (1924). Furthermore, she continued to write about these experiences throughout her life, ending with the essay "War Service in Perspective" (1968).

In *Testament of Experience* (1957), Brittain retrospectively claimed that having studied "numerous war books by men," she had conceived *Testament of Youth* in order to redress the gender balance.[1] As Jean Bethke Elshtain explains, tradition dictates that because

> women are *exterior* to war, [and] men *interior,* men have long been
> the great war-story tellers, legitimated in that role because they have
> "been there." ... The stories of women ... have sometimes been told
> but have [tended not to attain] ... the *literary* status of the great war
> novels by men ... nor have women written the most powerful war
> poems ... or memorable autobiographical accounts.[2]

Brittain's own idea that "war books" had only been written by men is problematic on two counts: first, many other women had already written *and published* their own war books; second, Brittain herself had already written and rewritten her own story in several formats. Brittain's crucial breakthrough, therefore, was not her decision to write a war book but her decision to write an autobiography.

Despite an inauspicious start to her writing career, Brittain believed herself capable of writing "the epic of the women who went to the war."[3] The foreword to *Testament of Youth* reveals something of her innovative autobiographical ethos, her writing process, and her understanding of subjectivity. She clearly viewed herself as a representative, or generational, autobiographer; her writing process was protracted, eclectic, and documentarist; and her understanding of subjectivity as something fluid and inconsistent was akin to that portrayed in the modernist texts of her male counterparts—the soldiers who survived the Great War. Each of these aspects of Brittain's work will be considered here, arguing that her wartime experiences and her repeated rewriting of these experiences contributed to her understanding of *female* subjectivity as something far from "universal." Moreover, this is to suggest that this understanding was intrinsically linked to her innovative layering of temporal perspectives and to her rejection of a wholly linear narrative. Brittain's autobiography will be contextualized by briefly sketching some of the major developments in the female autobiographical tradition since the seventeenth century.

Gender and Autobiography

Vera Brittain perceived "war writing" to be an inherently gender-biased genre. The gender bias within the ontological tradition has had an enormous impact on the autobiographical tradition—and of course, a good deal of war writing is autobiographical. One of the most problematic aspects of modern autobiography is that it seeks to fix the subject on the printed page. While this notion may accord with the humanist notion of the fixed, universal subject, it would seem discordant and difficult to reconcile with the various modern and postmodern notions of the unstable, fractured subject that create a sense that the autobiographical "I" must now represent a subject *artificially* unified, stabilized, and fixed for posterity. Different notions of subjectivity put forward by philosophers, theorists, and psychoanalysts have been disseminated and have created positions for the autobiographer either to embrace or resist. However, as Luce Irigaray observes, "Even when aspiring to a universal or neutral state, [the] subject has always been written in the masculine form, as man. . . . It is man who has been the subject of discourse, whether in the field of theory, morality or politics. And the gender of God . . . is always *paternal and masculine* in the west."[4]

This would suggest that the privilege awarded to the masculine, which is encoded within all notions of the subject, caused the autobiographical genre to develop along correspondingly exclusive and androcentric lines, thereby leaving "woman autobiographers self-evidently outside" what has come to be viewed as "the 'Great Men' tradition."[5] Indeed, to chronicle Western subjectivity from the seventeenth century to date is to chronicle the various notions and ideals of male disembodiment and their contrapuntal notions of apparently disadvantageous female embodiment and historical situatedness. A humanist notion of an apparently male transcendent subject has remained the dominant notion of subjectivity in the West, despite sustained and continuous theoretical attacks throughout the nineteenth and twentieth centuries.

Women's autobiography appears to have reached a crucial stage of its development in the seventeenth century. This is hardly surprising if autobiographical practice is indeed linked with the autobiographer's understanding of subjectivity. Since the rise to dominance of the Cartesian universal subject in the seventeenth century, any feminist appropriation of the autobiographical genre has necessarily involved both the gradual erosion and subsequent redefinition of extant notions of the autobiographical genre and the autobiographical subject.[6] By the seventeenth century, female subjectivity had come to be perceived as existing in oppositional relation to male subjectivity, if existing at all. The equation of "Woman" with "Nature" had effectively left the already inferior female mind both earthbound and body-bound and, as such, incapable of rational thought and transcendence. Furthermore, the dominant notion of the universal subject had compounded the inferiority of the female mind and highlighted the inadequacies of the female body by embracing the Cartesian idea that the body must act as an impermeable physical boundary. It was this separation of the mind from the outside world that facilitated the development of a transcendent, interior consciousness. To refer to Christine Battersby:

> The idealized equal, individualized and autonomous subjects of Enlightenment thought do not fit the position of a subject who is normatively female. . . . For the (normalized) "female" there is no sharp division between "self" and "other." Instead, the "other" emerges out of the embodied self, but in ways that mean that two selves emerge and one self does not simply dissolve into the other. . . . The "female" subject-position is linked to fleshy continuity, rather than to an autonomous and individualized "soul" or "mind" that merely inhabits the flesh. However, the dominant model of the human in

western modernity is disembodied: a "spirit," "soul," "conscious-ness" or *"cogito"* whose "personhood" is bound up with rationality and soul, rather than with flesh.[7]

So, if a woman cannot meet the exacting demands of Cartesian subjectiv-ity, how can she write a conventional autobiography in which, as C. Steed-man remarks, the "inchoate experience of living and feeling" is "marshalled into a chronology" so that the "central and unified subject" can be seen to reach "the conclusion of a life?"[8]

Domna C. Stanton's pioneering research in the 1980s facilitated the recovery from obscurity of many brilliant examples of women's autobio-graphical writing. In order to emphasize that women writers had devel-oped a very different autobiographical tradition from their male counter-parts, Stanton introduced the term "autogynography" to denote women's autobiographical practice. For Stanton, the "global and essential thera-peutic purpose" of autogynography had always been and indeed still was, "to constitute the female subject." Despite women having had little, if any, access to their autogynographical heritage, Stanton traced many similarities that traversed the centuries. Because autobiography is so in-extricably entwined with subjectivity, women's rejection of masculine subjectivity has created an alternative tradition of feminine narratives that would seem to deserve the distinctive term awarded them by Stanton.

Indeed, Stanton asserts that women have always found it difficult to see themselves as coherent subject identities; hence, they repeatedly "strove and failed to present the unitary and ordinary self." After exam-ining many examples of autogynographies from across the centuries, she concludes that

> the autogynographical narrative was marked by conflicts between the private and the public, the personal and the professional. . . . [T]here was a systematic tension between the conventional role of wife, mother, or daughter, and another, unconventional self that had ambition or a vocation. This dual and contradictory impulse . . . [can be] located in Lady Ann Fanshawe's seventeenth-century text . . . [but is] displayed much earlier in the . . . *Book of Margery Kempe.*[9]

Stanton's findings suggest that by the seventeenth century autogynograph-ical writing was, for many women, a conscious act of burgeoning femi-nism. Confined to the domestic sphere, except by vicarious association, women's autobiographies of this period are marked by their attention to quotidian detail, such as accounts of homemaking, descriptions of fashions, and transcripts of conversations. However, many women began to write in order to look beyond these "false" roles or selves imposed on them by society and to facilitate the definition of their "true" selves. They wrote in order to assert their own individuality and notoriety. As Valerie Sanders concludes, "The main exponents of the form undoubtedly [saw] themselves as distinct from the mass of conventional women who never step[ped] out of their appointed roles."[10]

This notion of a departure from quotidian experience forms a crucial link between the female autobiographical tradition and the male war narrative. War creates a break with the quotidian. Per Samuel Hynes (quoting Philip Caputo's *A Rumor of War*), war narratives tell of "the things men do in war" and "the things war does to them." Just as "no man goes through a war without being changed by it,"[11] no woman "steps out of her appointed role" without changing. However, both Sanders and Stanton note that even as far back as the seventeenth and eighteenth centuries, women's autobiographical accounts "share[d] certain likenesses that mark[ed] them out from the male mainstream,"[12] most notably "a *different* plotting and configuration of the split subject."[13]

The female autobiographical tradition almost faded away during the first part of the nineteenth century. Indeed, "not until the final quarter of the nineteenth century did a significant number of women . . . publish formal autobiography." Apart from these later formal autobiographies, nineteenth-century women created a "great mass of diaries, journals, autobiographical fiction, travel books and memoirs," a fact that, Sanders claims, "testifies to a widespread preoccupation with *individual* experience." These disparate texts demonstrate the burgeoning philosophical notions of many women writers. At a time when women's already precarious subject position was being still further undermined by theories of individualism, the genre of women's autobiography reemerged and was redefined by various Victorian women writers who sought to create a new and innovative form of self-writing capable of "accommodat[ing] the contradictions of their position."[14] While a historical, transcendent individualism became a valid *male* subject position, the formally innovative women autobiographers of the late nineteenth century sought alternative *female* subject positions. Though women may have been debarred from transcendent Cartesian subjectivity by their permeable, penetrable bodies, they consciously rejected the later contingent notion of abstract individualism. The rejection of individualism—the impetus behind most autobiographical writing by both men *and* women—inspired a new type of autobiography in the nineteenth century and subsequently facilitated the gradual development of an alternative subject position—that suited women but did not exclude men—by theorists such as Rosi Braidotti and Christine Battersby in the latter part of the twentieth century. Vera Brittain's claim to representative status places her within the female autobiographical tradition, but her understanding of subjectivity as something changeable prefigures recent feminist theory while also linking her autobiography with male-authored war narratives.

Brittain's Representative Status

Brittain's work can be viewed as innovative because she insisted that a war generation consisted of both sexes. Indeed, the opening sentence of Brittain's foreword clearly defines the parameters of her project: "For nearly a decade I have wanted . . . to write something which would show what the whole War and post-war period . . . has meant to *the men and women of my generation, the generation of those boys and girls who grew up just before the War broke out* (11, emphasis added)." Brittain sees herself as a representative of this generation and wants her autobiography to be a representative epic. She means "to write history in terms of personal life" and believes she is qualified to undertake such a task because of "the smashing up of . . . [her] own youth by the War" (11).

Brittain had always wanted to be a writer, and from an early age she had developed her powers of observation: "the seeing eye, the listening ear, and the conscious mind." Reviewing her First World War diaries, she unashamedly proclaimed: "I belong to the few who believe in all sincerity that their own lives provide the answers to some of the many problems which puzzle humanity."[15] Later, as an established, professional writer, she opined that prose fiction should deal with "the relationship of man to the world in which he lives, and to the problems and catastrophes which blind and bewilder him," while biography and autobiography should "increase our understanding of an age, class, nation or generation, or . . . enlarge our knowledge of mankind through the sincere study of one human being and his or her personal relationships."[16]

Following her own criteria, it would seem reasonable to identify Brittain as a representative of the "vast age of transition"[17] in which she lived; of the middle class; of the English nation; and of "the generation of . . . boys and girls who grew up just before the War broke out" (11). Yet despite her confused and contradictory claims, her main motivation for writing *Testament of Youth* was neither her belief in her keenly developed powers of observation nor her wish to commemorate the whole or part of a lost generation; rather, her main motivation was her belief in the importance of her own particular perspective, afforded not only by her age, class, nation, and generation but also by her *gender*, intellect, and education. Tellingly, she states, "I see things other than [men] have seen, and some of the things they perceive I see differently." Even in 1968, when she again tried to argue that the events described in *Testament of Youth* were "typical . . . not so much in terms of women's experience, as of that of an entire generation," Brittain immediately problematizes her assessment by acknowledging that "there was clearly a great contrast . . . between the stories of men and women," and by suggesting that "a woman could perceive the picture as clearly as a man—perhaps more clearly, owing to the inevitably greater detachment which a woman's wartime insignificance gave her."[18]

It would seem that because of her love for her brother Edward Brittain, for her fiancé Roland Leighton, and for their closest friends, Geoffrey Thurlow and Victor Richardson, Brittain was seduced by the concept of generational autobiography.[19] However, because of her feminist beliefs, she could not easily subordinate the issue of gender. Although *Testament of Youth* deals with Brittain's life from 1893 to 1925, her constant foregrounding of her "fairly typical" (12) personal wartime experiences led her to believe that she understood, and hence could represent, her whole generation simply because she had lived through the war.

Brittain's understanding of her own representative status was later illustrated more fully by her claim that though "the experience of one person . . . may be important in itself; its significance is doubled if the personal narrative is linked with the experience of many, and approaches the experience of all."[20] Sanders explains that this generational or representative mode of autobiography was utilized by several Victorian women who had found "the more formal and regular kinds of autobiography, which depicted the growth of a mind or the development of a career," both "alien and inappropriate, because women were not encouraged to view themselves in those terms." Hence,

autobiography, which most people would regard supremely as the narrative of an individual life, and the growth of an individual consciousness, became, for some Victorian women, the story of a generation, a slice of representative life in a specific period. This was clearly one way of minimising the egotistical impulses behind their writing. . . . Perhaps the best known example of this representative consciousness, though outside the Victorian period, is Vera Brittain.[21]

Thus Sanders views Brittain as a contributor to an extant female autobiographical tradition and Brittain's autobiographical aims would seem to echo those of Annie Besant in *An Autobiography* (1893) and Frances Power Cobbe in her *Life of Frances Power Cobbe. By Herself* (1894).

In her recent study, Anthea Trodd compares Brittain's *Testament of Youth* with Beatrice Webb's *My Apprenticeship* (1926)—both women draw extensively on their diaries and fall back on "perfunctory and difficult" romantic endings that cannot be fully reconciled with their preceding narratives. Trodd further notes that in the early twentieth century women who chose to write autobiography had to confront various "complex problems of self-presentation," because Victorian legacy still dictated that the "dominant paradigm was private and domestic, and the traditional antithesis between public life and women meant there were few narrative models." Consequently, Brittain's autobiographical "move away from individualism to incorporation within a group" may simply have been a form of self-effacement, prompted by her "acute consciousness of the antithesis between women and public life, coupled with a sense that women who rejected the paradigm of obscurity and privacy were breaking ranks with their fellows."[22] Similarly, Linda Anderson suggests that Brittain's representative mode of writing is a way of "effacing her own claim to fame behind the memorial she creates for the young men who died."[23]

Brittain's Writing Process

Ten years elapsed between Grant Richards's acceptance of *Not without Honour* and the publication of *Testament of Youth*. During those ten years, Brittain tried many different approaches to her "war book," experimenting with various writing techniques, drafts, and genres. Her descriptions of aborted projects explain this decade of delay:

> My original idea was that of a long novel, and I started to plan it. To my dismay it turned out a hopeless failure. . . . I found that the people and the events about which I was writing were still too near and too real to be made the subjects of an imaginative, detached reconstruction.

> Then I tried the effect of reproducing parts of the long diary which
> I kept from 1913 to 1918, with fictitious names. . . . This too was a
> failure. (11–12)

Here, Brittain is referring to the manuscript versions of "The Pawn of
Fate," "Folly's Vineyard," and "A Chronicle of Youth."[24] She later admitted that she had also spent several years planning and drafting a "dread-
fully autobiographical" novel titled *The Incidental Adam*.[25] In addition, the
Vera Brittain Archive holds the first draft of the manuscript that eventually became *Testament of Youth*—some 140 pages titled *The Kingdom of Endurance*.[26] These "failures" led Brittain to conclude that "there was only
one possible course left—to tell my own . . . story . . . against the larger
background" (12).

The fact that so many different versions of Brittain's wartime experiences existed prior to her embarking on *Testament of Youth* would seem
to problematize her claim to having reproduced "the exact truth" (12)
about herself and her life in this autobiographical volume. Having ex-
perimented with various genres, Brittain aimed to make her autobiographical account "as readable as fiction," and she advocated "the creative treatment of actuality." Furthermore, she aimed to make her account
"as truthful as history"—a rather ambiguous ambition, given that both
history and autobiography rely on limited and partial evidence in their
(equally fictional) reconstruction of the past.[27]

In the Foreword to *Testament of Youth*, Brittain acknowledges that
"it is almost impossible to see ourselves . . . as we really were" and that
"many of our contemporaries of equal age, in spite of their differences of
environment and inheritance, appear to resemble us more closely than
we resemble ourselves" (13). It might be argued that in any autobiographical account the construction of the self is inherently and merely representative. As Liz Stanley argues, "The apparently referential and unique
selves that autobiographical accounts invoke are actually invocations of
a cultural representation of what selves should be: these are shared ideas,
conventions . . . not descriptions of actual lives but interpretations within
the convention."[28] While such a representative technique may have afforded Brittain some comfort when recounting her early adulthood, its
efficacy does not extend beyond her war service, and it complicates the
rest of her autobiography.

Alan Bishop offers one reason why a representative technique may
have best suited the war years of Brittain's autobiography. Bishop quotes

Robert Jay Lifton's theory of psychological "doubling," which suggests that in times of extreme duress "the self [divides] into two functioning wholes." This prompts Bishop to suggest that "in wartime that mechanism is characteristically validated by official example and precept . . . and can be enforced by intense social and psychological pressure." Hence, Brittain can be seen to occupy both a conventional, representative position—that of "the compassionate nurse"—and a conflicting personal position, in this case, that of "the proud, anxious sister whose eyes are fixed on a heroic icon—Edward's Military Cross."[29]

As with any genre, autobiography is inherently intertextual, and in this respect Brittain's account is similar to Robert Graves's *Good-bye to All That*, which she later admitted to having studied "with scientific precision."[30] Indeed, *Testament of Youth* opens with two direct references to Graves's autobiography. Brittain writes, "I have . . . the honour of sharing with Robert Graves the subject of my earliest recollection, which is that of watching, as a tiny child, the flags flying in the streets of Macclesfield for Queen Victoria's Diamond Jubilee" (17). Graves claims to have included information about his early childhood and ancestry as "proof of [his] readiness to accept autobiographical convention."[31] In contrast, Brittain chooses to flout such convention and her debt to Graves by immediately qualifying her acknowledgement of his influence: "Fortunately there is no need to emulate my contemporary's *Good-bye to All That* in travelling still further back into the ponderous Victorianism of the nineteenth century" (18). Brittain is less concerned with lineage, indicating her disaffection with the androcentric "Great Man" tradition. Nevertheless, it would appear that both writers set out to create best-selling books. Like Graves, Brittain includes a great deal of documentary evidence that stands out clearly from the main body of her text. For example, the poster, headlines, and report from the *Star* (275–76); details from the Uppingham Speech Day program from July 1914 (88); and the "Special Order of the Day" notice (419). In addition, she includes dialogue, sheet music composed by her brother (79–80), song lyrics, extracts from books, and pieces of poetry. Every chapter is introduced by poems, written by Brittain or her fiancé, which "carry the authority of prophetic or retrospective insight." Brittain's inclusion of so much documentary evidence prompts Trodd to suggest that *Testament of Youth* can be considered not only to participate in an extant female autobiographical tradition but actually to further develop that tradition, thereby offering support of Brittain as a literary innovator. Trodd notes that Brittain's "massive accumulation of detail" was "in the spirit of the

1930s fiction of fact" and that Brittain's adoption of this contemporary literary style may well have provoked the unkind response that she was "a clever if unscrupulous artist who had produced . . . 'a novel masquerading as an autobiography.'"[32]

Brittain evolved her innovative writing process as a way of coping with the difficulties of making the private and personal stand as public and representative. She was aware, however, that representativeness created "difficulties of perspective" (13). In order to overcome these difficulties, she was compelled to theorize not only a "new type of autobiography"[33] but also a new type of fluid, inconsistent, and contradictory *female* subjectivity. Indeed, Brittain's redefinition of both the androcentric autobiographical genre and the exclusively masculine universal or fixed subject traditionally depicted therein seem to have been facilitated by her innovative layering of temporal perspectives.

Although *Testament of Youth* was written when she was in her thirties, Brittain consciously preserved the naïve perceptions of her youth by relying heavily on her lengthy war diary and the many letters she had written and received throughout the war. Her idea was that the "usual retrospective view" should "be combined with contemporary impressions and thus create the effect of a double dimension."[34] One immediately obvious manifestation of this idea is the way in which many incidents take on emblematic importance with the benefit of Brittain's hindsight. Brittain was by no means the first autobiographer to experiment with narrative structure in this way, though this important aspect of her autobiographical work is often overlooked.

As already noted, Brittain referred to many documents, including her school reports, juvenilia, diaries, newspaper cuttings, letters, and her own earlier attempts to fictionalize her wartime experiences. These documents allow contemporaneous access to her innermost thoughts throughout her comfortable prewar life, her devastating wartime experiences, her postwar alienation, her friendship with Winifred Holtby, and her early career. In her foreword to *Testament of Youth,* Brittain explains that "I have . . . made as much use as possible of old letters and diaries, because it seemed to me that the contemporary opinions, however crude and ingenuous, of youth . . . were at least as important . . . as retrospective reflections heavy with knowledge" (12). Brittain was therefore able to revive and revise herself and her experiences over and over again. By the time she wrote *Testament of Experience,* she was also able to draw on the detailed diary entries describing the process of writing and the publication of *Testament of Youth,* adding yet another perspective.

Brittain's careful layering of various temporal perspectives throughout *Testament of Youth* almost imperceptibly disrupts the linearity of her narrative, and her later references to this period depict her as a conscious innovator in the autobiographical form. Brittain records thinking that by including extracts from "the correspondence between myself and the four boys—lover, brother, and friends—who had been killed in the war . . . my new type of autobiography would become newer still."[35] Many people refer to their diaries when writing autobiographies and memoirs; however, two factors set Brittain apart: first, her recognition of the diary as an important literary form because of its "immersion in the horizontal, non-hierarchical flow of events and details—in other words, [its] radical parataxis";[36] and second, her utilization of her diaries, whether writing autobiographical or fictional accounts. Moreover, the ambiguous position of nurses at the front provided a crucial link between their diary writing and the modernist writing of the "men of 1914." Angela Smith observes that during the First World War even the work of "amateur diarists and letter writers, contains within it elements of stylistic change as these writers strive to find a way to articulate an experience which cannot be easily condensed into conventional language."[37] Brittain made such extensive use of her diaries and letters when writing her autobiography and her novels that she frequently transcribed lengthy passages with little or no alteration. The stylistic experimentation necessitated by Brittain's struggle to articulate her wartime experiences in her contemporary diaries, letters, and poetry also contributed to her later literary innovations.

The fragmentary, multilayered montage created by Brittain in *Testament of Youth* would seem linked to the ambiguous and discontinuous subject position she occupied during the First World War. Indeed, she became increasingly disillusioned and dehumanized, reaching a crisis point with the apparent onset of shell shock during General Erich Ludendorff's offensive on Étaples in 1918, when, unusually for a woman, she effectively experienced trench warfare. Afterward, she becomes explicit about her own process of dehumanization, stating, "My only hope now was to become the complete automaton, working mechanically and no longer even pretending to be animated by ideals. Thought was too dangerous. . . . On the whole it seemed safer to go on being a machine" (450). Moreover, she suffered from insomnia, nightmares, and hallucinations until 1925.

In her recent account of "feminist nomadic ethics," Rosi Braidotti implores women to "leave behind the linear mode of intellectual thinking . . . that most of us have been trained to respect and emulate."[38] For women writers, the development and deployment of a nonlinear style is an important feminist act. Indeed, *Testament of Youth* shows that Brittain consciously embraced a nonlinear, "feminine" narrative in order to broaden the limits of the androcentric autobiographical genre. Brittain's inability to contain herself within a linear narrative is illustrated by the fact that in just half a page she interweaves references to her birth, early childhood, adolescence, and recent working life (21). It is interesting to compare Brittain's narrative structure with her description of Miss Heath Jones's lessons at St. Monica's School—especially in light of the fact that Heath Jones was decidedly influential in introducing her to feminism:

> To this day I can remember some of the lessons which Miss Heath Jones gave us in History and Scripture—lessons which raced backwards and forwards in the same five minutes from the French Revolution to the liberal Victory in the 1910 General Elections, from the prophecies of Isaiah to the 1911 Italian invasion of Tripoli . . . they could hardly have been surpassed. (39)

This resistance to linearity is further evidenced in one of the key passages in *Testament of Youth*—Brittain's description of the Uppingham School Speech Day in "Chapter II. 8." Brittain juxtaposes her mature remembrance of the deaths of the Uppingham "old boys" she was close to, with a couple of arresting paragraphs written in the present progressive tense: "Edward and I *are standing* in a dark quadrangle outside the . . . prefects' studies. 'There are *boys about in various stages of undress,* so we can't go inside with you here,' Edward informs me" (86, emphasis added). This is an elaboration on Brittain's more coy diary entry for July 10, 1914, in which she states, "Edward said he could not take us indoors as there were *boys about in various stages of untidiness.*" This is an example of what Jean E. Kennard describes as "a reading of the diaries . . . by a second self," as Brittain has used her diary entry as a basis for her evocation of the past without quoting from it directly.[39] However, she then quotes directly and referentially from her diary—"I am waiting, as I admit afterwards in my diary, 'to get a glimpse of the person on whose account . . . I have come'" (86)—before reverting to a more "creative" use of her earlier account.

Significantly, Brittain glosses over the "perpetual discussion of Olive Schreiner and immortality" (90) in which she and Leighton were engaged. In *Testament of Youth* she writes that "Roland was deeply engrossed in explaining to me Immanuel Kant's theory" (90), implying her intellectual inferiority and passivity. However, her diary suggests that she played a far more active role in the discussion:

We started by discussing Olive Schreiner's idea of immortality; I said I was not sure I entirely agreed with her in thinking that the desire for, & in some cases belief in, conscious continuation implies pettiness or selfishness, but rather that it arose from the idea of any limit to our soul's growth being terrible to us. I said I thought that all religion arose from that fact, that it is impossible to imagine a limit set to our being. Roland said that Kant's theory was something like that.[40]

Kantian theory is central to Battersby's theory of female essence. Initially, however, Battersby draws on John Locke's notion of "nominal essences"— that is, that "'*Ideas* taken from particular Beings' gradually became 'general Representatives of all the same kind.'"[41] This notion accords with Brittain's belief that her wartime experiences could be both personal and representative. Battersby then combines this notion of essence with Kant's notion that essences were culturally and historically determined privileged norms and, as such, could change.

Vera Brittain's Understanding of Subjectivity

Brittain appears to understand individual subjectivity as the essence of each particular person. She wonders whether it is possible to write autobiographically, or to "make a book out of the very essence of one's self" (196), and worries that warfare will gradually destroy Leighton's essence: "These characteristics hardly seem . . . the real you. But the War kills other things besides physical life, and I sometimes feel that little by little the Individuality of You is being as surely buried as the bodies . . . beneath the trenches of Flanders and France" (218).

In addition, Brittain appears to accept sexual difference as a given but believes that the ideology based on such difference can, and should, change; hence, "the centre point of Brittain's approach to life [is] her unyielding faith that human nature can change."[42] The fact that even before the First World War Brittain was already beginning to consider the notion of an essential self that could change is evinced by another entry in her diary, dated June 4, 1914: "I might change . . . I might modify but the foundations would always remain the same."[43] Kennard writes that Brittain's account "moves backward and forward in time, her older self with her later knowledge recalling" her younger self.[44] However, having made this observation, Kennard neglects to afford it sufficient significance. By interweaving both "contemporary opinions" and "retrospective reflections" (12),

Brittain illustrates exactly how she herself has changed in the interim. Her writing process clearly reveals her awareness that subjectivity can change; furthermore, we might align her understanding of subjectivity with Julia Kristeva's theory of the "subject in process" and Braidotti's theory of the "nomadic subject." The subject must surely lie at the heart of any autobiographical narrative, yet Brittain's understanding of herself as a subject is seldom explored in depth.[45]

Brittain's unusual layering of temporal perspectives is both indicative of and crucial to her understanding of subjectivity. Kennard notes the significance of Brittain's temporal positioning "in the transition from the Victorian to the modern world" in shaping her understanding of her own subjectivity. Brittain's intention to "new type of autobiography" would not allow her to cling to the outdated notion of coherent subjectivity epitomized by the implicitly masculine universal subject.

As a VAD nurse, Brittain experienced firsthand women's changing role in society. The harrowing experience of nursing in France must have radically altered Brittain's perception of herself, although she may not have been fully conscious of this change at the time. However, as Sharon Ouditt explains, "the collision of established codes of femininity with the efforts of the VAD organization to advance women onto the battlefield" left most nurses with an "ambiguous subject identity."[46] On leaving the VAD, Brittain returned to her studies at Somerville College, Oxford, with a renewed commitment to feminism, socialism, and pacifism. After graduation, she embarked upon a career as a journalist and novelist before laboring to redefine a genre by creating what Rebecca West recognized immediately as a new "psychological sort of autobiography."[47] Consequently, it would seem unlikely that Brittain, an educated and emancipated feminist, would have chosen to reject "a modern perception of self" in her *Testaments*. Instead, by recording in detail the theoretical difficulties she encountered while writing *Testament of Youth, Testament of Experience,* and *Testament of Friendship,* Brittain actively and explicitly rejected the obsolete notion of coherent selfhood. Although she could not have seen herself in the terms of twenty-first-century psychoanalytical and philosophical discourses, by redefining autobiography and recognizing the inadequacy of traditional notions of subjectivity Brittain prefigured several important developments in recent feminist theory.

Brittain actively participated in the First World War, a "particular moment in history" that was "fraught with contradictions" and that left "aspirant nurses" to take "the strain produced by their being both 'in pro-

cess' as subjects and 'on trial' as women."[48] The First World War dominates the first volume of Brittain's autobiography; moreover, it remains a
constant theme, recurring throughout all of her other works, because it
shaped her understanding of her own subjectivity. Brittain came to understand her identity as an ongoing process, mediated by gender (the experiential divide between home and front, women and men, heightened her
commitment to feminism, prompted her to undertake increasingly dangerous war work, and strengthened her resolve to live independently);
sexuality (although their relationship was never consummated, she was
clearly sexually attracted to Leighton, as she recalls that "be[ing] alone
together" brought "all too quickly, the knowledge that being alone together
was not enough" (122); later she writes that "he made me, as I confessed
to my diary," nearly mad with longing for him, I wanted him so" [218]);
corporeality (both her burgeoning sexual attraction for Leighton and the
abject nature of her war work heightened her awareness of the subject as
embodied rather than transcendent); nation (her initial patriotic stance
was problematized when she had to nurse German prisoners, causing her
to question the whole concept of nationality); and, to a lesser extent, class
(although her war work brought her into contact with working-class men,
it was not until 1922 that she "realised, with a shock of poignant revela-
tion, the kinship between the men and women in these wretched homes
[in Bethnal Green], and the Tommies whom I had nursed" [576]).

Brittain was hardly alone in her struggle to redefine the female subject. Gill Plain suggests that because most women were subordinated to
men before the outbreak of the First World War, the prolonged absence
and death of so many men widely "raise[d] significant questions about
the precarious nature of female subjectivity." The war allowed women to
"begin the slow process of formulating an identity" free from "the subject" to which they had, until now, been "other." Although this gave

> them an unprecedented degree of mobility within the constraints of
> the symbolic order . . . [t]he opportunities open to women for a pub-
> lic redefinition of their subjectivity were controlled by the demands
> not only of the war machine, but also of a class hierarchy deter-
> mined to maintain the status quo. . . . But these limitations could not
> apply to the same extent to women's private exploration of a new
> subjectivity. . . . [A]n articulation of these changes in women's sense
> of self . . . gained [contemporaneous] access to the margins of the
> public sphere through the act of publication.[49]

Hence, it would seem significant that Brittain not only wrote repeatedly of her wartime experiences but sought to publish variations on this theme, in different genres, throughout her life, and that she bequeathed a great deal of her previously unpublished material to the public domain.

Testament of Youth should be considered an important text not only because Brittain does not achieve a consistent subject position but also because she appears to consciously reject the concept of the universal subject as inadequate and unsuitable for the postwar woman. While reflecting on her wartime experiences during her postwar writing career, Brittain came to accept that she had been changed dramatically by the war, although she had initially tried to resist the process of change in order "to preserve the integrity of the self that [Leighton] had loved" (174). Nursing at Camberwell, she had written to Leighton that "personally, after seeing some of the dreadful things I have to see here, I feel I shall never be the same person again" (215). Indeed, upon realizing that she was in the process of changing from an Oxford exhibitioner to "Nurse Brittain," she reacted by vowing "that at all costs I must . . . preserve the self which he loved and I have lost" (257).

However, Brittain found she could not resist the process of change thrust upon her by the war, and on her return from Malta she realized she had become "almost a stranger" (354) to her parents. Some of her war poetry also registers this process of change; for example, in "After Three Years," written on the third anniversary of Leighton's death, she asks, "What think you, now . . . / Of her you loved those endless years ago? . . . Have I so changed . . . ?"[50] She also recognized that the experiential divide between the front and England, men and women, had quickly changed Leighton's attitudes and beliefs; in fact, she became almost obsessed with the possibility of his changing. She describes "look[ing] carefully through his letters for every . . . phrase, which suggested that not merely the body but the spirit that I desired was still in process of survival" (143). On one occasion, Leighton informed her that he knew he had changed and wrote: "I wonder if your metamorphosis has been as complete as my own" (216). Brittain observed an even greater change in her brother. By 1916 she was able to remark, "The Battle of the Somme had profoundly changed him and added ten years to his age" (283). By June 1917 she was describing him as "an unfamiliar, frightening Edward, who never smiled nor spoke except about trivial things" (356). The fact that he, too, was aware that he had changed is evidenced by one of his letters to his sister in which he writes, "you find me changed, I expect, more than I find you" (361). Such pronounced changes in the people closest to Brittain must surely have heightened her awareness of subjectivity's instability.

Bishop's explanation as to why a stereotypical or representative notion of the self might have suited the war years of Brittain's autobiography has already been referred to here. After the war, however, she seems to have experienced something akin to the sense of alienation that, John H. Gagnon suggests, was widely experienced during the nineteenth century. Once the tendency to view the self as "a limited and seemingly coherent bundle of socially given roles" had been undermined, there remained

> a fundamental tension between the multiplicity of internal voices and the necessity . . . to speak in one voice . . . (this is what is meant by being "ladylike" . . . or "professorial"). This tension was probably more acute in the nineteenth century . . . [due] to a number of adaptive problems. In some cases, persons [found] themselves limited by the singular voice . . . and began to feel . . . [their public role was] alien to them.[51]

During the war, Brittain temporarily smothered her "selves"—her "multiplicity of internal voices"—in order to take on the only socially acceptable wartime role available to her, that of a VAD nurse. Indeed, in *Testament of Youth* Brittain contemplates "the spiritually destructive preoccupations of military service," writing, "I . . . realise[d] through my own mental surrender—that only a process of complete adaptation, blotting out tastes and talents and even memories, made life sufferable for someone face to face with war at its worst" (217). After the war, of course, the role of VAD nurse became obsolete; however, Brittain soon discovered that her pre-war role as Somerville exhibitioner had become similarly limiting and alien to her. She writes of having lived two lives: a "first life that ended with Edward's death in 1918," and a "second that began with Winifred's companionship in 1920" (495). She remarks that "although I was a student at Oxford in both my lives, it was not the same Oxford and I was not the same student" (495). Indeed, as Anderson observes, Brittain had changed so much that in *Testament of Youth* "distance is perceived . . . not only as an estrangement from the events of the past . . . but as an otherness within the subject." The war had robbed Brittain of her subordinate identity in relation to Leighton and had disrupted her independent identity as a professional writer. According to Plain, most women's writing of the First

World War exhibits a similar "grief that encodes not just the pain of personal loss but also the politics of personal identity."[52]

Brittain's ideas anticipated the work of such contemporary feminist theorists as Kristeva, Braidotti, and Battersby. Brittain identified certain traits or characteristics as being "exclusive" or essential to women and "also looked to a future which would see a synthesis" of these "separate qualities" attributed to men and women and the consequent "emergence of an 'organic type of human being.'" Indeed, Brittain hoped that both men and women "would at last be able to shed the stereotyped role[s] forced upon [them] by society and live according to [their] individual nature[s]."[53] In "Women's Time," Kristeva identified a (then burgeoning) third phase of feminism that presupposed "the deconstruction of the concept of 'identity'" and opened up "a space where individual difference" could be "allowed free play": "In this third attitude, which I strongly advocate[,] . . . the very dichotomy between man/woman as an opposition between two rival entities may be understood as belonging to *metaphysics*. What can 'identity,' even 'sexual identity,' mean in a new theoretical and scientific space where the very notion of identity is challenged?"[54]

Subsequently, as this third phase of feminism has progressed, Braidotti's reexamination of sexual difference has led her to advocate that both men and women adopt a "nomadic" mode of subjectivity that "cuts across the boundaries of race, class, gender, and sexual practice," while most recently, Battersby's study of feminist metaphysics has enabled her to theorize a new "model of identity that . . . is more adequate for men (as well as women) than the classical philosophical understanding of the subject."[55]

Braidotti's figuration of subjectivity would seem to align with Brittain's portrayal of her own subjectivity in *Testament of Youth*, because Braidotti focuses on the many similarities between the modern and the postmodern conditions. For example, Braidotti believes that "this new Europe . . . witnesses all of its old problems," including a "renewed and exacerbated sense of nationalism." For Braidotti, the construction of a "female feminist subjectivity in a nomadic mode" involves "a figurative style of thinking" that is "occasionally autobiographical" and occasionally creative and fictional. She writes:

> Were I to write an autobiography, it would be the self-portrait of a collectivity. . . . I would much rather fictionalize my theories, theorize my fictions, and practice philosophy as a form of conceptual creativity. . . . Letting the voices of others echo through my text is . . .

a way of actualizing the noncentrality of the "I" to the project of thinking, while attaching it/her to a collective project.[56]

Brittain's "generational" autobiography might easily be described as a "collective project"; by quoting directly from letters she had received, she clearly allowed the "voices of others to echo through her text"; she openly declared that through her autobiographies she aimed to "bring out the poetry in the private affairs of ordinary people" by the "creative treatment of actuality"; and she carefully blended historical "truth'" and feminist theory with a contemporary literary style in order to make her autobiography "as readable as fiction."[57]

Conclusion

Many critics have commented on the various conflicts and contradictions within *Testament of Youth*. Indeed, Brittain's feminist, socialist, and pacifist ideals are frequently compromised. Brittain is a feminist "glad to be spared the chattering, pervasive femininity" (147) of her female contemporaries; a socialist whose political allegiance is so tenuous that before giving a lecture on the Russian Revolution she remarks, "It will be a desperate matter if the Socialists throw eggs at my new black gabardine and satin frock" (542–43); and a pacifist who envisages a utopian future where women will be conscripted just like their male counterparts: "I find myself hoping that if . . . war breaks out on a scale comparable to that of 1914, the organisers of the [war] machine will not hesitate to conscript all women under fifty for service at home or abroad" (422). Such problems, however, would seem inherent in women's autobiographical struggle with subjectivity. Braidotti's theory of nomadism accommodates contradiction in a way that might also seem reminiscent of Brittain's autobiographical practice. Braidotti draws explicitly on Nietzsche and Deleuze in order to theorize a subject that consists of a "multiplicity . . . contained in a multilayered temporal sequence," where "discontinuities and even contradictions can find a place" because the subject "is split time and time again, over multiple axes of differentiation." Although Brittain makes no direct reference to Nietzsche and could not have been aware of Deleuze's work, her *Testaments* clearly advance an innovative multilayered temporal perspective. It is interesting to note that Layton detects "distortions of Nietzsche" in Brittain's wartime writing, while Anderson suggests that the "irrationality" of Brittain's nonlinear narrative "could perhaps be better described as folding the 'before' and 'after' within each other, as arranging them in an overlapping rather than consecutive fashion." Deleuze understood subjectivity as a process of folding, and Anderson's description would seem reminiscent of this. Furthermore, Brittain's autobiographical writing anticipates Braidotti's "challenge" to "feminist nomads . . . to conjugate [a] multilayered, multicultural perspective, with responsibility for and accountability to their gender."[58]

In many respects, Brittain's ideas seem to have been ahead of their time. Her autobiographical practice, in its rejection of a consistent subject position combined with espousal of the notion of female essence as incontrovertible, might also seem to anticipate Battersby's recent theoretical project to reconcile these two apparently disparate concepts—fluid or changeable subjectivity and female essence. Battersby's definition of an essence as "a rule or norm that can itself fluctuate, but which functions as a paradigm—a kind of idealized image or snapshot—that is used to arrest the fluid and the manifold into a temporary stability of form," might offer an alternative explanation for Brittain's subsuming of her individual subjectivity behind that of the representative, stereotypical nurse during World War I. Propaganda constructed women's conception of themselves as subjects for the duration of the war. As a young, unmarried woman, Brittain's adoption of the self-image of the nunlike nurse, probably the most idealized contemporaneous female image, might have allowed her to subsume her inconsistent subject position behind this "temporary stability of form" and helped her cope with her extreme trauma and grief. However, having effectively experienced trench warfare, Brittain could not hide behind this veneer of "stability" for the duration of her autobiography. Her narrative is, in some ways, a "soldier's tale" of "*inner* change."[59]

Anderson suggests that a "preoccupation with memory could be seen as a pathological or hysterical symptom," and this notion might apply equally well to Brittain, since according to Freud "the hysteric" was "unable to put the past behind her" and so "was condemned to live it, endlessly, repetitively, retreating from historical or linear time into a phantasmal past." In contrast, however, Braidotti suggests that such a process of repetition can have a positive outcome if it is a conscious undertaking. Braidotti calls this process "the practice of 'as if,'" explaining it thus:

> The practice of "as if" is a technique of strategic re-location in order to rescue what we need of the past in order to trace paths of transformation of our lives here and now. . . . What I find empowering in

the practice of "as if" is precisely its potential for opening up, through successive repetitions and mimetic strategies, spaces where alternative forms of agency can be engendered. In other words, parody can be politically empowering on the condition of being sustained by a critical consciousness that aims at engendering transformations and changes.

Since Brittain was conscious of the fact that she was changed by "two things[:] . . . [w]ar itself" and her "attempt to record it," her literary accounts were a form of positive parody that proved politically empowering as they helped her to understand and develop her political and philosophical beliefs.[60]

The constant public reassertion of her socialist, pacifist, and feminist ideals facilitated Brittain's awareness of her own subjectivity as something fluid, contradictory, and always in process. Moreover, the difficulty of adopting a representative technique throughout her narrative seems to have contributed to her unique and innovative autobiographical style. To some extent, the enduring popularity of her autobiography justifies its having been declared "the war book of the Women of England."[61] *Testament of Youth* has continued to appeal to readers for almost seventy years because Brittain succeeded in painting a prescient picture of female subjectivity. Her innovation was the synthesis of certain writing practices inherent in the female autobiographical tradition with other writing techniques gleaned while working as a journalist and novelist.

Notes

1. Vera Brittain, *Testament of Experience: An Autobiographical Story of the Years 1905–1950* (London: Virago, [1957] 1979), 76, hereafter cited parenthetically in the text. Brittain lists Robert Graves's *Good-bye to All That*; Richard Aldington's *Death of a Hero*; Erich Maria Remarque's *Im Westen Nichts Neues* (translated as *All Quiet on the Western Front*); Ernest Hemingway's *A Farewell to Arms*; Edmund Blunden's *Undertones of War*; and Siegfried Sassoon's *Memoirs of a Foxhunting Man*.

2. Jean Bethke Elshtain, *Women and War* (Brighton, U.K.: Harvesten, 1987), 212.

3. Brittain, *Testament of Experience*, 77.

4. Luce Irigaray, *The Irigaray Reader*, ed. Margaret Whitford (Oxford, U.K.: Blackwell, 1991), 166.

5. Laura Marcus, *Auto/Biographical Discourses: Theory, Criticism, Practice* (Manchester, U.K.: Manchester Univ. Press, 1994), 1.

6. While I accept that most women would not have read philosophical texts before embarking upon their autobiographies, I believe they would have assimilated some

widely received notions of subjectivity through cultural institutions, such as the church. John H. Gagnon's essay "The Self, Its Voices, and Their Discord" in *Investigating Subjectivity: Research on Lived Experiences*, ed. Carolyn Ellis and Michael G. Flaherty (Newbury Park, Calif.: Sage, 1992), 221–43, is persuasive in its explanation of the social and cultural dissemination of literary and philosophical ideas.

7. Christine Battersby, *The Phenomenal Woman: Feminist Metaphysics and the Patterns of Identity* (Cambridge, U.K.: Polity, 1998, 8–10).

8. C. Steedman, "Women's Biography and Autobiography: Forms of History, Histories of Form," in *From My Guy to Sci-Fi: Genre and Women's Writing in the Postmodern World*, ed. Helen Carr (London: Pandora, 1989), 103.

9. Domna C. Stanton, ed., *The Female Autograph* (Chicago: Univ. of Chicago Press, 1984), 14–15.

10. Valerie Sanders, *The Private Lives of Victorian Women: Auto-Biography in Nineteenth-Century England* (Hemel Hempstead, U.K.: Harvester Wheatsheaf, 1989), 37.

11. Samuel Hynes, *The Soldiers' Tale: Bearing Witness to Modern War* (London: Pimlico, [1997] 1998), 3.

12. Sanders, *The Private Lives of Victorian Women*, 46.

13. Stanton, *The Female Autograph*, 16 (emphasis added).

14. Sanders, *The Private Lives of Victorian Women*, 2, 47 (emphasis added).

15. "The seeing eye . . ." in Vera Brittain, *On Becoming a Writer* (London: Hutchinson, 1947), 97; "I belong . . ." in *Chronicle of Youth: Vera Brittain's War Diary, 1913–1917*, ed. Alan Bishop with Terry Smart (London: Gollancz, 1981), 13. This latter quotation is from a foreword written by Brittain in 1922 when she first tried, unsuccessfully, to publish her diary.

16. Brittain, *On Becoming a Writer*, 96, 90.

17. Brittain, "War Service in Perspective," in *Promise of Greatness*, ed. George Panichas (London: Cassell, 1968), 369.

18. Brittain, *Testament of Experience*, 77, and "War Service," 369.

19. Edward Brittain was killed in action on June 15, 1918; Roland Leighton died from wounds on December 23, 1915; Geoffrey Thurlow was killed in action on April 23, 1917; and Victor Richardson died from wounds on June 9, 1917.

20. Brittain, *Testament of Experience*, 16.

21. Sanders, *The Private Lives of Victorian Women*, 11.

22. Anthea Trodd, *Women's Writing in English: Britain, 1900–1945* (London: Longman, 1998), 148, 154.

23. Linda Anderson, *Women and Autobiography in the Twentieth Century: Remembered Futures* (London: Prentice Hall/Harvester Wheatsheaf, 1997), 13.

24. These manuscripts are held in the Vera Brittain Archive (hereafter VBA) as items A27, A28, and A29.

25. Brittain, *Testament of Experience*, 35.

26. Manuscript held in the VBA as item A37.

27. Brittain, *Testament of Experience*, 77, 16, 77.

28. Liz Stanley, *The Auto/Biographical I* (Manchester, U.K.: Manchester Univ. Press, 1992), 62.

29. Alan Bishop, "The Battle of the Somme and Vera Brittain," in *English Literature of the Great War Revisited,* ed. Michel Roucoux (Picardy, Amiens, Fr.: Univ. of Picardy, 1986), 125–42.

30. Brittain, *Testament of Experience,* 77.

31. Robert Graves, *Good-bye to All That* (London: Penguin, [1929] 1960), 9.

32. M. Joannou, *"Ladies, Please Don't Smash These Windows": Women's Writing, Feminist Consciousness and Social Change, 1918–38* (Oxford, U.K.: Berg, 1995), 44; Trodd, *Women's Writing in English,* 153; Brittain, *Testament of Experience,* 89. Anderson (*Women and Autobiography in the Twentieth Century,* 76) argues that *Testament of Youth* was a book that "made a virtue out of documentary realism."

33. Brittain, *Testament of Experience,* 77.

34. Ibid., 78.

35. Ibid.

36. Rebecca Hogan, qtd. in Angela Smith, *The Second Battlefield: Women, Modernism and the First World War* (Manchester, U.K.: Manchester Univ. Press, 2000), 56.

37. Ibid., 6.

38. R. Braidotti, *Nomadic Subjects: Embodiment and Sexual Difference in Contemporary Feminist Theory* (New York: Columbia Univ. Press, 1994), 29.

39. Jean E. Kennard, *Vera Brittain and Winifred Holtby: A Working Partnership* (Hanover, N.H.: Univ. Press of New England, 1989), 131; Brittain, *Chronicle of Youth: Vera Brittain's War Diary, 1913–1917,* ed. Alan Bishop with Terry Smart (London: Gollancz, 1981), 77.

40. Brittain, *Chronicle of Youth,* 131.

41. Battersby, *The Phenomenal Woman,* 29.

42. M. Mellown, "Vera Brittain: Feminist in a New Age," in *Feminist Theorists: Three Centuries of Women's Intellectual Traditions,* ed. Dale Spender (London: Women's Press, 1983), 332.

43. Brittain, *Chronicle,* 72.

44. Kennard, *Vera Brittain and Winifred Holtby,* 139.

45. To date, the most detailed analyses of Brittain's subject position in *Testament of Youth* are those by Kennard, *Vera Brittain and Winifred Holtby;* and Anderson, *Women and Autobiography in the Twentieth Century.* In addition, C. M. Tylee, *The Great War and Women's Consciousness: Images of Militarism and Womanhood in Women's Writings, 1914–64* (London: Macmillan, 1990); Joannou, *"Ladies, Please Don't Smash These Windows";* Trodd, *Women's Writing in English;* and L. Layton, "Vera Brittain's Testament(s)," in *Behind the Lines: Gender and the Two World Wars,* ed. Margaret Randolph Higonnet et al. (New Haven, Conn.: Yale Univ. Press, 1987)—all make some reference to this important issue.

46. Sharon Ouditt, *Fighting Forces, Writing Women: Identity and Ideology in the First World War* (London: Routledge, 1994), 8.

47. Brittain, *Testament of Experience,* 79.

48. Ouditt, *Fighting Forces, Writing Women,* 8.

49. Gill Plain, "'Great Expectations': Rehabilitating the Recalcitrant War Poets," *Feminist Review* 51 (1995): 44–46.

50. Brittain, *Verses of a V.A.D. and Other War Poems* (London: Imperial War Museum. [1918] 1995), 58.

51. J. H. Gagnon, "The Self, Its Voices, and Their Discord," in *Investigating Subjectivity: Research on Lived Experience,* ed. Carolyn Ellis and Michael G. Flaherty (Newbury Park, Calif.: Sage, 1992), 222, 234–35.

52. Anderson, *Women and Autobiography in the Twentieth Century,* 78; Plain, "'Great Expectations,'" 44.

53. Mellown, "Vera Brittain," 328.

54. Julie Kristeva, *The Kristeva Reader,* ed. Toril Moi (Oxford, U.K.: Blackwell, 1986), 188.

55. Braidotti, *Nomadic Subjects,* 2; Battersby, *The Phenomenal Woman,* 3.

56. Braidotti, *Nomadic Subjects* 1, 12, 14, 37–38.

57. Brittain, *Testament of Experience,* 16, 77.

58. Braidotti, *Nomadic Subjects,* 32, 171; Layton, "Vera Brittain's Testament(s)," 74; Anderson, *Women and Autobiography in the Twentieth Century,* 94.

59. Battersby, *The Phenomenal Woman,* 34; Hynes, *The Soldiers' Tale,* 3.

60. Anderson, *Women and Autobiography in the Twentieth Century,* 8; Braidotti, *Nomadic Subjects,* 6–7; Brittain, *Chronicle,* 15.

61. Brittain, "War Service," 367.

Five

Women's Confinement as Women's Liberation

World War II Civilian Internees in South Pacific Camps

Lynn Z. Bloom

There is too much fathering going on just now and there is no doubt about it fathers are depressing. Everybody nowadays is a father, there is father Mussolini and father Hitler and father Roosevelt and Father Stalin . . . and father Franco is just commencing now and there are ever so many more ready to be one. Fathers are depressing.

—Gertrude Stein, *Everybody's Autobiography*

Strangeness is the great constant in remembered wars. The young man who goes to war enters a strange world governed by strange rules, where everything that is not required is forbidden[—] . . . a violent and dangerous world where, out there in the darkness or just over the hill, strangers wait whose job it is to kill you. Strangest of all is the presence of death, and the ways it is present.

—Samuel Hynes, *The Soldiers' Tale*

I watched the [American] tanks and trucks roaring past Headquarters on the road toward Manila, and looked at all the thousands of trucks and jeeps and new kinds of equipment. In part of my brain . . . a shadowy voice saying, "We had the best time of our lives in here—sorry to leave."

—Natalie Crouter, *Forbidden Diary*

Prologue

Diary theory explains why those who kept diaries and other forbidden records in wartime internment camps are likely to be the very people who would find the experience of confinement the most memorable and the most valuable. These are the risk takers—adventuresome, adaptable, resourceful, eager for new experiences even if the consequences are unpredictable, dangerous, and even life-threatening. They are also analytical, capable of the split vision that enables them to write about their most passionately engaging experiences with cool, critical detachment. Their attitudes toward life make them willing to risk defying their captors by engaging in a variety of proscribed behavior, from clandestine sex with the high probability of pregnancy to keeping detailed records of camp life that, if discovered, are punishable by death.

Two wartime accounts, Natalie Crouter's *Forbidden Diary: A Record of Wartime Internment, 1941–1945* (1980) and Margaret Sams's *Forbidden Family: A Wartime Memoir of the Philippines 1941–1945* (1989),[1] buttressed by other works, reveal that for these women the physical confinement of wartime internment provided a paradoxically liberating context in which they found risky independence and self-fulfillment they might never have experienced in a more conventional but technically freer civilian life. As explained in "'I Write for Myself and Strangers,'" in reconstructing themselves through postwar editing and revising of these memorable works— their only publications—the authors have the opportunity in reflection to enhance their self-presentations as capable, intelligent women survivors who not only endured their wartime circumstances but prevailed over them.[2] The illustrations and analysis that follow explain who these remarkable women were and why they could find liberty in confinement.[3]

The Phenomenon of Authorship in Wartime Confinement

Sams and Crouter are among the small percentage—estimated at three in one thousand—of civilian prisoners of war in the Pacific who recorded their experiences. According to Esther Captain, the Japanese interned approximately a hundred thousand civilians during World War II, yet as of March 1998 the Rijksinstituut voor Oorlogsdocumentatie (RIOD) in Amsterdam possessed only 230 unpublished diaries. Recent works by Frances Cogan and Theresa Kaminski cite an additional forty-six published volumes of memoirs, letters, and diaries, and six unpublished works. Until recently, says Captain, historians did not recognize diaries as valuable or reliable primary documents because of their unofficial (and, amateur and unauthorized) status, and there was little incentive to save or pay much attention to them.[4] Hence the above figures are low and doubtless incomplete. What we have to date may be nearly all that can be recovered, for with every passing year, as survivors die and their estates are broken up, it is likely that undiscovered materials will simply be discarded or destroyed.

What impels some people in extreme and thoroughly strange circumstances to record their experiences, depleting scarce materials and precious time and energy when rest or sleep is a compelling alternative? Why are these few willing to risk their very lives to perform this clandestine and proscribed activity? Such authors want to make the most of their lives, whether they have chosen the circumstances or been thrust into them. Instead of regarding wartime confinement as a dead end, possibly culminating in death itself, they regard it as the chance of a lifetime—guerilla theater—its unknowns and improvisatory qualities the subject of unceasing drama. They are acutely aware of the strangeness of their lives in confinement and, paradoxically, of the potential richness of these extreme circumstances even in the context of deprivation. Their sense of history, combined with a strong sense of selfhood, fuels their will to survive and to resist whatever is demeaning or dehumanizing. In *The Soldiers' Tale* Samuel Hynes explains, "Helplessness is a condition of victim literature, perhaps the definitive condition. So long as you can *do* something, oppose your enemy somehow, you are not entirely a victim."[5] Thus keeping a clandestine record is a way to reaffirm every day the writer's individuality, independence, and resistance, and to flirt with danger in the process.[6]

Natalie Crouter and Margaret Sams before the War

Sams and Crouter share these personal characteristics, writing from the motives identified above and others more personal, as will be clear later. Although as wartime captives they could be classified as "victims," there is not a scintilla of victimhood, and rarely of self-pity, in the accounts that encompass their incarcerations throughout the entire span of World War II in the Philippines.

Both Natalie and Margaret were risk takers, with exactly the combination of characteristics that would lead them as young women to live in the Philippine provinces, half a world away from their native culture. Whereas not everyone would find liberation in captivity (most would not), their adventurousness, eagerness for new experience, resourcefulness, and adaptability allowed these women to do just that. Natalie, a feisty Bostonian born in 1889, had spent three resolute years of her childhood overcoming the consequences of polio and meningitis. Exercise and self-discipline left her with only a slight limp but a lifelong commitment to aid victims of injustice, such as Sacco and Vanzetti. In Manila in 1927, accompanying her realtor father on a trip around the world, she met Jerry Crouter, a transplanted Colorado lawyer turned businessman who had become enamored of the Philippines while stationed there during World War I and had returned to work there after his discharge. From Boston Natalie pursued this uncommitted bachelor by letter, returning to Beijing (then Peking) in 1927 to marry him. They soon settled in Baguio and had two children.

The idea that American middle-class wives in the prewar Philippines lived in Shangri-La was never truer than in Baguio, the Philippines' mountain-ringed summer capital. Their husbands' incomes as businessmen, clergymen, or engineers assured a high social status and a very comfortable life in an intimate community of 449 whites embedded in an Asian population of 21,857 Filipinos and 1,213 Japanese and Chinese.[7] Prices were low; even during the Depression many families who in the States would have had to do everything for themselves were accustomed to the full-time services of a live-in Filipino *amah* and a houseboy, often supplemented by a cook, a *lavandera* (laundress), a gardener, and a chauffeur. The lady of the house could, if she chose, become a lady of leisure, for the *amah* would care for the children and the remainder of her retinue would tend to the rest. Whether she spent that leisure playing bridge and sipping cocktails at the country club or, as Natalie did, raising money for Chinese war relief and rolling bandages for the Red Cross was a matter of temperament and social conscience.

No ascetics, the Crouters also enjoyed a full range of country club activities. Although they were aware that war was brewing in the South Pacific—the U.S. military had sent service families back to the States— the Philippines was their home, and there they chose to stay. At breakfast on December 8, 1941 (Pacific dating), the Crouters "heard a long ripping sound like the tearing of a giant sheet and saw an enormous burst of smoke and earth near officers' quarters at Camp John Hay—the first bombing of the Philippines before our eyes" (3). Soon another nearby military base, Camp Holmes, was captured by the Japanese and transformed into an internment camp for Baguio's entire Anglo American population of 350 people, along with some 150 missionaries who had been sent from China to the Philippines and the safety represented by the "impregnable" fortress of Corregidor.

Margaret Sams, born in 1916, the daughter and granddaughter of pioneer homesteaders, prided herself on her lifelong spirit of adventure, her motif being her mantra from the age of four—"Mama," she would say, "every time I hear a train I just want to get up and go" (24). At twenty, having completed two years at Riverside Junior College, she traveled from her Beaumont, California, home (on the legendary Route 66) to the Philippines to marry Bob Sherk, her hometown boyfriend who was circumventing the Depression economy by working as a mine supervisor at Nyac, on Luzon. Its romantic and remote location was enhanced by high pay and company housing that in four years metamorphosed from minimalist to American suburban bourgeois, with servants and a company car, in Syoc, where they moved after their son David was born in 1938. Margaret, befriended by another American woman in this small community, would have been content to stay there and fulfill her life's goals: "I simply wanted to be a nice wife . . . have a nice home, nice children and a nice husband" (7). Her world changed utterly when Bob enlisted in the U.S. Army and marched off to Bataan on New Year's Eve, 1942. She later learned, through smuggled notes, that he had survived the Bataan Death March only to be imprisoned in notorious Cabanatuan; he would die, skin and bones, of dysentery aboard a Japanese ship shortly before the war's end. She and David were first interned in Manila's five-thousand-person Santo Tomás on the campus of Santo Tomás University. During 1944–45, Margaret wrangled a transfer to Los Baños, a camp half that size, on the site of a former agricultural school, to which Jerry Sams had been transferred a year earlier.

The Double Helix Structure

In "The Double Helix," Margaret and Patrice Higonnet explain how and why "the social and economic roles of many women undergo rapid and radical transformation both at the onset of war and, in a symmetrically opposed direction, at its conclusion." Although war precipitates "radical changes for women," historians such as Alan Milward and Angus Calder claim that these changes are not permanent but "mere interruptions of 'normal' gender relations," which revert to the status quo ante bellum after the cessation of hostilities. The women the Higonnets discuss move from the "home" to the "home front," Rosie the Riveters working in war-related industries in "certain sectors that were temporarily reclassified as appropriate for women."[8] Their liberation and earning power are legendary but short-lived; when the war ends, so do their jobs. Returning servicemen are hired for new peacetime jobs, and women return once again to *Kirke, Küche,* and *Kinder.*

The two wartime accounts on which this chapter focuses reveal an analogous phenomenon for women in internment camps and a comparable double-helix narrative structure: a conventional prewar life in the Philippines (bourgeois for Crouter and pioneer with bourgeois overtones for Sams), followed by an explosive altering of those lives throughout the war—an alteration that is the heart and soul of the authors' stories. Both conclude with a brief account of postwar life that seems humdrum in comparison with the exciting, oddly liberating war years. The double-helix structure reflects, as well, a narrative pattern common to myth, folklore, and confession, as well as captivity narratives—the pattern of "separation, initiation, and return," as Susanna Egan notes in *Patterns of Experience in Autobiography,* that "begins in equilibrium, is disturbed by disequilibrium, and moves into a new equilibrium."[9]

The War Years: "There is too much fathering going on just now. . . ."

During wartime men rule, in a practice unchanged from Troy to Iraq. While "father Mussolini and father Hitler and father Roosevelt and Father Stalin" dominated international prewar politics, as Stein observed (she might have added "father MacArthur" for the South Pacific), two echelons of men ruled the internment camps. Both Santo Tomás in Manila and the camp outside Baguio were operated by Japanese commandants and their entourage of guards and other soldiers, usually Japanese and Manchurian soldiers on rest assignments after arduous fighting in China or the South Pacific. However, most of the internal organizational structure and regulation was provided by the inmates, by committees of civilian American (and occasionally British) men who had been leaders in the prewar business, clerical, and medical communities of Manila and Baguio. Although women's suffrage had been in effect in America since 1919, in Baguio women could vote only in elections for a separate Women's Committee but not in the general elections until halfway through the war, by which time policies and procedures were already well established. If women had a voice in the operations of Santo Tomás, Margaret was unaware of it.

At the war's outset, the narrators, like everyone else in the camps, were truly strangers in a strange land. The camps had sprung up overnight, like toadstools, with no models except the analogous camps for incarcerating Japanese in the United States—at Manzanar, the infamous Tule Lake, and other sites. Neither captors nor captives knew how to behave, for no one could adequately prepare in advance for an unimaginable experience—particularly when it was complicated by belief on both sides that the war would be over quickly. The earliest estimate, "three days," soon extended to three months, but no one expected three years— a serious miscalculation that, for instance, kept the camps from planting extensive gardens that could have prevented the near starvation that they experienced by the end of the war.[10] Although war is largely conceived of in terms of men,[11] the camps were bursting with women, children, and babies. Indeed, as a means of population control, cohabitation—"cubicilization," in Baguio argot—was one of the first prohibitions imposed by the Japanese (who forbade any physical contact), and as the war proceeded it became the most bitterly contested, as much for the sake of family closeness as for sex. Policies had to be established on the spot to allocate food, housing, clothing, blankets, medicine, and ultimately even the minutiae that make civilized life possible: "A straight pin, a safety pin, a needle, a piece of thread, a piece of string, a shoe lace, a bobby pin, a bottle, a can, a piece of Kleenex, a cup, a spoon, a plate, a washboard, toilet tissue, toothpaste, a toothbrush, a fingernail file, a piece of paper on which to write" (Sams 78–79). Because the Philippines' shipping lanes were blockaded as soon as the war broke out, every item eventually grew scarce (when available at all) and had either to be rationed, made in camp, jury-rigged, or done without.

The Men's Committee in the Baguio Camp established principles of governance that on the whole translated into relative fairness for the internees: an informal communistic system that required everyone except babies and children to perform between twelve and thirty hours of work for the common good, according to their ability and free of charge. Internees were assigned to work in the kitchen, the hospital, the school, and in the wood and sanitation crews, among other places. The best jobs were those closest to the food—the kitchen and garbage detail—and those went to the men. Hours and quality were constantly monitored by the internees themselves.[12] There was to be a "balance between personal and community duties" (Crouter 81). To ensure fairness, everything had to be regulated: the width of the beds; the amount of cubicle space in dormitories where people lived—thirty-three inches wide per adult (Natalie's cubicle had three inches less, and she groused about it); the number of sheets of toilet paper (or newspaper strips) in the bathroom line; the portions of food in the chow line; and by the end of the war even the handful of moldy rice. The machinist made a banana-dispensing machine to eliminate griping, which Natalie Crouter interpreted as the essence of democracy, for it embodied "cold fact, technical accuracy, with true justice and balance between the large and small bananas, the fresh and the bruised. The Banana Machine does away with favoritism, privilege, graft, politics, personal touch and hurt feelings," and indeed offered everyone an equal opportunity to get the perfect banana "under the law of averages" (140). The regulation necessary to ensure health and survival of some six hundred people (five hundred captives and their captors) on a military base built for half that number, as well as the constant surveillance by the Japanese (which slackened somewhat as the war continued), allowed precious little privacy, except for the life of the mind, which Natalie exercised primarily through writing daily in her clandestine diary.

Santo Tomás, ten times larger than Baguio, was far more heterogeneous, and—to a lone woman who had arrived with her child from an outlying area, as Margaret Sams had—indifferent and impersonal when not downright hostile. Manila residents were often interned with their families, as nearly everyone in the Baguio camp was; they could live in "shanties," some very fancy. They had friends, former servants, and bank accounts "on the outside" that could be drawn on for money and material comforts throughout the war except during its last days of hardship. Margaret had none of these supports. Assigned to a small room that housed some twenty-five mothers (who were offended by David's malodorous nightly bedwetting) and children, she felt besieged by constant hostility. "Every able bodied person" in Santo Tomás had to contribute two hours of work a day to the general welfare; other work was organized on a fee-for-service, pay-as-you-go basis. Although Margaret mended camp books from the camp's seven-hundred-volume library for three hours every morning while four-year-old David stayed in a "private kindergarten" (at a cost of two dollars per month, "sixteen books to be mended" [88]), she was poor. Inflation was rampant; Margaret paid a precious $1.50 for a box of cornflakes, which she stretched for a month of breakfasts to ease her constant dysentery. With or without David, she had to stand in line incessantly in tropical sunshine or monsoon rains for meals, harsh lye soap, toilet paper, showers, and laundry. She needed a friend and confidante, a helpmeet if not a protector (84–100).

Liberation in a Time of Disequilibrium

These women's accounts of their wartime experiences, therefore, provide space for the woman writer's voice that was either silenced, subdued, or ignored in the camps' day-to-day operations. Says Hynes, no one "goes through a war without being changed by it, and in fundamental ways. And although that process will not be explicit in every narrative—not all . . . are self-conscious or reflective enough for that—it will be there. Change —inner change—is the other motive for war stories: not only what happened, but what happened to *me*." Yet even in camps surrounded by hundreds of other people, wartime authors write as if they were in literary isolation, from a self-constructed sense of unique individuality, with no acknowledgment of other comparable records even when another author might be living in the same barracks, as some were in Baguio. Hynes observes, "In most war narratives there is nothing to suggest that the author is aware of any previous example: no quotations or allusions or imitations of earlier models, and no evident knowledge of previous wars, or even of other theaters in the war that he is recalling. War writing," he says, "is a genre without a tradition" for those who write it. Like the soldiers' narratives that Hynes analyzes, women's internment stories "are not concerned with *why*"; they are "experience books; they are about what happened, and how it felt." It is their "small-scale, detailed, and confined perspective" that keeps them from being histories, although these form the detailed matrix from which histories are written.[13]

For Natalie and Margaret writing behind (and between) the lines, this focus ultimately centers on their maturation as women, lovers, mothers, human beings. Both these authors underwent considerable change and growth, if in different ways. They were not the same people at the war's end as they had been at the beginning, and they would never be the same again. Their wartime circumstances affected them profoundly and were to remain a continual point of reference throughout their long lives afterward.

Natalie's life in camp was not as strenuous as Margaret's. Natalie had the continuous support of her husband and teenage children, a community that had been established for years before the war in which she was known and respected (if not always liked), and loyal former servants who during the war used the Crouters' confiscated bank account to bring extra supplies—coveted food, soap, medicine, clothing—into camp. In civilian life, as a community mover and shaper, Natalie's very busy schedule dictated by her upper-middle-class status and interests allowed too little time for writing and reflection, although her wide reading would earn her the reputation of a camp "intellectual," as it had in prewar Baguio. In camp, Natalie's unaccustomed leisure—much of it, to be sure, provided by long stays in the camp hospital recuperating from dysentery, dengue fever, and other afflictions related to dietary deficiencies as the war ground on—gave her plenty of time to write, sometimes four or more hours a day.

In her diary, similar in size, scope, and perceptiveness to *Mary Chesnut's Civil War,* she recorded her observations and experiences of camp life in microcosmic detail, replete with characters (good, bad, and indifferent), dialogue, minidramas, and settings ranging from Baguio's spectacular mountain views ("shade after shade of blue from dark crevices and valleys to light along the ridges, an enormous range of strength" [75]) to the minutiae of cubicle life. Although writing materials were scarce, Natalie developed a microscopic handwriting that filled envelope flaps, the margins of books, any scrap of paper that came to hand. The growing diary (which took her several postwar years to transcribe on four thousand typed pages) became her most precious possession, wrapped in waterproof pieces of an old raincoat and hidden in a straw basket that she could take onto the parade ground during barracks inspections. That the Japanese never investigated the contents of Natalie's basket may be compared to the endurance of Poe's "purloined letter," in such plain sight that its familiarity rendered it invisible.

As the war continued, Natalie's mission as self-appointed camp historian (she painstakingly copied into her diary the minutes of every one of the innumerable committee meetings throughout the war) gave her the same sense of self-worth that Bruno Bettelheim, in *The Informed Heart,* explains as his motive for writing about his imprisonment in the far more extreme context of Dachau: "To observe and try to make sense out of what I saw was . . . a way of convincing myself that my own life was still of some value, that I had not yet lost all the interests that had once given me self-respect. This, in turn, helped me to endure life in the camps"—a lifeline extending to the world beyond the camp and after the war.[14] Hynes observes that wartime narratives by women and by prisoners of both genders typically "don't regard the war as an evil inflicted on their helplessness, they don't say that what is happening to them is atrocious, they don't speak of hatred or of anger. For them, war is simply a catastrophe to be dealt with" (252). So it was for Natalie, who saw war as the source of enormous education under unparalleled circumstances in a natural laboratory. In the long run, it was not Natalie's survival but her *account* of that survival that mattered the most to her—to have written a magnum opus that she firmly believed would live beyond her as witness not just for her own children but for the world at large. This perspective explains how Natalie, reduced to eighty-five pounds and near death from starvation after three years in internment, could write on liberation day, "I watched the [American] tanks and trucks roaring past Headquarters on the road toward Manila [where the Baguio inmates had been evacuated six weeks earlier], and looked at all the thousands of trucks and jeeps and new kinds of equipment. In part of my brain . . . a shadowy voice saying, 'We had the best time of our lives in here—sorry to leave'" (February 5, 1945). This is the diary's most resonant sentence—paradoxical, haunting, and true to Natalie's sense of adventure, romance, and history.[15]

Margaret Sams's *Forbidden Family* is more unusual. It is the only extant South Pacific prisoner-of-war narrative that is at once a love story, a confession, and an apologia. After the first nine months, a break-in period, Margaret, at twenty-six, was beginning to enjoy newfound independence: "As soon as I made up my mind to the fact that no one in the world cared for David and me, I began to rather enjoy doing as *I* pleased, for the first time in my life. I had no one to account to. As long as I had lived I had had to consider either my family or my husband first. Now, all at once I had nothing in the world to prevent me from coming and going and doing as I pleased, within Japanese bounds, that is." During wartime Margaret, typical of many women internees with small children, had only one primary responsibility instead of many: "As long as I fed and clothed and took care of David to the best of my ability, I was on my own." Never a conscious feminist, she liked her new status: "I owed no man allegiance, and I began to enjoy the sensation," for "my child and I were surviving through the efforts of no one except myself" (102–3).

The plot of Margaret's passionate story is simple, its execution complex. In her newfound freedom she forged an extramarital alliance with Jerry Sams, "one of the most handsome men I have ever seen" (105). The cataclysmic consequences of their casual meeting at a camp baseball game ("What's the score?") included Margaret's unilaterally risky decision to bear a daughter out of wedlock in a prison, under deteriorating conditions, and to rear her by herself, if necessary, for the Japanese transferred her lover to another camp the day after Margaret became pregnant. Significantly, her entire story may be divided into nine-month segments: the liaison, pregnancy, living as a "forbidden family" in camp, and the postwar wait until Jerry's divorce was final and the couple could marry.

Liberated by the circumstances of her own confinement, a husband in prison himself, and no personally meaningful community sanctions against adulterous behavior, Margaret could allow herself to fall madly in love with a man whose motives were more ambiguous. Jerry—an ingenious operator and contriver of machines as well as meetings—first invited Margaret to visit his secret "home," a private platform under the high ceiling of a stairwell, equipped with unimaginable camp luxuries— a clandestine refrigerator, a Bunsen burner for cooking, a radio, a chess set, and two chairs—"something I had not sat on for eight months." He offered her food, "the first time I had an invitation to eat someone else's food." Also, he made her a washboard, "the thing I wanted most in the world right then. . . . I most likely would have fallen in love with the devil himself if he had offered me help and food" (104–10).

Margaret justifies falling in love on the grounds of passion and immediacy as well as proximity: "The circumstances were right for it. No one knew what the next day held; we might be dead, we might be liberated, anything might happen." Her "carpe diem" philosophy, clearly at variance with Crouter's upright moral standards (which internment served to intensify rather than diminish),[16] is much more characteristic of the public stereotype of men rather than of women in wartime; indeed, neither Cogan's nor Kaminski's works—both of which draw heavily on Sams and Crouter—identify anyone else like Margaret. The uncertainty, she says, "made one want to drain the last drop from the minute at hand. Right now, this minute, is the important thing. Live it. Enjoy it if possible." "Probably a poor philosophy," she says, implicitly acknowledging the fact that war does not necessarily ennoble its participants, men or women, but offering no excuses (110–11). Margaret, the Prodigal Daughter, hopes to write herself back into the conventional peacetime community from which she has risked exile. This "fallen woman," as she continually calls herself, confesses from, as Weintraub says of Rousseau, "a deep urge for self-justification."[17] She hopes, as Rousseau did, that by revealing her private experience to the public, she can lead not only her immediate family but posterity to understand and thus to love as well as to forgive her (Sams xi, 298). Telling that story thus became the ultimate act of self-definition as well as self-assertion.[18]

Conclusion

Writers who turn their notes and diaries into memoirs have the vantage point of hindsight, knowing the outcome from the start and being able to interpret the beginning—indeed every event and nuance of character— in light of the end. Natalie Crouter and Margaret Sams are well aware of the significance of their liberation in captivity; they know who they had been before the war, how they changed, and why. They have a clear sense of how they want their works to be read. Both had expected immediate publication after they revised their works at the war's end,[19] both were frustrated by publishers' indifference to civilian women's war stories ("Where are the rapes? Where are the murders?"), which, absent either rape or murder, did not emerge until the 1980s.[20] Evelyn Hinz expresses contemporary sensibility concerning such works: "We want indeed to see character issuing out of struggle," which is one major focus of these works of captivity. By "making sense out of one life for others to understand," as Egan says, these autobiographers translate "the unique and inexplicable into the universal"—another twist of the double helix with its culturally encoded DNA.[21] Just as the fundamental DNA structure contains the genetic code for both the continuity and development of future generations, the liberated voices of these engaging women have the potential to resonate for generations of readers to come, as through their works they are transmuted into the history they helped to make.

Notes

1. Natalie Crouter, *Forbidden Diary: A Record of Wartime Internment, 1941–45*, ed. Lynn Z. Bloom (New York: Burt Franklin, 1980). Also CD-ROM and print-on-demand in *North American Women's Letters and Diaries* (Alexandria, Va.: Alexander Street, 2002); Margaret Sams, *Forbidden Family: A Wartime Memoir of the Philippines, 1941–45*, Wisconsin Studies in American Autobiography, ed. Bloom, (Madison: Univ. of Wisconsin Press, 1989).

2. See my "'I Write for Myself and Strangers': Private Diaries as Public Documents," in *Inscribing the Daily: Critical Essays on Women's Diaries*, ed. Suzanne L. Bunkers and Cynthia A. Huff (Amherst: Univ. of Massachusetts Press, 1996), 23–37.

3. My understanding of these works has been greatly enhanced by thirty-five years of conversation with Natalie Crouter (who died in 1984) and her family; by discussions with Margaret and Jerry Sams in the late 1980s; by an ongoing dialogue with retired Foreign Service officer James Halsema, also a Baguio internee, and use of his extensive library of materials concerning World War II in the Far East; attendance at the 1989 Baguio Internment Reunion in Los Angeles; and published accounts: Tressa R. Cates, *Infamous Santo Tomás* (San Marcos, P.I.: Pacific, 1981); James J. Halsema, *Bishop Brent's Baguio School: The First 75 Years* (Baguio, P.I.: Brent School, 1988), and *E. J. Halsema: Colonial Engineer. A Biography* (Quezon City, P.I.: New Day, 1991); Ethel Herold, "War Memories of Ethel Herold," *Bulletin of the American Historical Collection* 10 (1982): 44–67; Judy Hyland, *In the Shadow of the Rising Sun* (Minneapolis, Minn.: Augsburg, 1984); Agnes Newton Keith, *Three Came Home* (Boston: Little, Brown, 1947); Fern Harrington Miles, *Captive Community: Life in a Japanese Internment Camp, 1941–45* (Jefferson City, Mo.: Mossy Creek, 1987); Frederic H. Stevens, *Santo Tomás Internment Camp* (n.p.: Stratford, 1964); Rokuro Tomibe, "The Secret Story of the War's End," *Bulletin of the American Historical Collection* 7 (1979): 37–45; and Elizabeth Vaughan, *The Ordeal of Elizabeth Vaughan: A Wartime Diary of the Philippines*, ed. Carol M. Petillo (Athens: Univ. of Georgia Press, 1985).

4. Esther Captain, "'Written with an Eye on History': Wartime Diaries of Internees as Testimonies of Captivity Literature," *Tydskrif vir Nederlands en Afrikaans* 5, no.1 (June

1999): 1–3. Dutch historian H. W. von der Dunk explained in 1970 the historian's skepticism about letters, diaries, oral history, and other autobiographical modes of recollection, claiming that such *egodocumenten* have a limited potential for true reconstruction of the past because they reflect only *dichtung*, the specific truth of the author, rather than *warheit*, the more generalizable historical truth (Captain, "'Written with an Eye on History,'" 3). Recent feminist scholarship has accorded diaries and letters a higher status. See my "'I Write for Myself and Strangers,'" and "Women's War Stories: The Legacy of South Pacific Internment," in *Visions of War: World War II in Popular Literature and Culture*, ed. M. Paul Holsinger and Mary Anne Schofield (Bowling Green, Ohio: Bowling Green State Univ. Popular Press, 1992), 67–78; Frances B. Cogan, *Captured: The Japanese Internment of American Civilians in the Philippines, 1941–45* (Athens: Univ. of Georgia Press, 2000); and Theresa Kaminski, *Prisoners in Paradise: American Women in the Wartime South Pacific* (Lawrence: Univ. Press of Kansas, 2000).

5. Samuel Hynes, *The Soldiers' Tale: Bearing Witness to Modern War* (New York: Viking-Penguin, 1997), 274.

6. See also Captain, "'Written with an Eye on History,'" 7–8, citing Laqueur Weiss (16–29) and Dresden (33–36).

7. *Census of the Philippines*, 1939, I, part 3, Manila, 1940.

8. Milward and Calder are quoted in Margaret R. Higonnet and Patrice L.-R. Higonnet, "The Double Helix," in *Behind the Lines: Gender and the Two World Wars*, ed. Margaret Randolph Higonnet et al. (New Haven, Conn.: Yale Univ. Press, 1987), 31–35. The Higonnets argue that even in wartime women's war-related jobs continued their "social and professional subordination" to men, for women were "barred from highly skilled and supervisory positions and were . . . given incomplete training and made to work without proper safety precautions" or appropriate day care arrangements for their children (35–36). The particulars of this argument are beyond the scope of this paper.

9. Susanna Egan, *Patterns of Experience in American Autobiography* (Chapel Hill: Univ. of North Carolina Press, 1984), 41.

10. From the outset Santo Tomás grew part of its food (see Sams, *Forbidden Family*, 89), but on the urban university campus that the camp occupied there was hardly enough space for the people it contained, let alone a farming operation extensive enough to feed everybody.

11. Analyses of writings about war continue to concentrate primarily on men's writing, as is reflected in Paul Fussell, *The Great War and Modern Memory* (New York: Oxford Univ. Press, 1975), and *Wartime: Understanding and Behavior in the Second World War* (New York: Oxford Univ. Press, 1989); Hynes, *The Soldier's Tale*; and various volumes by Stephen Ambrose, including *D-Day: June 6, 1944: The Climactic Battle of World War II* (New York: Simon and Schuster, 1994), *Americans at War* (Jackson: Univ. Press of Mississippi, 1997), and *Citizen Soldiers: The U.S. Army from the Normandy Beaches to the Bulge to the Surrender of Germany, June 7, 1994–May 7, 1945* (New York: Simon and Schuster, 1997).

There are some exceptions. In addition to Cogan's and Kaminski's books about civilian internments in the South Pacific during World War II, Holsinger and Schofield, eds., *Visions of War*, is about evenly divided between men and women, and Higonnet et al., eds., *Behind the Lines*, focuses entirely on women.

12. This thoroughgoing organization actually enabled the camp's residents to override Japanese edicts on many occasions. For instance, initially the Japanese had said "No schools for the children," but once the internees reached a consensus their collective behavior was so single-minded and insistent that the Japanese simply acceded. The internees set up an elementary school and a high school. There they taught even the "forbidden" subjects (those that included Japan)—history and geography—switching to safer subjects when guards came within earshot.

13. Hynes, *The Soldier's Tale*, 3–4, 12.

14. Bruno Bettelheim, *The Informed Heart: Autonomy in a Mass Age* (Glencoe, Ill.: Free Press, 1960), 111.

15. Laurie McNeill, whose analysis of Natalie Crouter's diary forms a significant section of her dissertation, "Public Designs for a Private Genre: Community and Identity in the Diary" (Ph.D., University of British Columbia, April 2004), made the same observation (personal conversation July 23, 2000).

16. Natalie also used her diary to blow off steam about unethical individuals and undemocratic practices that violated her strong code of personal ethics. A briefer than usual entry says, "I stopped writing because I felt drained and fed up with human beings. The constant furtiveness in camp, the low ebb of ethics, the general atmosphere of shrugging shoulders, camp riddled with petty graft—had me down for a few hours. How they can all be so swell and so rotten within a short space of time is incalculable and I give up. I like them and despise them all at once" (entry for August 29, 1942).

17. Karl Joachim Weintraub, *The Value of the Individual: Self and Circumstances in Autobiography* (Chicago: Univ. of Chicago Press, 1978), 298.

18. Some of this interpretation of Margaret Sams is derived from my analysis in "Women's War Stories," 71–72.

19. At the end of the war Natalie's diary was confiscated by the American military for evidence of possible war crimes. With great reluctance she relinquished this, the only material item she had saved from the war. Her husband spent two years tracking it down, finally locating the package, unopened, in a warehouse in Kansas City.

20. Since then movie and TV producers have recognized the dramatic possibilities of both of these stories and have commissioned scripts, though to date none have been produced. To ensure that the Japanese camp commandants were treated fairly rather than stereotypically, Natalie Crouter and her family have insisted on approval rights of the scripts of *Forbidden Diary*.

21. Evelyn J. Hinz, "A Speculative Introduction: Life-Writing as Drama," in *Data and Acta: Aspects of Life-Writing* (Winnipeg: University of Manitoba, 1987), x; Egan, *Patterns of Experience in American Autobiography*, 41.

Six

Myths of Unity

Remembering the Second World War
through Letters and Their Editing

MARGARETTA JOLLY

In the history of letter publishing, war letters are a particularly interesting case, partly because of the sheer scale of their reproduction. A search
through major research library catalogues registers a steady trickle of publications throughout the twentieth century, becoming a veritable stream
in the last twenty years.[1] War letters have also, of course, been extensively
archived everywhere from the attic to the British Imperial War Museum.[2]
Even ordinary letters gain poignancy and presence when penned in the
face of death or in the dramatic conditions of battle, wartime imprisonment, exile, or a transformed home front. It is not surprising that this is an
area where the amateur epistolarian can get public attention.

But the publication of war letters is also interesting for the multiple
interests it represents—personal, social, and ideological. In addition to the
perennial commercial conditions of a famous name and a complete, well-
written correspondence, letters can accrue interest through association with
national ceremonies of war commemoration, in debates over military history, and even with the advent of other wars. The letters of David Tinker,
killed in the Falklands, have been compared to the writings of First World
War poets.[3] Conversely, Paul Fussell, the eminent reviewer of Ronald
Blythe's 1991 edition of Second World War letters and diaries, worried
about its too-smooth integration into a glut of sanitized anniversary publications.[4] The publishing of personal documents is perhaps even more
entwined with generational, familial, and individual time spans. War letters are most often retrospectively consumed as personal commemorations by relations of their writers, although this auto/biographical frame
itself has social determinants in a culture of memoir and autobiography

making. A rather different context for publication has been the rise of cultural and women's studies over the last twenty years. The interest stirred by these disciplines in the private documents of the socially and literarily marginalized has been particularly powerful in facilitating the publication of women's war letters. In all three contexts, letters are positioned in relation to the symbolic place that wars play in public and personal memory, and they gather mythical as well as historical meanings.

This article will consider the publication of Second World War letters as a fragment of this special epistolary niche. It is not its intention to analyze the letters themselves—this has begun to be done elsewhere[5]—but rather to add to the history of what Janet Altman has called "the letter-book as a literary institution."[6] It will argue that the letter books of the Second World War take three characteristic forms, according to whether a national, familial, or academic "memory" is uppermost.

The first form, determined mostly within national memory, tends to be presented as military history or war writing aimed for a popular readership, usually with minimal introduction, little academic paraphernalia, and a lot of illustration. These books draw heavily on letters in archives but also on appeals made in the local media and on already published letter anthologies. Notable in Britain are the editions published by or in association with the Imperial War Museum.[7]

The second and largest category of publication represents personal, typically familial, war memory—books edited by a relative of the letter writer or by the letter writer themselves. When these are published commercially, the writers unsurprisingly tend to be prominent in public life, or their editors are academics or writers. These are also typically officers' rather than privates' or civilians' letters. It is certain that there exist many epistolary memoirs that failed to get published or that were compiled for personal circulation alone, as the number of privately published editions suggests.

Finally, there are a few collections that have a scholarly conception, being more critically oriented, often aimed at academic audiences and put together by academics for university presses. Yet these too can be said to represent a form of remembering, in seeking to create alternative social and political genealogies of the past. Although sometimes overlapping, these three categories bring with them distinctive agendas in proposing a public, long-term interest in the private, ephemeral letter. However, these "letter books" all feature a tendency to mythologize the unity of their letter writers in the face of war, whether that unity is national, familial, sexual, or political.

Popular Letter Collections: National Memories of War

While popular war-letter collections can range from the frankly coffee-table variety to the literary or sociohistorical highbrow, they share an editorial rhetoric that asserts the value of a private and "spontaneous" record of war. Yet on inspection it becomes clear that they work within a distinctly public discourse of national identity in which the reprinting of letters, even when they are not overtly patriotic, takes part in the complex politics of public war memory. While many eyewitness accounts were published during and between the First and Second World Wars in journalistic, propagandist, or memorial capacities, public interest in personal accounts after 1945 gained its first major boost in Britain in 1964 with the fiftieth anniversary of the start of the First World War. By the 1980s, half a dozen new collections were appearing each year, with increasingly specialized appeal. The fiftieth-anniversary commemorations, from September 1989 to August 1995, of the end of the Second World War gave further impetus to the publishing and filming of popular memories and records of the war.[8] The pattern of war-letter publishing thus can be tied to the cultural and ideological place of the world wars in national self-perception and to the waning and waxing of nationalism in general.

A 1964 BBC documentary series on the First World War signaled a new era in remembering war. In 1950s Britain, as elsewhere, memories of the war were contained within an evasive discourse of leadership and victory in a "righteous" war (quiet, by contrast, on concurrent anticolonial wars). The political sea change of the sixties, in which nationalist and liberal humanist orthodoxies were cracked on many fronts, began to generate more critical and even pacifist responses to war. George Mosse's history of war commemoration across the century provides a more specific context for thinking about the publishing of personal documents. His thesis is that public memory of the world wars reflects a decline in nationalism in Western Europe since 1945, precipitated by the ideological nature of the Second World War, the Holocaust, and the advent of the nuclear age. Compared to the sentimentalizing and sanctifying commemorative acts after the First World War, "the cult of the fallen was no longer of great importance for the worship of the nation; indeed, the close association of nationalism and the symbols of war was now regarded with some distaste. . . . Mourning for the dead stood in the foreground, and their resurrection for the purpose of stimulating a national revival had given way to the quest for consolation."[9]

One of the effects of this change in the style of mourning was to emphasize individual rather than collective representations of loss—for example, in the kinds of obituaries written on gravestones, the establishment of memorial parks rather than statues, and most dramatically, in the personal style of the Vietnam Veterans Memorial, the "wall of mourning," erected in Washington in the 1980s. Like the mementos (including letters) that cover this modern memorial, the publication of personal war memoirs, letters, and diaries since the mid-sixties is one symptom of this more individualized means of representing and commemorating sacrifice in war.

The cultural historian of war Paul Fussell, in his review of Mosse's book, warns us, however, that "despite these promising novelties, the trivializing and sanitizing are still going on."[10] This is particularly true since the swing back toward "pre–World War I rhetoric" of national sacrifice and unity with the rise of the New Right in the 1980s. This return was obvious with the Second World War remembrance commemorations in the early nineties but had been already starkly evident in Britain in the rhetoric used during the Falklands War in 1982. In Britain, representations of the Second World War, in contrast to those of the First World War, played a particular part in keeping this nationalist discourse alive. While the latter became a myth of tragic loss and the pointlessness of imperialism, the Second World War remained for the Allies the "Good War" fought against Nazism and for democracy.[11] In Britain, this rhetoric offered a "'last fleeting vision of greatness' from which both the left and right in British politics could take inspiration," particularly at moments of national crisis.[12] It is true that the war's association with an internal leveling of the class system, decolonization, the bombing of civilians, and the Holocaust has produced a politically ambiguous legacy. But these aspects of the war have increasingly been contained within equally strong associations of a collective national resistance in which all classes "pulled together" in a discourse often markedly more conservative than that current during the war itself.

War-letter books published since the 1960s for popular consumption express these ideological shifts and tensions. On the one hand, they mark the overall democratization and individualization of war commemoration, bringing out themes of social rather than national identity and exploring diversity of experience rather than the more straightforward emphasis on martyrdom and national unity that dominates letters published during both world wars and immediately afterward. But in comparison to, for example, oral histories and poetry,[13] in many ways letter books are framed within particularly nationalist terms, albeit often in "soft" form.[14] This tendency exists because letters are in themselves likely to be imbued with patriotic feeling and personal reassurance; Fussell and others have for that reason viewed them as the least conducive material for charting the real experience of war.[15] However, it is also because of the particular kinds of editors, publishers, and markets that frame them, in partial response to the politics of war memory in the resurgent nationalism of the last twenty years. Letters from the Second World War rather than the First World War are particularly likely to bear such messages.

Let us consider first two illustrated hardbacks produced by the British Imperial War Museum in 1988 and 1990. These were put together under the museum's own imprint as part of its "Personal Experience" series, inaugurated in 1969 with George Coppard's *With a Machine Gun to Cambrai: The Tale of a Young Tommy in Kitchener's Army, 1914–1918*. Like this highly successful diary-memoir, the two books considered here are introduced by the museum's director, Alan Borg, and keeper of education, Christopher Dowling, as valuable for their spontaneity but also for the point of view that they offer. While Coppard was considered to reveal a hitherto neglected "private's" perspective, the letters of a WREN (member of the Women's Royal Naval Service) to her fiancé, collected as *Entertaining Eric*, are, though "apparently inconsequential," in fact vital to "build[ing] up an accurate account" of "wartime life."[16] Borg reminds us in the foreword to *Special Relations: Transatlantic Letters Linking Three English Evacuees and Their Families, 1940–45*, that "one of the characteristics of modern war is that it affects everyone." These letter books clearly reflect the museum's dedication to representing the amateur or marginalized voice of war, and in this sense they continue that democratizing of war literature discussed as a post–Second World War phenomenon. But they also reflect the museum's overall mission to educate the visitor or reader into a sense of national identity. Lucy Noakes tells us that

> from its inception [in 1917], the Imperial War Museum was a consciously "national" museum, with the aim of creating a sense of inclusion and membership of the nation amongst its members. As many members of the nation as possible were to be included in the museum's presentation of a nation at war, including munitions workers and Land Army girls. These goals were made explicit in the King's dedicatory speech at the official opening of the museum in 1920, when he explained that it stood "not for a group of trophies

won from a beaten army nor for a symbol of the pride of victory, but as an embodiment and lasting memorial of common effort and common sacrifice." The museum, despite its name, thus represented the First World War less as a great imperial victory for Britain, and more as a time of national unity, shared suffering and shared effort. The institution was surrounded from its inception by the imagery and language of common sacrifice and effort.[17]

The museum's archive, from which the Personal Experience series is mostly drawn, represents an even more purely "educative" aspect than the displays and exhibitions offered to the public, and as such the letter collections distill this institutional rationale of "common sacrifice and effort" and "an inclusive sense of national . . . identity." This takes a particular form in relation to the Second World War, which we have shown has remained a powerful icon of Britain's social unity in a just cause.

Entertaining Eric, published in 1988 in the runup to the big commemorations of the start of the war, takes on a new perspective in this light. As the tale of an upper-middle-class woman turfed out of her career as a fashion designer to billet industrial workers in stately homes, then to work as a WREN courier in the secret service and thereafter as a stoker onboard a ship, it is well placed to comment on the upsetting of the class and gender order. At the same time, both her social background and the epistolary form work to contain this within the safe form of "entertainment." As Maureen Wells jokes about her disastrous placement of a bowler-hatted and portly "Mr. B" shouting "Pleased ter meetcher" in the big country house of languid, elegant "Mrs. S,"[18] or the affairs of married women with visiting servicemen, Mrs. Miniver appears to be alive and well.

Special Relations, published in 1990 two years after *Entertaining Eric,* equally responds to the myth of Second World War as a time of "national unity in a time of adversity . . . in which internal divisions, notably those of class and politics, were overridden as the nation coalesced behind high ideals to fight a just war."[19] As the book's title suggests, this tale of frightened middle-class English children evacuated to unknown Ohio makes them the bearers of national identities, little "ambassadors" to the United States. Through negotiations over these children, the correspondences between the British Mathews parents and their two host families trace a poignantly domestic meeting of British dry humor and stiff upper lip, and American expansiveness. But they also enact a symbolic drama of a poor "mother" nation reconciling itself with its wealthy offspring through a shared "rediscovery" of their democratic ideals. One American foster parent confesses their comfortable income and hopes that they don't spoil their "English child," pointing out that "accumulated wealth is just as dangerous as high explosive": a resonant metaphor for the times. "I'm thankful to say that . . . since 1931 we have been strong 'New Dealers,' supporting reforms in the capitalist system which are necessary, we think, to save it and American Democracy."[20]

Conversely, the English father suggests, "I cannot say just how we should feel about [Negroes] if the situation were the same in this country as in yours. From what I remember of history, it is entirely our fault that you have the problem today. As an outsider, I should say that if the negro pays taxes equivalent to the white, he should have access to the same educational facilities and the right to vote,"[21] while his daughter writes angrily home to him about hypocritical American anti-Semitism.[22] This mutual prodding of conscience partakes of a discourse of democracy as the prerogative of white, middle-class gentiles, a political version of enlightened parenting that was as resonant in 1990 as in 1940. In 1990–91 this discourse was being reemployed in more straightforwardly imperialist terms, as John Major's government emphasized its support of the United States in the Gulf War, affirming once again the nations' "special relationship" as elder stewards of democracy in the face of a Saddam Hussein constantly likened to Hitler. Letters from this noncombatant record represent "the People's War," but in a version more amenable to a liberalizing of national rhetoric for the interests of post-imperial Britain.

Two other editors of letters designed for a broad readership can be analyzed as representing this kind of double-edged reflection on the national identity. Sanger's 1993 *Letters from Two World Wars: A Social History of English Attitudes to War 1914–45* aims to offer "a socio-psychological study of English attitudes to war" through what he considers to be "the truest and most moving testimony."[23] Tapert views her 1984 *Despatches from the Heart: An Anthology of Letters from the Front during the First and Second World Wars* and 1987 *Lines of Battle: An Anthology of Letters by American Servicemen in World War II* as offering a "parallel history" of war from the point of view of the men and women who actually did the fighting and dying. Both editors create extremely rich anthologies by incorporating dozens of writers across varying backgrounds that represent the individual's experience of fear, suffering, and courage, as well as their views of military action. Tapert indeed declares a democratic principle of selection, specifically choosing letters that "spoke to her emotionally" or "provided vivid accounts of battles" rather than those that concerned famous writers, military leaders, or strategy.[24]

That Sanger's selection of letters aims at an impartial view is implicit in his sociological purpose:

> To provide a) a continuous selective narrative for the general reader of successive English wars . . . accompanied by brief summaries of the causes, principal actions and social features of the wars, as witnessed by our letter writers; b) a sourcebook for the student of history, with short details of the circumstances in which the letters were written and of the personalities involved; c) a socio-psychological study of English attitudes to war which are highlighted by significant quotations from the letters in the captions and comments, and by contemporary poetry (or prose) at the beginning of each chapter.[25]

At the same time, as these editors reject laudatory rationales, they construct a collective narrative that remains essentially nationalist in effect. This is in part the effect of their organization of the letters by the public (national) chronology of key strategic moments in the history of each war. It is also the result of the use of iconic photographs—for example, of the D-Day landing. The inclusion of last letters (i.e., the last written before the death of the writer) at the end of the book again betrays the celebratory tone of the "cult of the fallen soldier" that Mosse identifies as the basis for the more nationalist kinds of war commemoration characteristic of the period before the 1960s. Finally, their editorial comments suggest the slippage between heritage and history making.[26] Sanger, on the one hand, offers a brief summary of the changing themes of twentieth-century war letters in relation to those of previous centuries: "jingoism, looting[, and] . . . mutiny [disappear,] . . . while admission of fear, consciousness of the obscenity and insanity of war, cynical humour, or acceptance of self-sacrifice are larg[er] features]."[27] Sanger concludes the book with a sequence of letters that offer proof of this thesis. Yet he also invokes the character of the "Englishman" (singular, not plural, implicitly Anglo-Saxon) as a member of a "deeply humane race" with little appetite for brutality and a self-deluding idealism, a character that he sources in the "historic inviolability of the island's sea defences and the long experience of ultimate victory."[28] In comparison to Sanger, Tapert (who is more of a journalist than a historian) seeks letters that capture private and literary rather than public or military selves. Yet she too turns to the rhetoric of race and nation in defining it:

> This passion for letter writing is at odds with the *common assumption that Americans—and American men, in particular—are inarticulate and*

infrequent correspondents. . . . . As I began to collect letters from U.S. soldiers in World War II, I half expected to find that they would be terse and uncommunicative. Their real message, I thought, would be found between the lines: I miss you, I'm well, try not to worry. In the course of my research I read thousands of letters. They came via public appeal in over two hundred regional newspapers and military journals, by searching the archives of several military institutes, and by personal solicitation. And as I read each letter, I was struck by the constant eloquence—*especially the eloquence of men from the American heartland.* Most had not been to college. Few had ever been exposed to the vast literature of war. . . . For these men letters were the only links with the private worlds they had left behind."[29]

To argue that letter collections like these work in the way that wartime publications did, as a subtle form of propaganda, would obviously be to overstate the case.[30] Half a century on, there is far more scope for publishing admissions of fear, doubt, indifference, and even pleasure in violence—from the nursing sister who wonders if the wives of injured men will be able to recognize their husbands being shipped home[31] to the squabbling, unpatriotic Smith brothers.[32] More important still, "educative" determinants, and their accompanying ideologies, such as still strongly guide the Imperial War Museum, are relatively weak in relation to those of the market—the museum ceased publishing its Personal Experience series altogether in the 1990s due to lack of sales.[33] But precisely because letters are not the most commercially successful genres in which war is represented, they may reveal better than, for example, war-glorifying comics or thriller films, the more public state politics of war memory that guide the commissioning of war memorials, museum and archive collections, BBC documentaries, and school curricula. They form part of a discourse of the Second World War that combines a view of the war as social leveler, with war as national unifier, that is still very powerful strategically and culturally in Britain and, arguably to some extent in the United States too.

Before turning to consider the related personal resolution involved in familial editions of war letters, we should consider a contrasting "public" edition, notable for its resistance to incorporation by this myth. This is Ronald Blythe's 1991 *Private Words: Letters and Diaries from the Second World War.* Like Sanger and Tapert, Blythe amasses his "private words" from existing publications, archives, and friends,[34] yet the range and tone of his writers are strikingly different. Where Sanger's writers converge through military description and Tapert's through homesickness, Blythe offers dramatically contrasting voices: intellectual, sexual, begrudging, confessional, and (notably) the "unrelenting cheerfulness" that was perhaps the most characteristic voice of the war. It is not that the social backgrounds of his writers are more varied—although there are notably more prisoners of war and civilians than others represented—but that their writing styles are. It is this literary interest that emerges as Blythe's criteria for selection. Of the letters and journals of the Elliot siblings, he comments that in a "simple fugue-like way, . . . by centering what was happening on their parents' house in Suffolk, a family could unconsciously tell the whole story [of war,] . . . its novelty, its bloodying of the home fields, its commonplaces and its horrors."[35] Of "marriage by correspondence," he observes that "while at first it was natural and easy to write, it soon became apparent to many husbands and wives that letters could lead them into artificiality. It took time and either some literary ability or a pure ingenuous sincerity to push the marriage along." A simple means by which Blythe draws out our awareness of the creativity of letter writing—and reading—is to offer a sequence of letters from each writer rather than only one or two. Much of the effect of Ted Seckle's story is precisely the irony of letters that receive no reply. Secondly, Blythe offers editorial commentary on the contradictions behind epistolary rhetoric. The Hopkinsons, we are told, met after three years apart "on Hungerford Station on a bitterly cold February evening, he laughing and saying, 'My bride, my darling!' as if he had rehearsed it, she confused." A third factor in Blythe's literary conception is his thematic rather than chronological arrangement. Rather than the national story implied by chronology, his themes represent cultural aspects of wartime life that make no claim to collective representation: "Loyalties," "The Last Time I Saw Paris," "My Kingdom for a Book," "It's Being So Cheerful as Keeps Me Going," "Go Home, Yanks!," "Miniverism," and "Writing in a Blitz." This organization also disrupts the standard equation between letters and authenticity, representing them rather as genres, albeit genres of crucial psychological and emotional importance in war.[36]

Blythe, is, of course, well known as a literary anthologist and writer rather than a military historian like Sanger or a commercial editor of war letters like Tapert. Paul Fussell views his "absence of bellicose imagination" as a handicap to representing the bitterness and sadism of war, resulting in his having chosen over-wholesome correspondents.[37] Yet his aesthetic approach allows an acute historical understanding of letters, because the view it offers of them as psychological and social constructions, from the glitteringly creative to the blandly conventional, can better approach the multiple "myths" they represent. In relation to the public myth of wartime unity, his panoply of voices proposes a much more eclectic and internally riven portrait of Britain. Further, he thus allows the construction of more personal myths of family and sexual unity to become critically visible. These myths are crucial to both letter writing and to relationships in war. But they are also effects of editorial practice that are particularly evident in the many collections edited by the letter writer or a relative of the letter writer. It is this second category of collection we shall now consider.

Memorial Letter Books: War and Myth at Home

It is undoubtedly true that the main instigation for the publication of war letters comes from the relatives of their writers, or from the writers themselves. These books, like the anthologies or institutionally sponsored collections discussed as part of "national" memory, are symptoms of the individualization of mourning practices and a general rise in the writing and dissemination of autobiography in the postwar context. But here, of course, personal commemoration is the central motive, the collection being assembled very often after the writer's death. The missives of Roger Spicer and Caleb Milne, edited and privately printed by Spicer's father and Milne's mother, respectively, after their deaths in action, are typical in this regard:[38]

> I am publishing these extracts for private circulation for three reasons—firstly because I think they are well enough written to give a good description of a young subaltern's [junior officer's] life in an infantry battalion on active service; secondly, because I believe those who knew him well will enjoy this record; thirdly, to those of my friends who did not know him this may serve as some introduction to one whom I would like them to have met.[39]

Such editions were sometimes printed during the war in the vein of patriotic last letters. However, they partake of a long tradition of printing letters in memorial books,[40] and it is not surprising that a second crop of letter collections has been appearing with the aging and death of the World War II generation. Examples include the letters of a U.S. combat medic edited by his wife;[41] those of British diplomat and Women's Voluntary Service member David and Sybil Eccles, edited by David Eccles; those between Mirren Barford and her fiancé, edited by her son; Joyce Statler's presentation of her elder siblings' evacuation letters; Judy Barrett Litoff's of her aunt and uncles' epistolary marriage; and Nathalia Danesi Murray's collection of the letters of her lover, journalist Janet Flanner.[42]

Ellen MacRorie's unpublished "Bits and Pieces" exemplifies the layers of familial relationship being sustained in these compilations.[43] Her uncle created a mimeographed "family newspaper" from the letters of his four sons, who were all in the U.S. Army; he added other family news, circulating it to immediate family members as well as civilian relatives throughout the war. His jovial "editorials" were severely strained when one brother-in-law was killed. Thirty years later, a daughter-in-law came across the surviving "Bits" and "republished" them as a typed manuscript for her children, with copies for dispersed cousins. This manuscript finally received a third layer of family "publication" a further ten years on, as MacRorie decided to piece together its lost parts and supplement them with oral historical interview and archive materials. This project involved rediscovering now geographically distant American relatives as well as her family's past, even as she conceived it within the academic context of an evening class in life history research. If we count the decision to place a collection of letters in an archive as representing a kind of publication, there are many more such examples.

These editors of family or loved ones' letters usually present their letters as constituting more than simply family memoir but as at least a humble offering to the public record, much as Tapert described her intentions as showing "the contribution of the individual" to history.[44] However, the autobiographical, indeed psychoanalytic, dimensions of these projects inhibit criticism of the potential "myths" embedded in the "documents" they assemble. Rather, the messages of fidelity and longing between lovers, men and women, sisters and brothers, parents and children, are understood and portrayed simply as stories of personal transcendence over frightening situations or frustrating separations. Consider, first, that many young men and women in military service or war work are motivated, at least in part, by the wish to leave home and parents. Generational tensions may be confirmed but also displaced, counteracted, or simply postponed by wartime separation. Moreover, these desires were and still are clearly played upon by the military and the state employers, which package their appeals for young, strong labor in terms of a rite of passage to adulthood or independence, higher education, or preparation for a later job. In this light, letters between parents at home and children away in battle or war work are direct products of a generational and bodily division of labor that is both perennial and highly specific to the history of warfare.[45]

"Always looking forward to coming home, but wish to see a little more active service first," declares the young Spicer, who left school before graduating to join the army, in response to the British Secretary of State for War Anthony Eden's appeal to school boys to join up after Dunkirk.[46] "Please tell [Daddy] the news gently because I'm afraid I've been rather a disappointment to him," requests Lucia Lawson to her mother after having failed to become an officer,[47] while Mirren Barford is conversely disappointed that her family will not let her leave Oxford to join the WAAFS (Women's Auxiliary Air Force).[48] Jock Lewes puts it particularly explicitly in describing how he was able to preserve "the privilege of [a] wonderful relationship" with his parents through "six years of letter writing" precisely because they were physically apart.[49]

Of course, if there were real and deep divisions within families, the letters would not have been written in the first place.[50] But this only points up that letters are just where the terms on which war labor is organized will be mystified, either by their writers' fantasizing or fobbing off now-distant parents and children, or by editors' reconstructing a dead child's, parent's, or grandparent's letters. Spicer's father posthumously gives his son's fateful volunteering his blessing, notably pointing out that his son had not needed to "follow in his father's footsteps" in the regiment he joined. Michael Wise's edition of his mother's letters to a man killed before she met his father offers another version of family romance. It is not that he was unaware his mother had had a lover before his father, he says, for his brother had been named after the noble Special Air Service hero. Through editing them he "began to feel almost a part of [Jock's] family" and "determined to try to find [Jock's] brother." Having tracked him down, he discovered his mother had been an equal presence for his would-have-been family-in-law, as the woman that their lost one had loved. "The circle was complete," he tells us, in a therapeutically resonant image.

A rather different rationale might have motivated Joyce Statler's edition of her elder siblings' evacuee letters in *Special Relations*. As the child too young to have been evacuated with them, was Statler repairing the guilt of having had their parents to herself, or was she writing herself into their exclusive adventure? Her comment that "we did have great fun at times as a reunited family" after their return suggests as much, as does the explanation of her U.S. trip in 1958 to "go and see for myself what I had heard so much about from the others, and even to go a little further." It is obviously significant that this trip was provoked by her father's death.

If commemorative editing inevitably partakes of genealogical fantasies that obscure the political and personal dynamics of call up, so too does it risk perpetuating the military ideology of a natural sexual division of labor, upon which letters, even in the context of total war, persistently draw. Jock and Mirren's correspondence, for example, is a particularly articulate courtship in which Mirren's sexual as well as intellectual independence as a student at Oxford seduces the hero-officer and would-be philosopher Jock. At the same time, Mirren battles with her place in the private and protected sphere, and Jock takes for granted his self-definition in the public. He applauds her wish to leave Oxford to do her bit for England, but when she speculates that women can endure what men can or even that she may need her degree if she does not marry or is left a widow, he is utterly dismissive. "It is modern affectation among women to act as though they had no intention of ever getting married, to try and carve out a career for themselves in competition with men instead of in co-operation with them," he says; "Your true vocation [is] marriage."[51] His protestations of his desire for "the shape and colour and feel of your body" place the love letter as an attempt to manage the much broader contradictions in the wartime wish for women to take on male labor without challenging sexual ideology. Just as much so is her refutation:

> When your lust for beating Germans grants you time to feel trust and desire for me, I shall be around for a while longer anyway. I don't only mean physical desire, but all desire, nor do I mean merely blood lust, but a lust to crush all that you condemn. Your wife won't have a pleasant time when you, bearing the great weight of convictions and beliefs, treat her as a pretty porcelain figure. It would be soul killing for most women to know that your long, long way to Tipperary was quite lively, and that you ignored the passionate appeal of their flesh and blood, their brain and spirit, to walk the long way with you, even as lightly and inconspicuously as their shadow.[52]

One of the correspondence's distinguishing features is the unique sexual code in which each of their meetings is designated as a house on "Joy Street" populated by allegorical characters, such as the dangerous "beggar priest," who represents Lust, and the "little blind baby girl called Tears." Yet while they flamboyantly fetishize their letters as "a filter which rejects all that we most desire and passes on clear and clean all that we shall value most,"[53] they also lean on the most conventionally gendered literary war imagery: he as Paris, she as Helen, he as Ulysses, she as Penelope.[54] Of course Jock and Mirren were products of their time and class. Yet their "serial romance" is precisely that, a personal but also social—and even literary—mythmaking.

Their editor, Michael Wise, is clearly captured by the archetypal quality of the correspondence. He tells us that despite having first simply intended to create a private memoir of his mother's letters, "the task caught hold of me . . . and the letters begged for publication." What this restorative approach necessitates, however, is the rejection of any critical view of this myth. Wise—and his publishers—in fact, amply consolidate it, literally titling the book by genre as *Joy Street: A Wartime Romance in Letters*, providing facing portraits of his protagonists and marketing it as "the most romantic story you will ever read."

By Safe Hand: Letters of Sybil and David Eccles 1939–42 (1983) mythologizes a wartime relationship through letters less sympathetically. This correspondence stands out not only because of its astonishing completeness but because it seems to foreshadow its editing, forty or so years later. David, a Foreign Office diplomat, wrote to his wife Sybil from Spain November 17–18, 1940, that "I think your description of Wiltshire in war and mine of a mission abroad would make an amusing duet, and that we must string them together, and read them at a sitting, because it is astonishing how the evolution of events and ideas comes out when you take a big bite of papers written seriatim."[55]

It seems that everything this suave diplomat did was for posterity. Thus, it is unsurprising that we find him in the early 1980s deciding to publish the letters as a kind of elegy to Sybil, who had died several years earlier. Yet his letters dominate hers, not only in their content (negotiating trade deals to keep Spain and Portugal neutral and to get the United States into the war) but in the structuring of the narrative, suggested in his summary of "the pattern of the correspondence" as

> held together by three questions: Why did Franco's Spain remain neutral? How should we have treated France after the Armistice? And what may happen to a marriage when two people who have been so much in love are forced to live apart? The letters should provide some fresh material on the history of the Blockade, some clues to the character of men like Salazar, Franco, Petain, Weygand and Samuel Hoare, and point up the difference between real love and pot-luck desire.[56]

Eccles downplays the startlingly liberal elements in both his and his wife's record of that wartime economic and diplomatic policy, unsurprising for a retired Tory member of Parliament yet also reminiscent of that resurgent nationalism characteristic of the 1980s.[57] A more striking aspect of the letters' framing, however, is his dehistoricizing of Sybil's letters. In his schema, her account of "Wiltshire in war"—which in fact deals with rationing, illness, loneliness, war entertainment, and her own war job of promoting national nurseries—figures largely to "point up the difference between real love and pot-luck desire." Admittedly, her letters are complicit in this essentializing of the civilian wife's record, a "picture of wartime life in the country"—pullets and piglets and communal jam making.[58] But her morale-boosting letter writing breaks down when, near the end of the correspondence, she finally realizes his infidelity and abandons her epistolary role as his faithful Ariadne: "Your letters have been the anaesthetic that seduced and bewitched me through the first one and a half years of war. They have lost their power and make me dream no longer. . . . Neither at home nor abroad am I necessary any more—your letters are the dividend of a generous heart to capital invested long ago."[59]

In the light of the narrative's ending, David Eccles's repeated letters proposing to Sybil that "dovetailing" their letters would let them see the wood from the trees read as his sense that making the letters into one narrative would symbolically put their marriage back together. His eventual decision to publish the letters, particularly after she had died, and the editorial choices he made appear to be a posthumous fulfilment of that desire. The necessarily unfinished narrative of the letters is brought into a romantic closure that undermines the disruptiveness of their widening dialogue. It also potentially undermines the historical or indeed psychological import of a civilian woman's war.

Collections edited by family members or partners create a second moment of epistolary mythmaking, in which the letter writers' original fantasies of unity, of self-preservation through perfect communication, are once again played out by the editor. Such myths are a common and entirely understandable feature of the family memoir; indeed, they are probably the engine of its commemorative impulse (although debunking modes are becoming more common). It is perhaps more surprising that these questions have not been seriously taken up by academic editors. Let us finally consider this third group of letter collections and their own temptations for mythmaking.

Academic Collections: Antiheroic Veterans and Martyrs

If the context for popular editions is that of the culture of war memory and for family editions that of the memoir industry, a more specialized group of war letter books shows the influence of the rise of cultural and women's studies. A radical turn in the academy in the late sixties and early seventies away from canonical figures and forms to discover the history and culture of marginalized peoples has stimulated a new interest in letters, diaries, and other private writings. One effect is the appearance of letter books organized around themes of social and ethnic rather than national identity. Scholars have pursued wartime experiences through letters of African Americans,[60] Japanese Americans,[61] Jews,[62] and Japanese.[63] War experience has diversified from the prerogative of military men in action to a much broader spectrum, from evacuees[64] to concentration camp internees.[65]

Feminist researchers have led the turn to letters as oppositional war history. Olga Kenyon outlines the double-pronged impetus in stating that "women as letter-writers have been comparatively neglected, though often the letter was their main literary outlet," an outlet of exceptionally widespread application in wartime. Kenyon stresses the new perspectives that a "feminist approach" can bring, in which letters "can be read as disruptive texts, blurring binary definitions of gender attributes, between 'high' and 'low' registers," between cultures and subcultures.[66] Second World War collections with this kind of remit include those of American civilian women to servicemen,[67] American women who are in the armed services themselves,[68] and British women writing letters and journals,[69] as well as letters between women working as welders[70] and the extraordinary love letters between an erstwhile Nazi housewife and her Jewish woman lover in Berlin.[71]

Most dedicated to the cause are the American historians Judy Barrett Litoff and David Smith, who together archived ten thousand American women's war letters (having advertised over several years); out of this set they published four large, scholarly editions with the university presses of Georgia and Mississippi and the Oxford University Press. In the tradition of "rediscovering" a forgotten past and valuing previously dismissed "voices," they maintain correspondences themselves with many of the now elderly women who donated their letters, and they "publish" a newsletter for interested parties, in the form of a wartime "V-mail." Their book of civilian letters, *Since You Went Away: World War Two Letters from American Women on the Home Front*, is perhaps their most important, as the least previously documented type of war letter. The book is organized partly through the chronology of the war—from its opening for the States with Japan's bombing of Pearl Harbor to its end with Victory Day—but also partly through types of relationship, from courtship by mail to war brides. Nearly all of these are women writing to male partners, though a few are mothers to sons or children to fathers. Smith and Litoff preserve individual relationships with each letter writer by giving us the "end" of each letter writer's story, as provided by the writer. A few of these end in the death of the man at the front, most in the happy reunion of the couple. They inform us, for example, that Maurice and Isabel Kidder were reunited in the late summer of 1945, finished their education, and had a family; he became a parish priest, and she moved from library work to teaching English.[72]

However, Litoff and Smith ultimately capitulate to happy endings that are overdetermined by the circumstances of collecting as well as reading the letters. Influenced by the relationships with elderly women developed through the project, Smith decided not to include evidence of postwar breakdown of marriages represented through letters in *Since You Went Away*, as it was neither "relevant" to the historical period of the war nor respectful to the women who donated their letters to the project.[73] While this may be ethical in terms of editorial relationships to the women, it is less ethical toward the general readership—especially as he does not include this qualification in the editorial foreword. Within the laudable terms of recovering hitherto marginalized perspectives, the fantasies of communication and reunion of their writers are uncritically recycled. This also presupposes a view of the letter as literal communication, a faith in its "sincerity" and "presence." While Litoff and Smith comment that their letters "read like great literature," they seem unaware of their own construction of a historical romance of heterosexual and maternal unity.

This is not so different from the dynamic identified in familial collections, and it may be relevant that Litoff and Smith first became interested in war letters through publishing the marital correspondence of Litoff's aunt and uncle.[74] However their construction makes much more serious claims in the alignment of their correspondents' happy endings with the thesis that the war offered women new independence. This makes little acknowledgement of the patriarchal resistance this engendered or the patriarchal reaction that followed after the war ended. They state, for example, that "the woman war worker was highly lauded, and 'Rosie the Riveter' became a national heroine.... In their letters to loved ones, women war workers expressed pride in their jobs and often were enthusiastic about the new sense of responsibility and independence they were achieving."[75] This view is echoed by some historians, particularly Arthur Marwick and John Costello, but the extent to which the war was a liberating experience for women is still a subject of great contention. Feminist historians such as Penny Summerfield, Susan Hartmann, and Margaret Higonnet now consider that women's economic and political gains were mostly hedged with terms that ensured they would only last "for the duration." Hartmann and others have traced the high price women paid in autonomy during the immediate postwar years of demobilization, a price that helped delay the emergence of any organized women's movement for more than two decades.[76]

Over and above differences of interpretation of letters' accounts of work experience, new friendships or political awareness, the status of civilian letters to men in the forces begs us to question how the independence of women is encompassed within a medium defined by their relationship with men. Even as Smith and Litoff champion letters as a neglected source of the history of war, they treat the medium as neutral rather than heavily overdetermined by this fundamental fact. But their own editorial design of *Since You Went Away* suggests the problem of integrating the sexes' histories through letters:

> We have organised the letters around themes which were of especial importance to the women who wrote them. These themes are very different from those which are emphasized in traditional accounts of World War II. We would have been unfair to the letter writers had we organized this book around the great events of the Second World War. Instead, the book focuses on the responses of women to the outbreak of war, courtship by mail, the varied experiences of war brides and war wives, and the challenges faced by female war workers. In addition, it provides examples of home-front responses to the demands created by the war. The book concludes with an examination of how women were affected by the sacrifices which led to victory and how they perceived the larger meaning of the war.[77]

Servicemen and civilian women's wars remained far apart even in total war (and possibly servicewomen's too), mainly because men and women's lives were far apart anyway. Letters dramatize the same expressions of romantic and familial unity that in peacetime would seem easier, ironically, for academic deconstruction.

We can see the same conundrum in an edition by Eva Figes of British women's wartime letters written over five hundred years, from medieval civil wars to the Second World War. Figes herself has a history as a feminist academic and novelist; her book is presented as an uncovering of women's part in a "male defined" preserve. She draws this conclusion from her selection:

> The human race has always been a community of two sexes, living and working together, and for the most part they see their interests in common. Women, willy-nilly, have always been involved in war; it has touched upon their lives in a thousand different ways, and involved hardship, deprivation and grief. They also serve who only sit at home and wait, and keeping the home fires burning, the business going, the children healthy and the house safe is not exactly an easy option at the best of times, and at the worst of times, during the London Blitz, for instance, absent men worried more about their families than they did for their own safety. But very many women have, whether by chance or choice, found themselves more directly involved, and more actively engaged, in all sorts of different ways.[78]

It is telling that she emphasizes the unity of the sexes while stressing her efforts to represent the different perspectives of women from different class backgrounds.[79] But there is a serious difficulty with reading civilian women's letters to servicemen as assertions of unity of interest. For the relationships that the letters embody may not only inhibit the recording of women's independence or maturation in letters but actively undermine those steps to liberation. It is a paradoxical claim to see civilian women's letters to those in the services as evidence of their participation in war, given that they are the product of their institutional and social displacement from the military.[80] A more radical feminist perspective would go farther to view the correspondences that preserved men and women's relationships in war as part of a romantic mystification of deep cultural and economic divides between the sexes, divides that are as contradictory as they are sustaining.

The fact that such letter collections are proposed as women's participation in war without questioning its terms or the terms of their writing is evidence of a third kind of "myth" peculiarly dear to cultural historians, the myth of women's liberation through wartime and, more generally, the rationality and justness of the oppressed.[81] Such "antiheroic" heroic accounts may ironically bear as little relation to what really happened as histories that either ignore the importance of such relationships or dismiss the role of women in the period.

Conclusion: War Letters and the Uses of Mythmaking

Overall, the publishing of such documents charts a democratization of the means by which war is represented, celebrated, and mourned, and a pluralization of the historical record. But if academic and politically motivated editors who consciously reject facile nationalist, sexual, gender, or racial paradigms and who may attempt to control or expose personal investment find themselves presenting letters within "mythical" terms, letters must have a serious power to seduce their readers. One of the interesting aspects to analyzing such editions is the multiple determination of their myths. Very often commercial or academic editors initially cathect to the project because of personal attachments to wartime documents; conversely, familial editors often reach for patriotic rhetoric as a means to rationalize loss.

There are ways in which we might wish to "correct" for such epistolary bias. First, we can compare correspondences between male military and female civilians to other kinds of correspondences (for example, between civilian women or between gay military personnel).[82] Second, we can compare them to other evidence—official histories, military reports, censorship records, diaries, and oral histories. Third, we can include discussion of what happened after the correspondents reunited in the long term, as well as the short term. Fourth, we can read them "against the grain" for their unconscious testimony to the contradictory divisions of labor in wartime. In letters, ideologies of an essential division of labor or ritual separation between men and women, or even old and young, physically able-bodied and disabled, black and white, Jew and gentile, are *literally* materialized. On the other hand, there we can trace people's struggles to survive and make sense of such ideologies, where we can get access to a much wider range of experiences than if we stick with published and well-known writers.

Most important, perhaps, we can simply make explicit the fact that letters construct fantasies of identity and relationship, that they are kinds of creative writing that are also highly conventional and that may be particularly conventional in wartime. For, finally, letters spring from and codify ideal relationships, preserving the self through appeal to the other and practicing the conduct of civility. Letter editors, especially when motivated by personal ties, are often interested in the same "myths" of unity—of nation, family, sexual relationship, or alternative community. This can only testify to our need for such myths even as we must retain a skeptical attitude toward them in the context of a still dangerously nationalist, patriarchal, heterosexist, and generationally bound politics of war memory.[83]

Notes

1. A combined count of titles of personal letters from the two world wars in Princeton University Library catalogue, the British Library catalogue, and COPAC (Oxford, Cambridge, London, and other major United Kingdom universities) listed circa 283 entries between 1914 and 2000. Of these 121 were published between 1990 and 2000. The other cluster of publications was between 1915 and 1919, during which fifty-three titles are registered. These are certainly gross underestimates due to the limitations of search tools in library catalogues, particularly those in the United Kingdom. These listings also do not reflect the printing of sample or excerpts of letters in histories, biographies, and literary or war anthologies, which is an easier form in which to publish letters than an entire "letter book." A search in Bookfind (November 7, 2000), which lists works in print, forthcoming, and recently out of print from the United Kingdom, the United States, Europe, and elsewhere from a very large range of publishers, produced 753 titles that included "war letters" in the text out of 6,171 that included "letters" in the text. It should be noted that there is some degree of multiple listing of the same title under different editions, as well as some irrelevant listings. It should also be noted that of 153 books listed under "True Stories" of the Second World War, only one was a letter collection; memoirs and one diary comprised the rest. Letters represent only a fraction of the industry in publishing personal narratives of war.

2. Another important collection in Britain is in the Liddell Hart Centre for Military Archives. In the United States, major holdings are at the Military History Institute at Carlisle Barracks, Pennsylvania, and the Marine Corps Historical Center in Washington, D.C. Historian Andrew Carroll initiated a new archive in 1998 specifically to collect letters from American servicemen through all U.S. wars. He collected about fifteen thousand in the first year of the project. See Andrew Carroll, "American Soldiers Write Home: The Stories of the Twentieth Century's Wars," *New Yorker* (Dec. 27, 1999–Jan. 3, 2000): 89–99.

3. David Tinker and Hugh Tinker, *A Message from the Falklands: The Life and Gallant Death of David Tinker from His Letters and Poems* (London: Junction, 1982); Simon Featherstone, ed., *War Poetry: An Introductory Reader* (London: Routledge, 1995), 12–13.

4. Paul Fussell, "From the Front: Taking the Sting out of the World Wars," *Times Literary Supplement*, September 27, 1991.

5. See Judy Barrett Litoff and David C. Smith, "'Will He Get My Letter?': Popular Portrayals of Mail and Morale during World War II," *Journal of Popular Culture* 23, no. 4 (1990): 21–44; Detlef Vogel and Wolfram Wette, eds., *Andere Helme—andere Menschen?*

Heimaterfahrung und Frontalltag im Zweiten Weltkrieg (Tubingen, Ger.: Klartext, 1995);
W. Lee Nahrgang, "Journals and Letter Collections: The Best West German Literary
Representations of World War II," *Lamar Journal of the Humanities* 12, no. 2 (Fall 1986):
33–45; S. Narovchatov, "World War II Letters from a Soviet Soldier to His Mother,"
Novyi Mir 5 (1983): 186–98; W. Rohr, "'I Very Rarely Cried': Letters and Diaries by Ber-
liners from World War II," *Zeitschrift Fur Geschichtswissenschaft* 42, no. 3 (1994): 286;
Paul Sargent, "'Keep Smiling, Keep Those Chins Up and God Bless': Filmed Messages
Home from Service Personnel in the Far East during the Second World War," *Imperial
War Museum Review*, no. 7 (1992): 23–33.

6. Janet Gurkin Altman, "The Letter Book as a Literary Institution 1539–1789: Toward a Cultural History of Published Correspondences in France," *Yale French Studies* 71
(1986): 17–62.

7. The Imperial War Museum—Britain's premier military museum but also a key
site of memorial culture—was first established in 1917 as a national, state-sponsored
commemoration to the collective effort of the First World War. See Gaynor Kavanagh,
"Museum as Memorial: The Origins of the Imperial War Museum," *Journal of Contemporary History* 23 (1988): 77–97.

8. Roderick Suddaby, a keeper of documents in the Imperial War Museum, considers print runs to have been 1,500–2,000 in the 1970s. Personal communication, 2000.

9. George L. Mosse, *Fallen Soldiers: Reshaping the Memory of the World Wars* (New
York: Oxford Univ. Press, 1990), 222–23.

10. Fussell, "From the Front," 3–4.

11. Particularly interesting in this context is Laurence Housman's 1930 *War Letters
of Fallen Englishmen*, in which its introduction explicitly posits the letters as the "voice"
or speaking stones of the British Cenotaph, in a remarkably antimilitarist strain. See
Wolfgang Natter, *Literature at War, 1914–1940: Representing the "Time of Greatness" in
Germany* (New Haven, Conn.: Yale Univ. Press, 1999), for a fascinating discussion of
the different politics of editing German soldiers' last letters in the famous collection of
Philipp Witkop (first edition, 1916).

12. David Cesarani, "Lacking in Convictions: British War Crimes Policy and National Memory of the Second World War," in *War and Memory in the Twentieth Century,*
ed. Martin Evans and Ken Lunn (Oxford, U.K.: Berg, 1997), 27. Margaret Thatcher's
reworking of antitotalitarian and "People's War" rhetoric for the Falklands War in
1982 was the most evident point in this revival, but it continues. Witness John Major's
pronouncements on the Gulf War and even Tony Blair and Foreign Secretary Robin
Cook's spin on the war in Bosnia (see Kenneth O. Morgan, *The People's Peace: British
History since 1945* (Oxford, U.K.: Oxford Univ. Press, 1999); Lucy Noakes, *War and the
British: Gender, Memory and National Identity* (London: Tauris, 1998).

13. For critical oral histories, see Alessandro Portelli, *The Death of Luigi Trastulli and
Other Stories: Form and Meaning in Oral History* (New York: State Univ. of New York
Press, 1991); Luisa Passerini, *Fascism in Popular Memory: The Cultural Experience of the
Turin Working Class*, Studies in Modern Capitalism (Cambridge, U.K.: Cambridge Univ.
Press, 1987); Dorothy Sheridan, "Ambivalent Memories: Women and the 1939–45 War
in Britain," *Oral History* 18, nos. 1–2 (Spring 1990): 32–40; Penny Summerfield, *Recon-*

structing Women's Wartime Lives: Discourse and Subjectivity in Oral Histories of the Second World War (Manchester, U.K.: Manchester Univ. Press, 1998). The enormous amount of scholarship on oral histories of the Holocaust is especially illuminating on the constructed nature of memory, personal and collective.

14. Here they can certainly be contrasted with genres such as film, television, and comics, which have preserved unreconstructed heroic chauvinist views of war.

15. See Paul Fussell, *The Great War and Modern Memory* (Oxford, U.K.: Oxford Univ. Press, 1975), and David Keshen and Jeff Mills, "'Ich bereite mich auf den Tag vor, da es zu Ende geht!': Briefwechsel von Kanadierinnen und Kanadiern im Krieg," in *Andere Helme—andere Menschen? Heimaterfahrung und Frontalltag im Zweiten Weltkreig*, ed. Vogel and Wette, 257–82. For an analysis of cultural constructions of self in war letters see Christa Hammerle, "'You Let a Weeping Woman Call You Home?' Private Correspondences during the First World War in Austria and Germany," in *Epistolary Selves: Letters and Letter-Writers, 1600–1945*, ed. Rebecca Earle (Aldershot, U.K.: Ashgate, 1999), 152–82, and Margaretta Jolly, "Everyday Letters and Literary Form: Correspondence from the Second World War," (Ph.D. diss., University of Sussex, 1996).

16. The "Personal Experience" series contains thirteen volumes to date, most of which are memoirs.

17. Lucy Noakes, "Making Histories: Experiencing the Blitz in London's Museums in the 1990s," in *War and Memory in the Twentieth Century*, ed. Evans and Lunn, 92–93.

18. Maureen Wells, *Entertaining Eric: Letters from the Home Front, 1941–44* (London: Imperial War Museum, 1988), 18.

19. Noakes, *War and the British*, 23.

20. Jocelyn Statler, ed., *Special Relations: Transatlantic Letters Linking Three English Evacuees and Their Families, 1940–45* (London: Imperial War Museum, 1990), 75–76.

21. Ibid., 101.

22. The extremely limited nature of this liberalism is evident when, a paragraph later, he says, "Frankly, though, I do not think I should care to work under a negro boss, so you see I haven't the courage of my own convictions." Ibid., 102.

23. Ernest Sanger, ed., *Letters from Two World Wars: A Social History of English Attitudes to War, 1914–45* (Phoenix Mill, U.K.: Alan Sutton, 1993), ix.

24. Annette Tapert has also edited letters by servicemen during the American Civil War, in her *The Brothers' War: Civil War Letters to Their Loved Ones from the Blue and Grey* (New York: Times, 1988).

25. Sanger, *Letters from Two World Wars*, ix.

26. See Patrick Wright, *On Living in an Old Country: The National Past in Contemporary Britain* (London: Verso, 1985), on the distinction between these two ways of constructing the past.

27. Sanger, *Letters from Two World Wars*, x.

28. Ibid.

29. Tapert, *The Brothers' War*, xvi–xvii (emphasis added).

30. From 1940 until 1942, British-American correspondences were published in the United States on the covert orders of the Ministry of Information as a form of "soft" propaganda, alongside specially commissioned literary works and Ed Murray's

"Britain speaks," to lobby the then still heavily isolationist Americans. See Nicholas John Cull, *Selling War: The British Propaganda Campaign against American "Neutrality" in World War II* (New York: Oxford Univ. Press, 1995). As I have argued elsewhere, such personally articulated appeals for mutual understanding in the generically positive and reassuring tones of a letter were ideal for putting the case in an apparently unpolitical and unmediated form. See Margaretta Jolly, "Between Ourselves: The Letter as Propaganda," in *Propaganda: Political Rhetoric and Identity, 1300–2000*, ed. Bertrand Taithe and Tim Thornton (Phoenix Mill, U.K.: Alan Sutton, 1999), 239–61.

31. Sanger, *Letters from Two World Wars*, 168.

32. Tapert, *The Brothers' War*, 90. See Joanna Bourke, *An Intimate History of Killing: Face-to-Face Killing in Twentieth-Century Warfare* (London: Granta, 1999), for the use of letters to chart soldiers' pleasure in murdering.

33. The Imperial War Museum does continue to publish in association with publishers and individuals, and the pressures on the public sector may be reflected in an increasingly commercial note. The museum began charging a visitor's entrance fee in 1989, and it would seem that newer books that include letters from their collections, published in association with it—such as *The Imperial War Museum Book of the First World War* (1991) and *Forces Sweethearts: Wartime Romance from the First World War to the Gulf* (1993)—are more commercially oriented. See Margaretta Jolly, "Love Letters versus Letters Carved in Stone: Gender, Memory and the 'Forces Sweethearts' Exhibition," in *War and Memory in the Twentieth Century*, ed. Evans and Lunn, 105–21.

34. Unlike Sanger and Tapert, Blythe does not appear to have advertised in order to uncover other sources.

35. Ronald Blythe, ed., *Private Words: Letters and Diaries from the Second World War* (London: Penguin, 1993), 69.

36. Ibid: 14.

37. Fussell, "From the Front."

38. Caleb Milne, *'I Dream of the Day . . . ': Letters from Caleb Milne*, ed. Marjorie Kinnan Rawlings, 2d ed. (New York: Longmans, 1945); L. Spicer, ed., *Letters from My Son, 1942–1944, Roger Lancelot Spicer* (London: Unwin, [1955?]).

39. Spicer, *Letters from My Son*, n.p.

40. Richard Altick, *Lives and Letters: A History of Literary Biography in England and America* (New York: Greenwood, 1979).

41. PFC Keith Winston and Sarah Winston, eds., *V-Mail: Letters of a World War II Combat Medic* (Chapel Hill, N.C.: Algonquin, 1985).

42. Natalia Danesi Murray and Janet Flanner, eds., *Darlinghissima: Letters to a Friend* (London: Pandora, 1988).

43. Ellen MacRorie, personal communication (1999).

44. Tapert, *The Brothers' War*, xx.

45. The history of candidates rejected from service on the grounds of age or disability would make an important context for thinking about this, as would the letters from disabled who did find opportunities in war work.

46. Spicer, *Letters from My Son*, 25.

47. Eva Figes, ed., *Women's Letters in Wartime*, 1st ed. (London: Pandora, 1994), 276.

48. Mirren Barford and Lieutenant Jock Lewes, *Joy Street: A Wartime Romance in Letters*, ed. Michael T. Wise (London: Little, 1995), 38–39.

49. Ibid.,106.

50. Red Cross volunteers attempted to get American GIs in Britain to "write home to mother." See Juliet Gardiner, *Over Here: The GIs in Wartime Britain* (London: Collins, 1992).

51. Barford and Lewes, *Joy Street*, 40–41.

52. Ibid., 166–67.

53. Ibid., 52.

54. The Hopkinsons also designate themselves "Ulysses and Penelope." See Blythe, *Private Words*.

55. David Eccles, ed., *By Safe Hand: Letters of Sybil and David Eccles, 1939–42* (London: Bodley Head, 1983), 202–3.

56. Ibid., 11.

57. One reviewer comments: "These letters of two score years ago tantalizingly show that the intervening decades might truly have had another pattern, and a better one." Alistair Forbes, "To Be with a Happy Marriage Is So Rare," *Listener*, January 20, 1983.

58. See Alan Bell, "Wykehamical," *Spectator*, February 12, 1983.

59. Eccles, *By Safe Hand*, 387.

60. Phillip McGuire, ed., *Taps for a Jim Crow Army: Letters from Black Soldiers in World War II* (Santa Barbara, Calif.: ABC, 1983).

61. Louis Fiset, *Imprisoned Apart: The World War II Correspondence of an Issei Couple* (Seattle: Univ. of Washington Press, 1997); William Shinji Tshchida, *Wear It Proudly: Letters of a Japanese-American Soldier in Europe 1944–5* (Berkeley: Univ. of California Press, 1947).

62. Renata Polt, ed., *A Thousand Kisses: A Grandmother's Holocaust Letters* (Tuscaloosa: Univ. of Alabama Press, 1999).

63. Frank Gibney, ed., *Senso: The Japanese Remember the Pacific War—Letters to the Editor of Asahi Shimbun* (Armonk, N.Y.: Sharpe, 1995); Jean Lartéguy, *The Sun Goes Down: Last Letters from Japanese Suicide-Pilots and Soldiers* (London: New English Library, [1956] 1975).

64. Martin Parsons, *Waiting to Go Home: Letters and Reminiscences from the Evacuation 1939–45* (London: DSM, 1999).

65. Richard S. Geehr, *Letters from the Doomed: Concentration Camp Correspondence, 1940–1945* (Lanham, Md.: Univ. Press of America, 1992).

66. Olga Kenyon, ed., *Eight Hundred Years of Women's Letters* (Phoenix Mill, U.K.: Alan Sutton, 1992), ix, xx.

67. Judy Barrett Litoff and David C. Smith, eds., *Dear Boys: World War II Letters from a Woman Back Home* (Jackson: Univ. Press of Mississippi, 1991); Judy Barrett Litoff and David C. Smith, "Since You Went Away: The World War II Letters of Barbara Wooddall Taylor," *Women's Studies* 17, no. 3–4 (1990): 249–76.

68. Judy Barrett Litoff and David C. Smith, eds., *We're in This War, Too: World War II Letters from American Women in Uniform* (New York: Oxford Univ. Press, 1994).

69. Jenny Hartley, ed., *Hearts Undefeated: Women's Writing of the Second World War* (London: Virago, 1995); Figes, ed., *Women's Letters in Wartime*, 1st ed. (London: Pandora, 1994).

70. Margaretta Jolly, ed., *Dear Laughing Motorbyke: Letters from Women Welders in the Second World War* (London: Scarlet, 1997).

71. Erica Fischer, *Aimée and Jaguar: A Love Story, Berlin, 1943*, 1st ed. (New York: HarperCollins, 1995).

72. Judy Barrett Litoff and David C. Smith, eds., *Since You Went Away: World War Two Letters from American Women on the Home Front* (Oxford: Oxford Univ. Press, 1991), 100.

73. David Smith, personal communication (June 1995).

74. Judy Barrett Litoff and David C. Smith, eds., *Miss You: World War II Letters of Barbara Wooddall Taylor and Charles E. Taylor* (Athens: Univ. Press of Georgia, 1990).

75. Litoff and Smith, *Since You Went Away*, 145.

76. Susan M. Hartmann, "Prescriptions for Penelope: Literature on Women's Obligations to Returning World War II Veterans," *Women's Studies* 5 (1978): 223–39.

77. Litoff and Smith, eds., *Since You Went Away*, 145, ix–x. It is interesting that Litoff and Smith in their edition of the marital correspondence entitled *Miss You* abandon their editing as a dialogue when Charles is posted overseas, to separate it into two monologic chapters, "The Home Front: June 1944–August 1945" and "Western Front: June 1944–August 1945." Although this structure suggests doubts about their own celebration of the letter as link, it also allows the reader to observe the therapeutic uses of letter writing for servicemen, upon which the editors interestingly comment.

78. Figes, *Women's Letters in Wartime*, 11.

79. She represents three servicewomen (discussed above) and three civilians: a Bristol bus conductress confessing terror in the Blitz to her soldier husband in Cornwall, the wife of a bombardier in North Africa, and an upper-class mother who sends painfully buttoned-up bulletins of mourning for a son to another of her sons in action.

80. See Cynthia Enloe, *Does Khaki Become You? The Militarization of Women's Lives* (London: Pandora, 1988), for an excellent discussion of this.

81. I do not exempt myself from these fantasies. See the epilogue to *Dear Laughing Motorbyke*.

82. For an example of gay letter writing in the military see Allan Berube, *Coming Out under Fire: A History of Gay Men and Women in World War Two* (New York: Plume, 1991).

83. As I have suggested, this politics is also racist and invested in a politics of the able-bodied and disabled, but these may affect the politics of letter editing less.

Seven

War Elegy

PAT C. HOY II

As I sit here on this flagless Memorial Day overlooking Washington Square Park from my apartment in the city of New York, my mind turns naturally to war and to E. B. White. This was, after all, his city, and it is impossible, still, to write here apart from him, especially on a national holiday like this one. During the 1930s and stretching all the way into the late sixties his *New Yorker* pieces reflect a continuing impatience with national fervor. In 1933 he calls on Einstein, speaking "not about relativity but about nationalism," to warn us of "forces inimical to life," and as late as 1969 White frets about a similar concern during a moment of national celebration. The moon, he grumbled, is "a poor place for flags"—"What a pity that in our moment of triumph we did not forswear the familiar Iwo Jima scene and plant instead a device acceptable to all: a limp white handkerchief, perhaps, symbol of the common cold, which, like the moon, affects us all, unites us all." It was unity that interested White—world unity—and were he with us today, still writing, I suspect that India and Pakistan would replace Leipzig in his mind; and he would try once again to make us see how "a single day's development" could take us back "a thousand years into the dark."[1]

But White would also be concerned, as he was when he buried his pig, about forgetfulness, a failure to mourn those who have suffered and with whom we should be bound. He would not have us cast national unity aside, even though we are inclined to misuse it politically. "The Death of a Pig" remains fresh and provocative because it plays against our deep-seated, but often ignored, need for communal purgation. For White the tragic scene that he and his cast enact over the pig's death is "slapstick—the sort of dramatic treatment that instantly appealed to my old dachshund, Fred, who joined the vigil, held the [enema] bag, and, when all was over, presided at the interment."[2]

But there is a serious undercurrent in this ritual. The death is not about the loss of nourishment, White tells us, but about the pig who "had suffered in a suffering world." White brings in a host of characters from the rural community to bear witness to the suffering, and at the end, despite the slapstick and the rhetorical hyperbole, we know that White's "deep hemorrhagic in tears" express a loss that is bigger than a pig—that this death is a "departure which the community marks solemnly on its calendar, a sorrow in which it feels fully involved." White assures us, finally, that he and Fred will visit the unmarked grave in the woods "singly and together, in seasons of reflection and despair, on flagless memorial days of our own choosing."[3]

Flagless memorial days—suffering and death recounted privately, throughout the year, rather than on specified days of national mourning—that is White's idea about the authenticity of mourning. My concern today, as I look out over Washington Square, is that most of those sauntering happily around the park—pushing as they often do the very limits of free expression—know, as the years pass, less and less about the suffering that others have done on their behalf. As the past recedes from memory, these inheritors of freedom have little basis for remembering, often no basis at all except the stories that others have left, and are leaving, behind.

The definitive history of those stories has been written by Samuel Hynes in *The Soldiers' Tale: Bearing Witness to Modern War*. Hynes's elegant book extends the work that Paul Fussell did so well in *The Great War and Modern Memory* and less well in the polemical *Wartime: Understanding and Behavior in the Second World War*. Hynes gains distinction because of the broader scope of his investigation—the two world wars and the war in Vietnam—and the narrower focus on the soldiers' tales within each of the wars. In an earlier book, Hynes, like Fussell, investigated the relationship between war and culture. In *The Soldiers' Tale* he distills the essence of the tales themselves, subordinating culture to the experience of war. The larger tale that he eventually constructs emerges from his evenhanded analysis of the personal stories—memoirs, letters, journals—of men who actually fought. Beginning with the particulars of their experiences, he reaches for "the recoverable past of war" rather than making a higher claim on "historical truth." What he grasps is a heightened sense of how war feels, what it is like for the soldier.[4]

The power of Hynes's accomplishment derives in large part from the way he uses his own war experiences and from the attitude he brings to the task of recovery; the two go hand in hand. To illustrate just what I mean by these strengths, I want to juxtapose Hynes and Fussell a moment longer. Their own memoirs of war provide the clues we need to understand just how Hynes elicits the reader's trust as he constructs the larger tale.

In *Doing Battle: The Making of a Skeptic* Fussell recovers a persona he had cast aside in 1987 as he began to collect and republish many of his earlier pieces on war, just as he also began to conceptualize *Wartime*. He identified that persona as "the pissed-off infantryman, disguised as a literary and cultural commentator."[5] When Fussell deliberately removed that infantryman from the collected essays, affecting a more appealing form of reasonableness, the writing ironically became more polemical, less persuasive. He lost touch with his own teasing ambiguities.

In his memoir Fussell restores that same infantryman but strips him of his military title, leaving us with what seems to be the real McCoy—the veteran "skeptic" who seems still to be riding high on the crest of a wave of unspent anger. Fussell takes us from his privileged early life in Pasadena (1924–43) all the way to the publication of *Wartime* (1989) and his final years of teaching at the University of Pennsylvania, but the central story of the memoir is the "extirpation of Boy Fussell" at the hands of the U.S. Army.[6] From that story we see how war can strip away entitlement and turn innocent fascination into rage. In this most lonely of the soldier's tales, we see too how far war continues to fuel Fussell's anger, feed his contempt, set him apart from others, and undercut his ironic stance. He can't get war out of his system.

Fussell is at his best as a writer when he pushes the anger below the surface and dispassionately rubs our noses in the grim reality of war, asking only that we sit up and take notice. To those inclined to forget the horrors of war, Fussell seems to say, *I will not permit it.* For those without experience, he provides it, delighting as he does in how "wonderfully absurd, bizarre and unforgettable" the sights of war can be:

> The spectacle that caused my mouth to open in wonder, and almost in admiration, consisted of five German soldiers spread out prone in a semicircular skirmish line. They were still staring forward, alert for signs of the maquis. Behind them, in the center of the semicircle, was an equally rigid German medic with his Red Cross armband

who had been crawling forward to do his work. In his left hand, a roll of two-inch bandage; in his right, a pair of surgical scissors. I could infer a plausible narrative. One or more men in the group had been wounded, and as the medic crawled forward to do his duty, his intention was rudely frustrated by an unspeakable loud sharp crack [of artillery] overhead, and instantly the lights went out for all of them. . . . The little waxwork squad, its soldiers unbloody and unmarked, had all left life at the same instant.[7]

We are left with an eerie image, one of a kind that Hynes will call Battlefield Gothic.[8] Fussell, left with a "sight that somehow brought art and life into strange relation," intensifies the image for us: "It was so cold that the bodies didn't smell, and they'd not begun visibly to decompose, but their open eyes were clouded, and snow had lodged in their ears and the openings in their clothes and the slits in their caps. Their flesh was whitish green. Although they were prone, their knees were bent, as if they were athletes terribly surprised while sprinting. They looked like plaster simulacra excavated from some chill white Herculaneum. No one but me, apparently, saw this sight."[9]

Now, owing to Fussell, we have all seen it, and because of the transfiguration we wonder with him whether to interpret it "as an image of the whole war and its meaning, less a struggle between good and evil than a worldwide disaster implicating everyone alike, scarcely distinguishing its victims in the general shambles and ruin." For him the image and the experience linger in his mind "as a prime illustration of modernism, not that it occurred but that it seemed so normal, and that no one seemed to care."[10]

There in that last bit of imagining, we see Fussell taint the image with his own personal suffering—so normal no one seemed to care—as he points to the emblematic source of the unbalancing anger that causes him during the war to grow "unpleasantly snotty and sarcastic" and years later to see his less gifted, less experienced academic colleagues as "dolts." Out of Harvard and on the way to his first academic job, he "insisted on playing [his] transfigured self, that is, impudent, insolent sarcastic, and ostentatiously clever and supercilious."[11] Even though that transfigured self is tempered often by a yen for irony and occasionally by a deep, contradictory strain of sentimentality, the angry critic prevails, dominating and wearying us as he goes about his work.

Hynes's memoir, *Flights of Passage: Reflections of a World War I Aviator* (1988), reveals a very different kind of man, one who took with him from the war a more settled and settling resolution. His war in the Pacific, while no less isolating than Fussell's in Europe, took place in the sky, and that, coupled with an inherited emotional restraint, seems to have made all the difference. From the outset Hynes is a "true believer in the religion of flight,"[12] and his lyrical descriptions retain a romantic flavor whether he is training stateside or flying combat missions in the Pacific:

Over Memphis
Below me light began to come on in houses and farms, and every thing that was not a light became dark and indistinct, so that the ground was almost like a night sky. But still I flew on in sunlight. The surface of the plane seemed to absorb and hold the light and color of the sunset; brightness surrounded me. It was as though the earth had died, and I alone was left alive. A sense of my own aliveness filled me. I would never die. I would go on flying forever.

Over the Pacific
And then the island appears ahead, the planes slide into attack formation, the high-speed descent begins, the first plane peels off and you really see the island for the first time, in your bombsight—a grove of trees on the right, an airstrip, a few buildings—and tracers begin to rise lazily toward you, and little clouds of AA bursts hang in the air as you dive past, and you have dropped and are pulling away, over the trees toward the beach and safety.

They were classic, beautiful strikes, the feeling of planes and men relating in the intricate choreography of a strike-formation, the gutknotting climax, and the long, calm return. What memory returns to me is images.[13]

How different these images are from Fussell's and yet Hynes is no giddy flyboy. He suffered the loss of friends, "felt the rage that other pilots felt," and, in the memoir, he exposes the U.S. Navy's complicity in these losses. But from the outset there is something besides the lilt of flying that holds Hynes steady. "After preflight," he tells us, "we would never quite join the Navy; we had joined instead a smaller, more independent and anarchic group, the community of fliers. The Navy was our antagonist, musclebound and dumb like those football-coach officers; but because it was dumb we could beat it. With a little imagination we could circumvent, muddle, and exploit the regulations, and we could fly."[14]

Home from the war, Hynes chose to be discharged in Pensacola because he "wanted to return just once, just for a few days, to that place where I had learned the only skill I had, and where I had been happy in that timeless world of young men, before the dying began." "Perhaps," he goes on, "the impulse to return is a sign that one has grown up, an acknowledgment of the way the good times pass us. We go back in space because we can't go back in time." Some forty years after the war, summing up the experience of his last four-hour flight there in Pensacola, Hynes recalls the end of that wartime adventure: "We had become men with families and responsibilities and futures. The end of flying had made us mortal."[15] And yet the war has not ended for Hynes either. Like Fussell he can't seem to be done with it, but the distance he has acquired from it allows him to elicit trust when he writes about it.

Hynes's discerning judgment, tempered by the claims of war, informs all that he says in *The Soldiers' Tale*. The book's supreme accomplishment lies in the multiplicity of voices—each of the individual soldier's voices that Hynes permits us to hear, accompanied always by the deft analytical voice of the soldier-scholar, making of the many tales the one definitive story about modern war. It is a delicate act of witnessing and reconstruction, complicated by the fragility and whimsicality of memory and language; but, by the end of this book, I have already begun to know what I could never have known through my own soldierly experiences. I know where I fit into the larger narrative of war, where my brothers who fought in Hynes's war fit into that same long, continuing tale. I know how the tale varies from war to war and from theater to theater; and because of Hynes's own discerning presence in this scholarly reconstruction of war, I also know something about the worth of the soldiers' collective investment in the nation's life. I know better what to mourn and what to revile in that common experience that binds us all together as a nation.

Hynes's own witnessing takes two different but related forms. The first consists of the subtle discerning commentary that permits us to understand each witness's contribution to the larger tale. In that commentary Hynes must weigh the value of those other tales, necessarily different from his own. As he creates the collective tale, a tale never heard until now, he must do justice to the others if his own is to be believed.

Here, then, is just a glimpse of how Hynes does that essential work of weighing and valuing. The war, in this example, is my war, Vietnam; the soldier's tale under examination is Philip Caputo's. The particular detail under scrutiny is Caputo's account of the death of Captain Frank

Reasoner, a man I knew almost forty years ago when we were both cadets at West Point.

Before turning to the death itself, or even to Caputo, Hynes establishes the context for viewing the death, reminding us that Vietnam narratives, unlike the narratives from other wars, were written after various myths about the war had already been established within our culture. "The soldiers' tale of the war, when it took shape in the postwar years, would draw on [an] . . . existing myth, affirming or denying it, but acknowledging that it existed, that before the war ended it had been judged." Hynes has two myths in mind: "the Myth of the Bad War, which said it was an immoral adventure that should never have begun, in which American boys were killed and a nation was devastated; and the Myth of the War That Was Lost, which said the army could and would have won, if it had been allowed to fight as it wished." Hynes sees in the two myths a common thread: "bitterness and a sense of national shame."[16]

One of the many things about these myths that interests Hynes is the "way the narratives use the traditional language of military values, the Big Words like 'courage' and 'duty' and 'heroism.' Those words survive, but without a clear moral base; they are simply words for extra ordinary kinds of behavior." To demonstrate his point he turns, finally, to Caputo's description of "'the hero's' death of Captain Reasoner":

> We split a beer and talked about the patrol he was taking out in the afternoon. His company was going into the paddy lands below Charlie ridge, flat, dangerous country with a lot of tree lines and hedgerow. Reasoner finished his beer and left. A few hours later, a helicopter brought him back in; a machine gun had stitched him across the belly and the young corporal who had pulled Reasoner's body out of the line of fire said, "He should be covered up. Will someone get a blanket? My skipper's dead."[17]

Hynes then goes to work, analyzing this description, emphasizing what it reveals to us about the revised language of war: "How flat and workmanlike that sounds, just a story of a Marine going out to do his job and coming back dead. But then there is the touch of tenderness for the dead captain: 'He should be covered up. . . . My skipper's dead.' The emotional links between soldiers, and between officers and their men, are difficult to render because though attachments between men in war can be strong—stronger than peacetime friendships—they are mostly inarticulate. Caputo does it delicately here."[18]

Hynes has more to show us about what happened to Reasoner, about his Medal of Honor and the official citation; but he is most concerned about the absence in Caputo's language of the "brave adjectives." Nevertheless, this glimpse is enough to reveal the acute witnessing that Hynes does, the way he insinuates himself into the larger account of war, as he explains the narratives that others have written. And there is yet another dimension to his witnessing. In "Agents and Sufferers," the last chapter of his book, Hynes turns his attention to the victims of the Holocaust and the bombing of Hiroshima and to the prisoners whose long confinements deprived them of their status as active soldiers, made them helpless like the others. Asking whether these victims' stories should be included in the soldiers' tale that he is constructing, Hynes focuses our attention on the brutality surrounding what he considers the ultimate "war against humanity." We see the corpses, experience the torture inflicted on the prisoners in the Japanese camps, and look straight at the disfiguring damage of the Bomb. It is Hynes's way of intensifying questions about the moral complexity of war that have been largely implicit throughout the rest of the book, muted by his own dispassionate and workmanlike analysis of the hundreds of individual tales. But here Hynes points to our darkest side, reminding us that the "elements of our nature as human beings that we thought were immutable can be diminished or destroyed, and that the human heart may be colder and crueler than experience has shown us." He wants us to *see* clearly that "the process of disillusionment within progress and civilization reached its lowest depth there, in those camps designed by reason and by science for the efficient destruction of human lives."[19]

At the end, as he brings together the experiences of the Holocaust victims, the denuded soldiers in the prison camps, and the innocent civilians at Hiroshima, Hynes also calls our attention to a variation on witnessing that makes us see in a different light what he had been doing throughout the book. He reminds us that "remembering is an action: to witness is to oppose. If you make the truth survive, however terrible it is, you are retaliating against inhumanity, in the only way the powerless have." These stories of suffering, Hynes tells us, "close the soldiers' tale of our century: not because they stand at the chronological end of modem war narratives (wars and their stories go on, as I write, as you read) but because they mark the extreme edge of military destructiveness in our time—as far as humankind has been able to extend the idea of war toward pure victimhood, beyond imaginable conflicts of armies to mass annihilation of the helpless and the innocent, and the end of war stories."[20]

Focused as Hynes is at this moment on a particular aspect of the tale, we cannot help looking back on the inhumanity and the suffering that is always and everywhere an integral part of the soldiers' tale. There in that final chapter, we come to see how subtly he has woven his own opposition into the fabric of the book—as if by giving us that felt sense of war, he can somehow help us learn to stop the killing and the destruction, to bring an end to the long tale.

Whether we have it in us to be that wise remains to be seen. The legacy of war is compelling, and the evidence of these memoirs suggests that something deeper than politics and nationalism draws us inexorably into the fray. In acknowledging war's power to call us out of our ordinary selves, I want to touch briefly on James Salter's *Burning the Days*, the most beautifully written memoir I've ever read—dangerous in its seduction, compelling in its presentation of the allure of war, and unsettling in its implications.

Salter knows only too well how the deep allure of war is like an obsessive love affair, and in the first half of this haunting book he sweeps us through the seductive phase of his life when love and war tempt him and pull at his spirit. The second half takes us into the aftermath of youthful romance, where the spell of writing competes with the afterglow of the war, and loses. Nothing, not even a woman, can quite measure up to the feeling of grandeur that the war, at certain moments, can deliver. Salter calls it "the single daring act" that transforms a man, makes him godly, gives him satisfaction, gives him, as Hynes demonstrates again and again, the sense that he is a part of history.[21] Listen as Salter pinpoints the ecstasy and then draws out the loss:

Over Korea

The flight has split up, we're in two's. By this time MIGS are being called out everywhere. The radio is brimming with voices, among them someone calling out MIGS south of the river at twenty-four thousand feet. How many, someone asks?

"Many, many!"

We head that way and see two, far out, sail past us on the left. We turn to follow, and they climb and begin to turn also. The sky is a burning blue, a sky things seem black in. I am on my back, Immelmanning up to get between them and the river, rolling out slightly beneath the leader, who is turning hard to the right and cannot see me. I duck my head and try to find the gunsight, which is an image projected onto a thick, slanted piece of glass that serves as the wind-shield. There's nothing there—turning has pulled it all the way off the glass. The MIG begins to level out and the sight drifts into view. About a thousand feet back I press the trigger. The tracers fall be-hind him. He begins to climb again and I am cutting him off, clos-ing, glancing quickly back to see if my wing-man is still there, firing again. A few hits in the right wing, then tremendous joy, at closer range a solid burst in the fuselage. The flashes are intense, brilliant, as of something vital shattering. He abruptly rolls over and I follow, as if we are leaping from a wall. He begins to pull it through. I am still shooting and something flies off the plane—the canopy. A mo-ment later a kind of bundle, the pilot, comes out.

Loss
In the end there is a kind of illness. A feeling of inconsequence, even lightness, takes hold. It is, in a way, like the earliest days, the sense of being an outsider. Others are taking one's place, nameless others who can never know how it was. It is being given to them, the war with all its fading, romantic detail, its disasters and lucky chances. They will be coming home through the intense skies of autumn, settling gracefully in over the boundary of the field. The smooth black runway floats up to meet them. The ships are empty, feather-light, the fuel tanks almost drained, the belts of ammunition van-ished; they are bringing back nothing except that thing we prized above all.[22]

How, Salter asks us to consider, can anything ever match it? How can a young man turn away from it? War, Salter implies, is the only experience that is sure to rescue him from "obscurity."

As I turn from these memoirs and Hynes's magisterial tale back into my ordinary life, I feel the snap. It is better, I think, that the people out-side the window sauntering in the park do not know what I know, what other soldiers know, else they too might ease their resistance and be drawn to it. On the other hand I have feelings akin to those of Hynes and Fussell. I do not want them to forget.

This past summer at my sister's house I chanced to find a box of my older brother's belongings, all that's left of a tail gunner's physical life: a handful of letters, a scrapbook, trinkets from Paris, a boy's parapherna-lia. I have not yet had the courage to read these letters, written some fifty-odd years ago before his life ended, in the skies over Germany, on a New

Year's Day. I do not know what the contents of that box will tell me, but I do know that those scant remains will bind the two of us even closer and that once more I will suffer his loss. I know too that I will mourn again and again at a time of my own choosing. And I will never forget.

Notes

1. E. B. White, *Writings from the* New Yorker, *1927–1976*, ed. Rebecca M. Dale (New York: HarperCollins, 1990), 102.

2. White, *Essays of E. B. White* (New York: Harper and Row, 1977), 17–18.

3. Ibid., 23–24.

4. Samuel Hynes, *The Soldiers' Tale: Bearing Witness to Modern War* (New York: Viking-Penguin, 1997), 25.

5. Paul Fussell, "My War," *Harper's* (Jan. 1982): 40.

6. Fussell, *Doing Battle: The Making of a Skeptic* (New York: Little, Brown, 1996), 171.

7. Ibid., 133–34.

8. Hynes, *The Soldiers' Tale*, 26.

9. Fussell, *Doing Battle*, 134.

10. Ibid., 134–35.

11. Ibid., 168, 209, 225.

12. Hynes, *Flights of Passage: Reflections of a World War II Aviator* (New York: Pocket, 1998), 14.

13. Ibid., 60, 239.

14. Ibid., 37.

15. Ibid., 269–70.

16. Hynes, *The Soldiers' Tale*, 212.

17. Ibid., 212–13.

18. Ibid., 213–14.

19. Ibid., 269.

20. Ibid., 269, 277.

21. James Salter, *Burning the Days: Recollections* (New York: Random House, 1997), 127.

22. Ibid., 157–58.

Eight

The "Atrocious Privilege"

Bearing Witness to War and Atrocity
in O'Brien, Levi, and Remarque

CHRIS DALEY

In the 1998 Francesco Rosi film *The Truce*, Primo Levi, played by
John Turturro, is told by a fellow survivor that he must have been spared
in Auschwitz by God in order to write. The character Levi replies, "If I
was saved in order to write, then writing is an atrocious privilege." Levi
himself comments on this idea in his collection of essays, *The Drowned and
the Saved*: "And why me? . . . Perhaps because I had to write, and by writing bear witness. . . . Such an opinion seemed monstrous to me."[1] This
issue of an atrocity survivor's "privilege" to write runs throughout the
work of Levi, specifically in *The Drowned and the Saved*; it can also be found
in Tim O'Brien's *The Things They Carried* and Erich Maria Remarque's *All
Quiet on the Western Front*.

To survive is to be allowed the opportunity to bear witness, yet how
can words describe a system in which language has lost its meaning? An
account of atrocity is a narrative of lost words, of what James Dawes calls
"the mutual exclusivity of language and violence."[2] To attempt to tell the
story of a condition in which language has forfeited its power of signification, in which the essential emptiness of language has been revealed, is
to attempt to explain the inexplicable. The meaning of language has been
maimed and destroyed along with the bodies and souls of the victims.
The only message that retains materiality is the flesh that witnesses the
violence. It is understandable that Levi would recoil from the idea that
his survival was preordained by a higher power in order for him to bear
witness. "Even if they had paper and pen," Levi reminds us, "the drowned
would not have testified because their death had begun before that of
their body. Weeks and months before being snuffed out, they had already

lost the ability to observe, to remember, to compare and express them-selves" (84). True witnesses would not have the language with which to tell their experiences, having lost the ability to observe, remember, and express, and finally having lost the corporeality that would be the only true embodiment of memory. Though Levi speaks as a survivor of the concentration camps of World War II, Remarque of the German experi-ence of World War I, and O'Brien of the U.S. "conflict" in Vietnam, each writer addresses the atrocious privilege of the survivor and the futility of language in the face of horror.

Limits of Genre

I write fiction and I'm told it's autobiography, I write autobiography and I'm told it's fiction, so since I'm so dim and they're so smart, let them decide what it is or it isn't.

—Philip Roth

Language's failure in any narrative form to communicate the truth of ex-treme physical and moral violence means that writers can at best circle around the inexpressible and come at it from multiple narrative ap-proaches in the hope that each approach might reveal some new dimen-sion of the experience, that the many approaches combined might pro-vide a greater sense of the truth. Different genres are one way writers can vary their approaches.

The discussion of various genres in this essay—expository essay, screenplay, novel, and short story—speaks to the slippage in the concept of war memoir. As postmodern autobiographical theory has established, the labels "memoir" and "autobiography" do not preclude a text from containing fictional embellishments, nor does fictionalization of events disqualify a narrative from possessing autobiographical elements. Tim O'Brien's Vietnam memoir *If I Die in a Combat Zone* begins with the caveat that "names and physical characteristics of persons depicted in this book have been changed," while his work of fiction *The Things They Carried* stars a character and sometimes narrator named Tim O'Brien who closely resembles his creator.[3]

Why do bookstores and publishers locate *If I Die in a Combat Zone* in the "Literature" section when very similar memoirs—such as Michael Herr's *Dispatches* and Tobias Wolff's *In Pharaoh's Army*—are categorized and shelved as "Military History" and "Memoirs/NonFiction"? To bring corporate book retail logic into this analysis might lead us farther astray, but perhaps we can use this distinction to underscore the difficulty we face when discussing autobiographical and fictional narratives. Is autobiography a retelling of people and places? Of events? Does a designation of fiction imply only a reworking of plot? If so, where do we place Robert Graves's technically autobiographical memoir *Good-bye to All That*, which uses the same real "character" Siegfried Sassoon and many of the same events in his life as Pat Barker's "novels" in the *Regeneration* trilogy?[4] The determination between fiction and autobiography is finally somewhat arbitrary and driven by the need for false divisions between life and life story. Written autobiography has been arranged with the purpose of narrative teleology and a sense of audience, both of which contribute to necessary embroidery of language and description of events. When the complications of memory and the limitations of language are added to the complex perception of war and its experiences, the capricious boundaries between truth and fiction blur.

Narratives of war and other atrocities pose a dilemma for the literary theorist as the genre itself calls into question the nature of language and what it means to tell a story. In one story from *The Things They Carried*, "How to Tell a True War Story," O'Brien introduces the dilemma inherent in the title: "In many cases a true war story cannot be believed. . . . In other cases you can't even tell a true war story. Sometimes it's just beyond telling" (71). O'Brien's short-story collection comes closest to illustrating the assertion that stories of war and atrocity cannot be told with any accuracy, that bearing witness is frequently impossible. By a constant return in the work to the construction of his narratives and the ambiguity of the original events, O'Brien addresses the issues at the heart of any representation of violence that extends beyond reason. At the same time, his constant narrative returns in different genres and forms allow him to explore different dimensions of his actual experience, to approach truth from new angles. The story "On the Rainy River," for example, achieves a truth about why both the quasi-fictional Tim O'Brien and the real Tim O'Brien went to war—"I was a coward"—that the memoir's version of this incident could not.[5] Fictional versions of the self are still versions of the self, and they frequently reveal quite a bit about the actual self's attempt to reconcile the "facts" of his or her life (assuming anyway a working "actual" self).

Limits of Language

> *It is an obvious observation that where violence is inflicted on man it is*
> *also inflicted on language.*
>
> —Primo Levi

It is a trope of poststructuralist theory to challenge the capacity of language to convey with any accuracy the nature of the metaphysical Real beyond the Symbolic. As Saussure famously points out, "The bond between the signifier and the signified is arbitrary. Since I mean by the sign the whole that results from the associating of the signifier with the signified, I can simply say: the linguistic sign is arbitrary."[6] Saussure's "tree" example of the ambiguous representation of linguistic signs is a blatantly benign example compared to the signified represented by Levi's "anguish," or O'Brien's "dead," or Remarque's "madness." To write or speak the signs "war" and "atrocity," whose signified meanings include the various experiences of trench warfare, concentration camps, and the ravaged jungles of Vietnam, is in O'Brien's language to seek meaning along "the border between trivia and bedlam, the mad and the mundane" (89). There is no possible representative relation between what occurs on the outskirts of human morality and the language we use to connote "tree." One needs only to visualize the Great War's blasted tree of no-man's-land or O'Brien's "Lemon Tree" to recognize this linguistic fact. Without language to signify the events of war and its traumas and atrocities, we have no method for a "true" accounting of these events.

In the chapter "Communicating" from *The Drowned and the Saved*, Levi addresses this conundrum of incommunicability:

> "Incommunicability" supposedly was an inevitable ingredient, a life sentence inherent to the human condition, particularly the life style of industrial society: we are monads, incapable of reciprocal messages, or capable only of truncated messages, false at their departure, misunderstood on their arrival. Discourse is fictitious, pure noise, a painted veil that conceals existential silence.

Levi then goes on to state that such a condition "originates in and points to mental laziness" (88–89). The antidote to the incommunicability of language is the communicability of silence. We are urged to look at signs that allow us to communicate outside of linguistic sign systems, a practice also recognized by Erich Maria Remarque. As *All Quiet on the Western Front*'s narrator Paul Baumer explains, "The attack does not come, but the bombardment continues. We are gradually benumbed. Hardly a man speaks. We cannot make ourselves understood."[7] The force of silence is demonstrated through the benumbing of the body; even the organs, limbs, and skin have failed to speak. More often than not, silence—the silence of guilt, shame, memories of unspeakable terror, or the corpse—becomes the transmission of emotion or the symbol of the futility of articulation.

In Remarque's novel, Paul Baumer's frustrations with language as he tries to express the horrible and tragic nature of trench warfare make the reader more aware of how little can be understood without actual bodily participation. Remarque's novel is indeed a war story, but Baumer never lets the reader forget his limitations in capturing the narrative "essence" of war. According to Baumer, a war story cannot be properly written during war, or possibly even after, because the writer is not able to achieve tranquil objectivity or even sufficient strength of rational analysis to assume the authority necessary to vouch for authenticity, to accurately witness. There is a reason why all is quiet on the western front and elsewhere.

O'Brien's "On the Rainy River" describes O'Brien the narrator's failure of will when about to dodge the draft by fleeing to Canada. During his stay at an inn on the Rainy River (which divides the United States and Canada), Tim O'Brien the character refrains from revealing the truth about his visit to his benefactor, the proprietor of the Tip Top Lodge. Part of the difficulty O'Brien the character experiences is his inability to know the truth himself: Is someone who refuses to fight in Vietnam an unqualified coward or a man of principle? However, his not speaking with the old man also involves an awareness of the limits of verbal communication: "I think the man understood that words were insufficient. The problem had gone beyond discussion" (51).

The death of Kiowa and the disappearance of his corpse in the sludge described in O'Brien's story "Speaking of Courage" lead to silence in the character of Norman Bowker. Essentially and ironically, Bowker does not speak of courage or much of anything else. The verbalization of the incident is prevented by a lack of desire to speak with meaningless words: "There was nothing to say. He could not talk about it and never would" (153). Silence becomes a refuge, yet as Levi reminds us, when constructing the narrative of an event where language has proven inept, "silence, the absence of signals, is itself a signal, but an ambiguous one, and ambiguity generates anxiety and suspicion" (89). Bowker ultimately acknowledges and submits to silence's supreme dominion over his soul by killing himself. After the narrator O'Brien has killed a man outside the village of My Khe, as told in the story "The Man I Killed," he sits for hours staring silently at the corpse. "'Why not talk about it?' . . . 'Come on, man, talk.' . . . 'Talk,'" pleads Kiowa (130). O'Brien's refusal to give verbal expression to his vision of a corpse he created seems somehow unnatural.

Levi also sees this silence as a signal of something else. Both war and the Holocaust can be seen as routes to the rapid dehumanization of its victims. In each situation, the "use of the word to communicate thought, this necessary and sufficient mechanism for man to be man, had fallen into disuse. This was a signal: for those people we were no longer men" (91). For the prisoners of Auschwitz, "those people" were their German captors; for the soldiers of twentieth-century warfare, "those people" were themselves. To sit in silence before the corpse of a man one has killed, as O'Brien's character did, is for Levi a step toward animality: "Not to suffer from it, to accept the eclipse of the word, was an ominous symptom: it signaled the approach of definitive indifference" (101).

Remarque also gestures toward silence's relation to dehumanization. We are unable to see what might become of Baumer, because he finishes his narrative as yet another casualty, but we do see the fear, remorse, and guilt that accompany the one hand-to-hand killing he commits. Symbolically, he stabs to death in a shell hole an enemy soldier who turns out to be a French printer, a distributor of language and possibly of the propaganda that had led them to the crater in the first place. Baumer initially vows to write to the dead man's wife but reconsiders when he recalls the futility of words to express anything that happens in war. He realizes that language provides security from the truth; when he is required to console his dead comrade Kemmerich's mother back in Germany, he recognizes he would have to "invent a story" of Kemmerich's death and almost believe it himself (181). Language is distant and unreal; only war has presence: "Life is simply one continual watch against the menace of death; —it has transformed us into unthinking animals in order to give us the weapon of instinct—it has reinforced us with dullness, so that we do not go to pieces before the horror, which would overwhelm us if we had clear, conscious thought" (273–74).

This lack of clear, conscious thought adds an element of necessary fiction to any war narrative that claims authenticity. Even with conscious thought restored, an accurate narrative could not be written after the war, because the writer is restricted to language to express the events that have robbed him of expression and left him with silence.

Limits of Morality

A thinking man's true answer to the question whether he is a nihilist would probably be "Not enough."

—Theodor W. Adorno

As far back as Horace, we have been informed that a piece of writing should entertain, but more importantly that it should instruct. According to Sir Philip Sidney, "This purifying of wit, this enriching of memory, enabling of judgement, and enlarging of conceit, which commonly we call learning, under what name soever it come forth, or to what immediate end soever it be directed, the final end is to lead and draw us to as high a perfection as our degenerate souls, made worse by their clayey lodgings, can be capable of."[8]

The moral of the story should lead us to higher virtue and enlightenment. Ideally, a narrative of war or atrocity would effectively persuade us to do whatever we could to prevent such an event from ever occurring again. Yet we are not that naïve. We have just ended a century that has produced a plethora of wars, war narratives, and still more wars, and we have just embarked on a century that promises much more of the same. Stories of war and atrocity do not serve as prophylactics. Besides, a narrative with a simplistic moral would not approach the "truth" needed to engage the reader in the first place. In "How to Tell a True War Story," O'Brien declares,

> A true war story is never moral. It does not instruct, nor encourage virtue, nor suggest models of proper human behavior, nor restrain men from doing the things men have always done. If a story seems moral, do not believe it. If at the end of a war story you feel uplifted, or if you feel that some small bit of rectitude has been salvaged from the larger waste, then you have been made the victim of a very old and terrible lie. There is no rectitude whatsoever. There is no virtue. As a first rule of thumb, therefore, you can tell a true war story by its absolute and uncompromising allegiance to obscenity and evil. (69)

The lack of a clear political agenda at the core of the Vietnam War consigns any narrative that seeks to express a lesson in virtue to the realm of the absurd, where it will find company with narratives from the two world wars, which together could not find a moral center between them. This decentering further complicates the tale and removes the narrative of atrocity from the conventional purpose of fiction of providing a moral of some fashion, instead illustrating how such a moral, constructed by language, is ridiculous when the violence goes beyond language.

Even as *All Quiet*'s Baumer narrates his story, he reinforces how futile verbal communication is when the horrors of war are beyond words: "How senseless is everything that can ever be written, done, or thought, when such things are possible. It must all be lies and of no account when the culture of a thousand years could not prevent this stream of blood being poured out, these torture chambers in their hundreds of thousands. A hospital alone shows what war is" (263). A hospital alone shows what war is because only its collection of bodies carries the true meaning of war, which cannot be expressed through rhetorical plaints or casualty lists. The materiality of blood and pain cannot be replaced by the pedantic attempts at cultural enlightenment through empty masterstrokes.

An important element in Baumer's disillusion with language is his conclusion that language, in some ways, is directly responsible for the war.[9] As he discusses the reasoning behind the war with his comrades, he places the blame on the propaganda produced on both sides:

> We didn't want the war, the others say the same thing—and yet half the world is in it all the same.
> "But there are more lies told by the other side than by us," say I; "just think of those pamphlets the prisoners have on them, where it says that we eat Belgian children. The fellows who write those lies ought to go out and hang themselves. They are the real culprits." (206)

The separation is apparent between those making the war with language and those fighting the war with their bodies, those who design propaganda and those who stand accused of eating children. Baumer correctly identifies the gulf between his generation, who die daily in the trenches, and the previous generation, who create ideologies and implements of war: "I see how peoples are set against one another, and in silence, unknowingly, foolishly, obediently, innocently slay one another. I see that the keenest brains of the world invent weapons and words to make it yet more refined and enduring. . . . What will happen afterward? And what shall come out of us?" (263–64). Words thus become synonymous with weapons as tools of destruction even as they also demonstrate their inability to function as tools of expression. The question as to what will happen afterward is the clamor for a moral, any moral, to provide a rationale for the relentless massacre of soldiers on both sides of the Great War, and to allow this story to be told.

In *The Drowned and the Saved*, Levi offers one answer. Levi's chapter "The Gray Zone" deconstructs the notion of a morality that could provide an instructional center: "The network of human relationships inside the Lagers was not simple: it could not be reduced to the two blocs of victims and persecutors" (37). Without the ability to distinguish between good and evil—a driving impulse in all humans engaged in conflict with others, and termed "the adversary atmosphere" by Fussell (86)—the idea of a moral that instructs is absurd. Levi denies this binary opposition, calling attention to "the space which separates . . . studded with obscene or pathetic figures . . . whom it is indispensable to know if we want to know the human species" (40). In this space, any concept of morality and any possibility of a "true story" become necessary fictions in the face of machinations of power even beyond the boundaries of the power: "Where power is exercised by few or only one against the many, privilege is born and proliferates, even against the will of the power itself" (42). Levi uses the narrative of Chaim Rumkowski, ghetto collaborator, to typify the desire for power that "gives birth to that ill-defined sphere of ambiguity and compromise" (67). This sphere is the location from which one must try to portray accurately the atrocious nature of the gray zone, but from which it is almost impossible to generalize or to achieve an objective position: "Like Rumkowski, we too are so dazzled by power and prestige as to forget our essential fragility. Willingly or not, we come to terms with power, forgetting that we are all in the ghetto, that the ghetto is walled in, that outside the ghetto reign the lords of death, and that close by the train is waiting" (69).

If it is true, as Michel Foucault posits, that "this multiplicity of force relations can be coded—in part but never totally—either in the form of 'war,' or in the form of 'politics,'" it is within that incomplete coding that we can locate "true" accounts of war and atrocity.[10] Sidney's purifying, enabling, enriching, and enlarging morality cannot take place in this space. As Levi states in *The Truce*, "God cannot exist if Auschwitz exists."

Limits of the Witness

The Greek word martur, meaning "witness," became the English word
"martyr," which eventually acquired the meaning "witness by blood."
—Charlotte C. Morse

The texts explored here interrogate the constitution of the writer as witness and that position's effect on his or her ability to give a true account of the witnessed event. Remarque, Levi, and O'Brien each argue that the victimization preceding survival retains its power long after its experiential conclusion. Remarque prefaces his novel, in which the narrator is killed in battle during World War I, with a statement on the lingering effects of witnessed warfare: "This book is to be neither an accusation nor a confession, and least of all an adventure, for death is not an adventure to those who stand face to face with it. It will try simply to tell of a generation of men who, even though they may have escaped the shells, were destroyed by the war." The destruction implicit in witnessing death "face to face" necessarily colors all subsequent accounts of the atrocity. This coloring interferes with the tale of the witness by implicating the witness in his own survival, an issue Remarque's dead narrator obviously cannot address. Only Remarque, in his preface, can warn the reader of the complicated nature of survival.

On the other hand, O'Brien and Levi both comment on the guilt and shame that confound a simple recollection of the witnessed event. Levi, by his own account, was dehumanized along with the other prisoners of the numerous concentration camps, but he does not feel any relief: "When all was over, the awareness emerged that we had not done anything, or not enough, against the system into which we had been absorbed. . . . [T]here should not have been much to be ashamed of, but shame persisted nevertheless" (76–77). Innate to this shame was the thought that there were others, now dead, more deserving of life than the living. The portrait given of Kiowa after his death in the O'Brien story "In the Field" also speaks to the shame of the survivors:

> Kiowa had been a splendid human being, the very best, intelligent and gentle and quiet-spoken. Very brave, too. And decent. The kid's father had taught Sunday school in Oklahoma City, where Kiowa had been raised to believe in the promise of salvation under Jesus Christ, and this conviction had always been present in the boy's smile, in his posture toward the world. . . .
> A crime, Jimmy Cross thought. (164)

Though not explicitly stated, the shame of living can be found in the ever self-doubting Lieutenant Cross's conviction to write Kiowa's parents immediately, in Mitchell Sanders's determination to assign blame, in Norman Bowker's endless circling of the lake, and Bowker's assertion that Kiowa's death was "Nobody's fault[—] . . . [e]verybody's" (176). In traditional narrative, to refuse to designate fault in a young man's death is to tell the story improperly: "When a man died, there had to be blame" (177). To be factual and honest, according to O'Brien, there must be shame as well as blame. "You can tell a true war story if it embarrasses you" (69).

To assign or assume culpability in a war is less fraught than in a concentration camp, but the guilt and shame remain. Levi asks questions that might have arisen in the face of Kiowa's death but result from surviving the Holocaust. "Are you ashamed because you are alive in place of another? And in particular, of a man more generous, more sensitive, more useful, wiser, worthier of living than you? You cannot block out such feelings" (83). To believe that you are not a true witness and that others may have been more deserving impedes the true aim of any atrocity narrative. A "true" witness does not survive; it is for this reason that Levi forces himself to write "in their stead, by proxy," even as he knows that his words are insufficient: "I must repeat: we, the survivors, are not the true witnesses. . . . [T]hose who saw the Gorgon have not returned to tell about it or have returned mute" (84). Here Levi introduces the idea that witnessing is too often a corporeal activity beyond words.

In seeking a "true" witness to war, one cannot lose sight of the fact that language loses its power in the face of the violence done to the body. From the beginning of Remarque's novel, Baumer develops a new language based on the more tangible experience of his body:

> The soldier is on friendlier terms than other men with his stomach and intestines. Three-quarters of his vocabulary is derived from these regions, and they give an intimate flavor to expressions of his greatest joy as well as of his deepest indignation. It is impossible to express oneself in any other way so clearly and pithily. Our families and schoolteachers will be shocked when we go home, but here it is the universal language. (8)

Occurring early on in the novel, this passage reveals the distance Baumer is already beginning to feel toward the traditional concept of language and the newfound proximity he feels toward his body. When Baumer finds himself lost and separated from his company in the midst of a fiery battle, words come to his rescue, but it is not the words' signification that offers his salvation—it is the fact that the words represent the disembodied voices of his fellow soldiers. The meaning of the words is once again inconsequential in the face of death: "These voices, these quiet words, these footsteps in the trench behind me recall me at a bound from the terrible loneliness and fear of death by which I had almost been destroyed. They are more to me than life, these voices, they are more than motherliness and more than fear; they are the strongest, most comforting thing there is anywhere: they are the voices of my comrades" (212). The voices, as representations of the bodies from which they originate, are stronger than language or even the emotions behind language. Baumer's deliverance is the sound of the voices rather than the meaning of the words. The inability to express oneself follows Baumer home on leave, where he is once again thrust into a world where language feigns accuracy. As he tries to relate to his mother and sister, who attempt to sympathize with the young narrator, Baumer realizes, "They understand of course, they agree, they may even feel it so too, but only with words, only with words" (169). They cannot understand with their bodies, not having witnessed the fragility of the human form in the line of fire.

Similarly, Levi describes how the Nazis counted on the distance between the witness and his audience. He cites Simon Weisenthal quoting an SS soldier, "However this war may end, we have won the war against you; none of you will be left to bear witness, but even if someone were to survive, the world will not believe him. . . . [P]eople will say that the events you describe are too monstrous to be believed" (11–12). *The Drowned and the Saved* as well as history itself is rife with examples of how true the above statements could become. Mitchell Sanders in O'Brien's "How to Tell a True War Story" intimates that this disbelief in the listener is actually a property by which to gauge the verity of a story. As he tells the story of soldiers losing their capacity to reason in the dense fog of the Vietnam jungle, where they feel as if they "don't even have a body" (73), he introduces the notion of credulity:

> "This next part," Sanders said quietly, "you won't believe."
> "Probably not," I said.
> "You won't and you know why?" He gave me a long, tired smile.
> "Because it happened. Because every word is absolutely dead-on true." (74)

The inversion of potential disbelief as foundation for verisimilitude is one of the characteristics of the narrative of atrocity's unconventionality as a genre. In the same story, O'Brien writes of how "in many cases a true war story cannot be believed. If you believe it, be skeptical. It's a question of credibility. Often the crazy stuff is true and the normal stuff isn't, because the normal stuff is necessary to make you believe the truly incredible craziness" (71). Determining factors of this revision of conventional form include the distinction between survivor and witness, the significance of witnessing with the body, and the threat of incredulity on the part of the auditor. Yet as fundamental as these details of witnessing may be, it cannot be denied that the memory of the witness plays an even more influential role.

Limits of Memory

> What sticks to memory, often, are those odd little fragments that have no beginning and no end.
> —Tim O'Brien

For a memory to be transcribed into a story, it must cease to be a memory and become something else, something constructed rather than remembered. If the memory grows distant, its evocation will be partial unless repeated—at which point, according to Levi, it runs the risk of becoming a "stereotype." Traumatic memory, on the other hand, "is itself traumatic because recalling it is painful or at least disturbing" (24). This condition often results in repression. In *Beyond the Pleasure Principle*, Freud explains:

> The patient cannot remember the whole of what is repressed in him, and what he cannot remember may be precisely the essential part of it. Thus he acquires no sense of conviction of the correctness of the construction that has been communicated to him. He is obliged to *repeat* the repressed material as a contemporary experience [often through traumatic dreams] instead of . . . *remembering* it as something belonging to the past.

Toleration of the traumatic memory can be increased, according to Freud, by "an appeal to the reality principle" (18–21). Psychoanalysis and writing are two practices that may bring this toleration, but they may not end the need to repeat the memory. Due to the need for repetition of traumatic memory, the torture of that memory and the chance that a memory repeatedly told will solidify into something other than the truth of that memory, the act of remembering events of war or atrocity through narrative is a sensitive and intricate maneuver.

Both Levi and O'Brien visualize memory as a burden. For O'Brien, because the soldiers of Alpha Company "shared the weight of memory," they "would never be at a loss for things to carry" (14, 16). The presence of memory is a constant encumbrance that is useless to attempt to discard. Levi sees his act of bearing witness as a potential desire to be free of memory: "I could not say whether we did or do so out of a kind of moral obligation toward those who were silenced or in order to free ourselves of their memory" (84). Yet this is not within the realm of human agency, as O'Brien the character's daughter Kathleen in the story "Field Trip" has yet to discover. "Sometimes you're pretty weird, aren't you?" she says to her father. "Some dumb thing happens a long time ago and you can't ever forget it" (183). At times even the memory of pleasure can be a grievous weight. Levi learns this upon his incarceration, O'Brien's Jimmy Cross learns this prior to burning Martha's letters and photographs, and Remarque's Baumer learns this on his first trip to the home front.

For Baumer, not only do the spoken words of his relatives and former associates ring false in the context of his memories of the front, but any meaning he may have taken from written language in the past has also lost its meaning. As the young soldier on leave stands before his bookshelves and imagines a time when he once again will feel what he refers to as the "quiet rapture" from his books, he remains unmoved (171). His connection to language has been lost, as we see here in his alienation from the literature that used to bring him pleasure:

I stand there dumb. As before a judge.
Dejected.
Words, Words, Words—they do not reach me.
Slowly I place the books back in the shelves.
Nevermore.
Quietly I go out of the room. (173)

The word "nevermore" signifies how far removed Baumer has become from any belief he previously had in the integrity of language. He now resides in an intellectual no-man's-land where language has no place, and memory is false.

The comments of Freud and Levi on traumatic memory introduce some of the complications involved in drawing on memory for narrative in general. In the first chapter of *The Drowned and the Saved,* Levi issues the following disclaimer: "An apology is in order. This very book is drenched in memory; what's more, a distant memory. Thus it draws from a suspect source and must be protected against itself" (34). Here the gap between memory and "truth" is marked in order to disabuse the reader of the illusion of accuracy. In the work of Levi and O'Brien (memory is rarely addressed in *All Quiet on the Western Front,* because Baumer does not survive to bear witness), the spurious texture of memory is dissected to demonstrate its complexity. Memory has a different shape than narrative. For one thing, per O'Brien, "You can tell a true war story by the way it never seems to end. Not now, not ever" (76). Memory does not have a conventional genesis and closure; it needs to be reshaped in order to function as story. Through this reconstruction and revision of memory, both O'Brien and Levi argue that a form of falsification takes place. Levi claims that with memory, "no reliable answers exist, because states of mind are by nature labile and even more labile is the memory of them" (30). O'Brien, on the other hand, attributes to memory not a sense of unreliability but a sense of the unreal: "Eight months in fantasyland, it tends to blur the line. Honest to God, I sometimes can't remember what real *is*" (204). The result of this blurring is often manipulation of the self. Evocation of memory for O'Brien is a "kind of self-hypnosis . . . partly willpower, partly faith," while for Levi it is the way the Nazis dealt with the memory of their crimes (244). As he writes, "The silent transition from falsehood to self-deception is useful. . . . The further events fade into the past, the more the construction of convenient truth grows and is perfected" (27). The route from memory to narrative is strewn with obstacles.

Regardless of this specious transcription of memory, the need to remember and share memory remains a compulsive force, for a number of reasons. Obviously, Freud's notion of trauma reinforces the necessity of revisiting the memory, but doing so also serves the purposes of catharsis and clarification. For O'Brien the narrator, "Telling stories seemed a natural, an inevitable process, like clearing the throat. Partly catharsis, partly communication, it was a way of grabbing the people by the shirt and explaining exactly what had happened to me, how I'd allowed myself to get dragged into a wrong war, all the mistakes I'd made, all the terrible things I'd seen and done" (157–58).

Keeping the dead alive, resurrecting the silent victims of war and atrocity, also serves as a motive for the referral to memory. Levi comments upon this motive as both an obligation and liberation. O'Brien discusses it in depth at various points in his story collection. In "The Man I

Killed," O'Brien the narrator builds an entire fictive life for the title character based upon nothing but his own guilt-ridden imaginings. In "Ambush," O'Brien's daughter surmises, "You keep writing these war stories . . . so I guess you must've killed somebody," intuitively sensing the method behind her father's madness (131). "The Lives of the Dead" is the most poignant revivification through memory, this time not of a fellow soldier but a young cancer victim from O'Brien's past: "But in a story, which is a kind of dreaming, the dead sometimes smile and sit up and return to the world" (225). This process is later described as "memory and imagination and language [combining] to make spirits in the head" (230). Yet the dead only *seem* to return, and one is left to remember alone. For O'Brien, whether one gains from the act any consolation beyond momentary respite remains unclear.

Limits of Truth

> *Communication of knowledge gained through experience . . . has also occasioned a crisis for orthodox history, by multiplying not only stories, but subjects, and by insisting that histories are written from fundamentally different—indeed irreconcilable—standpoints, no one of which is complete or completely "true."*
>
> —Joan W. Scott

Perhaps inseparable from the evocation of memories of war and atrocity is a search for truth, and as slippery and evasive as memory may be, the concept of an originary truth is even more onerous. As Walter Benjamin observed, "To articulate the past historically does not mean to recognize it 'the way it really was.'" Often, the linguistic challenge described earlier is complicated by a prior crisis of epistemology. In order to approach a possible conception of truth, one must realize that truth does not assume the form of knowledge prettily wrapped up in a cogent narrative. It isn't just that language, as representation, can never entirely express experience but that the experience itself can never entirely be known. Limited subjective perception and the vagaries of memory preclude access to what O'Brien calls "happening-truth." In other words, we simply can't know. To "tell the truth" in the guise of a story requires literary invention, some glossing of the details, some choice—that is, equivocation.

Language becomes the initial obstacle, as we can see in *All Quiet in the Western Front*. As the battles become more frequent and bloody, language fails as a satisfactory expression of reality. "Attack, counter-attack, charge, repulse—" exclaims Baumer—"these are words but what things they signify!" (129). The actual truths signified by these words are so remote from the language used to express them, emphasizing the distance between signified and signifier, that Baumer loses faith in the expression and begins to see the words themselves as abhorrent. His disgust is apparent when he states, "Bombardment, barrage, curtain-fire, mines, gas, tanks, machine-guns, hand-grenades—words, words, but they hold the horror of the world" (132). Baumer is actually underscoring the fact that it is the reality behind these words and the effect they have on the bodies of soldiers that truly contains the horror.

The division between participant and nonparticipant, between combatant and noncombatant, comes across most clearly in Baumer's hostile criticism of the leaders of the armed forces, who do not actually ever engage in battle, and the fathers and grandfathers and teachers of the soldiers, whose lack of any sense of the truth of actual battle leads them to buy into the empty language of the state: "While they continued to write and talk, we saw the wounded and dying. While they taught that duty to one's country is the greatest thing, we already knew that death-throes are stronger. . . . We loved our country as much as they: we went courageously into every action; but we also distinguished the false from the true, we had suddenly learned to see" (13).

While the noncombatants construct additional rhetoric, the soldiers see body upon body destroyed. The soldiers distinguish between the language of war and the language of the body, between the false and the true. The distinction between what is spoken and what is seen underscores the vacuity of the speech of the older generations. When Baumer remarks that the soldiers had suddenly learned to see, he is describing the newfound and unwelcome knowledge of the witness. To see is to be able to attest to the authenticity of an experience, but language fails to provide a vehicle to express that truth.

As the twentieth century's endless wars progressed, any sense of the actual attainment of "truth" became more and more suspect. Both Levi and O'Brien comment on the frequent occurrence of simplification when attempting to tell a true story and the existence of various "truths." Levi frowns on this tendency: "Simplifications are proper only for textbooks; the whys can be many, entangled with one another or unknowable, if not actually non-existent" (150). O'Brien sees some form of invention as inescapable when attempting to narrate the past: "Yet even if it did happen—and maybe it did, anything's possible—even then you know it can't be true, because a true war story does not depend on that kind of truth. Absolute occurrence is irrelevant. A thing may happen and be a total lie; another thing may not happen and be truer than the truth" (83). To tell a story is necessarily to try to create a metonymic relationship, which O'Brien feels moves it farther from the truth:

How do you generalize?

War is hell, but that's not the half of it, because war is also mystery and terror and adventure and courage and discovery and holiness and pity and despair and longing and love. War is nasty; war is fun. War is thrilling; war is drudgery. War makes you a man; war makes you dead. The truths are contradictory. It can be argued, for example, that war is grotesque. But in truth war is also beauty. . . .

To generalize about war is like generalizing about peace. Almost everything is true. Almost nothing is true. (80–81)

When the event to be narrated is full of mystery, horror, and ambiguity, possible truths and falsehoods multiply and frequently overlap.

Levi describes the contrast between various truths developed around the fate of his friend Alberto. Alberto has disappeared, and Levi believes the "truth" that Alberto has perished at the hands of the Nazis; his family believes he is safe, in hiding, somewhere. He writes, "More than forty years have passed. I did not have the courage to show up again and to counterpose my painful truth to the consolatory 'truth' that, one helping the other, Alberto's relatives had fashioned for themselves" (34). If war and atrocity do nothing else, they help to reveal that all truth is fashioned. As Levi sets up the distinction between two sets of "truths," O'Brien makes a different discrimination between "story-truth" and "happening-truth," calling attention to two nuances, one being that story-truth is constructed, the other that happening-truth is no more reliable because human perception is by nature unreliable (179). Levi comments on this when he writes, "For purposes of defense, reality can be distorted not only in memory but in the very act of taking place" (33). O'Brien calls this "surreal seemingness," which "makes the story seem untrue, but which in fact represents the hard and exact truth as it *seemed*" (71). Trying to connect with this distortion often takes the shape of repetition, once again invoking Freud's ideas of trauma, as can be seen in the telling and retelling of the deaths of Kiowa, Ted Lavender, and Curt Lemon:

In any war story, but especially a true one, it's difficult to separate what happened from what seemed to happen. What seems to happen becomes its own happening and has to be told that way. The angles of vision are skewed. When a booby trap explodes, you close your eyes and duck and float outside yourself. When a guy dies, like Curt Lemon, you look away and then look back for a moment and then look away again. The pictures get jumbled; you tend to miss a lot. And then afterward, when you go to tell about it, there is always that surreal seemingness. (71)

These questions of visualization and disembodiment that occur during the event can only further serve to pervert the memory of the event. The more horrific the memory, the more unsettling the truth. When Levi states that "uncomfortable truths travel with difficulty," it could be this blurred space between witnessing, remembering, narrating, and telling the truth to which he refers (159).

Atrocious Privilege

Try. Fail. Try again. Fail better.

—Samuel Beckett

As atrocious as the privilege of writing may be for the survivor, the atrocity-narrative genre testifies to the fact that such a privilege becomes a profound need in the witness. As this essay demonstrates, writing perseveres despite the barriers that interfere with its expression. If we add to these obstacles the necessary limits of language, subjectivity, and truth, it becomes clear that the story may be told—and will be told, and in many different ways—but the "truth" never can be. In O'Brien's "Sweetheart of Song Tra Bong," this conundrum even becomes the object of humor as Mitchell Saunders demands that Rat Kiley be aware of his "obligations" as a storyteller and maintain a consistent "tone" during his description of a young woman consumed by the physical and spiritual jungle of Vietnam (113, 107). O'Brien the character's comments on his written exchange with Norman Bowker also illustrate this slippery search for the truth. Yet the search continues, because "this too is true: stories can save us" (225).

Stories serve the same purpose as life for Remarque: "Let the months and years come, they can take nothing from me. . . . The life that has borne me through these years is still in my hands and my eyes. Whether I have subdued it, I know not. But so long as it is there it will seek its own way out, heedless of the will that is within me" (295). Writing with the hands and witnessing with the eyes is power. There is a reason why Holocaust survivors repeatedly command their audience, "Never forget." Because sometimes remembering *can* save us. No longer is there any room in human consciousness for the idea *"Nicht sein kann, was nicht sein darf* (What may not be cannot be)."[11] Any attempt to witness brings knowledge, with which we will do what we will. But we can no longer claim ignorance.

Notes

1. Francesco Rosi, director, *La Tregua/The Truce* (film), Telegraph S. L. (Spain/Italy), 1996; Miramax (U.S.), 1998. *The Truce* is based on the book of the same name but was published as *The Reawakening* in its English translation. Primo Levi, *The Drowned and the Saved* (New York: Vintage, 1988 [1986]), 86.

2. Dawes describes here what he calls the *emancipatory model* of the relationship between language and violence; it is emancipatory because, if the two are mutually exclusive, then just as violence renders language moot, so is "the volitional use of language . . . miraculously an assault upon violence." Language, conceived of as the foundation of "normative social practices," becomes society's chief weapon against violence. Dawes contrasts this model with the *disciplinary model,* which primarily draws on Foucault to suggest that language constructs ideologies and organizations and therefore the most basic act of language, "naming, is also the most basic and simple act of coercion." James Dawes, *The Language of War: Literature and Culture in the U.S. from the Civil War through World War II* (Cambridge, Mass.: Harvard Univ. Press, 2002), 2–3, 17.

3. Tim O'Brien, *If I Die in a Combat Zone, Box Me Up and Ship Me Home* (New York: Dell, 1973); and *The Things They Carried* (New York: Broadway, 1998 [1990]).

4. See also Paul Fussell's discussion of the highly creative and manipulated aspects of Graves's book in *The Great War and Modern Memory* (London: Oxford Univ. Press, 1975), 203–20. For Fussell, *Good-bye to All That* is "fiction disguised as memoir" (220).

5. O'Brien, *Things*, 61. Compare with chapter 6, "Escape," in *If I Die.*

6. Ferdinand Saussure, *Course in General Linguistics* (New York: Philosophical Library, 1916), 68.

7. Erich Maria Remarque, *All Quiet on the Western Front* (New York: Ballantine, 1928, repr. 1982), 107.

8. Sir Philip Sidney, "An Apology for Poetry," in *The Critical Tradition*, ed. David H. Richter, 2d ed. (Boston, Mass.: Bedford, 1998), 139.

9. Dawes's disciplinary model—see note 2 here.

10. Michel Foucault, *The History of Sexuality: An Introduction*, vol. 1 (New York: Vintage, 1990), 93.

11. Levi, *The Drowned and the Saved*, 164.

Nine

On the Battlefield and Home Front

American Women Writing Their Lives on the Vietnam War

Bettina Hofmann

The dedication of the Women's Memorial in Washington, D.C., on Veterans Day, 1993, drew the attention of a wider general public to the fact that American women had also served in Vietnam. Most of the estimated 7,500 to 11,000 women did so in the Nurse Corps. Additionally, civilian women worked in Vietnam for relief organizations. Furthermore, the war deeply affected the mothers, sisters, wives, and children of the male soldiers. While the tales of men, presented in writing or on screen, have received considerable attention, the life stories of women have often been neglected. None of the three texts studied here, for example, receive individual entries in M. Paul Holsinger's *War and American Popular Culture* (1999) or Philip K. Jason and Mark A. Graves's *Encyclopedia of American War Literature* (2001).[1] This essay will partly try to fill this gap by considering in detail three exemplary military life stories of the Vietnam War by American women:[2] one by an army nurse, Lynda Van Devanter's *Home before Morning* (1983); one by an officer's wife, Marian Faye Novak's *Lonely Girls with Burning Eyes* (1991); and one cowritten by an officer's wife and her husband, a former prisoner of war, Jim and Sybil Stockdale's *In Love and War* (1990).[3]

In order to evaluate the chosen texts properly, we must situate them within the broader context of Vietnam War literature. The main question to each of the texts will be addressed in turn: How does gender inform the representation of the Vietnam War by nurses and wives? This question is both a literary and an historical one, for as Penny Summerfield stresses, "Experience cannot exist outside discourse, agency cannot exist independently of language."[4] These texts offer a new perspective within the genre of war narratives while making use of traditional narrative forms.

Vietnam War autobiography is primarily associated with texts produced by men who participated in combat. Quite often the narratives follow the pattern of a journey from innocence to experience, from enthusiasm to disillusionment. Examples of such narratives include Philip Caputo's *A Rumor of War* (1977) and Ron Kovic's *Born on the Fourth of July* (1976). While Caputo's book deals with the experience of being "in country," Kovic's focuses on the homecoming of a soldier whose wounds have disabled him for life. Both texts, along with many others, participate in a particular tradition established in autobiographical first-person nonfiction narratives during the First World War. In his classic study on the literature of World War I, *The Great War and Modern Memory* (1975), Paul Fussell shows that many writers of the war employed vulgar language to expose the official euphemistic language of war propaganda. Writers who identify with the powerless foot soldiers challenged the language used by those who profit from the war—the upper military ranks, politicians, businesspeople, and other civilians. These writers retell the war from the perspective of the people who acted it out. The polished language of officials and of official war propaganda is supplanted with the vulgar, graphic language of soldiers. According to Evelyn Cobley, this counterversion aims at rewriting history, at setting "the record straight by providing an alternative history which is scrupulously accurate in its description of everyday events."[5]

While dismantling the myths produced by the propaganda, however, these writers were themselves creating a new mythology of their own. "And despite the fact that their writings exposed the mythical quality of received notions of masculinity," observes Margaret Higonnet, "they could not help creating fresh myths that were also identifiably masculine."[6] One of these masculine myths is the myth of authenticity. It implies that only the eyewitness on the battlefield is granted the authority to talk about war. Conversely, it implies, no one who has not been to the combat zone may assume any competence to speak about it. Thus a narrow definition of war experience has emerged that equates war with combat, a definition that has led to an exclusion of women's voices and stories. Even if one disregards that the state of war encompasses a variety of home-front activities (involving women *and* men), one cannot deny that women, in and out of uniform, at home or at war, have been directly touched by war and combat. Yet women's experiences have consistently been regarded as secondary. Cynthia Enloe convincingly explains this phenomenon:

> Women as *women* must be denied access to "the front," to "combat,"
> so that men can claim a uniqueness and superiority that will testify
> their dominant position in the social order. And yet because women
> are in practice often exposed to frontline combat . . . the military has
> to constantly redefine "the front" and "combat" as wherever "women"
> are not. Women may serve the military, but they can never be permit-
> ted to *be* the military.[7]

The same mechanism also operates in the literature of the Vietnam War,
from which women's writing has by and large been excluded.

The separation of the public male versus the domestic female spheres
reaches to the core of Western civilization—to what Nancy Huston calls
the "reciprocal metaphorization" of women's and men's roles.[8] While the
woman becomes the preserver and nurturer of life, the man becomes the
master of sacrificial killing and death. These are mutually exclusive
spheres, yet both men and women are expected to sacrifice their own ego-
istical impulses for the interest of others—the soldier for his country, the
mother for her children.[9] In order to form a meaningful whole, both functions need to be fulfilled: "Love is the feminine counterpart to, not the
opposite of war."[10] But the male experience has been given precedence
and has been deemed the more important. Susan Jeffords deftly summarizes the situation: "War is the most severe consequence of mystification
of gender and the concomitant mystification of power relations that occur
within patriarchy."[11]

What consequences follow? This essay will examine how the three
female autobiographers under examination affirm or undermine these
assumptions about gender roles.

An exemplary text for life stories by nurses is the narrative by Lynda
Van Devanter, *Home before Morning* (1983). The subtitle of Van Devanter's
Home before Morning—"The True Story of an Army Nurse in Vietnam"—
underscores the text's presumed authenticity according to the male criterion of "the man who was there," as Samuel Hynes phrases it in his critical study *The Soldiers' Tale: Bearing Witness to Modern War*.[12] Van Devanter
describes herself growing up as an all-American Catholic girl in a middle-
class family in Washington, D.C. Her training as a nurse at a hospital may
be considered the female equivalent to boot camp. It shares with its male
counterpart the emphasis on discipline, military-like roll calls, isolation
of trainees from civilian life, and a single-sex environment, though at the
hospital nuns instead of officers and sergeants rule. Van Devanter then
exchanges this world of regulated conduct and service for a similar one in

the army. One source of motivation for joining the army is the family configuration. As the oldest of four girls, she had assumed the role of substitute son for her father early in her childhood: "I became one of the boys. . . . I picked up a football and saw my father smile" (18). By joining the army, she further pleases her father by compensating for a missing part of his own life, as he had not been accepted into the military in the Second World War. Among her friends, fantasies of male heroic adventure—dreams of climbing the Himalayas or going to the Amazon—compete with more traditional visions about their future as mothers and homemakers in peaceful, affluent suburban homes (50). Nursing in Vietnam promises Van Devanter a respectable combination of these two impulses as well as a delay of the inevitable family constraints following marriage. Uniform service represents to her "probably the only chance we'll ever have to be as free as the wind" (16).

The recruiting officer assures the women that all hospitals in Vietnam are in the rear area and are perfectly safe (47). Van Devanter soon enough discovers otherwise, as the first American nurse killed in the war dies on the very day Van Devanter arrives; her assigned hospital is regularly under attack. Her experience is typical for nurses in Vietnam: a "Harris poll found that 75 percent of women veterans had been 'in or exposed' to hostile fire and combat. Noncombatant status, said one nurse, simply meant that 'we couldn't shoot back.'"[13] According to Enloe, the "front line" is defined not according to the presence of danger but according to the absence of women—an official attitude that denies women the status of being in a combat zone. The recruiting officer's false assurance becomes a motif of official betrayal, reenacting the soldiers-versus-leadership antagonism familiar to soldier-writers of World War I. Nor does the antagonism stop with this man. "Lifers"—career military personnel—prove a constant threat in the medical corps as well as the combat units. These figures are often portrayed as embodying the worst qualities of arbitrary power. Bureaucrats, self-apotheosized demigods, also stand in efficiency's way and cause needless suffering. As an officer, however, Van Devanter is not as helpless in the face of their decisions, as are the enlisted technicians who, at the bottom of the hierarchy, turn to her for protection.

Once at her hospital, Van Devanter is assigned to assist in the operating room, where the men brought in are severely wounded and often undergo amputation. Psychological stress on the staff is extraordinarily high because they do not have the opportunity to see their patients improve; after initial care the patients are transferred immediately to Japan for further treatment. Van Devanter's narrative delivers detailed medical accounts of the kinds of wounds the soldiers suffered and the different operational procedures employed to treat them. The clinical terminology highlights Van Devanter's professional competence. She presents herself as a specialist and participant the same way a male soldier-writer authenticates himself through military jargon. In other words, her strategy matches that of the male soldier-writers, whose narrative style is described by Hynes:

> Whatever their dates, they have nearly all been realists, adopting a common style that would come as close as language can to rendering the things of the material world as they are. . . . [T]hey have reported their wars in a plain, naming vocabulary, describing objects and actions in unmetaphorical terms, appealing always to the data of the senses. . . . War is details, to be put down plainly.[14]

Thus it comes as no surprise that the glossary at the back of Van Devanter's book includes both military and medical technical terms. The medical language also strips the war of any glamour or glory. There are no heroic wounds, just medical diagnoses. These precise accounts of medical procedures add to the vivacity and poignancy of the scenes while conveying the depths of Van Devanter's sympathy, as she can still recall names and the corresponding diagnoses.

The endless flow of mutilated bodies into the operating room causes not only physical exhaustion but also overwhelming despair. Among the numerous mortally wounded soldiers Van Devanter describes, one stands out. Gene's face has literally been blown away; the medical staff cannot save him. What Van Devanter remembers about him is the picture he had carried with him everywhere. It shows a young healthy man with a girl, obviously taken at a high school prom: "Gene and Katie, 1969." The photo emphasizes for Van Devanter the youth of most of the soldiers; more significantly, it reinforces the motif of romantic love that will not be fulfilled, of lives that will no longer experience love. It reminds Van Devanter too of those suffering at home. This image of innocent and hopeful romantic love contrasts sharply with the kind of intimate relationships she experienced and watched in the hospital. For the reader, the photo functions as an identification device.

As one might expect, the shared intensity of circumstances led to love affairs between doctors and nurses. Fully aware of the widespread sexual stereotypes of women in the military as "either whores or lesbians" (117), Van Devanter nonetheless engages in several affairs. For her, the affairs she and the other nurses have with the doctors are not prompted by romantic love, desire for sexual pleasure, or a quest for a suitable husband but rather by a need for camaraderie and bonding. Repeatedly she stresses that this kind of human bonding was the only way to feel like a human being in the midst of an openly inhuman and hostile world. Van Devanter feels no guilt or shame for breaking moral conventions: "What we did need was love, understanding, friendship, and companionship; the things that would keep us human in spite of all the inhumanity practiced around us" (122). Again, this need for close intimate connection and affection as a mechanism against the war milieu mirrors the same need as expressed in male soldiers' tales, where one can often find overtones of the homoerotic—which Paul Fussell defines as "a sublimated (i.e., 'chaste') form of temporary homosexuality" marked by admiration, sentimentality, and idealization of the other.[15] Intimate relationships, however, harbor danger as well as comfort. The fear of losing the other, either by death or through the end of one's tour, is enormous. Furthermore, as Van Devanter's story shows, the military during the Vietnam War completely ignored women's emotional and sexual needs. A double standard prevailed. The women had no personal hygiene equipment, and birth control pills were hard to come by since women were expected to behave like "ladies." Meanwhile, the men had the ready option of spending off-duty time in brothels.

As in narratives by male soldiers, Van Devanter's tale relates her progress from "fucking new guy" to "short-timer." In her case, however, the narrative also traces the gradual development of an antiwar stance. Looking at Gene's prom photograph serves as something of a turning point; afterward, Van Devanter for the first time signs a letter home with "peace" (203). She had entered the war with strong feelings of public spirit and patriotism, like Caputo citing President Kennedy as an inspiration. While in one of her first letters home she tells her parents to fly the U.S. flag as a symbol of solidarity, she later throws away the rhinestone on her uniform that symbolizes her patriotism. On Thanksgiving, an organized antiwar fast takes place in the hospital. The event shows that she is not alone in her new feelings about the war. Humanitarian reasons, not political ones, have led to her changed position. Her attitude toward the moon landing illustrates her diminished patriotism. The race to the moon between the Americans and the Russians was not simply a question of technical superiority; it also involved national and ideological competition. The medical staff in the hospital, however, remains unimpressed by the U.S. victory. After the event, laconic graffiti appear on the wall, like "U.S. lands on moon . . . Who cares?" (126). Van Devanter shares this feeling, but in a letter communicates something different to her parents: "The pride in our country filled us to the point that many had tears in their eyes" (127). This is an especially vivid case of the divide between "Nam" and "the World." Van Devanter understands that she cannot communicate her state of mind to her family at home. She dares not express to them her frustration and anguish. She does not admit how her attitude to the war is changing.

Van Devanter's tale of her journey from innocence to experience does not take a happy turn at her homecoming. Reintegration into civilian society is extremely difficult. The gap between her and the others is epitomized when her mother refuses to look at slides of the wounded. By averting her gaze, the mother refuses to acknowledge her daughter's experience. Like her male Vietnam counterparts, Van Devanter suffers from nightmares, severe periods of depression, and thoughts of suicide—from post-traumatic-stress disorder (PTSD). Van Devanter and the other nurses' difficulties are exacerbated by the denial of professionalism accorded to them back in the States, where they are no longer treated as competent partners of the doctors but as handmaids. They are also rejected by other veterans. When Van Devanter tries to join the Veterans Against the War, the men deny her participation for fear that it might jeopardize their project by leading the public to question their manhood. Only in the absence of women can the men appear as real men. Perhaps against their better judgment, the men nevertheless comply with the established myth that only the soldier who fought on the battlefield may take a stand on the war. They accept the ideology that does not grant women authenticity and competence to talk about the war. Being excluded by her fellow veterans at home is more devastating to Van Devanter than the failure of establishing meaningful intimate relationships in Vietnam. Bonding, as with the male soldier-writers, again proves to be more important than any notion of romantic love—her own marriage does not heal her emotional troubles. But male veterans at least have opportunities for postwar bonding; however similar the woman soldier's war narrative might be to theirs, her homecoming narrative has this radical difference. Eventually, male veterans do accept her, and she travels back with them to Vietnam to attempt reconciliation with the Vietnamese. This conventional "happy ending" aside, Van Devanter's experience of coming home was markedly different from those of her male comrades.

Marian Faye Novak's *Lonely Girls with Burning Eyes: A Wife Recalls Her Husband's Journey Home from Vietnam* exemplifies military life stories by women who watched their men go off to the war.[16] The very first sentence of her narrative, "I am the wife of a man who went to war" (3), shows that Novak defines herself through her husband, a marine officer. The title of her narrative is taken from *Requiem für die Gefallenen von Europa*, a dirge by Yvan Goll on the dead of the Great War. Allusions to poets of the First World War appear as mottos in front of her chapters, a framing technique already used by Caputo. Her indebtedness to the tradition of soldier-writers is quite evident. Both in life and literature she follows male predecessors.

Novak's part is to endure until her husband David's return from Vietnam and meanwhile to master pregnancy and childrearing—the life-nurturing principle—on her own. She accepts that her role as a woman is of secondary importance compared to her husband's role as a man. Typical of other middle-class U.S. women of her generation, she had never envisioned a career for herself and went to college in order to find a suitable husband. Teaching and nursing were socially acceptable occupations to bridge the time between high school and starting a family. While courting, Novak finds David most attractive in his uniform. Clearly, one function of a uniform, to impress others and transform its bearer into something else, is demonstrated here. Marian is politically unaware, and in no way does she connect his uniform with the ongoing war. She is prepared to play the subordinate role of a supportive wife in a military environment. She even phrases her commitment in the language of the military: "My own active duty began with adjusting—nothing more and nothing less seemed required of me. When I married Dave, I had agreed to accept whatever it was that had to be done, no matter how inconvenient or unpleasant. This was my service" (107). In contrast to Van Devanter, who adopts the vulgar language of the troops, Novak uses the polite, official code of the military and thus expresses her positive identification.

Still, Novak's feelings about the military remain ambivalent. She finds herself no longer part of the regular civilian world, yet not really integrated into the military either. The military ID card becomes a token of acceptance: "I don't think the Marine Corps had the slightest idea what to do with the wives of these young, war bound junior officers. But by issuing us the military ID, they did recognize us as their own. When I got my ID card, it did not matter whether the Corps wanted or welcomed me or not. Emotionally, I began to feel that I belonged" (84). In her eagerness to be accepted, she gives the military the benefit of the doubt. What Novak still tries to justify—the expectation that as a matter of course the wives will adapt to their husbands' careers—is severely criticized by the sociologist Cynthia Enloe.[17] Benefits for military wives come in the form of privileges, not wages, and thus the wives' dependence on their husbands is reinforced. Cheap shopping facilities and health benefits can be obtained only through the husband's status, through having an ID card linking her to him.

The military community very much determines the social life of the wives. At one meeting of officers' wives, no one talks to Novak; she feels excluded and miserable until later, when she realizes that she had put her maiden name onto the tag and therefore nobody recognized her. Only when she is identified as a particular officer's wife does her peer group accept her. Within the women's parallel military hierarchy, spontaneous and genuine interest in another person hardly arises. As this scene illustrates, the women are completely defined by their husbands' identity and they willingly submit to this arrangement. It is interesting to note that even in retrospect Novak seems more embarrassed about her social blunder than ready to criticize the underlying attitude. Novak befriends and bonds with other young military wives, though this occurs largely by virtue of their shared circumstance: "We were all we had beside our husbands, and they were going away" (118). While the men are initiated into their new status as officers in an official graduation ceremony, Novak and two of her friends undergo a similar change of status as they become pregnant. Yet in contrast to their husbands, the women's new social roles are not publicly acknowledged. Once, when these three couples go for an outing in the woods, the men and the women take separate paths. The men forge ahead in buoyant spirits, while the women follow at slower pace and in a more subdued, more cautious mood. While the men look forward to lives of autonomy, challenge, and self-fulfillment, for the women the future holds confinement, passivity, and responsibility for their offspring. The contrast between the social expectations of the men and the women is literally inscribed on Marian's and David's bodies. When the Novaks meet on an R&R (rest and recreation period) in Hawaii, husband and wife show each other the marks they have acquired during their separation. David bears scars from the war on his arms, while Marian is marked by the episiotomy scars on her belly. Their bodies have come to signify the gendered narratives they have lived, the gendered initiations they have undergone.

When the men depart for Vietnam, the women exchange one kind of dependence for another. They do not even consider staying together as a group and supporting one another; instead, each goes back to her parents. The bonds between the women endure only as long as the men are around. If a husband is killed overseas, contact between the widow and the other wives breaks off. With the solidarity of the military breaking apart, the women find themselves isolated from civilians as well. From others they encounter no understanding but at best indifference, at worst open hostility. Despite the altogether different circumstances, then, they have only one person left with whom they can identify—their respective husbands. Linguistically, Novak continues to use military terms and metaphors to describe her experience as a wife. While this stylistic strategy might be considered an effective way of emphasizing her burdens and raising them to the level of his, it needs also to be read as an act of subordination. The terms she uses, after all, come from *his* world. There is no need to find words of her own.

When Novak's husband eventually returns, however, the couple's bond does not prove to be as strong as either had imagined. Her sense of isolation remains. They do not talk about the war, and he develops symptoms of PTSD. He is finally able to talk about his experiences with another veteran (Philip Caputo, incidentally). While the men are talking, Marian Novak, pressed to the margins, listens on the stairs to their conversation. Once again she assumes a secondary position, and like Van Devanter, she seems to experience a minor case of PTSD of her own. Again as in Van Devanter's narrative, what is perhaps most surprising about Novak's is not the wartime tale but the postwar experience. The men have each other; the women no one but their lonely selves.[18]

Jim and Sybil Stockdale's *In Love and War* (1990) demonstrates the plight of families whose husbands were declared POWs or MIAs. Another example of such cooperation is Anne and Ben Purcell's 1992 *Love and Duty,* which is modeled after the Stockdales', as the Purcells acknowledge.[19]

Both husband and wife in both families are educated, white, and middle-class, and their lives revolve around the military. Both men are career officers, both families have four children, and both texts follow the same pattern of alternating chapters narrated by husband and wife. The dichotomy in the two titles reflects the two perspectives and would appear to attest to the thesis that love is the counterpart, not necessarily the adversary, of war. Yet if we read the titles in this dichotomous way, the gendered subtext replays the conventional social roles of woman as responsible for love and man as responsible for war and duty. Another way to read the titles distributes the responsibilities more equitably, with each couple's husband and wife recording their experiences of both loving and suffering during war. The center of the Stockdales' life story, however, is Jim's career. He was a senior pilot and squadron commander in the navy when he was shot down over North Vietnam in 1965. After his release in 1972, he was promoted to vice admiral. His narrative begins and ends the book—framing and enclosing hers. Jim tells his male adventure story as a life full of challenges, trials, personal growth, and rewards. In the extremely adverse circumstances of capture, captivity, and torture in the "Hanoi Hilton," he feels bound to follow the code of conduct and, oddly, fears less his present situation than the possibility of shame back home: "What brought the most fear, however, was my imaginative extrapolation of where I seemed doomed to go after the war into a life of continuous shame without friends or self-respect" (176).

Jim Stockdale comments extensively upon the entire enterprise of the U.S. war in Vietnam. As a professional soldier and patriot proud of his skills and his country, he does not necessarily question policy decisions. On the other hand, he is well educated and not without opinions. His military identity leads him to blame not the military but the political leaders at the Pentagon (especially Robert McNamara) for the country's faulty and fatal policy. He is a hard-liner whose "jeremiad" is "directed at the careerism, legalism, and managerial ethos" of Washington. While Lynda Van Devanter feels that the military shares responsibility with the civilian administration for the war's conduct and for the vast human suffering, Jim Stockdale refuses to blame it. For him, the politicians and the peace movement unnecessarily prolonged the war (and his captivity). He regards the Tonkin incident, in which he participated as a pilot, as provoked by American politicians as a pretext for intensifying the war, and as typical of the erroneous decisions driving U.S. strategy. He does not contradict the North Vietnamese official who tells him, "We will win this war on the streets of New York" (181).

The chapters narrated by Sybil are shorter, and they follow the chronology established by her husband's. To set the tone for her tale, Sybil Stockdale starts with the motif of romance, with memories of how as a child she dreamed about her coming prince. Like Novak, Sybil is attracted by her spouse's splendid uniform. They marry in 1947. She reads *The Navy Wife* and is ready to identify herself with her new role. Jim's approval of her actions is of utmost importance to her. Phrases like "I didn't want to fail him in any way" (48) or "I'd try to make him proud of my behavior" (121) abound. Also as with Novak, it is a matter of course for Sybil to give up her career in order to raise her four sons.

Her husband's captivity, though, shakes these foundations of an idyllic traditional family life. The indefinite period of waiting and uncertainty about Jim's whereabouts is most difficult to endure. As with other women in her situation, "normal patterns of coping with father-husband absence were disturbed by the unprecedented and indeterminate length of the absence."[20] Without her husband, she must keep the family together. She reorganizes her life and starts working again, assuming the roles of both father and mother for the time being. Even in times of despair, the responsibility for the children helps her to structure the day and carry on. As if mimicking her husband, Sybil is most terrified of the possibility of a postwar public trial for war crimes. Much of her narrative, in fact, echoes his. Her pride in the coverage of the Tonkin episode in the local paper, *The New Haven Register*, which she promptly shows to her family (58), reveals her patriotic pride in her husband's career. She constantly calls the North Vietnamese simply "communists," and she blames U.S. politicians for not allowing the military to make use of its power—without which "it made no sense whatsoever for our country to be struggling to overcome that tiny country" (217). She shares her husband's opinion about McNamara. It comes as no surprise that she regards the antiwar movement and other counterculture movements as her husband does, with skepticism. She concedes that "they may have meant well" (208) but claims they are mistaken for their undermining and declares them responsible for prolonging the war. In a letter in 1968 to friends calling them to action, she writes, "I also told them I planned to vote for Nixon if he was nominated, wouldn't have a copy of Dr. Spock's book in my house (Spock was a baby doctor turned vocal war protester), and felt that Eugene McCarthy had prolonged the war" (298). She herself nicely establishes a link between the political and the private by referring to Benjamin Spock, at the time the most progressive authority on childcare. As a mother of four, she has the competence to deny him authority in her domain of childrearing and, as a wife of a POW, in the domain of politics as well.

Though she is lucky that her husband is an identified POW and not MIA, and though she receives an occasional letter from him, waiting idly for word of her husband is not her path. After fighting to ensure that his pay is continued so she can financially survive, she must struggle to get him officially listed as a POW, and she then fights to induce the government to insist on North Vietnam's obligation to adhere to the Geneva Conventions. Over the course of her battles with military and civilian officials, she develops from a dependent wife to a self-confident and active woman.

While at the beginning she is "anxious to please" her husband's commander (135) and continues to call on the benevolence and acceptance of superior male authority, later she becomes more dismissive of all kinds of power, to the point of openly confronting an admiral. She never, however, condemns the navy or military in general, only the incompetent performance of political authorities—in this again, her narrative very much echoes her husband's. His rank and status certainly lends her voice much of its authority, for she is more likely than wives and relatives of men of lower rank to be listened to and is thus more in control, and she is quite content with her assigned function of helping younger wives.[21]

Sybil's method of coping thus consists of her leaving the role of the passively suffering wife. Most visibly, she founds the National League of Families of American Prisoners and Missing in Southeast Asia, which "was the catalyst that catapulted the long-invisible POW issue to the forefront of public awareness."[22] Her new attitude can also be seen in her reaction to the treatment of her husband's letters. At first she is very upset about the intrusion of privacy when she finds out that intelligence analysts have read them as well. Later she chooses to become an active participant in this process, gladly conveying covert information and encoding messages in her letters. In order to directly confront the Vietnamese, she and other members of her organization travel to Paris, the site of the peace talks. Even though she has by now acquired self-confidence in her public role, she leaves the public speech to a man: "I was thankful our marine father was a spokesman" (322). It had not been by choice that Sybil entered the public sphere. As soon as a man can assume the leading role, she happily hands it over.

Despite all her energy and efforts not to become victimized, the psychological toll is great. One son suffers from emotionally induced blindness and she herself reluctantly undergoes therapy when she cannot cope with her depression any longer. Yet unlike Van Devanter, Sybil Stockdale does not vividly depict her suffering. She displays instead a conscious self-restraint in her refusal to exhibit her emotions on the page. This technique preserves a degree of privacy, but it fails to involve the reader in her emotional despair, and it seems to be another case of her mimicking her husband's attitude.

One of the first things she notices about her husband when he finally returns home is his new uniform (441). The book has come full circle, for it was the uniform that had attracted her when they first met. Romance can begin anew—she overcomes her genteel reticence when she admits to having sexual intercourse with her husband the first night after his return, but another motive seems to impel this breach of manners. She wants to stress that the prison experience has not undermined her husband's manhood. The narrative focus ends as it began, with him, and her image of him, her prince. After all the years of separation and hardship, their resumption of family life gives this story its fairy-tale happy ending.[23]

The life stories of Van Devanter, Novak, and Stockdale show a tripartite structure of before, during, and after the time when the Vietnam War affected their lives. In this they share the general model of the male soldier-writer's tale, which Eric Leed, after Arnold Van Gennep's anthropological study of initiation rites, identified as possessing three stages: separation, liminality, and incorporation[24]—similar to what Joseph Campbell called, mythically speaking, the Hero's Journey.

These women's journeys all also share a therapeutic function, yet another defining feature of men's postwar writing.[25] All three texts discuss the aftermath of the war in terms of healing and recovery. Ironically, the wives depict themselves as more successful than the nurse in integrating this part of their past meaningfully into their lives. Neither Novak nor Stockdale ask further questions about underlying politics or the meaning of the Vietnam War for other victims—for instance, the Vietnamese—apart from themselves. Van Devanter's is the most challenging of these texts, for it contains silences and gaps that prevent the narrative closure she so desires. Her life story is the most fractured and suggests that some wounds may never be healed, not even by love. In this she deviates from the normative construction of a woman's gendered experience; at the same time, she resembles more closely the men with whom she went to war.

Even though Novak and Stockdale affirm their secondary position toward their husbands, their lives and their acts of writing nonetheless have feminist implications. Although they would probably deny any feminist agenda, they expand the gender boundaries and claim their own voices. These voices are highly indebted, as are many of the male Vietnam War narratives, to the male soldier-writers of the Great War. This is underlined by their linguistic identification with the soldiers. All three writers use military language and jargon to authenticate their stories and their own authority. While the men prove themselves on the narrowly defined battlefield, the women prove themselves through their endurance. By relying on traditional male strategies for representing war, these women writers expand the genre of writing on war.

Notes

1. One of the three, Lynda Van Devanter's *Home before Morning*, is listed in Jason and Graves's entry "Vietnam War." Studies of American women's Vietnam War writing include Bettina Hofmann, *Ahead of Survival: American Women Writers Narrate the Vietnam War* (Frankfurt, Ger.: Peter Lang, 1996); Margaret Perri, *Witnesses to War: The War Stories of Women Vietnam Veterans* (Ph.D. dissertation, University of Massachusetts, 1998), 98–23; M. Salvatore, *Women after War: Vietnam Experiences and Post-Traumatic Stress Contributions to Social Adjustment Problems of Red Cross Workers and Military Nurses* (Ph.D. dissertation, Simmons College of Social Work, 1992), 55–12A.

2. Thus my discussion will exclude texts by women journalists (Mary McCarthy, Susan Sontag, and Gloria Emerson come to mind), narratives by civilian relief workers, and fictional texts by American women writers (such as Joan Didion or Bobbie Ann Mason).

3. That two texts are by officers' wives reflects the sociohistorical situation. The husband's rank becomes a criterion because officers' wives usually received a comparable college education. Furthermore, the enlisted men usually were extremely young and unlikely to be married.

4. Penny Summerfield, *Reconstructing Women's Wartime Lives: Discourse and Subjectivity in Oral Histories of the Second World War* (Manchester, U.K.: Manchester Univ. Press, 1998), 11.

5. Evelyn Cobley, "Narrating the Facts of War: New Journalism in Herr's *Dispatches* and Documentary Realism in First World War Novels," *Journal of Narrative Technique* 16, no 2 (Spring 1986): 98.

6. Margaret Higonnet, et al., eds., *Behind the Lines: Gender and the Two World Wars* (New Haven, Conn.: Yale Univ. Press, 1987), 13.

7. Cynthia Enloe, *Does Khaki Become You? The Militarization of Women's Lives* (London: Pluto, 1983), 15.

8. Nancy Huston, "The Matrix of War: Mothers and Heroes," in *The Female Body in Western Culture*, ed. Susan Rubin Suleiman (Cambridge, Mass.: Harvard Univ. Press, 1986), 165.

9. Jean Bethke Elshtain, *Women and War* (Brighton, U.K.: Harvester, 1987), 22.

10. Helen M, Cooper, Adrienne Auslander Munich, and Susan Merrill Squier, eds., *Arms and the Woman* (Chapel Hill: Univ. of North Carolina Press, 1987), 10–11.

11. Susan Jeffords, *The Remasculinization of America: Gender and the Vietnam War* (Bloomington: Indiana Univ. Press, 1989), 181.

12. Lynda Van Devanter with Christopher Morgan, *Home before Morning: The Story of an Army Nurse in Vietnam* (New York: Warner, 1983). Samuel Hynes, *The Soldiers' Tale: Bearing Witness to Modern War* (New York: Allen Lane/Penguin, 1997), 1.

13. Carol Lynn Mithers, "Missing in Action: Women Warriors in Vietnam," in *The Vietnam War and American Culture*, ed. John Carlos Rowe and Rick Berg (New York: Columbia, 1991), 84.

14. Hynes, *The Soldiers' Tale*, 25–26.

15. Fussell, *The Great War and Modern Memory* (New York: Oxford Univ. Press, 1975), 173.

16. Marian Faye Novak, *Lonely Girls with Burning Eyes: A Wife Recalls Her Husband's Journey Home from Vietnam* (Boston, Mass.: Little, Brown, 1991).

17. Enloe, *Does Khaki Become You?* 50.

18. The Novaks had four daughters, the oldest of whom—like Van Devanter, also the oldest of four daughters—considered herself something of the son her father never had and joined the army, serving as a communications officer for a support battalion assigned to the Twenty-fourth Infantry Division during the First Persian Gulf War.

19. Jim and Sybil Stockdale, *In Love and War: The Story of a Family's Ordeal and Sacrifice during the Vietnam Years* (Annapolis, Md.: Naval Institute Press, 1990). The Purcells' book is given an entry in M. Paul Holsinger, ed., *War and Popular Culture: A Historical Encyclopedia* (Westport, Conn.: Greenwood, 1999). According to that entry, the book is "one of the few Christian-based narratives to emerge from the Vietnam War. Neither author is bitter over the ordeal, instead viewing it as a gift from God, who made them stronger people and better Christians in spite of their hellish experiences" (400). The book is subtitled *The Remarkable Story of a Courageous MIA Family and the Victory They Won with Their Faith.* Ben Purcell was a POW from January 1968 to March 1973.

20. Hamilton J. McCubbin, Edna J. Hunter, and Barbara B. Dahl, "Residuals of War: Families of Prisoners of War and Servicemen Missing in Action," *Journal of Social Issues* 31, no. 4 (1975): 104.

21. Joan Silver and Linda Gottlieb's *Limbo* is a fictionalized account of the plight of relatives of POWs and MIAs; most of the soldiers are of lower rank.

22. Maureen Ryan, "Pentagon Princesses and Wayward Sisters: Vietnam POW Wives in American Literature," *War, Literature, and the Arts* 10, no. 2 (1998): 141.

23. Here they prove stronger than the odds. Indeed, the divorce rate of returned prisoners of war was quite high. Ironically, couples who had adapted best to the period of separation had many problems to deal with when reunited (McCubbin et al., "Residuals of War: Families of Prisoners of War and Servicemen Missing in Action," 107).

24. Leed, Eric J. *No Man's Land: Combat and Identity in World War I* (Cambridge, U.K.: Cambridge Univ. Press, 1979).

25. See Peter Ehrenhaus, "Cultural Narratives and the Therapeutic Motif: The Political Containment of Vietnam Veterans," in *Narrative and Social Control Critical Perspectives,* ed. Dennis K. Mumby, Sage Annual Reviews of Communications Research 21 (Newbury Park, Calif.: Sage, 1993), 77–96.

Ten

The African American Autobiography of the Vietnam War

Jeffrey Loeb

The stereotype of the black serviceman from the Vietnam era is that of angry misfit or rebel, an individual who probably served time in the brig and quite possibly received a less-than-honorable discharge. Statistically speaking, there is some accuracy to this image—African American soldiers, marines, sailors, and airmen did fare more poorly than their white contemporaries in terms of how they were treated by the military.[1] However, by 1970 the services themselves—reluctantly to be sure, with much foot-dragging—had begun to recognize the structural inequities inherent in their systems, and by the end of the next decade, with the advent of the all-volunteer army, this situation was changed considerably. The military had begun to become for black citizens what it had long promised to be—a career opportunity in which race was minimalized as a factor in promotion.

The Vietnam War itself was perhaps the critical circumstance in impelling this change. African American participants often came from deeply patriotic backgrounds and entered the service with high hopes of advancement and opportunity, only to have these hopes challenged both by the service and by changing popular opinion at home. Placed in line units at higher rates than their white contemporaries and put under the control of a command system comprising white noncommissioned officers (NCOS) of mostly southern heritage, black servicemen found themselves fighting an unpopular war that more and more appeared to be race based. At the same time that they were dying in greater numbers than whites, they were watching people of color in the United States beginning to rebel against continued denial of their basic rights. Thus, African American servicemen and women found themselves self-divided in important ways, often undergoing enormous changes in their own personal identities, though, interestingly, just as often choosing to reaffirm the basic values with which they went to war.

While there are but a handful of memoirs by African American participants in the war, they explore the full range of political and social positions. Some deeply affirm more conservative values, while others are essentially revolutionary in outlook. Of the eleven known self-generated memoirs by black veterans, four clearly recapitulate "establishment" mores: Samuel Vance's *The Courageous and the Proud* (1971), Norman A. Mc-Daniel's *Yet Another Voice* (1975), Phill Coleman's *Cannon Fodder* (1980, 1987), and Colin Powell's *My American Journey* (1995).[2] Four more challenge the status quo in qualified fashion: David Parks's *GI Diary* (1968, reissued 1984), Fenton A. Williams's *Just before the Dawn* (1970), Eddie Wright's *Thoughts about the Vietnam War* (1984), and Albert French's *Patches of Fire* (1997). The other three advocate radical change or reenvisioning of a system that engages in racial conflict at home and abroad: Phillipa Schuyler's *Good Men Die* (1969), Terry Whitmore's *Memphis-Nam-Sweden* (1971, reissued 1997), and James A. Daly's *Black Prisoner of War* (1975, reissued 2000).

It should probably come as no surprise that three of the four memoirists who argue for conservative values—McDaniel, Powell, and Vance—were also career servicemen, with Wright, a "moderate" of sorts, also having retired from the army. The majority of the books, six in all, were written by people "just passing through"—those of Coleman, Daly, French, Parks, Whitmore, and Williams. One—the only book in this group by a woman, Schuyler—was composed by a civilian reporter. At least four are coauthored, all with white writers, and one, Coleman's, has been "published" only on the Internet. Over half of the memoirs—seven in all—were penned almost immediately after the experiences depicted. While this fact adds immediacy to their exposition, it also reduces their perspective, not only in political and social terms but also in matters pertaining to the impact of trauma and its consequent effect on the form of the narrative.

Accommodation or resistance, affirmation or negation of the status quo—the essential choice faced by African Americans since they found themselves on these shores—is also the motivating theme of these eleven memoirs. Each writer at some point or another faces this problem and provides his or her individual opinion on its ramifications for black people, sometimes in very unexpected ways—one is a conscientious objector, and another "votes with his feet," which is to say, deserts. In the end, though the black-authored memoirs are relatively few in number (compared with over five hundred white first-person accounts), the memoirists themselves are as diverse in viewpoint and mode of expression as any group of Americans can be. Together, these works, few though they are, tell a collective African American story of Vietnam that is not only an alternative to white versions of the black experience there (whether these white representations be overly romanticized ones, like James Webb's novel *Fields of Fire*, or stereotyped ones, like Oliver Stone's film *Platoon*) but that also differs in kind in important ways. In particular, these black-authored memoirs show an almost constant awareness of racial difference, an awareness that is absent or negligible in white accounts.

Narratives of Affirmation

Vance's, McDaniel's, Coleman's, and Powell's memoirs are the most affirmative of what each writer feels are basic American values, yet they are hardly homogenous, as each takes quite a different stance toward racial difference.

In *The Courageous and the Proud*, Vance, a career NCO who was twice wounded and won the Silver Star, tells his story in order to demonstrate the worth of the black soldier in an army that in many ways seems to doubt it. In fact, he signals this intent in his first chapter: "I felt that Vietnam was the place for all black soldiers to make a stand that the world would read and hear about. I asked for war because I wanted to be one of the blacks that history would capture."[3] Vance presents his story as a series of tests designed to refute stereotyped notions of African American soldiers as uncourageous (hence the title). In doing so, he recounts incidents that show blacks as not only the equal of whites in combat but, in many cases, better. Also, as a career soldier proud of his service (he retired in 1969), Vance is anxious to show how the American military, in spite of its history of racial discrimination, is nevertheless a viable place for those African Americans able to measure up to a certain mark of excellence.

In the events he depicts, Vance recounts a variety of situations in which courage, leadership, and resourcefulness by African Americans win the day. He discovers, however, that such qualities are not sufficient by themselves for him in his effort, as platoon sergeant of the most successful platoon in his company, to prevail in a white-controlled world. In fact, they only make things worse in some ways, because they result in his having to lead more and increasingly dangerous patrols, while the white-led platoons are able to stay in the company command post. Ironically, it is after having unsuccessfully confronted the company commander on this very subject that Vance wins the Silver Star for heroism. Learning that his platoon has been assigned a patrol only hours after returning from one, he approaches the captain to ask why it has not been given to one of the others. He is summarily dismissed by the captain after an insulting rebuff, and his platoon goes out. While the voice of white authority seems to have the last word, Vance is nevertheless vindicated. The platoon gets into a vicious firefight, and Vance distinguishes himself by saving a wounded forward observer even though he himself is hit in the process. After being released from the hospital, he is awarded the Silver Star in front of the entire battalion, taking satisfaction from the fact that the unsympathetic captain is grudgingly compelled to watch him receive the award. Though he is thus victimized by the viciousness and stupidity that he represents as accruing to whites, Vance is able to prevail through courage and perseverance.

The Courageous and the Proud ends with an assertion of the possibilities for racial harmony. Vance closes with a sort of dream incident in which he is lecturing a group of "new guys," black and white, about what to expect in Vietnam and how the army can offer an environment where racial difference can be overcome. He says, "All of you were taught various things about one another in the past. Your cultural standards are different, and so are your backgrounds. But in Vietnam you will look at a man and you will judge that man not by what you see on the surface. You will judge him by what he does."[4]

Norman A. McDaniel, a major in the air force and one of two African American POWs to have written autobiographies, was, like Vance, a career military man and is similarly disinclined to be critical of the service. Unlike Vance, however, or any of the other memoirists, McDaniel barely mentions race in his book, *Yet Another Voice*; most curious of all, he never indicates in the text the fact that he is black. Only the picture of him and his family on the dust jacket reveals his race.

Yet Another Voice begins with McDaniel's capture, in 1966, when the B-52 that he is navigating is shot down. The bulk of the story thereafter is of his ordeal in North Vietnam over the next seven years, how he both resisted his captors and retained his faith in God. McDaniel's emphasis is thus on the trial and its aftermath rather than any sense of loss. In addition, he essentially makes the book a vehicle for discussing his religious convictions, frequently referring to ways in which he was sustained by his faith as well as ways in which the society and family to which he returned have rejected that same faith. He makes clear in his introduction this intention for the book: "Also discussed are some of the perils that we face as a country for failure to serve God and the responsibilities of those who are trying to lead Christian lives." Furthermore, McDaniel takes pains to represent himself throughout his captivity, which he calls his "ordeal at the mercy of a cruel enemy," as being sustained by a "deep belief in God and the promises of the Bible." As a result of this sustenance, he feels that he has remained stable while "the rest of the world [has] moved on," and that, despite attempts to make him "current" and to "update" him, this admittedly retrograde position is not at all negative. In fact, he feels, it is his family and his society that have become aberrant and that they need, as he terms it, "correction."[5]

Because McDaniel feels repelled by his family and by the general state of affairs in the United States, he is in effect left with no community, only his religious faith and his loyalty to the military remaining as a bulwark against the uncertainties that assail him. At the same time, because he apparently refuses to acknowledge his African American heritage, he effectively denies himself that community as well. Thus, of the eleven memoirs, McDaniel's, while on the one hand among the most affirmative of the "system," is ironically among the most traumatically alienated as well.

Phill Coleman's Internet autobiography, *Cannon Fodder*, is on a massive site that he calls the *American War Library*. Here, a viewer might peruse statistics of dubious source on the Vietnam War, search for veterans of any war, review the medals awarded for various engagements, or read highly sentimentalized accounts of battles. *Cannon Fodder*, Coleman states, "describes the experiences of U.S. Army service during the Vietnam War from Induction—during the beginning growth of the antiwar movement in 1968—to Discharge in 1971." It was, as he says on the *American War Library* site, "completed in 1980 and accepted by Paragon House Publisher in 1987," though there is no evidence that it has ever been published in book form by Paragon House or any other publisher.[6]

In the memoir Coleman situates himself as a Vietnam survivor who has grown from his experience, which includes certain racially charged incidents, and who embraces his country fully. Among other self-advertisements contained within its electronic covers is a testimonial attributed to William C. Westmoreland: "Your comments are well thought out and I generally agree with them. It seems to me that you have written a worthy book and I wish it success." Though Coleman's critics—and he seems to have many—dispute the authenticity of this statement, its inclusion provides a basic sense of his conservative political orientation toward the war.[7]

Coleman, from the time he enters the army, encounters incidents that attest to his growing realization that it is a fertile ground for racism. For instance, while in training he encounters systematic physical mistreatment that is directed specifically toward African Americans; he and other black soldiers protest, but to no avail. They are told, in fact, by their drill instructor, "You assholes are the ones who are racist because you're trying to make a couple of accidents appear to be race-related." For his trouble, he is given the derogatory nickname "Lips Lancaster." Nevertheless, he decides that he will protest no further and make the best of his situation: "I decided that if the Army was going to let racism be one of its problems, it could. But it wasn't going to be one of mine. . . . I saw nothing to gain if I fought with a racist supervisor, and my self-respect to lose if I played 'Uncle Tom.'"

From this point, Coleman becomes, in effect, a covert apologist for the army's systemized racism. In one of the more revealing set pieces, he encounters another black soldier who has supposedly studied the "history" of the black military experience. The soldier tells Coleman that it is "black leaders," beginning with A. Philip Randolph, who have been responsible for the inequities that obtain in the army, mainly because they have worked closely with military authorities to establish and maintain the racist status quo. This "information" reinforces Coleman's decision not to practice even mild resistance; he concludes, "My decision turned out to be the right one. It relieved me of a lot of needless concern trying to prove something as a black, accomplish something as an 18 year-old, or fulfill something as an American. I reasoned it would be a whole lot easier for me to try doing my 3-year tour slightly better than the best I could do." Thus, Coleman, though more willing than McDaniel to recognize the racial inequities he has encountered, does not go a great deal farther in repudiating the enterprise of which he has been a part.

When Colin Powell wrote *My American Journey* in 1995, he had recently retired from the army after an illustrious career in which he had ascended to the position of chairman of the Joint Chiefs of Staff, the top position in the U.S. military. He was also being courted by the Republican Party as a potential presidential candidate (and, of course, then becomes secretary of state in the George W. Bush administration). Thus his book has a different political purpose and, as a result, different rhetorical strategies than any of the other memoirs considered in this article. In form, it resembles what Paul John Eakin calls a political testament, one conveying a sense of self as "completed," as opposed to struggling to locate personal identity in the wake of trauma that marks most other Vietnam War memoirs.[8] For instance, though the book chronicles at great length Powell's life from childhood to the writing present, he frequently steps outside the text to assume the voice of a finished self who knows and understands all of the events being described. As a result, we witness the writing self, struggling to make sense of circumstances while in their midst, in tension with the written self, who is able simultaneously to explain the events that perplex the writing self.

This split perspective becomes crucial in terms of Powell's true stance toward the effects of racial difference on the war's participants. On the one hand, he witnesses with dawning outrage racial incidents that he, with his all-black, somewhat sheltered upbringing, has thought to be a thing of the past; on the other hand, he writes as follows on the occasion of seeing members of Vietnam Veterans Against the War throwing their medals at the Capitol Building: "I still believed in an America where medals ought to be a source of pride, not shame, where the uniform should be respected, not reviled, and where the armed forces were an honorable part of the nation, not a foreign body to be rejected by it."[9] In asserting these values, Powell comes to resemble Vance, even Coleman, in that he shows himself willing to ignore racism and make the best of the situation in which he finds himself.

A careful analysis of his depictions of racism reveals its intractability only in civilian circumstances, such as when he is denied off-base housing in Georgia (107) or is stopped by an Alabama state trooper (113), and it implies a belief that the army (at least following 1948) is an inherently fair place where "equality of opportunity has followed" for African Americans who have "answered their nation's call" (62). Thus Powell, in asserting, like Vance, that blacks can find a home in the military, claims that the army has been "living the democratic ideal ahead of the rest of America" (62). In addition, as he makes clear in several narrative intrusions into his descriptions of the war, he has the qualified opinion that Vietnam was a worthwhile enterprise, teaching most importantly that "you do not squander courage and lives without clear purpose, without the country's backing and without full commitment" (158).[10]

Narratives of Criticism

None of the remaining memoirists is quite as sanguine about the opportunities for African Americans in the military or as affirmative of America's presence in Vietnam. Four of them, David Parks in *GI Diary*, Eddie Wright in *Thoughts about the Vietnam War,* Fenton Williams in *Just before the Dawn,* and Albert French in *Patches of Fire,* are all ultimately critical of the war in Vietnam and of the military's treatment of black soldiers, though each stops short of outright condemnation, and none takes any action, beyond writing about it, to counter the racism he witnesses. One, Williams, goes even farther in linking the war itself to U.S. racism exported to the rest of the world, a position also taken by the remaining three—Schuyler, Whitmore, and Daly.

Though resembling earlier wartime diaries like Oliver Wendell Holmes's Civil War account *Touched with Fire* and Richard Tregaskis's WW II *Guadalcanal Diary,* the content of Parks's *GI Diary* differs markedly from these white-authored works because of an undercurrent of racial difference.[11] Even while in basic training, Parks, the son of noted African American photographer and writer Gordon Parks, encounters instances of overt racial bias: "Never had such bad feelings against white guys before. But then I've never met white guys like these before. They don't let you forget that you're colored and they're white for one minute."[12] This bias obtains in the civilian communities where Parks is stationed as well; even the commercial districts are segregated, with blacks restricted to seedy, tumbledown red-light districts for off-base entertainment.

Although he arrives in Vietnam with a highly developed feeling of obligation to the U.S. cause, Parks's sense of duty begins to flag in the face of racial inequality. For instance, he comments on the propensity of the white sergeant of his mortar platoon to make race the basis of assignments to either the relatively safe fire-direction (FDC) position or the more dangerous forward observer (FO) jobs: "So far he's fingered only Negroes and Puerto Ricans for [the FO] job. I think he's trying to tell us something. I do know he gives me a sour look every time he sees me at the FDC controls. Every time he comes around I get the feeling I should have been born white."[13]

Parks returns home safe but disillusioned in mid-1967. As he tells us in the afterword of *GI Diary's* second edition, issued in 1984, he returned to school, became a photographic journalist, and ended up covering several antiwar rallies at about the same time as the book was originally published. Even though in the second edition he is commenting several years later—the only one of the early memoirists to have the opportunity to do so—his sympathies are clearly split between his newly developed antiwar sentiments and the soldiers being asked to police the demonstrators. At the 1968 Washington, D.C., demonstration, he notes, for instance, that when the demonstrators broke through the lines of troops, "the soldiers didn't retaliate because they were tired, sick, and broken. I couldn't take pictures. It was impossible to do anything."[14] Clearly with Parks, writing these words seventeen years after leaving Vietnam, the ambivalence of his experience there still remains.

Fenton Williams was a physician just out of medical school who was drafted and assigned to Vietnam in late 1969. He immediately encounters the army's racism in an incident that begins for him a radicalization process that grows throughout his story. After being inducted, Williams learns of three openings for residencies at Beaumont Army Hospital in El Paso. He applies and, on the basis of his credentials and recommendations, is accepted, pending a face-to-face interview. Following this interview, however, his orders are inexplicably changed, and he is instead assigned to Fort Sam Houston for training for Vietnam. He afterward learns that three white physicians have been assigned the slots; he reflects, "That I was victimized by the old American practice of discrimination was incandescently clear." Later, while departing for Vietnam, Williams bitterly notes, "It was extremely difficult for me to accept the fact that I was bound for Vietnam to assist the South Vietnamese in their struggle for freedom when I could not enjoy the same in my own country."[15]

In Vietnam, Williams has the fortune to go on frequent MEDCAPS, field medical clinics, to assist villagers. Between this fact and his avid interest in learning whatever possible about the history of Vietnam and the American presence there, he begins noting the disparities between official policy and the realities he observes around him. Ultimately, he determines that racism not only is responsible for the quasi–Jim Crow environment of the army but also underlies the war itself.

At this point Williams's story undergoes a shift in form, from a narrative of events in his life to an essay on racial injustice, both in the United States and around the world. He appends statistics about black casualties in Vietnam and cites evidence to bolster his case against America's being in Vietnam, drawn almost certainly from the *New York Times* reprinting of the *Pentagon Papers*, perhaps the earliest literary use of that evidence. He singles out Central America, for instance, as an area where American involvement should be carefully monitored. In closing, Williams utters words that might easily have been heard in the last decade in the U.S. Congress, ironically from conservatives, in the various debates over military intervention in the Balkans: "If America learns nothing else from the loss of 44,000 lives in Vietnam, she should learn that in this day and age she cannot police the world and force her values on other people."[16]

With respect to form, Parks, Wright, and Williams craft what Robert Stepto terms "eclectic narratives," not totally integrated. The other eight fall into Stepto's category of "generic narratives," fully self-integrated works with purposes "far more metaphorical than rhetorical"—which is to say, mostly linear and paradigmatic.[17] Parks wrote what his title suggests, a diary, to which he appends a number of his photographs. However, his diary, while perhaps the most readable of the eleven memoirs, remains, because of the limitations of the diary form, in some ways the most restricted in scope.

Wright's memoir, on the other hand, consists basically of a series of essays and interviews with other veterans.[18] It has value as a collection of commentaries on various black-oriented issues related to Vietnam, but at the same time its irregular form and ambiguous purpose make its inclusion in the category of narrative questionable. Williams begins with a narrative of his experience but changes modes to analysis of how the United States blundered into Vietnam, concluding with a polemic on world political conditions.

What is lost in these so-called eclectic accounts is a sense of a self-seeking subjectivity through narrative, a hallmark of African American autobiography dating back to at least *The Narrative of the Life of Frederick Douglass*. For instance, while Williams quite clearly traces his progress from a naïve draftee, trusting the government's sense of fair play and integrity, to a man who understands the insidious role that racism plays in determining foreign policy in places like Vietnam, in so doing he almost totally removes himself from the text as a first-person voice. Parks, having published his diary within a year of his return from Vietnam, chose nearly twenty years later merely to reissue it with additional commentary rather than writing a more integrated narrative, one giving him the opportunity to reflect on himself and the war. Wright, while not totally eschewing the personal, nevertheless chooses an objective form in which to pursue even the most self-reflective of observations. It was as if each of these narrators somehow felt that the appearance of objectivity, rather than subjectivity, was necessary to establish their authority.

Albert French's *Patches of Fire* represents a departure from this removal of the subjective self that marks the narratives in the second group.[19] All others, save those by Powell and Wright, were published soon after the events they describe and so tend to be more polemical than self-reflective. French's work, however, probably because of its long gestation period, reverses this relationship, and the aftermath of trauma—in particular his serious wound, in general his total experience in Vietnam—rather than the politics of race becomes the central focus. *Patches of Fire* is also significant, however, because it augments French's other literary achievements, the novels *Billy* and *Holly*, in important ways, mainly by serving as the story of their composition. Since the memoir was actually written before the two novels but published after them, French is able in it to reflect upon its inception, and *Patches of Fire* is thus in a curious way a commentary upon itself, especially as examination of the repressed trauma that precipitated its writing.

Events such as French's wounding and the violent deaths of several Marine Corps friends, the effects of which pervade the narrative, are clearly the major reasons for its composition, in that he describes them in painstaking detail. Yet, as many veterans have done, he later represses his traumatic memories as he pursues a career in journalism and publishing. Only at age forty, when he reaches a crisis—the magazine he had founded is on the verge of going under, and his personal life is a shambles—does French begin dealing with the long-buried effects of the war.

The title event of *Patches of Fire* is a hillside burning with napalm, an image that later mnemonically triggers French's imagination. This scene imprinted itself on his psyche as he lay writhing in pain for the several hours it took to evacuate him after being wounded, yet only years later does it return to him. His attempts to come to terms with this image, and the memories for which it provides the leading edge, make up the second half of the book. First in a veterans' outreach group of the type that proliferated in the eighties, then by the writing of several drafts of *Patches of Fire*, he slowly begins to deal with the traumatic aftermath of twenty years before. Before he is finished, he suffers a total breakdown and a painful reconstruction of his personal life, both romantic and familial, but in the process he also discovers his literary voice, producing not only this book but *Billy* and *Holly*.

The style of *Patches of Fire* is impressionistic. French employs an early version of the free indirect discourse that marks his novels to render both the innocence of childhood and the growing pain of racial self-awareness. The effect, at least in the book's first half, is symphonic, with a return to common themes, notably the realities of racial difference, at several levels. This technique of multivocal narration also underscores a dichotomy between writing and written selves that marks Powell's work as well. Thus, French smoothly represents the impressions of an innocent eighteen-year-old with no seeming consciousness of the traumatized writing self poised years in the future, yet he accentuates the tension between the two through italicized intrusions by that later self's reflections. In the book's second half, which chronicles French's self-recovery, this dual-voiced quality is, if anything, accentuated, though turned around so that the boy now speaks to the man. The result is an emphasis on the traumatic self-division caused by Vietnam and his growing up black in white America.

Witnessing Racism

The three most accomplished memoirs, along with *Patches of Fire*, are Phillipa Schuyler's *Good Men Die*, Terry Whitmore's *Memphis-Nam-Sweden*, and James A. Daly's *Black Prisoner of War*. It is perhaps no coincidence that each work takes an avowedly oppositional stance toward U.S. policies in Vietnam or that each situates at its center American racism, both that of whites toward blacks and that experienced by Asians at the hands of Americans.

On May 9, 1967, Philippa Schuyler, a thirty-five-year-old journalist, a "stringer" for the archconservative *Manchester Union Leader,* was killed in a helicopter crash in the vicinity of Da Nang. Schuyler was the second woman journalist to die in Vietnam and the tenth overall. At the time of her death, she was in the process of writing a book, part memoir and part critique of the U.S. role in Vietnam; the work was already near enough to completion to be published posthumously some two years later, under the title *Good Men Die.*[20] It would have been her fifth book. The remarkable thing about Schuyler, however, is that she was in Vietnam at all. The daughter of a black man, George Schuyler, a noted conservative journalist and protégé of H. L. Mencken, and of a white woman from the South, Josephine Cogdell, also a writer, Schuyler had been a child prodigy musician, winning her first national piano competition at age four with one of her own compositions. At the time of her death, she was still engaged in a career of composing and performing in addition to journalism. She had been around the world several times on concert tours and had, since the late fifties, been writing from an anticommunist point of view about the political and social conditions she found in various third-world locales, notably Africa, then emerging from colonialism. Her original trip to Vietnam, in 1966, had been part of a worldwide concert tour for American servicemen, sponsored by the U.S. State Department, and she had been feted at that time by Ambassador and Mrs. Ellsworth Bunker personally.

This was a year later, however, and neither the Bunkers nor other U.S. officials, including the military command, were happy to see her back; she had been extremely critical of the way the war was going in a series of articles emanating from her previous journey. These articles were not, however, written from the point of view that the war was wrong or unwinnable, as many journalists covering the war at that point were beginning to feel; rather, they reflected the more reactionary position that the United States was not doing enough to win, including invading the North or, conceivably, using nuclear weapons. The result of inept political and military strategies, Schuyler felt, was that the Vietnamese culture was being ravaged and American troops were dying futilely.

This was an eccentric stance and one especially strange coming from a black woman, whom our cultural reflexes would expect to be liberal, but Schuyler was an unusual woman, and her book *Good Men Die* reflects that uniqueness. An eclectic mix of personal memoir, political analysis, cultural anthropology, and right-wing polemic, the book has something of Park's or Wright's form about it but ultimately is a true anomaly. Among Schuyler's gifts were the ability to learn languages rapidly—she had become nearly fluent in Vietnamese in about a month—and a brashness and a commitment to her self-appointed task of chronicling the folly and misery that confounded U.S. officials. Presented sanitized versions of the situation by American officials, she used her knowledge of the language and the fact that her skin tones and facial features resembled those of the Vietnamese to disguise herself in an *ao dai* and conical hat and light out into the countryside to gain a truer measure of the war's progress.

The result is a memoir very sensitive in its stance toward the Vietnamese people and American servicemen, both of whom Schuyler felt were caught between the pincers of U.S. ineptitude and communist rapacity. It combines personal sensitivity with the type of rabid polemic that one might see today in, say, a Phyllis Schlafly. It is clear, however, reading her book in the present, that Schuyler was in the process of reexamining her political opinions in the light of what she was learning in the countryside. While the bulk of the text contains these reactionary political observations, the last section, the one she was working on at the time of her death, displays a markedly different tone and contains an agenda for action, one calling for replacement of American military by a huge humanitarian mission that might have been composed by the Friends Committee, as opposed to an organization representative of the right. One wishes that Schuyler had lived to revise what was obviously a work in progress.

Terry Whitmore's *Memphis-Nam-Sweden* takes perhaps the most critical stance toward American racism. Whitmore joined the Marines in 1967 in order to get "off the block" in Memphis and away from an oppressive family life; for him, the Marines represented "freedom," a concept much explored in the book. The crisis for Whitmore occurs after he is seriously wounded and sent for recovery to Japan. There he is told that he will soon be returning to the States because of the severity of his wounds. However, unlike the white soldiers around him who are also scheduled to be medevaced to the United States, Whitmore is inexplicably ordered back to Vietnam. He deserts instead, eventually managing to escape to Sweden with the help of Beheiren, an international peace organization.

The meaning of freedom, the major question in African American literature since the first slave narratives, thus changes for Whitmore, and an exploration of its elusive nature becomes the point of his story. "Why are you sending me back?" he asks rhetorically, increasingly unable to understand the logic of the war:

> To help the Vietnamese people? Hell, I just helped them to commit suicide, that's all. . . . Because the doc says in I'm in A-1 condition, that's why. Nigger, you don't need a better reason than that. Now just haul your black ass back to that jungle and do as you're told. The Man don't dig Charlie [the Vietcong], so you shoot some gooks for him and if you get shot doing it, sorry 'bout that.[21]

At the point of deserting, he reflects on how freedom is ultimately related to race:

> I'm not coming up with any good reason for going back except that if I don't get my ass back in the Nam, it has to be back to America and a Marine prison for at least five years at hard labor and then the rest of my life as an ex-convict. A black ex-convict. There are a hell of a lot of those cats running around America and I don't have to tell you how most of them end up. . . . Do I have the brains and balls to tell Sam [i.e., Uncle Sam] to take his goddamn war and shove it up his big fucking white ass? . . . And if I say *no* to Sam and *no* to America and its jails, then it has to be *no* to everything I know, my family, my block, everybody. Either spend the rest of my life on the run or get lucky enough to find someplace where the man will never be kicking my black ass into doing his dirty work.[22]

Whitmore ends his story in Sweden as a sort of exotic black pet for the all-white peace community, an irony that he does not miss: "It's a country of blond-haired, blue-eyed *white* people. So I wasn't completely without my doubts about Sweden." At the same time that he regrets never being able to see his baby daughter, he ponders the racial situation in the States, recent site (in 1970) of the Jackson State massacre, and closes by saying, "Do I ever want to go back to America? No, thanks. I'm just not that dumb anymore."[23]

In contrast, James Daly's autobiography, *Black Prisoner of War*, ends on an affirmative note, despite his years of mistreatment by the U.S. Army.[24] In writing it, he adopts an ethical stance that results in part from his religious background but equally from his innate sense of right and wrong; in many ways, *Black Prisoner of War* is the story of Daly's moral growth and testing as much as of what happens to him. Daly begins the memoir with a portrait of himself as a member of a warm, supportive family that opposes violence. He becomes a Jehovah's Witness and declares conscientious-objector status at age eighteen. When his draft board challenges this declaration, he seeks counsel from his local recruiter, who is also black. Naturally, such a move is ill advised, and it turns out to be exactly the wrong thing to do. The recruiter advises Daly to join, assuring him that if he does he will be able to name his own job, thus avoiding combat, possibly even Vietnam. Of course, the recruiter is lying, and Daly ends up a "grunt." Once in the army, when Daly realizes his error, he asserts his convictions as a CO, talking to his commanders and chaplains and writing letters requesting a discharge. The army refuses at every point; one commander even throws his requests away. Eventually, in 1967, he is sent to Vietnam. There he first refuses to carry his weapon and, later, when forced to do so, to load it. Astoundingly, he is still sent on patrols, and on one of these, after a firefight in which he is wounded, he is captured by the Vietcong.

After being shuttled from place to place for two years, during which time he is starved, beaten, and generally mistreated, he is taken to North Vietnam, to the "Hanoi Hilton," where conditions improve marginally for him. During this period, Daly's consciousness of the war as racially based is enhanced by his frequent conversations with his captors, and he undergoes something of a prison conversion. He now is able to see his own life and circumstances of an incipient American racism that victimizes everyone who is not white. Eventually, unlike his fellow captive McDaniel, Daly joins the "Peace Committee" and cooperates with the North Vietnamese on a limited basis, making antiwar statements. At the end of five and half years, he returns to the United States, but unlike most other former Peace Committee members, who sought immediate release from the military, he decides to stay in the army for a time. As a result, he makes himself vulnerable to charges of treason and collaboration with the enemy.

In fairly short order, these charges are brought by fellow captive Theodore Guy, an air force colonel. Although initially dismissed for lack of substance, the charges are reinstated by another air force officer. After interviewing sixty-seven witnesses, a military court again dismisses all charges against Daly; he chooses to exit the army immediately in order to preserve the disability pension that the army otherwise threatens to take away. Daly is thus left in an uncertain situation at the end of *Black Prisoner of War*. Rather than reflecting bitterness at his treatment, however, he remains true to the ethical tone of the entire book in never criticizing anyone—not the recruiter who lied to him, or the army who mishandled and mistreated him in many ways, nor his captors, or even the implacable officers who brought charges against him. Only the war itself, and America's part in it, continues to anger him.

Conclusion

Without question, the twentieth century's most tumultuous era in race relations was the one now referred to as "the sixties." Though this decade's strife immediately proceeded from that of the previous decade, the fifties, and certainly spilled over into the seventies, most key events in the civil rights, black power, and black arts movements are somehow rooted in its years. Central to the racial unrest of the sixties—seldom discussed in this context, yet impossible to separate from it—was Vietnam. The war, which came to be viewed in succeeding decades by white America as merely ignominious, was absolutely disastrous for black America. Yet despite—or perhaps because of—this calamitous effect on the black community, the war has remained almost totally unexamined by its African American participants. Nonetheless, few in number though these memoirs are, they form a complete canon of African American responses to the war, one that should be regarded more closely by its students. I feel that it is no accident, given the common upbringing of the writers in a deeply religious black culture, that many of these authors take religious or ethical positions that bear careful review in today's pragmatic society. Each has something of the country church about it; together they form a cathedral of words.

Notes

1. See Ronald H. Spector, *After Tet: The Bloodiest Year in Vietnam* (New York: Free Press, 1993), 242–60, for a fuller discussion of the legal problems faced by blacks in Vietnam. Also, there is a great deal of pertinent material on this subject in Lisa Hsiao, "Project 100,000: The Great Society's Answer to Military Manpower Needs in Vietnam." *Vietnam Generation* 1, no. 2 (1989): 14–37.

2. Since writing this article, I have discovered, via the efforts of David Willson, Vietnam War bibliographer extraordinaire, two other memoirs, but I had no time to include them in this analysis. They are: Richard A. Guidry, *The War in I Corps* (New York: Ivy, 1998); and Clifton Johnson, *GI* (New York: Vantage, 1980). Readers might also be interested in Wallace Terry's *Bloods: An Oral History of the Vietnam War by Black Veterans* (New York: Random House, 1984).

3. Samuel Vance, *The Courageous and the Proud* (New York: Norton, 1970), 5.

4. Ibid., 165–66.

5. Norman A. McDaniel, *Yet Another Voice* (New York: Hawthorn, 1975), viii, vii, 86, 93. For another Christian faith-based POW memoir, see Anne and Ben Purcell, *Love and Duty* (1992)—though these authors are white.

6. Phill Coleman, *Cannon Fodder: Growing Up for Vietnam*, members.aol.com/warlib/cf.htm, and the *American War Library*, members.aol.com/veterans/index.htm. (Both accessed June 10, 2004).

7. Coleman is often mentioned in discussion groups such as Alt.War.Vietnam and rarely positively. Unfortunately, for many active participants on such sites, Coleman's name becomes synonymous with the African American literature of the war. As an example, I received the following message to a general query I made trying to locate any new or unknown works: "Good luck with your project! If you monitor Alt.War. Vietnam (groups.yahoo.com/group/alt-war-vietnam/), you will have come across Phillip R. Coleman. He is the individual behind the American War Library. Although he has shown himself to be both a crook and a kook, his ramblings in his online book 'Cannon Fodder' illustrate just how clueless some of McNamara's 100,000 actually were. You might find it humorous to compare his perceptions with those of intelligent African American authors" (e-mail from Tom Rau, July 12, 1997).

8. John Paul Eakin, "Malcolm X and the Limits of Autobiography," in *African American Autobiography: A Collection of Critical Essays*, ed. William A. Andrews (Englewood Cliffs, N.J.: Prentice Hall, 1993), 151.

9. Colin Powell, with Joseph E. Persico, *My American Journey* (New York: Random House, 1995), 154.

10. Ibid. Housing in Georgia (107); Alabama state trooper (113); "equality of opportunity . . . living the democratic ideal" (62); lesson learned (158).

11. It would seem more relevant to compare these works with earlier wartime memoirs by African Americans, but there are very few available, and these do not seem relevant. The ones I have been able to locate include the following: James A. Dunn and Mansel G. Blackford, eds. *On Board the USS Mason: The World War II Diary of James A. Dunn* (Columbus: Ohio State Univ. Press, 1996); Charity Adams Early, *A Black Woman*

Officer Remembers the WAC (Corpus Christi: Texas A&M Univ. Press, 1996); Susie King Taylor and Patricia W. Romero, *A Black Woman's Civil War Memoirs: Reminiscences of My Life in Camp with the 33rd U.S. Cavalry Troops, Late 1st South Carolina Volunteers* (New York: Markus Weiner, 1988). For a general history of African American participation in war, see Gerald Astor, *The Right to Fight: A History of African Americans in the Military* (Novato, Calif.: Presidio, 1998).

12. David Parks, *GI Diary* (Washington, D.C.: Howard Univ. Press, 1984), 24.

13. Ibid., 76.

14. Ibid., 135.

15. Fenton A. Williams, *Just before the Dawn: A Doctor's Experiences in Vietnam* (New York: Exposition, 1971), 15–16.

16. Ibid., 127.

17. Robert B. Stepto, "Narration, Authentication, and Authorial Control in Frederick Douglass' *Narrative* of 1845," in *African American Autobiography*, ed. Andrews, 27.

18. Eddie Wright, *Thoughts about the Vietnam War: Based on My Personal Experiences, Books I Have Read, and Conversations with Other Veterans* (New York: Carlton, 1984).

19. Albert French, *Patches of Fire: A Story of War and Redemption* (New York: Anchor, 1997).

20. Philippa Schuyler, *Good Men Die* (New York: Twin Circle, 1969).

21. Terry Whitmore, *Memphis-Nam-Sweden: The Autobiography of a Black American Exile* (Garden City, N.Y.: Doubleday, 1971), 119–20.

22. Ibid., 120–21.

23. Ibid., 168, 189.

24. James A. Daly and Lee Bergman, *Black Prisoner of War* (Lawrence: Univ. Press of Kansas, 2000; originally *A Hero's Welcome: The Conscience of Sergeant James Daly versus the U.S. Army*, 1975).

Eleven

The Life Writing of a
Military Child

JENNIFER SINOR

The trajectory of recent scholarship about personal narratives of war and the military has shown that while soldiers' stories are important, they are not the only ones. The recovery of women's war stories, in particular, has provided a more complicated picture of military service, moving our attention away from tales of death and sacrifice to the more mundane, to what a life writer in Margaret Higonnet's collection calls the "backwash" of war.[1] The testimony of nurses, female machinists, female soldiers, and female journalists provides, as Diane Fessler suggests, a "counterpoint" to the chronicles of the "male warrior."[2] Higonnet's recent collection of women writers of World War I includes women from all over the world, from different educational backgrounds, from different races, and from different classes. Such a broad spectrum of women writing about their experience of war in powerful and compelling ways—some witnessed publicly for the first time ever—certainly calls into question how narrowly we can cast our net when determining the boundaries of military life writing. These "counterpoints" demonstrate that military experience is an experience shared by many more than those who carry the guns and expand the boundaries of what (and who) counts when compiling military autobiography.[3]

Having said that, though, gaps in military life writing continue to exist. These gaps include single-authored narratives by military wives, by children from other countries left behind by American soldier–fathers, and narratives by gay servicemen, as well as those by civilian contractors, who are playing increasingly greater roles in military operations. By far, one of the largest gaps is writing by and about military children.

At first, perhaps, such a gap may seem quite appropriate. After all, children of U.S. military personnel do not fight wars. They do not readily appear to be the bearers of war stories and would fail miserably as witnesses with firsthand war experience. They have not enlisted, and they do not fight, train, test, shoot, order, strategize, or deploy. It is for this very reason that their stories need to be told. They do not choose to serve, yet their lives, often from birth, are conscribed by both the possibility and the paraphernalia of war. They may not see, hear, feel, or taste war, but their entire lives are lived under its threat. To suggest they have no war stories is to ignore the costs necessary for war.

The absence of military children as subjects within the military system as well as in current scholarship duplicates their demographic absence, a gap Mary Edwards Wertsch measures when she describes "military brats" as "America's most invisible minority."[4] In history, in the military, and in academic research, they are unaccounted for. When considered at all, the children of military personnel are most often subsumed under the umbrella of "the military family." Both within the military itself and within scholarship, military children are often viewed as "an extension of the father."[5] Literally and metaphorically, children are not deemed separate individuals with unique experiences deserving attention. In addition, any professional attention given them is often framed in terms of securing "a strong, deployable military force," again placing the emphasis not on the child but on the father/soldier/fleet.[6] Because of their doubly disenfranchised status as both military dependents and as children, they are rarely given status as individuals and, more importantly, are never viewed as complicated subjects with conflicting desires and needs.

As a result, we know very little about the experience of military children and even less about their own self-representation. In general, the military child is afforded only two subject positions within the scholarship. These roles—either victim or warrior—represent military children in static, one-dimensional ways. The first role, one supported by social scientists like Don M. Lagrone and writers like Pat Conroy and Mary Edwards Wertsch, suggests that the military child is a victim of the "military family syndrome." Authoritarian fathers, repeated geographical displacement, alienation from the civilian world, and the rule-bound life of the military work to build what Wertsch terms "the Fortress," generating psychological legacies military children bear for the rest of their lives. In these studies, the military is something children must recover from. Such a view can give very little agency or control to children in terms of how they resist or reproduce the cultural scripts that surround them, a failing that characterizes much of the research about marginalized subjects.

The second role afforded to military brats in current scholarship, and one predictably perpetuated by researchers who work for the military (for example, Jensen, Hunter, and Kaslow), is that the military offers exciting and unique opportunities to children, opportunities that make them healthier and better able to cope with the real world. Adult military children themselves often reproduce the image of child as warrior. In Mary R. Truscott's *Brats: Children of the American Military Speak Out*, most of the adult military brats she interviewed see military children as "aggressive, outgoing, resilient, and well adjusted."[7] The great majority are thankful for the experience and claim hardship has made them stronger. Of the outcome of a military upbringing, one states, "I have no fear."[8]

In these studies, military children overcome what would initially appear as obstacles (frequent relocation, deployed parents, etc.) to demonstrate remarkable flexibility and responsibility from an early age. They eventually outstrip their civilian counterparts in terms of psychological adjustment, claiming that they have "come out ahead, in spite of and because of [their] background."[9] These warriors, when faced with adversity, rise to the occasion. However, what goes unnamed in these analyses—indeed, the knowledge that haunts these studies—is the fact that these children, unlike civilians, are raised in a culture whose explicit purpose is armed defense. In this line of research, the context in which military children are raised is virtually neutralized.

The concern here is not the validity of the evidence that military children are either "weaker" or "healthier" than their civilian counterparts but the fact that these are the only two positions afforded military children. Neither representation is complicated or convincing. The main reason that these pictures of military childhood are so one-dimensional and static is that they often rely on secondhand or removed evidence. Much of the work by scholars both inside and outside the military relies on information gathered from parents, health care providers, hospital records, or adult military brats, not military children themselves. There is very little attempt made to interact directly with those being studied. In the rare case study or memoir-fictional account, military childhood is accessed only through the eyes of adult military children. Both Wertsch and Truscott rely on interviews with adults who have "survived" the military. Writers like Pat Conroy *(The Great Santini)* and Elizabeth Berg *(Durable Goods)* must recreate the drama of the military childhood through memory. Few studies capture how the military child represents her self and her experiences *as a military child.*[10]

Even when working directly with military children, research is difficult and complicated. Nancy Ryan-Wegner, whose own research with military children was compromised by too few participants, notes that military parents are hesitant to allow their children "to think about war and what it means to their family."[11] They appear less willing than civilian parents to allow researchers access to their children. In addition, my experience in working with military children suggests that it is difficult for an "outsider" to gain access to this population. Wertsch and Truscott have extensive connections to the military, providing a ready pool of research subjects. Truscott, in particular, comes from a long line of military officers, several of whom have themselves written books about the military (*Dress Gray*, for example). Because it is difficult for an "outsider" to gain access, most of the work on military children, including Ryan-Wegner's, is partially or solely supported by the Department of Defense. In addition, military children often relocate, making extended research difficult. Last and most significant, acknowledging the complicated position of the military child and the cost of their service would demand an examination of our own complicity in the formation of that position. We would have to assume partial responsibility for the less visible outcomes of being a military superpower.

Rather than rely on the stories told by adult military children or on research conducted within the military, an examination of military children's life writing brings us as close as possible to the sights and sounds of duty. It provides what Samuel Hynes means when he stresses the narrowness and fallibility of statistics and calls instead for "the personal witness" of those who serve.[12] Life writing documents a life in progress—regardless of whether the text is a note left on the kitchen table, a full-length autobiography, or a diary kept during adolescence. How an individual makes a text offers one opportunity—though not a transparent one—to examine how she manufactures her world. Texts that might illuminate the world of the military child include diaries, scrapbooks, school assignments, notes, lists, letters, and creative writing. While each of these texts obviously follows certain generic conventions (for example, a story written for school is not the same kind of text as a note written to a friend), they also share important commonalties. Not only do they inscribe a moment in a life, but they are written within the powerful context of military childhood, and they bear evidence of that context.

By examining the work the military child conducts while still within "the fortress," we can begin to understand the experience of one of the

most invisible members of military service, the experience of one conscripted by birth. Such an examination begins with an understanding that
while these children do not fight in combat, their daily lives are nevertheless marked by war.

Ordinary Trauma

Military childhood is spent in paradox, where the extraordinary passes
as the ordinary. It is lived within a system dedicated to rendering as ordinary the act of making and preparing for war, with the result that one
does not question sacrifices made for defense. That the paraphernalia
and possibility of war becomes as commonplace as a stop sign produces
"ordinary trauma." At first such a term may seem like an oxymoron—
after all, as Judith Herman writes, "traumatic events are extraordinary
not because they occur rarely, but rather because they overwhelm the
ordinary human adaptation to life."[13] Discussions of acute psychological
trauma focus on acts of atrocity and natural disasters. Enormous, extraordinary, awful events like rape, incest, abuse, and battle unmake individuals, forever. These can be one-time cataclysmic events or cases of
chronic trauma. In either instance, the sheer enormity of the event pulls
trauma from the realm of the everyday and places it in the extraordinary.[14] However, what sets ordinary trauma apart from acute psychological trauma is not simply its nonextraordinary status, but that it *passes*
as ordinary. The active and ongoing construction of ordinary trauma
makes it invisible. Those within the context of ordinary trauma do not
and cannot perceive the extraordinariness of their situation, because to
them it is unexceptional.

Ordinary trauma merges with everything else in our lives that passes
unnoticed, unmarked, and unnamed. That does not mean that our modern world has not made us all, in some way or another, "survivors" of
trauma.[15] Charles Anderson and Marian MacCurdy suggest, in the introduction to their edited collection *Writing and Healing*, that "even witnesses"
to a traumatic event can suffer acute psychological trauma.[16] They list
two world wars, the spread of HIV, the *Challenger* disaster, and the bombing of the federal building in Oklahoma as part of an "apparently endless
succession of virtual and actual encounters with great traumatic potential."[17] To this list, of course, we could add September 11, the most recent
shuttle disaster, the Columbine shootings, and the ongoing war on terrorism. But the apparent endlessness of traumatic events and the expan-

sion of PTSD (post-traumatic-stress disorder) to include witnesses as well as participants is *not* ordinary trauma. Anything newsworthy, noteworthy, or exceptional cannot be mundane. Ordinary trauma, on the other hand, accounts for the extraordinary events and possibilities that are masked as ordinary. For the military child, the possibility of war is so ordinary that it receives no notice.

Ordinary trauma illuminates, among other things, why the current research on military children is so misleading. To ask a military child about her experience of war is like asking a civilian child about her experience with breakfast cereal. No anxiety that the military child experiences about the possibility of war, a possibility lived every day of her life, will register, because it, like the milk she drinks in the morning, is her ordinary—more importantly, even, it is with great effort made to be ordinary by the military scripts that abound. The paraphernalia of war—missiles, guns, tanks—are as common as fire hydrants or shrubbery. Sandboxes sit upon bomb shelters. Fathers can be deployed without notice. Antiterrorist explosives fill the neighborhood speed bumps. Guard gates let you in or keep you out. Dependents go on submarine cruises and feel the reverberations of torpedo slugs sounding through their chests.

In the same way that the endless succession of traumatic events in our modern world does not amount to ordinary trauma, to say that military childhood is lived within the context of ordinary trauma is not to say that the experience of military childhood is synonymous with acute psychological trauma. While certainly some military children experience acute psychological trauma from abuse or neglect, the most recent research suggests that this percentage is not any higher than that of civilian children who are abused or neglected.

Being a military child does not equate with being in a war.[18] Yet the experience of the military child rests somewhere between the extraordinary experience of being in battle and the "ordinary" experience of civilian children, for whom war is typically both abstract and remote. Unlike their parents, who have preservice memories that act as counternarratives to which they can compare the military experience, military children have no touchstones outside their lives in service. For the military child, the possibility of war is the only ordinary reference, even as it also remains staggering. The fact that war is a concrete, immediate possibility (one that parents prepare for every day) throws the shadow of the battlefield across the daily experiences of children from military homes, moving their everyday experience more surely toward the pole of trauma.

In defining ordinary trauma there is a middle space that is not squarely inside conventional definitions of trauma or clearly outside it. Likewise, it is a space that is neither ordinary nor wholly extraordinary. In current trauma theory, the insistence on the sheer extraordinariness of trauma (in contrast to the ordinariness of the rest of experience) means that a memory or experience is either ordinary, and therefore narratable, or atrocious and therefore outside language. In these discussions nothing exists in between. There is no continuum of experiences, where memories range between the unknown and the narrated. Space does not exist for thinking about an experience that is articulated as ordinary but bears close connection to the extraordinary.

How the possibility of war gets constructed by the military, and by the military child, as ordinary is at the center of ordinary trauma, as well as the center of this essay. As argued elsewhere, the ordinary, while unmarked and unnoticed, is nevertheless rhetorically constructed and ordered.[19] Not only will the life writing of a military child duplicate this paradox but, in fact, her work as a writer will perpetuate it—reproducing, to a greater and lesser extent, the message she receives that this missile, like this mailbox, is simply a thing on the side of the road.

In recent years the fields of life writing and trauma studies have moved closer together. For reasons that will become apparent below, life writing is productive for locating something that is seemingly without location—traumatic memory. It is equally productive for evidencing ordinary trauma. Defining the connection between trauma (both ordinary and acute) and life writing begins with understanding the conventional definition of trauma. The study of trauma has been slow in coming. In 1980 PTSD was institutionally defined, and hence validated, by the American Psychiatric Association as a psychological reality.[20] For years, soldiers had been diagnosed as "shell shocked" when they returned from war and had trouble integrating their experiences on the battlefield with domestic life. The APA's acknowledgement finally gave these soldiers' experience legitimacy. It is worth noting that the first professional recognition of the inexpressibility of traumatic memory came in the wake of the Vietnam War. War and the resulting inability to integrate its experience into everyday life become a definitive example of trauma.

Trauma, from the Greek for "wound," can be both a physical wound or psychological shock that has lasting effect. The shock is so great that, Suzette Henke writes, it forever "threatens the integrity of the body."[21] In that way, trauma is a totalizing experience. The one who has been traumatized can no longer experience the world except through his or her wound. But trauma totalizes in another way as well: it is endless. Cathy Caruth writes that it is an "event that one cannot leave behind."[22] Similarly, Dori Laub says of Holocaust survivors that they "bear witness not just to a history that has not ended, but, specifically, to the historical occurrence of an event that, in effect, *does not end*."[23]

Sigmund Freud was one of the first researchers to document and study the totalizing effects of trauma. His qualitative analyses of women in the late nineteenth century opened the door for the often episodic work that would follow. From the very start, what was most clear and perplexing about working with survivors of trauma was the paradoxical nature of traumatic memory. While survivors often cannot recall the traumatic event at all, they constantly revisit the event through repeated images, ritual action, icons, or dreams. In this way, the event is both known (because it keeps recurring) and not known (because it is inaccessible).

Recently, physiological psychologists have learned that traumatic memory is stored in the brain differently than ordinary memory, shedding light on the paradoxical nature of trauma. Marian MacCurdy suggests in "From Trauma to Writing" that unlike ordinary memory, which is stored in verbal, linear ways in our brain and is therefore fully assimilated into the ongoing narrative of our lives, traumatic memory is stored in the amygdala, a more "primitive" part of our brain that stores experience as image rather than language. The memory, then, not held in language, is linguistically inaccessible, is not known in any conscious, meaningful way by the survivor. While psychologists may disagree about what counts as trauma and what recovery involves, they agree that a defining principle of trauma is the fact that the sheer force, the immediacy of the experience (rape, battle, abuse, car accident) and how the brain registers that experience ensures that its effects are not experienced at the time. Instead, the event arrives belatedly to form what Herman calls an "indelible image."[24] Survivors return again and again to the event via these images, trying to establish meaning by reliving the trauma. Possessed by something that they cannot name, they remain haunted.

Breaking this cycle requires the aid of an outsider, a witness, someone to help bring the experience into language. Shoshana Felman writes, referring to Freud's work, that "it takes two to witness the unconscious."[25] Bringing the experience into language orders the memory, assimilates it, and makes it known. For Freud, such healing happens in therapy, through what he calls the "talking cure," where the therapist helps the survivor, through word associations or hypnosis, eventually to name what haunts him or her. Shoshana Felman suggests that artists can serve as mediators, that they can through the visual arts, literature, and film serve as vehicles for healing. Most recent is theoretical work suggesting that writing itself is therapy—that survivors can heal themselves through the writing process.[26] What is even more interesting is that recovery through narrative, almost by definition, must happen in the field of life writing, the genre of writing in which the narrator represents, and re-represents, herself in relation to her world. Suzette Henke suggests that life writing heals because the autobiographical act of telling "mimics the scene" of psychoanalysis.[27] The writer becomes, through revision, both the analyst and the analysand.

Traumatic memory, stored in images or icons, is prenarrative. It exists as fragments. In logotherapy or scriptotherapy, theories of narrative recovery, survivors of trauma begin to order the experience into a narrative that, Charles Anderson writes, "holds the possibility of meaning and therefore wholeness."[28] What was formerly unknown, static, frozen, and totalizing becomes not only known but something that can be revised and therefore drafted, multiplied, changed, and reseen. Revision is a key part of narrative recovery.[29] Writers gain power by complicating the self, seeing themselves at the locus of multiple discourses and no longer frozen in one moment. By taking charge of their self-representation, they ultimately gain power over that which formerly imprisoned them. T. R. Johnson writes, "Writing that heals is often writing in which the writer names, describes, and takes control of the experiences in which the writer's powers of naming and controlling have been explicitly annihilated" (86). Johnson focuses our attention on the intricate relationship between writing and healing—the manipulation and control of both language and self-representation. Johnson's work causes us to look for traces of agency in what a writer is doing even when the writing might typically pass unnoticed, even when we do not see "trauma," even when we know that the writing does not tell a story, let alone a war story, but feel it is saying something about the removes of war.

Life writing, then, is text and healer, testimony and witness, record and recovery. It documents trauma, and it heals. The tendency, however, is to focus on extraordinary accounts of naming and healing, where writers testify to acute psychological trauma. Most recent books that seek the intersection between trauma and life writing examine famous, literary authors, whose writing and trauma are both extraordinary.[30] Such a focus parallels our desire to read extraordinary and literary examples of life writing in general. In doing so, we miss much. The "backwash" of war, like the "backwash" of everyday experience itself, is not found in these texts.

Ordinary trauma registers in ordinary ways. To understand how the extraordinary passes as the ordinary, to understand the work undertaken by institutions (specifically, here, the military) and individuals to ensure that the context of ordinary trauma is maintained, to understand what makes such trauma both powerful and insidious, we must look at ordinary writing. Only as a writer distills experience into text can we see the close relationship between the two. Only then will the ordinary writing of a military child testify to the efforts to reproduce the message that all is well.

The Diary of a Military Child

It is a haunting experience to come upon the diary you kept as a child. The diarist, like the grandparent you never visited, feels both familiar and strange. On the floor of my parent's attic, amid dust motes flocking to a nearby light, I read the cramped, penciled writing of a ten-year-old girl that was me. The entries are sporadic, fraught with resolutions to be a more consistent diary keeper, and plagued with misspellings and inventive grammar. In terms of factual content, I certainly recognize myself at ten, eleven, and twelve struggling with recurrent military relocations between the Pentagon and Pearl Harbor and with the onset of adolescence. Names of familiar friends appear: Karen, Stacy, Lisa. These are the friends with whom I played, fought, and built tree forts. On the last page of the diary, they come together along with others to form a list of names and addresses. It is my attempt to keep track of those the military has asked that I leave behind. Two names appear without addresses: Suzette and Kate. It is not that I did not know where they live. Rather, it is that at the time of this diary I had not left them yet. By recording their names, I prepared literally and emotionally for the fact that in a year or so they too would be left behind. They entered both my diary and my life as an inscribed absence.

With daily entries often stretching across decades, diaries provide the closest approximation of the "metaphor of the self," becoming, as Suzanne Bunkers writes, "the most authentic form of autobiography."[31] Felicity Nussbaum notes that the diurnal form allows the contradictions of selves to exist on the page. By recording the daily, by simply writing on the page, the diarist creates both a continuous sense of self (what Nussbaum calls "an enabling fiction of a coherent or continuous identity") and a discontinuous, changing self (I am not the same as I was yesterday).[32] To read the diary as life writing, as writing that documents moments in life, allows us to see the making of a self and the making of a text. *The Extraordinary Work of Ordinary Writing* argues that how a diarist, or any writer, orders that text—what she chooses to "order in" and what she chooses to "order out"—tells us a great deal about writer, culture, text. Like literary life writing (memoir, diary literature, and autobiography), ordinary writing, the kind of writing that litters our lives and is most often disregarded or tossed out, equally documents the tenuous making (and remaking) of experience. Ordinary diaries, specifically, document that making on a daily basis, taking the measure of self and experience. While we often overlook the diaries by the not so famous because they tend to be boring, bare, and plain, when we learn to read them, we find a document that literally vibrates with the extraordinary work required for both identity and text formation.

I turn to the diary I kept as a military child to begin to sketch the possibilities of reading life writing produced in the context of ordinary trauma. By examining the self-representation of a military child and military childhood, we can see the work undertaken by both institutions and individuals to reproduce as ordinary the extraordinariness of war. To this end, I look at three entries from my early teenage years, moments that lay, not insignificantly, in the midst of a series of moves and at the height of a nuclear mania in the United States. Clearly, the goal here is not an in-depth exploration of my diary or diaries in general but rather to suggest a place to begin to articulate how ordinary trauma is inscribed on the page.

In many ways, my diary is like any adolescent diary in the way that, as Suzanne Bunkers writes, "structure, spelling, and punctuation are fluid and changeable" and topics addressed range from "writing about daily events" to "relationships and feelings."[33] The entries, like those of many contemporary young diarists, are short, periodic, and not given to elaboration. I make no claims that my diary is structurally any different from other adolescent diaries. What I do claim is that while all diarists undertake the challenge of distilling experience into text, the lens through which I articulate my experience is one shaped by military scripts demanding that the extraordinary context of my Cold War childhood and the hardships that resulted from military service were in no way extraordinary. I claim, in other words, evidence of ordinary trauma.

My military service began in the midst of the Vietnam War—the reason my father entered the service—and ended a year after the collapse of the Berlin Wall. It was, then, dominated by the Cold War, nuclear deterrence, military buildup, and the Reagan years. Like all military childhoods, it was both typical and unique. We moved repeatedly but not as often as others. My dad wore a uniform every day of my childhood but did not carry a gun. We lived in military housing but never actually on a base. I am like and unlike the millions of other military children. When I meet other military brats or read about their childhoods, I am struck by the familiarity of the experiences, a familiarity that appears often at the level of language. For someone who has no home, these intersections become the closest I have to roots.

When I was growing up, my father always responded to those who asked us about home by saying that we were gypsies. The word would curl from his lips draped in colorful scarves and gold hoop earrings. The gypsy life was romantic, daring, and bold; it made me proud to think I was too. Military life—the moves, the losses, the relocations—was what I was taught to call "an adventure."[34] Yet the diaries I find in the attic, the two I kept irregularly as a child, are not wound with the colorful and the exotic but rather with fear and sadness. While I easily remember the events that are named—the camping trips and going to the mall—in reading my diary it is the anxiety that sounds most clearly. While for years I too called myself a gypsy, my diary is an exploration of loss.

The first diary, a tiny blue book entitled "My Diary" in which I inscribed my friends in terms of their absence, was kept from the ages of ten to fourteen. It is empty more than filled, marked mostly by entries in which I account for giant gaps in time. The second diary, the one kept throughout high school, is much more regular and, not surprisingly, longer. It is in this diary that sadness and anxiety are named more openly. While I still spend much of my time recording the daily events of school and work, there are many moments when I write, "My parents have been talking about moving. I don't think I want to but what do I know. I feel so lost most of the time. I can feel myself slipping into a world of blackness where nothing exists." Meeting these words for the first time in twenty years, my desire is to console this girl, comfort her. She is and is not me.

The first entry that I will look at is one of the final entries from the small blue diary, written when I was fourteen, in the fall of 1983. My family had just moved back to the mainland from Hawaii, a route I would replicate no less than three times in my life as a military dependent. In the throes of starting both a new school and high school, I write:

October 5, 1983
Life is hard right now. I have no friends. I miss my old ones. I probably can't get contact lens and I feel very low at times. I enjoy talking to God and should do it more. I think there may be a nuclear war which we will deserve because the world is falling apart.

In many ways, this could be read as a typical entry in an adolescent's diary. There is no overt evidence, other than the reference to moving, that this diary is one kept by a military child; the worries expressed are not atypical among adolescents. What is significant, though, and what causes me to pause, is the way in which the extraordinary possibility of nuclear war is embedded within the ordinary, to the point where nuclear war is nearly unmarked in the entry. The entry is not about either getting contact lenses before the start of school or about the promise of nuclear war—it is about both. The two concerns are rhetorical equals. Neither receives extended attention or commentary. Neither is made more or less significant than the other. Neither is marked the unusual. Within the laundry list of the daily, it seems both will appear.

The appearance of the extraordinary and the ordinary side by side in my diary is not surprising, given the way they met in my life. At any moment, as things go in the military, one may be asked to die. Like its warships, the entire military community floats in a steady state of readiness. Coming and going from the base and from our house we would note the DefCon (Defense Condition) chart posted at the gate, alerting us to the level of readiness. Most of the time we were in an "Alpha" state; latitude was generally shown at the gates into the housing communities. If I forgot my ID card and the guard recognized me, chances were he would let me go home. When we hit level Charlie (due to violence in the Middle East or an act of terrorism somewhere in the world), my family would be asked to get out of our car at the gate. The guards then searched the family minivan with flashlights, sliding mirrors mounted on wheels underneath the chassis to look for bombs. We might be returning home from the movies.

This was my daily experience. I could not make it from school to home without considering the possibility of war, if never on a conscious level.[35] The regulations, the procedures, the discipline were all part of the ongoing readiness. Orders by commanding officers to their sailors to shine the brass on their ships were discipline measures taken in preparation for the time when the order would be to stay behind and protect the retreat. At least that was what my dad said when I would ask about the yelling and the screaming I saw on base, the soldiers humping, the barbed-wired brig. He would carefully explain how in time of war—bombs exploding, people dying, smoke, and debris—an officer had to know that any order would be followed without question. The discipline to die.

My duty as a military dependent was to help maintain the community necessary to ensure that an eighteen-year-old from Mississippi would, without questions, sacrifice his life. That he would respond only, "Sir, yes sir." To ensure that response, we painted the walls in our houses white, kept the lawn trim, and flew the flag on all major holidays. To ensure his response, I spent great emotional energy in the eleventh grade defending the Strategic Defense Initiative and the nuclear option. I would sit at the dinner table and tell my father what I had heard that day from the teacher and students in my Global Relations class. He would tell me exactly how to respond, what to say to those communists who did not understand. Sitting in class the following day, my father's words would pour from me—Star Wars, Mutually Assured Destruction, Nuclear Deterrence. With all my body, I would argue for war to the point of tears.

It was more than a child learning her views from her parents. It was a script, a vocabulary that I was given to translate the evidence around me—absent fathers playing war games at the bottom of the sea, neighborhood buildings with corrugated exteriors designed to prevent spying—into the ordinary. Dinner-table conversations, centered on world events, the threat of communism, and nuclear weapons, became a place where the rhetorical work of ordinary trauma was learned and tested, to be reproduced later in my diary. It all blurred together: eating the casserole my mother had made, kicking my younger brother under the table, and articulating the importance of first-strike capability. The certainty of war was everywhere. It thrummed steadily beneath my days, like a steady breeze off the ocean, unnoticed until it ceases. Hunched over my diary late at night, worrying about a new school or about my appearance, war appears like a comma or a breath.

The veneer of ordinariness—on a military base or in the diary of a military child—is the result of a great deal of work. The mistake in reading any writing that registers ordinary trauma, and indeed ordinary writing in general, is to see the "ordinariness" of the writing as somehow not constructed, simply because it is not constructed in literary and storied ways. It appears uneventful and plain only because we forget that what initially appears ordinary is actively constructed as such. For the military child, it is constructed by a writer schooled in upholding paradox. I write:

> *April 23, 1984*
> When will the time come when I'm no longer depressed? Do I just use the move as an excuse to be depressed? Am I being too particular in choosing my friends? I wish these and more answers could be answered. I hate to blow up at my brothers. It makes me feel awful. Any little thing seems to make me fly into a rage. It also always seems like my dad is putting us kids down in front of others just for a laugh. I know this isn't true, but it seems like it. I am really beginning to hate how people look down on me. I get it at school, home and from friends. They all seem not to respect me as a person, only an image or object that is theirs to do what they want with. I know it is not that bad. So why do I make it seem like it is? I wish someone would answer these questions.

The above entry comes from the blank book I kept as a diary in high school. I am fifteen. Reading this entry, I remember how hard that time in my life was. We had lived in Virginia for about six months, my dad working at the Pentagon, between two tours of duty in Hawaii. I had few friends and still felt a stranger in a school of over two thousand students. Yet in my writing I do not allow my life to be hard. In fact, I work toward the opposite effect. I work to make that which is exceptional into that which is ordinary. By neutralizing the enormity of my circumstances, by scolding myself for "using" the move as an excuse, I attempt to ensure rhetorically that the extraordinary, the potentially traumatic, remains ordinary. In effect, I reproduce the messages around me. Any attempt to mark my experience as something other than ordinary, as something capable of making me depressed, is rhetorically met by statements that my situation is "not as bad as it seems," self-accusations that I am trying to "make it seem" worse. I work against the impermissible and allow myself no justifiable room to be sad, scared, or lonely.

The attempt is not completely successful. In the effort to render all as ordinary, there are moments of slippage, moments where I consider the possibility that my experience is far from ordinary, even though I work to inscribe it as such. Twice in this entry I wish for outside answers to my questions, indicating that my depression may have real, though unknown, causes, that I am not just making things harder than they seem. In the plea at the beginning and end of the entry, I read the need for someone to legitimate my experiences, to say that the self-inscribed ordinary in my life is far from ordinary. The questions themselves—the very act of asking questions—tends toward resistance of the military scripts surrounding me. Even as I work hard to replicate the paradox of ordinary trauma, to reinscribe the paradox into the pages of my diary, I allow a small space to question my position as military child, the "object" that others "do what they want with."

Unlike the first entry, in which I contain the extraordinary possibility of war within the ordinary of the day, in this entry I deny the existence of anything extraordinary altogether. It is a tactic I use again and again in the diary. For example, only a week prior to the above entry I write: "I am very depressed, but you can't really tell what that is. Actually it's a reasoning fallacy." Here again, I name something extraordinary but quickly discount its status as such, relying literally on the rhetorical terms that I have learned in my ninth-grade speech class. My feelings, I write, suffer from "vagueness as Mrs. Phillips says." To be depressed is a fallacy, an inappropriate and incorrect way of viewing my situation.

What is too enormous to handle is either rhetorically controlled or left unnamed. Overwhelming loss and the seeming objectification of my body haunt the above entry. The work is to make everything ordinary, correct my misperceptions, get back in line. In the third and final entry, the extraordinary is named more explicitly, though still veiled behind the slant of metaphor.

In this last entry I am sixteen. We have moved back to Hawaii very suddenly, two weeks into my junior year of high school. A newly appointed admiral wanted my father as his legal advisor. My mom had left to visit her mother who was ill, and I had the responsibility of "packing out" the entire house while my dad finished at work. Back in Hawaii, we lived in a hotel for three months because no housing was available. I shared a room with my two brothers. Dinner was often bologna sandwiches or whatever could be grilled at the park next to the hotel. The new school I had begun attending had already been in session for weeks when I arrived. Because I missed school pictures in both schools, my junior year would go undocumented. The friends I had made—the ones I blamed myself for not trying hard enough to make—remained in Virginia. I write:

March 1986
The knife sliced through the dew-kissed skin. Piercing the hardened gourd. The watermelon surrendered to the steel blade—raped. The inner secrets harshly exposed, the innocent flesh melting the callous

air—sting. Again the knife clearly glides, once a unified body now separate entities. The cool juices run crazily down the shell—escape. The knife drips guiltily with blood. The pulp glimmers in the boring sun—violated. Again the knife, again the blood. Over and over—it is done.

There is no reason given for this entry's atypical, creative form. Without the specificity of a date, it signifies all of March, all of spring, all of my days. I read the entry and recoil at the violent images and language used to describe a very ordinary event. The mundane act of cutting a watermelon becomes equated with rape at knifepoint. Were this kind of violent image absent from the rest of my diary, I would dismiss it as a creative whim. Yet this is not the only time that I move into horrible fictions in my diary. In the same way that my concern over nuclear war is registered again and again, such short, violent pieces collapsing the extraordinary into the ordinary appear often. There is a piece, for example, that describes the suicide of a small boy by hanging, but it concentrates on the shoestrings that dangle to the floor. Unlike the first two passages, where the extraordinary passes as ordinary, here the ordinary becomes transformed into the extraordinary. War and the everyday are not only equalized. They are indistinguishable.

It is the rawness of both the writing and the image in the entry about the watermelon that most startles me when I read it: *flesh, pulp, juice, blood*. The action is syntactically isolated and rhetorically heightened by dashes. In this way, the verbs, the acts, claim their own space: *raped, sting, escape, violated*. The watermelon—that staple July Fourth fruit—is acted upon. Not only do I, as the diarist, not appear, but no agent appears. Rather, the knife acts alone. No one is to blame for this abuse. The fact that the watermelon is acted on by an invisible force echoes not only the position of the military child, forced to uproot constantly, but the position of the population faced with a missile launch. The image figures a loss of control and the inability to name what or who is acting. The body eventually yields to the force.

In this final entry, the ordinary is made extraordinary and, therefore, comes closest to literally naming trauma. While my body and my position ghost the passage, I appear only as a watermelon, a common thing. My own presence is a well-rehearsed absence. Although the language and approach is unusual in comparison to much of my diary, the experience of being acted upon is commonplace, as is the fact that such action is violent.

It is difficult to describe to anyone outside the military the paradox of military childhood how hard you work to uphold the fact that your life is no different from anyone else's, no matter how many weapons abound around you. As one military brat has said of the experience, "In retrospect, it's a really ideal environment for a child. That's what I remember about the Army, aside from the other crazy part of it, the 'kill, kill.'"[36] How to rectify the ideal with the "kill, kill"? How to relocate once again and have it be okay? How to feel safe in your yard but have that safety ensured by force? How to tell yourself day after day after day that all of this—the uniforms, the guns, the nuclear submarines, the bomb shelters, the deployed fathers, the playing of Taps, the rules and regulations, the missiles and the tanks, the chain of command, the discipline to die, and the need for an arsenal that will destroy the world ten times over—that all of this is as ordinary as rain?

As a child I could not have articulated this paradox. It was my ordinary. There was nothing else. But I reproduced it in my writing. Less often, I resisted it. In those moments, when I questioned whether this was indeed "normal," I created some room for myself. I was neither warrior nor victim, but there were costs to my service, just as there are other hidden costs to being a military superpower. What I will claim is my ownership of the war story I tell here. For while my diary entries do not and cannot claim status as testimony, my understanding of my experience does testify to the paradox of military childhood and to the legacy of ordinary trauma.

Notes

1. Margaret R. Higonnet, ed., *Lines of Fire: Women Writers of World War I* (New York: Plume, 1999), xxi.

2. Diane Burke Fessler, *No Time for Fear: Voices of American Military Nurses in World War II* (East Lansing: Michigan State Univ. Press, 1996), 1.

3. There are others who are naming the reaches of war. In particular, Susan Griffin's powerful and personal book *A Chorus of Stones* documents the civilian cost of being a military superpower. The voices of those at home, those who waited for their husbands or fathers to return, can be heard in books like *Love and Duty,* by Ben and Anne Purcell; *Snake's Daughter: The Roads in and out of War,* by Gail Gilberg; and *The Souvenir: A Daughter Discovers Her Father's War,* by Louise Steinman. Even military memoirs—like *Faith of My Fathers* by John McCain and *The Autobiography of Lewis B. Puller,*—that focus on the experiences of soldiers and officers do give passing attention to those at home.

4. Mary Edwards Wertsch, *Military Brats: Legacies of Childhood inside the Fortress* (New York: Harmony, 1991), xii.

5. Don M Lagrone, "The Military Family Syndrome," *American Journal of Psychiatry* 135 (Sept. 1978): 1041. Although outdated, Lagrone's study continues to play a key role in the professional discussion surrounding military children. Most of the research in the wake of his study is in response to his diagnosis of the military family syndrome. He is consistently cited in work on military children, and the syndrome is revisited several times. See, for example, Peter S. Jensen, Stephen N. Xenakis, Perry Wolf, and Michael Bain, "The 'Military Family Syndrome' Revisited," *The Journal of Nervous and Mental Disease* 179 (1991): 102–7; and Nancy A. Ryan-Wegner, "Impact of the Threat of War on Children in Military Families," *American Journal of Orthopsychiatry* 71 (April 2001). Last, while the military continues to be made up of mostly men, more and more women are the sponsors in military families. See Seth Stern, "New Worry: Kids with Both Parents in Combat," *Christian Science Monitor* 93 (Oct. 2001). The point is not that the child is subsumed by the father necessarily but that the child is subsumed at all.

6. Lindsay B. Paden and Laurence J. Pezor, "Uniforms and Youth: The Military Child and His or Her Family," *The Military Family in Peace and War*, ed. Florence W. Kaslow (New York: Springer, 1993), 21. There are suggestions that the military is beginning to pay more attention to all military dependents but in particular to the health and well-being of military children. For example, the U.S. Army declared 1984 "The Year of the Military Child" and 1985 "The Year of the Military Family." More importantly, there have been increases in the numbers of family services provided to military families.

7. Mary R. Truscott, *Brats: Children of the American Military Speak Out* (New York: Dutton, 1989), 230.

8. Ibid., 216.

9. Ibid., 208.

10. Arguing "the need for further research from children's perspectives," nurse and social scientist Nancy A. Ryan-Wegner, qtd. ibid., 236, attempts to fill the absence by studying children who are currently in the military. In this case, though, the conclusion that she draws—that a military childhood lived under the threat of war creates resilient and adaptive individuals who are no more anxious about war than their civilian counterparts—does little to complicate the picture of military childhood.

11. Ibid., 243.

12. Samuel Hynes, *The Soldiers' Tale: Bearing Witness to Modern War* (New York: Penguin, 1997), 229.

13. Judith Herman, *Trauma and Recovery* (New York: Basic, 1992), 32.

14. Though, as Herman points out, with cases of sexual and domestic abuse the sheer numbers indicate that the experience, far from extraordinary, is all too commonplace.

15. Charles Anderson and Marian M. MacCurdy, eds., *Writing and Healing: Towards an Informed Practice* (Urbana, Ill.: NCTE, 2000), 5.

16. Ibid., 4.

17. Ibid., 5.

18. Statistics exist for the increased number of cases of post-traumatic-stress disorder in wartime children. For example, PTSD increased 87 percent in children who lived through

the Iraqi assault on its Kurdish population in the 1970s and 1980s. See A. Ahmad, M. A. Sofi, V. Sundelin-Wahlsten, and A.-L. von Knorring, "Posttraumatic Stress Disorder in Children after the Military Operation 'Anfal' in Iraqi Kurdistan," *European Journal of Child and Adolescent Psychiatry* 9 (Apr. 2000). Although Derek Hudson and Kenneth Miller trace the dramatic rise in birth defects in children born to servicemen who fought in the Gulf War, for the most part military childhood is not directly affected by the battlefield. Hudson and Miller, "The Tiny Victims of Desert Storm," *Life* 18 (Nov. 1995): 46–59.

19. See my *The Extraordinary Work of Ordinary Writing: Annie Ray's Diary* (Iowa City: Univ. of Iowa Press, 2002).

20. Anderson and MacCurdy, *Writing and Healing*, 3.

21. Suzette Henke, *Shattered Subjects: Trauma and Testimony in Women's Life-Writing* (New York: St. Martin's, 1998), xii.

22. Cathy Caruth, *Unclaimed Experience: Trauma, Narrative, and History* (Baltimore, Md.: Johns Hopkins Univ. Press, 1996), 2.

23. Dori Laub, "Bearing Witness or the Vicissitudes of Listening," in *Testimony: Crises of Witnessing in Literature, Psychoanalysis, and History*, ed. Shoshana Felman and Dori Laub (New York: Routledge, 1992), 67.

24. Herman, *Trauma and Recovery*, 166.

25. Shoshana Felman, "Education and Crisis, or the Vicissitudes of Teaching," in *Testimony*, ed. Felman and Laub, 15.

26. See, especially, Anderson and MacCurdy, *Writing and Healing*, as well as Henke, *Shattered Subjects*.

27. Henke, *Shattered Subjects*, xii.

28. Charles M. Anderson, with Karen Holt and Patty McGady, "Suture, Stigma, and the Pages that Heal," in *Writing and Healing*, ed. Anderson and MacCurdy, 57–58. Discussions of writing as healing may appear to reify the notion of an essential self by using words like "self," "integration," and "wholeness." Nothing could be farther from the truth. Traumatic memory freezes one moment by refusing to assimilate it. Healing occurs only in revision, in multiplying possible selves, possible stories, possible outcomes. Likewise, it is important to remember that telling the trauma story is crucial in narrative recovery not because the story is "the truth" but because a story is told at all.

29. See Tilly Warnock, "Language and Literature as 'Equipment for Living': Revision as a Life Skill," in *Writing and Healing*, ed. Anderson and MacCurdy, 34–57; Anderson, Holt, and McGady, "Suture, Stigma, and the Pages that Heal"; and T. R. Johnson, "Writing as Healing and the Rhetorical Tradition," in *Writing and Healing*, ed. Anderson and MacCurdy, 85–114.

30. See, for example, Leigh Gilmore, *The Limits of Autobiography: Trauma and Testimony* (Ithaca, N.Y.: Cornell Univ. Press, 2001).

31. Suzanne Bunkers, "What Do Women Really Mean? Thoughts on Women's Diaries and Lives," in *The Intimate Critique*, ed. Diane P. Freedman, Olivia Frey, and Frances Murphy Zauhar (Durham, N.C.: Duke Univ. Press, 1993), 211.

32. Felicity A. Nussbaum, "Towards Conceptualizing Diary," in *Studies in Autobiography*, ed. James Olney (Oxford, U.K.: Oxford Univ. Press, 1988), 134.

33. Bunkers, ed., *Diaries of Girls and Women: A Midwestern American Sampler* (Madison: Univ. of Wisconsin Press, 2001), 41.

34. Truscott, *Brats,* 209. Military children speak about their experiences in scripted ways. Like recovering alcoholics or the religiously converted, military children tell— or at least begin to tell—the same stories. See, specifically, Robyn Warhol and Helena Michie, "Twelve-Step Teleology: Narratives of Recovery/Recovery as Narrative," in *Getting a Life: Everyday Uses of Autobiography,* ed. Sidonie Smith and Julia Watson (Minneapolis: Univ. of Minnesota Press, 1996), 327–50; and Smith and Watson, *Getting a Life,* in general. For example, many of the military brats in Truscott's book (who grew up during the Vietnam War) speak specifically of the adaptability that the military taught them or the adventure of moving, often calling themselves "gypsies" (229). For years, I used the same language to negate the hardships of repeated relocation. The military children that I interviewed in the summer of 2000 (children who had lived through the Persian Gulf War) often began talking about their experiences with similar language, citing increased adaptability and the love of adventure.

35. As one military brat in Truscott's book says in reference to learning as a child that a plane carrying nuclear weapons had made an emergency landing on a nearby runway, this was the "day-to-day stuff. It didn't shock me at the time or upset me," *Brats,* 24.

36. Ibid., 16.

Twelve

Writing against the Vietnam War in Two Gulf War Memoirs

Anthony Swofford's *Jarhead* and
Joel Turnipseed's *Baghdad Express*

Elisabeth Piedmont-Marton

As Rick Atkinson explains in the prologue to his history of the first Gulf War, *Crusade: The Untold Story of the Persian Gulf War,* the national euphoria immediately after the swift and decisive defeat of the Iraqi forces soon gave way to a "certain hollowness," which manifested itself as "disdain for a feeble foe; disaffection at the terms of peace; [and] a preoccupation with domestic ills." The war, Atkinson writes, "would dwindle in public consciousness to an expedition of flimsy achievements launched under dubious pretexts—a footnote, a conflict as distant as the Boxer Rebellion of 1900. For most Americans, the Persian Gulf War became irrelevant."[1] And yet, despite, or possibly because of, the diminishing stature of the war in public consciousness, those who served feel called on to tell their stories.[2]

Anthony Swofford's *Jarhead,* published at the start of the 2003 war in Iraq, benefited from a big publisher's mighty publicity machine and arrived at the right moment for readers who were eager for war stories with conclusions. Reviewers were effusive in their praise, and not one failed to mention the book's genealogical relationship to the memoirs of writers such as Tobias Wolff and Tim O'Brien. Michiko Kakutani in the *New York Times* called *Jarhead* a "searing contribution to the literature of combat, a book that combines the black humor of *Catch-22* with the savagery of *Full Metal Jacket* and the visceral detail of *The Things They Carried.*"[3] Joel Turnipseed's *Baghdad Express,* however, also issued in 2003 but from a small press in Minnesota, toiled in the shadows of the *Jarhead* juggernaut and received a fraction of the ink and airtime. A brief review in the *Library Journal* noted, "The image of Turnipseed, a reservist called involuntarily to duty, harks back to that Vietnam-era truism: the college student drafted to fight but not really wanting to."[4] The reviewer for *USA Today* argued that

Baghdad Express "should not be overlooked" in the press frenzy surrounding *Jarhead*.[5] Both books certainly benefited from the outbreak of a new war in the Gulf region, as reviewers, television and radio hosts, and commentators expressed a desire to be associated with a recognizable and oddly reassuring sensibility, a desire to contain the noises and images from an unfamiliar war within the contours of a now-familiar one. For such readers Swofford's and Turnipseed's books seemed to promise that war and death will offer at the very least the compensation of literature, that in the end discontinuity will become continuity and chaos will become order—if only textually.[6]

This essay is not intended to be a definitive critical reading of the texts but rather a set of observations that seeks to map out the interpretive field within which these books and others can continue to be investigated. These soldier-narratives not only tell individual stories of war experience, but they also take up the work of other social discourses, including narratives of previous wars, especially the Vietnam War, as well as the discourses of addiction and recovery and of contractual work, the economic exchange between the body of the worker and the ideas and beliefs of the employer.

Vietnam in the Desert

In *The Wars We Took to Vietnam: Cultural Conflict and Storytelling*, Milton J. Bates identifies five cultural conflicts that soldier-writers of the Vietnam War carried in their rucksacks and their consciousness and within which they inscribed their own stories of the war. These include "the war between those who subscribed to different visions of American territorial expansion, the war between black and white Americans, the war between the lower classes and the upper, the war between men and women, and the war between the younger generation and the older."[7] Because the Vietnam War and the narratives that emerged in its aftermath did not, of course, resolve these conflicts, soldier-writers like Swofford and Turnipseed carried them into a new war, the 1990–91 Persian Gulf War. Swofford's *Jarhead* and Turnipseed's *Baghdad Express* both extend and break from the narrative tropes of the Vietnam War memoir. To paraphrase Ezra Pound's ambition to write a poem "containing history," both books contain war, certainly, but they also contain books that contain war. These two first-person accounts vibrate between two representational poles: the impulse to map the new war onto the former—to write the Gulf War in the vocabulary of Vietnam—and the impulse to make sense of the individual experience in a new kind of war.

Much has been written in this volume and elsewhere about the genre of the Vietnam War narrative, and there are a few of the characteristic features that also make their way into the Gulf War memoirs of Swofford and Turnipseed. Both books share Tobias Wolff's blend of dark humor and heady sweetness, Philip Caputo's tendency toward swagger and self-pity, and Tim O'Brien's blurring of fiction and memory. In fact, *Jarhead* seems at first glance to *be* a Vietnam War memoir, only in desert cammies and gas masks. This passage will strike many readers as familiar:

> Three men were squatting atop the rise and staring at us. We're within one hundred feet. I could, in two to three seconds, produce fatal injuries to all three of the men. This thought excites me, and I know that whatever is about to occur, we will win. I want to kill one or all of them, and I whisper to Johnny, but he doesn't reply. In a draw to our right I see five camels, obviously belonging to these men. The camels are as always, indifferent.[8]

This prose has the hallmarks of the genre—the black humor; estrangement of the intellectual narrator from his fellows, coupled with a longing for a lost masculine collective; and the surprising pleasure of violence. In other passages we encounter the defensive perimeter of irony, the starched and capricious commanding officer, the otherness of women, and the distrust of bureaucracy and authority. Turnipseed also dips into the familiar discourse of semidetached irony combined with longing for an authentic combat experience:

> I was in the *real war*—or, if that didn't exist, I was closer to enemies with guns. I had tried, on the drive up, to wrap my philosophy around this unsettling fact: even though I felt within me that this was a stupid war, an avoidable war, I wanted very badly to see the worst of war. As a would-be philosopher, I knew Pascal's line, "The heart has its reasons which reason does not know," and as a smart-ass I knew Freud's "The dick has its reasons which reason does not know," but a part of me didn't want to buy the fact that the fist, too, had its reasons.[9]

What is more significant than the stylistic similarities to the Vietnam narratives, however, are the ways in which Vietnam representations intrude on the texts, adumbrate, and sometimes threaten to appropriate them. The war that "nobody gives a fuck about" (165), in Swofford's words, the war that lasted barely one hundred days, acquires legitimacy by its association with the narratives of Vietnam, but it also struggles for its representational autonomy.

Swofford begins his story at the Marine base at Twenty-nine Palms, California, where his unit is preparing to ship out to Saudi Arabia. And how do the marines prepare for deployment? He writes:

> We send a few guys downtown to rent all the war movies they can get their hands on. They also buy a hell of a lot of beer. For three days we sit in our rec room and drink all of the beer and watch all of those damn movies, and we yell *Semper fi* and head-butt and beat the crap out of each other and we get off on the various visions of carnage and violence and deceit, the raping and killing and pillaging. We concentrate on the Vietnam films because it's the most recent war, and the successes and failures of that war helped write our training manuals. (5–6)

Not only did that war help write the manuals, it also wrote the master narrative within which Swofford and others will understand their experience. In this instance, however, they watch the movies in new ways. Instead of reading the films as cautionary tales, that they are "anti-war, that the message is war is inhumane and look what happens when you train young American men to fight and kill, they turn their fighting and killing everywhere," Swofford concludes that "actually, Vietnam war films are all pro-war, no matter what the supposed message, what Kubrick or Coppola or Stone intended," because "the magic brutality of the films celebrates the terrible and despicable beauty" of fighting (7). After the movies and the heroic drinking, Swofford is ready: "I take my seat and return to the raging battle. The supposedly anti-war films have failed. Now is my time to step into the newest combat zone. And as a young man raised on the films of the Vietnam War, I want ammunition and alcohol and dope, I want to screw some whores and kill some Iraqi motherfuckers" (7). This is a rhetorical gesture that points in two directions: it claims its lineage and asserts its independence. But like a domineering older brother, the story of Vietnam refuses to yield its place and continues to insert itself in the new drama.

One of the most striking examples of this kind of textual appropriation occurs in the middle of the book, when several years after the war Swofford and other members of his platoon travel to Michigan to attend the funeral of one of their own, Troy, who's been killed in a drunken one-car accident on an icy road. This episode, to which Swofford devotes eight pages, shows us how these marines grieve, and the grieving process looks a great deal like the preparing-to-deploy process: a violent, collective drunk-fest. The one-page chapter that follows the funeral chapter begins and ends with the same sentence: "We stayed drunk for many months" (83). The prodigious drinking begins before they even arrive at the Detroit airport: "The five of them had been drinking for thirty-six hours and I'd been drinking for thirty," Swofford reports. Then they pile into a rental car to make their way to the grimy postindustrial town of Greenville. With Swofford, the soberest one, driving, they "passed the whiskey and schnapps and brandy and Scotch around, and this way we stayed warm and were able to continue a buzz" (75). They are drunk for the viewing, drunk for the funeral, and drunk for the graveside service. Afterward, they find themselves as angry outsiders in a town Swofford describes as "the site of a gross failure of industry," and "largely alcoholic and religious" (78), looking for the next place to get drunk again. A family dinner at a Lions or Kiwanis Club is the next stop, then they drink beer and "a few bottles of whiskey" before they even enter the hall (78) and inevitably get into an altercation with a local reservist. The spectacle of drunken grief escalating to violence is believable and familiar, but what happens next in Swofford's narrative of the events in Greenville goes beyond the familiar trope. Swofford's depiction of their last raging night in town is a startlingly faithful reenactment of the 1979 film *The Deerhunter,* in which he and his buddies seem to have been transported back in time to a dingy steel town in the 1970s to mourn the death of the Russian-roulette playing Nicky. The older story so completely takes over Swofford's text that he seems to lose control of the details that would anchor the scene in the mid-1990s. It's a testament to the power of the *Deerhunter* images that neither Swofford nor any of the editors or readers would have noticed that the men would not have been legally able to "buy a bottle" of whiskey in a bar in the 1990s. It may seem a small detail, but it's indicative of a larger tendency in the book to merge, or even submerge, the narrator's experience in the now-canonical stream of the Vietnam War narrative.

The concluding episode in *Jarhead* marks another striking instance of the intrusion of Vietnam War representation into the Gulf War narrative. Swofford, a child conceived when his parents meet in Hawaii while his father is on brief leave from Vietnam; who claims to have been "raised on the films of Vietnam"; and whose experience in boot camp reproduces scenes from *Full Metal Jacket,*" interrupts his own homecoming after the war with the intrusion of a drunk and homeless Vietnam veteran. On a bus toward Twenty-nine Palms, the returning marines are cheered and feted by adoring crowds along the route: "People threw cases of cheap beer and bottles of cheap booze and plastic yellow ribbons and flags into the buses, and occasionally a marine lifted a willing woman into the bus" (250). At one point in this carnivalesque episode, someone "pulled a Vietnam vet onto the bus, a hard Vietnam vet, a man obviously on and off the streets for many years, in and out of VA hospitals." But this is no cautionary tale, no warning about the shallowness and transience of the hero's welcome. Instead it's an opportunity for the troubled vet from an earlier war to bestow his blessings on the fresh crop of vets: "The bus quieted. He closed his mouth and licked his cracked lips and yelled to the bus, 'Thank you, thank you, jarheads, for making them see we are not bad animals.'" Incongruously, Swofford expresses hope that the vet's gratitude will help "heal *his* wounds" (251; emphasis added).

Baghdad Express also exists in the shadow of the Vietnam War narratives, but it manages to wriggle free more often than *Jarhead* does. Turnipseed is able to do this in part because, as a reservist stationed in the rear-rear, his war doesn't even remotely resemble the Vietnam War, and he makes no effort to claim that it does. Turnipseed, a bookish unenthusiastic Marine, living and studying philosophy in Minneapolis, is sent to the Gulf to drive and maintain the trucks that will move the largest amount of materiel in history. He never fires his weapon, nor is he ever fired on, but his job is dangerous, exhausting, and frustrating, and, unlike *Jarhead*, almost all of *Baghdad Express* takes place in the Gulf.

But like Swofford, Turnipseed also views war through the lens of the movies and books he's grown up watching, most of them about Vietnam. Turnipseed, however, does not appear to want to recast his war experience in the mold of Vietnam narratives. Or to be more accurate, perhaps he *wants* (as does Swofford) to locate his war memoir in the tradition of O'Brien and Caputo and others but—unlike Swofford—recognizes the impossibility of doing so. The result is a war memoir that derives its power from marking its distance from what we have come to expect from the war memoir. In *Baghdad Express* narratives of the Vietnam War appear as they do in *Jarhead*, but they don't threaten to take over. In fact, Turnipseed recounts a conversation in which a fellow marine reservist at Camp Pendleton asked Boomer, an older, more experienced man, "What was it like, Vietnam?" In *Jarhead*, this question would likely have evoked tales of alienation and brutality and, above all, would have asserted its own ineffability. Vietnam is a secret you can't have known unless you were there. But in Turnipseed's account, Boomer says, "Boring." He goes on to describe a kind of boredom-induced trauma: "Ninety-nine percent of the time you just sat around, waiting for the shit to hit the fan. Boredom creeps up on you like a sickness. It makes you stupid" (41). As a truck driver, Turnipseed certainly experiences boredom, which he combats with "a mask of irony" (88), a bunker of books, and an endless chain of cigarettes. "This is how I fought much of my war," he says. "In silence. At two A.M. on a guard post or three A.M. out on a highway hauling a load of 155 mm shells. Alone. Without guns" (111).

But it is a war, nevertheless, and *Baghdad Express*, like *Jarhead*, evokes the specter of the misused Vietnam War veteran at the conclusion of the book. Whereas Swofford allows the possibility that the older veteran will derive some solace from his momentary and condescending inclusion on the bus of happy homecoming Gulf War vets, Turnipseed suggests that the occasion might provide for just the opposite: a chance to sever the connections, to release the younger generation from ties that bind with guilt. On their return to cheering crowds, Boomer exhorts them "to eat this up, really take it in, every fuckin' second. Every half-second. These folks are going to be cheering for you guys like you're the greatest American heroes that ever lived. And you deserve it. Even if you don't feel like you deserve it, you do" (196). Unlike the vet on Swofford's bus, Boomer recognizes that there will be no consolation in this welcome: "No matter if the ladies have double-dee swingin' tits, or how many flags are waving, or how many cases of cold beer they pass our way, they can never give us back the reception we missed. We had our war, and we can't have it back. Now you Marines had yours, and you came home heroes" (196). But Turnipseed and his fellows on the bus will not be able to differentiate themselves that easily. "And how would we have known," he writes, "standing in the shadows of Boomer and Benson, that we would have our turn at unease and untruth. That we would not be making jokes about Agent Orange, but clinical studies of PB, anthrax, depleted uranium, smoke, pesticides" (197). Turnipseed cannot fully escape the Vietnam War, and he knows that he can't reenact it, either, nor reinscribe it in his narrative. But in linking his possible chemical exposure to Agent Orange, he assumes a burden of anxiety that the previous generation has long been carrying—and writing about.

Despite these moments when the stories of an earlier war intrude into the narrative fabric, however, *Jarhead* and *Baghdad Express* also limn some new territory for American war narrative. Two features seem to be very much artifacts of the last decade of the twentieth century: the trope of the contract and the predominance of the recovery narrative as autobiography.

The Contract

At the heart of many narratives of the Vietnam War is the act of conscription, the draft, whereby individual bodies are appropriated to serve the state's purposes. As philosopher Elaine Scarry argues so persuasively in *The Body in Pain: The Making and Unmaking of the World*,[10] the structure of war requires the undeniable solidity of individual bodies to lend substance to its unsubstantiated fictions. In other words, the state confers weight and credibility on its "national fictions" by appropriating the bodies of its citizens, and in Vietnam this mechanism was the draft. In *Jarhead* and in *Baghdad Express* the contract, instead of the draft, is the point of articulation between the individual and the collective, between the body and the fiction.

In *Jarhead* the contractual nature of the ties between the individual and the Corps, or the "Suck," as Swofford and his buddies like to call it ("because it sucks dicks to be in it and it sucks the life out of you" [52]), emphasizes that what binds the two is an economic exchange rather than an ideological one. This is soldiering as business arrangement in which each party determines what he is willing to give for what he values but each retains certain rights. On occasion these two understandings clash. Working from an older model, Swofford's drill instructor (who seems to have walked out of *Full Metal Jacket*) berates him and then knocks his head through the chalkboard and into the cinderblock wall behind it. Swofford later refers to this event as an "assault" and chooses to file a complaint against the drill instructor, because he "believed no one had a right to put his hands on me" (31). This is a very strange thing to say, since the essence of agreeing to be a soldier is the recognition that people *will* put their hands and other weapons on you, as you will on them. His objection derives much less from the traditional discourses of the barracks and the battlefield than it does from the discourse of the workplace (or even the courtroom); it reveals a necessary new discourse in a peacetime, volunteer, corporate military "workplace" environment. Eventually, however, Swofford adjusts and decides that despite the realization that "joining the Marines had been a mistake," he would "handle it like a man," and honor his "contractual obligation" (46).

The contract between Swofford and the Marines is also a site of ambivalence where he can dramatize conflicting ideas about belonging and not belonging to the collective, a site of social as well as economic exchange.[11] One of the persistent themes of *Jarhead* is Swofford's ambivalence toward the Marine Corps and the masculine collective. During a staged perfor-

mance for the benefit of reporters, Swofford and his platoon are ordered
to play football in full MOPP (chemical protective) gear in the desert heat
of Saudi Arabia. To the horror of the officers, the game devolves into a
"field fuck: an act wherein marines violate one member of the unit, typically someone who has recently been a jerk of abused rank or acted anti-
social, ignoring the unspoken contracts of brotherhood and camaraderie
and esprit de corps and the combat family" (21). Despite his assertion, "I
hated the Marines and I hated being a marine" (33), the football game
brings him into the collective: "The exhilaration isn't sexual, it's communal—a pure surge of passion and violence and shared anger, a pure distil-
lation of our confusion and hope and shared fear" (21). In this instance
Swofford's conflicted feelings about belonging divide along predictable
lines: he can hate the Marines, represented by the overbearing officer and
his unreasonable demands, but love his fellow marines and express his
love in mock acts of sexual violence. Elsewhere his ambivalence is less
manageable, where he seems to want both things at once, to belong and to
separate himself. "The sad truth," he claims "is that when you're a jarhead, you're incapable of *not* being a jarhead, you are a symbol. . . . Though
you might be an individual, first you are a symbol. . . . Sometimes this is
correct, sometimes this is foolish. But either way, you are part of the
goddamn thing" (119). Yet Swofford also takes great pains to distinguish
himself from his fellow jarheads. After he tells other marines about an
encounter with some Bedouins who've pantomimed a complaint that
Americans have shot some of their camels, they think the story is funny
and "make jokes about 'camel jockeys.'" Offended, Swofford discovers
he's more empathetic to the Bedouins than to his fellow marines: "I'm not
happy to be in the Triangle, and I'm even less happy about going to war as
a hired man for another government, but I find their heartlessness particularly disturbing. I want to defend the Bedouins against this assault
from these ignoramuses" (139).

The trope of the contract emerges again in the description of a harrowing friendly-fire episode in the climactic chapter of the book. This incident is the defining event in Swofford's combat experience, and he narrates it with equal parts irony and terror: "Unlike the minor enemy assaults
we've experienced over the days prior, we know our own guys will not
stop until the entire convoy and all nearby personnel are annihilated, because that is the way of the Marine Corps." But it's not just the fear and
the cruel irony of being shot at by your own that fuels their "astonish-
ment and rage," it's the idea that the contract has been abrogated. Johnny,
Swofford's sniper team partner, is outraged and screaming: "Because of

all the things that Johnny believes in, the superiority of the sniper and the importance of the small unit, first he believes in the Marine Corps and that the Marine Corps takes care of its own, as in does not kill its own" (219). Swofford is not quite the true believer that his partner is, but he too feels not just that he's the victim of a terrible accident but that he's been betrayed: "No matter the numbers and statistics that the professors at the military colleges will put up on transparency, friendly fire is fucked fire and it makes no sense and cannot be told in numbers" (219). In other words, Swofford reads the friendly-fire incident as the apotheosis of the fear of betrayal that lies at the heart of every contract: that the other to which you pledge yourself—in marriage, in business, in war—will ultimately turn its terrible, intimately knowing power on you.

Finally, Swofford asserts that the contract itself confers the narrative authority on which the credibility of his book depends:

> I have gone to war and now I can issue my complaint. I can sit on my porch and complain all day. And you must listen. Some of you will say to me: You signed the contract, you crying bitch, and you fought in a war because of your signature, no one held a gun to your head. This is true, but because I signed the contract and fulfilled my obligation to fight one of America's wars, I am entitled to speak, to say, *I belonged to a fucked situation*. (254)

What's interesting about this passage is that the contract can be used to warrant silence or speech, confirming its role as site of conflict and ambivalence. The troubling implication remains, of course, that those of us who did not sign the contract have no authority to speak or to challenge the stories of those who do.

Turnipseed's relationship to the Marine Corps is also fundamentally contractual and economic. As a reservist, he's arguably even more motivated by sheer self-interest than Swofford admits to being. In fact, Turnipseed's relationship with the Corps had been, until the war became imminent, casual, intermittent, and long-distance. Having joined right out of high school, he completed boot camp, trained as a truck mechanic, and served in North Carolina for a few months. And then he simply went home and remained on Unauthorized Absence status for months. He eventually worked out a deal and returned to the Corps as a reservist, and once Iraq invaded Kuwait, he writes, "There was no going back for either of us" (23). Theirs is a contract based on mutual suspicion and raw self-interest. The Marine Corps wants all it can get out of Turnipseed, who is, in his own words, a "dream recruit: messed up enough that [he] had nowhere else to go; smart and aggressive enough to want to prove something" (23). And Turnipseed is determined to get what he wants from his deal with the corps: a paycheck and time and space to read, smoke, and sleep. Like a surly worker in a dead-end job, moreover, Turnipseed develops bad work habits when his employer, the U.S. Marines, fails to provide him with safe and adequate tools with which to perform his job. He is required to ride with foreign contract drivers who at best speak no English and at worst steal the trucks, has to steal safety straps from the army because they don't have enough, and is forced to drive a truck with a leaking fuel tank. Turnipseed and his fellow Marine drivers derive their own version of semper fi: FIDO—Fuck It, Drive On (126).

War and Recovery

While many war memoirs are survival narratives and coming-of-age stories, *Jarhead* and, to a lesser extent, *Baghdad Express*, it could be argued, are also recovery narratives—that most popular genre of the late twentieth century—overlaid on a war or, to use the language of a recent war, embedded in it. Both authors, Swofford more so than Turnipseed, locate their war memoirs in a culturally resonate stream about recovery from family trauma, struggles with substance abuse and addiction, and depression and suicide.

 Jarhead opens with a prologue in which the narrator describes the acts of remembering and self-disclosure that will become the basis for the book. He is in the basement of his house in Iowa (Swofford attended the Iowa Writer's Workshop after his discharge), and he is opening his ruck, taking out the tokens of war: "I've been working toward this—I've opened the ruck and now I must open myself" (1). As a sniper-scout, Swofford claims that he "saw more of the Gulf War than the average grunt." He also says that his memoir is "neither true nor false, but *what [he] know[s]*," in a gesture that invokes Tim O'Brien's "How to Tell a True War Story" in *The Things They Carried*. But *Jarhead* has more in common with an article O'Brien wrote for the *New York Times* in which he weaves together the stories of a return trip to Vietnam and of a break-up with his girlfriend and his subsequent suicidal contemplations.[12] In both cases war is part of—neither all nor the sole cause of—a journey through a troubled psyche. Swofford's characterization of himself is a catalog of late-twentieth-century dysfunction: war-damaged, undemonstrative and ultimately abandoning father; needy and manipulative mother; institutionalized suicidal sister; domineering and deceitful brother; unfaithful girlfriends; prodigious drinking habits; and suicidal impulses of his own. All these elements of his background converge one afternoon when he's obsessively cleaning his rifle and contemplating his girlfriend's infidelity. "But Kristina's various infidelities are not the reasons I'm standing in the middle of my small barracks room, placing the muzzle of my M16 in my mouth and tasting the cold rifle metal and the smoky residue of gunpowder," he writes. There are multiple reasons that he's come to this point, Swofford speculates: "The history of my family and the species? The reports that the enemy to the north are elite fighters who learned how to throw grenades when I was barely off the tit? To move closer toward my sister? Cowardice? Fatigue? Boredom? Curiosity?" (70). Having introduced the typical recovery narrative scene in which the subject finds he has "hit bottom," Swofford then omits the expected narrative counterpart in which the individual begins the painful, self-dismantling yet ultimately therapeutic journey toward recovery. Instead of counseling or rehab or medical intervention, Swofford treats his suicidal contemplations with physical exertion:

> We run and run and the hours pass, and even though we're going in circles, I'm running away from whatever I left back in the barracks. I'm swirling around the thing until it becomes part of the swirl, and the swirl becomes part of me, and I'm still a part of that small sickness, and that sickness is still a small part of me, but it no longer has me bent over at the waist, chewing on the muzzle of my rifle. Maybe someday in the future I will revisit the sickness, but for now I'm done with it. (73)

Although *Jarhead* does not follow the familiar arc in which the individual spirals into darkness and addiction, hits bottom, and journeys toward recovery through self-awareness, the narrative is nevertheless shaped and shaded by these elements, drawn from a discourse of recovery that has dominated so much of the popular media in the last decade or so.

There is no ascension to sobriety from the depths of addiction nor any other kind of renunciation at the end of *Jarhead*, and, if anything, his conclusion suggests just the opposite and excludes the possibility that writing the book has been a healing act:

> I remade my war one word at a time, a foolish, desperate act. When I despair, I am alone, and I am often alone. In crowded rooms and walking the streets of our cities, I am alone, and full of despair, and while sitting and writing, I am alone and full of despair—the same despair

that impelled me to write this book, a quiet scream from within a buried coffin. (254)

And yet, by the end of the book Swofford has offered several examples of men who are not faring as well as he is. There's the homeless and dirty Vietnam vet who momentarily shares their parade ride, Troy who drinks himself head-on into a tree, and poor Fergus, Swofford's drinking buddy, who can't find his way back into the world and ends up shooting a man on the streets of San Francisco. Swofford may be damaged, he suggests, but not as badly as some others, and the reason may be his willingness to "open himself up." For all the book's displays of hyper-masculinity—shooting, tests of physical strength, heroic amounts of drinking—there are surprisingly numerous accounts of vulnerability, fear, and tenderness among the men. During the Vietnam War film-fest that he describes at the beginning of the book, he and others are overcome with emotion: "We watch our films and drink our beer and occasionally someone begins weeping and exits the room to stand on the catwalk and stare at the Bullion Mountains, the treacherous, craggy range that borders our barracks. Once this person is me" (7). Much later, in the moments before they will go on their first real mission of the war, they exchange hugs and massages, suggested by the "loudmouth" Welty. "And through the hugs," Swofford explains, "Welty has helped make us human again. He's exposed himself to us, exposed his need, and we in turn have exposed ourselves to him, and for that we are no longer simple grunt savages in the desert ready to jump the Berm and begin killing" (214). The language here wavers between irony and sincerity, but ultimately Swofford seems to validate the therapeutic "men's group" gestures of Welty.

Baghdad Express is both a gleeful and at times hilarious repudiation of the standard recovery narrative, as well as a tracing of its familiar trajectory. If Swofford has to remake himself word by word after the war, if the war has undone him or finished the job of undoing begun by the dysfunctional family, then Turnipseed's war is a self-making enterprise fueled by a ferocious nicotine addiction. At the same time, his book also takes dead aim at the genre of recovery. Turnipseed comes to the Marines with some of the same dysfunctional family baggage that Swofford does. His father drank and beat up his mother; he learns later in life that even the abusive man he learned to think of as his father is just the guy whose "one good and gracious act of his life [had been] the adoption of a forlorn bastard baby" (32). He was "a total freak" in school, whose recurrent childhood nightmare "about running from an exploding car. Just flat-fuck streaking down a highway in the middle of nowhere" (26), turns out to be a true story about the time his mother's old car caught on fire, and she had to drag him and his brother from the flames. As a young adult he's still a loner: no friends to speak of, no girlfriend, no permanent home, only the consolations of philosophy in coffeehouses. Rather than dwell on his situation, however, he proposes to transplant these consolations to the desert, "where wisdom has always been achieved," and work on the "great labor of building an unassailable happiness." And that's more or less what happens. After the end of the war and near the end of the book, he claims a "new world had come into being, where [he] could simultaneously be a nasty drunk Marine and a philosopher manqué." As if, he says, he "had passed some invisible boundary; that certain things, previously contradictory, didn't have to matter much anymore" (198).

Beneath the surface of Turnipseed's journey toward self-knowledge, however, is a sharp critique of exactly the kind of self-involved recovery narrative that Swofford engages. Turnipseed's first action after being summoned back to duty in the Marines is to buy his first pack of cigarettes, thus setting in motion one of the fiercest tobacco addictions in recent war literature. He smokes so much and so obsessively that he can tell time by his smoking and his desire to smoke. He smokes on guard duty, smokes on night patrols, and smokes when wasted and feverish with bronchitis. His unapologetic addiction to cigarettes is so instantaneous, so extravagant, and so consuming that it invites reading it as a critique of addiction narratives.

What's undeniably a critique of addiction and recovery discourses is the chart designed to mimic the official Marine Corps table regarding the effectiveness of certain bunker materials in withstanding specific munitions.[13] The USMC Combat Engineer Instruction Company guidelines state, for example, that one needs eight inches of sand to withstand 82 mm mortars, but protection against the same mortars will require only 4 inches of brick, but 60 inches of snow, and so on. The USMC Philosophy Instruction School plots "time spent alone with, in hours, required to recover from: Child Abuse, Drunk Father, A Shitty Life, Ayn Rand," along the horizontal axis and a range of recovery tools along the vertical: Plato, St. Augustine, Kierkegaard, Nietzsche, and Bourbon. It will take, for example, 170 hours spent with Plato's *Apology* to recover from Ayn Rand, but only 60 with the same text to recover from a drunk father (148). Or, in Swofford's case, though it does not appear on Turnipseed's table, the desire to shoot oneself in the mouth can be cured with several hours of nighttime running and perhaps a hug.

Conclusion

Both *Jarhead* and *Baghdad Express* are important contributions to the genre of American war memoir and go a long way toward our understanding of the 1990–91 Persian Gulf War, a conflict that we urgently need to interrogate more closely, especially at a time when we are involved in another, increasingly fraught war in the region. But war narratives are not like exotic travel or explorer accounts: at their most powerful they do much more than tell of arms and men from a land far away. They are stories about us, and they demand our attention even when we wish to turn away from them. Swofford's and Turnipseed's memoirs are not without their problems as literary texts, certainly. Swofford's narrative voice is sometimes derivative and self-involved, and the style is occasionally mannered and gratuitously swaggering and crude. Turnipseed fails to develop other characters fully, lapsing too often into predictable stereotypes, especially racial ones.

Ultimately, however, *Jarhead* and *Baghdad Express* engage not only the discourse of war but also take up other persistent and complex discourses in American culture at the millennium: the making and unmaking of the self in the language of childhood and family trauma; addiction, recovery, and depression; and anxieties about the individual body as site of economic exchange in employment and in relation to government and corporate entities.

Notes

1. Rick Atkinson, *Crusade: The Untold Story of the Persian Gulf War* (New York: Houghton Mifflin, 1993), 4, 5–6.

2. Other Gulf War memoirs include Geoffrey Frankel, *Desert Storm Diary: An American Soldier's Personal Record of the Gulf War in Words and Pictures* (Rosemont, N.J.: Morris-Lee, 1997); David S. Pierson, *Tuskers* (Darlington, Md.: Darlington, 1997); Dominic J. Carccilo, *The Ready Brigade of the 82nd Airborne in Desert Storm* (Jefferson, N.C.: McFarland, 1993); Rafael J. Garcia Jr., *Paladin Zero Six* (Jefferson, N.C.: McFarland,1994); Alex Vernon with Neal Creighton, Greg Downey, Rob Holmes, and David Trybula, *The Eyes of Orion: Five Tank Lieutenants in the Persian Gulf War* (Kent, Ohio: Kent State Univ. Press, 1999); Martin Stanton, *Road to Baghdad* (New York: Ballantine, 2003); Keith Rosenkranz, *Vipers in the Storm: Diary of a Gulf War Fighter Pilot* (Atlanta, Ga.: Turner, 1997); Buzz Williams, *Spare Parts* (New York: Gotham, 2004); Sean T. Caughlin, *Storming the Desert* (Jefferson, N.C.: McFarland, 1996); and Elizabeth Kassner, *Desert Storm Journal* (Lincoln, Mass.: Cottage, 1993). Rhonda Cornum's *She Went to War* (Novata, Calif.: Presidio, 1992) is the story of a woman flight surgeon who was captured during

a combat search-and-rescue and was held by the Iraqis as a POW. Barry McWilliams' *This Ain't Hell . . . but You can See It from Here: A Gulf War Sketchbook* (Novato, Calif.: Presidio, 1992) is a direct descendant of Bill Mauldin's classic World War II comic narratives. Cynthia B. Acree with Cliff Acree co-wrote *The Gulf between Us: Love and Terror in Desert Storm* (Washington, D.C.: Brassey's, 2003).

Steven Manchester's *The Unexpected Storm: The Gulf War Legacy* (Central Point, Oreg.: Hellgate, 2000) is a fictionalized memoir, as is Charles Sheehan-Miles's *Prayer at Rumayla* (self-published, 2001). Among the Gulf War narratives written by journalists are Molly Moore's *Woman at War* (New York: Scribner's, 1993); Peter Arnett's *Live from the Battlefield* (New York: Simon and Schuster, 1994); John J. Fialka's *Hotel Warriors* (Washington, D.C.: Woodrow Wilson Center, 1992); and Michael Kelly's *Martyr's Day* (New York: Random House, 1993)—Kelly was killed while working as an embedded journalist in the 2003 U.S. war against Iraq. John Sacks, the award-winning author of *M* (about an infantry company fighting in Vietnam), wrote *Company C* (New York: Morrow, 1995), the story of an armored company's Gulf War experience. Tom Clancy coauthored two narratives of the Gulf War—*Into the Storm*, with 7th Corps commander Frederick Franks (New York: Putnam, 1997), and *Every Man a Tiger*, with Air Force general Chuck Horner (New York: Putnam, 1999).

3. Michiko Kakutani, review of *Jarhead* by Anthony Swofford, *New York Times Book Review* (June 6, 2003).

4. Charles M. Minyard, Review of *Baghdad Express* by Joel Turnipseed, *Library Journal* 128, no. 8 (May 1, 2003): 136.

5. Bob Minzesheimer, *USA Today*, April 4, 2003.

6. For a critical overview of the reviews, see my "Gulf War Memoir Syndrome," *Texas Observer*, September 12, 2003.

7. Milton J. Bates, *The Wars We Took to Vietnam: Cultural Conflict and Storytelling* (Berkeley: Univ. of California Press, 1996), 5.

8. Anthony Swofford, *Jarhead: A Marine's Chronicle of the Gulf War and Other Battles* (New York: Scribner, 2003), 137.

9. Joel Turnipseed, *Baghdad Express: A Gulf War Memoir* (Minneapolis, Minn.: Borealis, 2003), 62.

10. Elaine Scarry, *The Body in Pain: The Making and Unmaking of the World* (New York: Oxford Univ. Press, 1985).

11. The drama between belonging and not belonging to the soldiering collective is a major feature of Tim O'Brien's *If I Die In a Combat Zone, Box Me Up and Ship Me Home* (New York: Dell, 1973). See Alex Vernon, "Submission and Resistance to Self as Soldier: Tim O'Brien's Vietnam War Memoir," *a/b: Auto/Biography Studies* 17, no. 2 (Winter 2002): 161–79; reprt. in *Soldiers Once and Still: Ernest Hemingway, James Salter, and Tim O'Brien* (Iowa City: Univ. of Iowa Press, 2004): 201–19.

12. O'Brien, "The Vietnam in Me," *New York Times Magazine* (Oct. 2, 1994): 48–57.

13. One of the innovations of Turnipseed's book is the inclusion of graphics, including paneled cartoons and charts and tables.

Works Cited

Ahmad, A., M. A. Sofi, V. Sundelin-Wahlslen, and A.-L. von Knorring. "Posttraumatic Stress Disorder in Children after the Military Operation 'Anfal' in Iraqi Kurdistan." *European Journal of Child and Adolescent Psychiatry* 9 (2000): 235–43.

Aichinger, Peter. *The American Soldier in Fiction, 1880–1963: A History of Attitudes toward Warfare and the Military Establishment.* Ames: Iowa State Univ. Press, 1975.

Allen, M. D. *The Medievalism of Lawrence of Arabia.* University Park: Pennsylvania State Univ. Press, 1991.

Altick, Richard. *Lives and Letters: A History of Literary Biography in England and America.* New York: Greenwood, 1979.

Altman, Janet Gurkin. "The Letter Book as a Literary Institution, 1539–1789: Toward a Cultural History of Published Correspondences in France." *Yale French Studies* 71 (1986): 17–62.

Ambrose, Stephen. *Americans at War.* Jackson: Univ. Press of Mississippi, 1997.

———. *Citizen Soldiers: The U.S. Army from the Normandy Beaches to the Bulge to the Surrender of Germany, June 7, 1994–May 7, 1945.* New York: Simon and Schuster, 1997.

———. *D-Day: June 6, 1944: The Climactic Battle of World War II.* New York: Simon and Schuster, 1994.

Anderson, Charles M., with Karen Holt and Patty McGady. "Suture, Stigma, and the Pages That Heal." In *Writing and Healing*, ed. Anderson and MacCurdy, 58–82.

———, and Marian M. MacCurdy, eds. *Writing and Healing: Towards an Informed Practice.* Urbana, Ill.: NCTE, 2000.

Anderson, J. K. *Xenophon.* New York: Scribner's, 1974.

Anderson, Linda. *Women and Autobiography in the Twentieth Century: Remembered Futures.* London: Prentice Hall/Harvester Wheatsheaf, 1997.

Atkinson, Rick. *Crusade: The Untold Story of the Persian Gulf War.* New York: Houghton Mifflin, 1993.

Badian, Ernst. "Alexander's Mules." *New York Review of Books* (Dec. 20, 1979): 54–56.

Barford, Mirren, and Jock Lewes. *Joy Street: A Wartime Romance in Letters.* Ed. Michael T. Wise. London: Little, 1995.

Bates, Milton J. *The Wars We Took to Vietnam: Cultural Conflict and Storytelling.* Berkeley: Univ. of California Press, 1996.

Battersby, Christine. *The Phenomenal Woman: Feminist Metaphysics and the Patterns of Identity.* Cambridge, U.K.: Polity, 1998.

Beatson, Robert. *Naval and Military Memoirs of Great Britain, from the year 1727, to the present time.* 6 vols. London: Longman, 1804.

Beidler, Philip D. *American Literature and the Experience of Vietnam.* Athens: University of Georgia, 1982.

Bell, Alan. "Wykehamical." *Spectator* (Feb. 12, 1983): 23–24.

Berg, Elizabeth. *Durable Goods.* New York: Random House, 1993.

Berg, Rick, and John Carlos Rowe, eds. *The Vietnam War and American Culture.* New York: Columbia Univ. Press, 1991.

Bérubé, Allan. *Coming Out under Fire: The History of Gay Men and Women in World War Two.* New York: Plume, 1990.

Bettelheim, Bruno. *The Informed Heart: Autonomy in a Mass Age.* Glencoe, Ill.: Free, 1960.

Bishop, Alan. "The Battle of the Somme and Vera Brittain." In *English Literature of the Great War Revisited,* ed. Michel Roucoux, 125–42. Picardy, Amiens, Fr.: University of Picardy, 1986.

Bloom, Lynn Z. "'I Write for Myself and Strangers.' Private Diaries as Public Documents." In *Inscribing the Daily: Critical Essays on Women's Diaries,* ed. Suzanne L. Bunkers and Cynthia A. Huff, 23–37. Amherst: Univ. of Massachusetts Press, 1996.

———. "Women's War Stories: The Legacy of South Pacific Internment." In *Visions of War: World War II in Popular Literature and Culture,* ed. M. Paul Holsinger and Mary Anne Schofield, 67–78. Bowling Green, Ohio: Bowling Green State Univ. Popular Press, 1992.

Blythe, Ronald, ed. *Private Words: Letters and Diaries from the Second World War.* London: Penguin, 1993.

Bond, Douglas D. *The Love and Fear of Flying.* New York: International Universities, 1952.

Borg, Alan. Foreword to *Special Relations: Transatlantic Letters Linking Three English Evacuees and Their Families, 1940–45,* comp. Jocelyn Statler. London: Imperial War Museum, 1990.

Bosworth, A. B. *A Historical Commentary on Arrian's History of Alexander.* Oxford, U.K.: Clarendon, 1980.

Boucher, Arthur. *L'Anabase de Xénophon (Retraite des Dix Mille) avec un commentaire historique et militaire.* Paris: Berger-Levrault, 1913.

Braidotti, Rosie. *Nomadic Subjects: Embodiment and Sexual Difference in Contemporary Feminist Theory.* New York: Columbia Univ. Press, 1994.

Bray, Robert, and Paul Bushnell, eds. *Diary of a Common Soldier in the American Revolution, 1775–1783: An Annotated Edition of the Military Journal of Jeremiah Greenman.* De Kalb: Northern Illinois Univ. Press, 1978.

Breitenbach, H. R. "Xenophon von Athen." *Paulys Realencyclopädie der classischen Altertumswissenschaft* 9.A.2 (1967): 1569–928.

Brink, Elsabé. *1899: The Long March Home: A Little-Known Incident in the Anglo-Boer War.* Cape Town, South Africa: Kwela, 1999.

Brittain, Vera. *Chronicle of Youth: Vera Brittain's War Diary, 1913–1917.* Ed. Alan Bishop with Terry Smart. London: Gollancz, 1981.

————. *On Becoming a Writer.* London: Hutchinson, 1947.

————. *Testament of Experience: An Autobiographical Story of the Years 1925–1950.* London: Virago, 1979.

————. *Testament of Youth: An Autobiographical Study of the Years 1900–1925.* London: Virago, 1978.

————. *Verses of a VAD and Other War Poems.* London: Imperial War Museum, 1995.

————. "War Service in Perspective." In *Promise of Greatness,* ed. George Panichas, 363–76. London: Cassell, 1968.

Bunkers, Suzanne. "What Do Women Really Mean? Thoughts on Women's Diaries and Lives." In *The Intimate Critique,* ed. Diane P. Freedman, Olivia Frey, and Frances Murphy Zauhar, 206–21. Durham, N.C.: Duke Univ. Press, 1993.

————, ed. *Diaries of Girls and Women: A Midwestern American Sampler.* Madison: Univ. of Wisconsin Press, 2001.

Busch, Fredrick C. *A Dangerous Profession: A Book about the Writing Life.* New York: St. Martin's, 1998.

Calvino, Italo. *Why Read the Classics?* Trans. Jonathan Cape. New York: Pantheon, 1999.

Captain, Esther. "'Written with an Eye on History': Wartime Diaries of Internees as Testimonies of Captivity Literature." *Tydskrif vir Nederlands en Afrikaans* 5, no. 1 (June 1999): 1–20.

Caputo, Philip. *DelCorso's Gallery.* New York: Holt, Rinehart, and Winston, 1983.

————. *Indian Country.* New York: Bantam, 1987.

————. *A Rumor of War.* New York: Holt, Rinehart, and Winston, 1977.

Cartledge, Paul. *Agesilaus and the Crisis of Sparta.* London: Duckworth, 1987.

————. *The Greeks: A Portrait of Self and Others.* Cambridge, U.K.: Cambridge Univ. Press, 1993.

Caruth, Cathy, ed. *Trauma: Explorations in Memory.* Baltimore, Md.: Johns Hopkins Univ. Press, 1995.

————. *Unclaimed Experience: Trauma, Narrative, and History.* Baltimore, Md.: Johns Hopkins Univ. Press, 1996.

Carver, Jonathan. *Travels through America, 1766–1768.* Ed. Norman Gelb. New York: John Wiley and Sons, 1993.

————. *Three Years' Travels through the Interior Parts of North America, in the Years 1766, 1767, and 1768.* Charlestown, Mass.: West and Greenleaf, 1802.

Cates. Tressa R. *Infamous Santo Tomás.* San Marcos, P.I.: Pacific, 1981.

Cesarani, David. "Lacking in Convictions: British War Crimes Policy and National Memory of the Second World War." In *War and Memory in the Twentieth Century,* ed. Martin Evans and Ken Lunn, 27–42. Oxford, U.K.: Berg, 1997.

Chandler, David, ed. *Military Memoirs of Marlborough's Campaigns, 1702–1712, by Captain Robert Parker . . . and the Count de Mérode-Westerloo.* London: Greenhill, 1998.

Chen, Edgar, and Emily Van Buskirk. "The Czech Legion's Long Journey Home." *Military History Quarterly* 13, no. 2 (2001): 42–53.

Churchill, Winston S. *Marlborough: His Life and Times.* London: Sphere, 1967.

Clinton, Sir Henry. *Narrative of Sir Henry Clinton, K. B., Relative to His Conduct during*

Part of His Command of the King's Troops in North-America. New York: Sower, Morton, and Horner, 1783.

Cobley, Evelyn. "Narrating the Facts of War: New Journalism in Herr's *Dispatches* and Documentary Realism in First World War Novels." *Journal of Narrative Technique* 16, no. 2 (Spring 1986): 97–116.

Cogan, Frances B. *Captured: The Japanese Internment of American Civilians in the Philippines, 1941–45*. Athens: Univ. of Georgia Press, 2000.

Coleman, Phill. *American War Library*. members.aol.com/veterans/index.html. Accessed June 10, 2004.

———. *Cannon Fodder: Growing Up for Vietnam*. members.aol.com/warlib/cf.htm. Accessed June 10, 2004.

Conroy, Pat. *The Great Santini*. Boston, Mass. Houghton Mifflin, 1976.

Cooper, Helen M., Adrienne Auslander Munich, and Susan Merrill Squier, eds. *Arms and the Woman: War, Gender, and Literary Representation*. Chapel Hill: Univ. of North Carolina Press, 1989.

Corti, Eugenio. *Few Returned: Twenty-eight Days on the Russian Front, Winter 1942–1943*. Columbia: Univ. of Missouri Press, 1997.

Cronin, Cornelius A. "Lines of Departure: The Atrocity in Vietnam War Literature." In *Fourteen Landing Zones*, ed. Philip K. Jason, 200–216. Iowa City: Univ. of Iowa Press, 1991.

Crouter, Natalie. *Forbidden Diary: A Record of Wartime Internment, 1941–45*. Ed. Lynn Z. Bloom. New York: Burt Franklin, 1980.

Cuneo, John R. *Robert Rogers of the Rangers*. New York: Oxford Univ. Press, 1959.

Dale, Colin [C. D.]. "D. H. Lawrence's Novels." *Spectator* (Aug. 6, 1927): 223.

———. "Hakluyt: The First Naval Propagandist." *Spectator* (Sept. 10, 1927): 390–91.

Daly, James A., and Lee Bergman. *Black Prisoner of War*. Lawrence: Univ. Press of Kansas, 2000. Originally published as *A Hero's Welcome: The Conscience of Sergeant James Daly versus the U.S. Army*. Indianapolis, Ind.: Bobbs-Merrill, 1975.

Dawes, James. *The Language of War: Literature and Culture in the U.S. from the Civil War through World War II*. Cambridge, Mass.: Harvard Univ. Press, 2002.

Dawson, Joseph G., III. *Doniphan's Epic March: The 1st Missouri Volunteers in the Mexican War*. Lawrence: Univ. Press of Kansas, 1999.

Delebecque, Édouard. *Essai sur la vie de Xénophon*. Paris: Librairie C. Klincksieck, 1957.

Didion, Joan. *Democracy*. New York: Simon and Schuster, 1984.

Dillery, John. *Xenophon: Anabasis*. Cambridge, Mass.: Harvard Univ. Press, 1998.

———. *Xenophon and the History of His Times*. London: Routledge, 1995.

Dougan, Clark, and Samuel Lipsman. *A Nation Divided*. Boston, Mass.: Boston, 1984.

Dowie, William. *James Salter*. New York: Twayne, 1998.

Dupuy, R. Ernest. *Perish by the Sword: The Czechoslovakian Anabasis and Our Supporting Campaigns in North Russia and Siberia, 1918–1920*. Harrisburg, Pa.: Military Service, 1939.

Dürrbach, Félix. "L'apologie de Xénophon dans l'*Anabase*." *Revue des Études Grecques* 6 (1893): 343–86.

Eakin, John Paul. "Malcolm X and the Limits of Autobiography." In *African American Autobiography: A Collection of Critical Essays*, ed. William A. Andrews, 151–61. Englewood Cliffs, N.J.: Prentice Hall, 1993.

Eccles, David, ed. *By Safe Hand: Letters of Sybil and David Eccles, 1939–42*. London: Bodley Head, 1983.

Egan, Susanna. *Patterns of Experience in American Autobiography*. Chapel Hill: Univ. of North Carolina Press, 1984.

Ehrenhaus, Peter. "Cultural Narratives and the Therapeutic Motif: The Political Containment of Vietnam Veterans." In *Narrative and Social Control: Critical Perspectives*, Sage Annual Reviews of Communications Research, vol. 21, ed. Dennis K. Mumby, 77–96. Newbury Park, Calif.: Sage, 1993.

Elshtain, Jean Bethke. *Women and War*. Brighton, U.K.: Harvester, 1987.

Enloe, Cynthia. *Does Khaki Become You? The Militarization of Women's Lives*. London: Pluto, 1983.

Erskine, David, ed. *Augustus Hervey's Journal: Being the Intimate Account of the Life of a Captain in the Royal Navy Ashore and Afloat, 1746–1759*. London: William Kimber, 1953.

Estess, Ted. *Elie Wiesel*. New York: Ungar, 1980.

Featherstone, Simon, ed. *War Poetry: An Introductory Reader*. London: Routledge, 1995.

Felman, Shoshana, and Dori Laub. *Testimony: Crises of Witnessing in Literature Psychoanalysis, and History*. New York: Routledge, 1992.

Fessler, Diane Burke. *No Time for Fear: Voices of American Military Nurses in World War II*. East Lansing: Michigan State Univ. Press, 1996.

Figes, Eva, ed. *Women's Letters in Wartime*. London: Pandora, 1994.

Forbes, Alistair. "To Be with a Happy Marriage Is So Rare." *Listener* (Jan. 20, 1983): 22–23.

Forster, E. M. *Abinger Harvest*. New York: Doubleday, Doran, 1936.

Foucault, Michel. *The History of Sexuality: An Introduction*. Vol. 1. New York: Vintage, 1990.

Fox, John Charles, ed. *The Official Diary of Lieutenant-General Adam Williamson*. London: Royal Historical Society, 1912.

Francklin, William, ed. *Military Memoirs of Mr. George Thomas*. Calcutta, India: [W. Francklin], 1803.

Franklin, Benjamin. *Autobiography and Other Writings*. Ed. Ormond Seavey. Oxford, U.K.: Oxford Univ. Press, 1993.

Franklin, H. Bruce. *MIA or Mythmaking in America*. Brooklyn, N.Y.: Lawrence Hill, 1992.

Frederick II. *The Art of War*. London: G. Riley, 1782.

———. *Military Instructions . . . for the Generals of his Army, being his Majesty's Own Commentaries on His Former Campaigns*. London: T. Becket and P. A. De Hondt, 1762.

French, Albert. *Patches of Fire: A Story of War and Redemption*. New York: Anchor, 1997.

Freud, Sigmund. *Beyond the Pleasure Principle*. New York: Norton, 1961.

Fussell, Paul. *Doing Battle: The Making of a Skeptic*. Boston, Mass.: Little, Brown, 1996.

———. "From the Front: Taking the Sting Out of the World Wars." *Times Literary Supplement* (Sept. 27, 1991): 3–4.

———. *The Great War and Modern Memory*. New York: Oxford Univ. Press, 1975.

———. "My War." *Harper's* (Jan. 1982): 40–49.

———. *Wartime: Understanding and Behavior in the Second World War.* New York: Oxford Univ. Press, 1989.

Gagnon, J. H. "The Self, Its Voices, and Their Discord." In *Investigating Subjectivity: Research on Lived Experience*, ed. Carolyn Ellis and Michael G. Flaherty, 221–43. Newbury Park, Calif.: Sage, 1992.

Gibbon, Edward. *Memoirs of My Life.* Ed. Betty Radice. New York: Penguin, 1984.

Gilberg, Gail H. *Snake's Daughter: The Roads In and Out of War.* Iowa City: Univ. of Iowa Press, 1997.

Gilman, Owen, Jr., and Lorrie Smith, eds. *America Rediscovered: Critical Essays on Literature and Film on the Vietnam War.* New York: Garland, 1990.

Gilmore, Leigh. *The Limits of Autobiography: Trauma and Testimony.* Ithaca, N.Y.: Cornell Univ. Press, 2001.

Goll, Yvan. *Requiem für die Gefallenen von Europa: Dichtungen.* Darmstadt, Ger.: Luchterhand, 1960.

Goodwin, Sarah Webster, and Elisabeth Bronfen. Introduction to *Death and Representation.* Baltimore, Md.: Johns Hopkins Univ. Press, 1993.

Graves, Robert. *Good-bye to All That.* London: Penguin, 1960.

Griffin, Susan. *A Chorus of Stones: The Private Life of War.* New York: Anchor Doubleday, 1992.

Gruber, Ira D., ed. *John Peebles' American War: The Diary of a Scottish Grenadier, 1776–1782.* Stroud, Gloucester, U.K.: Sutton for the Army Records Society, 1997.

Gruner, Elliott. *Prisoners of Culture Representing the Vietnam POW.* New Brunswick, N.J.: Rutgers Univ. Press, 1993.

Gyles, John. *Memoirs of Odd Adventures, Strange Deliverances, &c. in the Captivity of John Gyles, Esq.* Boston: S. Kneeland and T. Green, 1736.

Halsema, James J. *Bishop Brent's Baguio School: The First 75 Years.* Baguio, P.I.: Brent School, 1988.

———. *E. J. Halsema: Colonial Engineer. A Biography.* Quezon City, P.I.: New Day, 1991.

Hamilton, George. *A Voyage Round the World, in His Majesty's Frigate* Pandora. Sydney, Australia: Hordern House, 1998.

Hartmann, Susan M. "Prescriptions for Penelope: Literature on Women's Obligations to Returning World War II Veterans." *Women's Studies* 5 (1978): 223–39.

Hasek, Jaroslav. *The Good Soldier Svejk and His Fortunes in the World War.* Trans. Cecil Parrott. New York: Penguin, 1985.

Hasford, Gustav. *The Short-Timers.* New York: Bantam, 1979.

Haswell, Janis E. Review of *The House on Dream Street* by Don Sachs. *Viet Nam War Generation Journal* 1, no. 1 (April 2001): 122–26.

Heberle, Mark A. *A Trauma Artist: Tim O'Brien and the Fiction of Vietnam.* Iowa City: Univ. of Iowa Press, 2001.

Heckler, Jonellen. *Safekeeping.* New York: Putnam, 1983.

Henke, Suzette A. *Shattered Subjects: Trauma and Testimony in Women's Life-Writing.* New York: St. Martin's, 1998.

Herold, Ethel. "War Memories of Ethel Herold." *Bulletin of the American Historical Collection* 10 (1982): 44–67.

Herman, Judith Lewis. *Trauma and Recovery.* New York: Basic, 1992.

Herr, Michael. *Dispatches.* New York: Knopf, 1977.

Higgins, W. E. *Xenophon the Athenian: The Problem of the Individual and the Society of the Polis.* Albany: State Univ. of New York Press, 1977.

Higonnet, Margaret R., ed. *Lines of Fire: Women Writers of World War I.* New York: Penguin, 1991.

———, Jane Jenson, Sonya Michel, and Margaret Collins Weitz, eds. *Behind the Lines: Gender and the Two World Wars.* New Haven, Conn.: Yale Univ. Press, 1987.

———, and Patrice L.-R. Higonnet. "The Double Helix." In *Behind the Lines: Gender and the Two World Wars,* ed. Margaret Randolph Higonnet, Jane Jenson, Sonya Michel, and Margaret Collins Weitz, 31–47. New Haven, Conn.: Yale Univ. Press, 1987.

Hinz, Evelyn J. "A Speculative Introduction: Life-Writing as Drama." *Data and Acta: Aspects of Life-Writing.* Winnipeg: University of Manitoba, 1987. v–xii.

Hoffman, Daniel. *Zone of the Interior: A Memoir, 1942–1947.* Baton Rouge: Louisiana State Univ. Press, 2000.

Hofmann, Bettina. *Ahead of Survival: American Women Writers Narrate the Vietnam War.* Frankfurt, Ger.: Peter Lang, 1996.

Holcroft, Thomas, trans. *Posthumous Works of Frederic II, King of Prussia.* London: G. G. J. and J. Robinson, 1789.

Holsinger, M. Paul, ed. *War and Popular Culture: A Historical Encyclopedia.* Westport, Conn.: Greenwood, 1999.

Holsinger, M. Paul, and Mary Anne Schofield, eds. *Visions of War: World War II in Popular Literature and Culture.* Bowling Green, Ohio: Bowling Green State Univ. Popular Press, 1992.

Housman, L., ed. *War Letters of Fallen Englishmen.* London: E. P. Dutton, 1930.

Howes, Craig. *Voices of the Vietnam POWs: Witnesses to their Fight.* New York: Oxford Univ. Press, 1993.

Hoy, Pat C., II. "Once More into the Breach." *The Sewanee Review* 98, no. 2 (Spring 1990).

Hudson, Derek, and Kenneth Miller. "The Tiny Victims of Desert Storm." *Life* (Nov. 18, 1995): 46–59.

Hunter, Edna J., and D. Stephen Nice. *Children of Military Families: A Part and Yet Apart.* Proceedings of Military Family Research Conference, September 1–3, 1977, San Diego. Washington, D.C.: U.S. Government Printing Office, 1978.

———. *Military Families: Adaptation to Change.* New York: Praeger, 1978.

Hyland, Judy. *In the Shadow of the Rising Sun.* Minneapolis, Minn.: Augsburg, 1984.

Hynes, Samuel. *Flights of Passage: Reflections of a World War II Aviator.* New York: Frederic C. Beil; Annapolis: Naval Institute Press, 1988.

———. *Flights of Passage: Reflections of a World War II Aviator.* New York: Pocket, 1998.

———. *The Soldiers' Tale: Bearing Witness to Modern War.* New York: Penguin, 1997.

Irigaray, Luce. *The Irigaray Reader.* Ed. Margaret Whitford. Oxford, U.K.: Blackwell, 1991.

James, Lawrence. *The Golden Warrior: The Life and Legend of Lawrence of Arabia.* New York: Paragon, 1993.

Jason, Philip K., and Mark A. Graves, eds. *Encyclopedia of American War Literature.* Westport, Conn.: Greenwood, 2001.

Jefferson, Thomas. "Letters: August 3, 1771." In *Thomas Jefferson, Writings*, ed. Merrill D. Peterson, 740–45. New York: Library of America, 1984.

———. "Letters: March 14, 1818." In *Thomas Jefferson, Writings*, ed. Peterson, 1411–13.

Jeffords, Susan. *The Remasculinization of America: Gender and the Vietnam War.* Bloomington: Indiana Univ. Press, 1989.

Jensen, Peter S., Stephen N. Xenakis, Perry Wolf, and Michael Bain. "The 'Military Family Syndrome' Revisited." *Journal of Nervous and Mental Disease* 179 (1991): 102–7.

Joannou, Maroula. *"Ladies, Please Don't Smash These Windows": Women's Writing, Feminist Consciousness, and Social Change, 1918–38.* Oxford, U.K.: Berg, 1995.

Johnson, T. R. "Writing as Healing and the Rhetorical Tradition." In *Writing and Healing*, ed. Anderson and MacCurdy, 85–114.

Jolly, Margaretta. "Everyday Letters and Literary Form: Correspondence from the Second World War." Ph.D. Diss., University of Sussex, 1996.

———. "Love Letters versus Letters Carved in Stone: Gender, Memory and the 'Forces Sweethearts' Exhibition." In *War and Memory in the Twentieth Century*, ed. Martin Evans and Ken Lunn, 105–21. Oxford, U.K.: Berg, 1997.

———, ed. *Encyclopedia of Life Writing.* London: Fitzroy Dearborn, 2001.

Kakutani, Michiko. Review of *Jarhead* by Anthony Swofford. *New York Times Book Review* (June 6, 2003): 23.

Kaminski, Theresa. *Prisoners in Paradise: American Women in the Wartime South Pacific.* Lawrence: Univ. Press of Kansas, 2000.

Kane, Richard. *Campaigns of King William and the Duke of Marlborough.* 2d ed. London: J. Millan, 1747.

Karlin, Wayne. "Those Dying Generations," *Washington Post Book World*, March 9, 1997, 5.

Karnow, Stanley. *Vietnam: A History.* New York: Penguin, 1991.

Kaslow, Florence W., ed. *The Military Family in Peace and War.* New York: Springer, 1993.

Kaslow, Florence W., and Richard Ridenour, eds. *The Military Family: Dynamics and Treatment.* New York: Guilford, 1984.

Kavanagh, Gaynor. "Museum as Memorial: The Origins of the Imperial War Museum." *Journal of Contemporary History* 23 (1988): 77–97.

Keeley, Lawrence H. *War before Civilization.* New York: Oxford Univ. Press, 1996.

Keenan, Barbara Mullen. *Every Effort a True Story.* New York: St. Martin's, 1986.

Keith, Agnes Newton. *Three Came Home.* Boston: Little, Brown, 1947.

Kennard, J. E. *Vera Brittain and Winifred Holtby: A Working Partnership.* Hanover, N.H.: Univ. Press of New England, 1989.

Keshen, David, and Jeff Mills. "'Ich bereite mich auf den Tag vor, da es zu Ende geht!': Briefwechsel von Kanadierinnen und Kanadiern im Krieg." In *Andere Helme—andere Menschen? Heimaterfahrung und Frontalltag im Zweiten Weltkreig*, ed. Detlef Vogel and Wolfram Wette, 257–82. Tubingen, Ger.: Klartext, 1995.

Kermode, Frank. *Not Entitled: A Memoir.* London: HarperCollins, 1996.

Kinney, Katherine. *Friendly Fire: American Images of the Vietnam War.* New York: Oxford Univ. Press, 2000.

Knightly, Phillip, and Colin Simpson. *The Secret Lives of Lawrence of Arabia.* New York: McGraw-Hill, 1970.

Kovic, Ron. *Born on the Fourth of July.* New York: Pocket, 1976.

Krentz, Peter. *Xenophon: Hellenika II.3.11-IV.2.8.* Warminster, U.K.: Aris and Phillips, 1995.

Kristeva, Julie. *The Kristeva Reader.* Ed. Toril Moi. Oxford, U.K.: Blackwell, 1986.

Lagrone, Don M. "The Military Family Syndrome." *American Journal of Psychiatry* 135 (Sept. 1978): 1040–43.

Langellier, Kristin M., and Eric E. Peterson. "Family Storytelling as a Strategy of Social Control." In *Narrative and Social Control Critical Perspectives,* Sage Annual Reviews of Communications Research, vol. 21, ed. Dennis K. Mumby, 49–76. Newbury Park, Calif.: Sage, 1993.

Lartéguy, Jean. *The Sun Goes Down: Last Letters from Japanese Suicide-Pilots and Soldiers.* London: New English Library, 1975.

Laub, Dori. "Bearing Witness, or the Vicissitudes of Listening." In *Testimony: Crises of Witnessing in Literature Psychoanalysis and History,* ed. Shoshana Felman and Dori Laub, 57–74. New York: Routledge, 1992.

Lawrence, A. W., ed. *Men in Print: Essays in Literary Criticism by T. E. Lawrence.* London: Golden Cockerel, 1940.

———, ed. *T. E. Lawrence by His Friends.* New York: McGraw-Hill, 1963.

Lawrence, T. E. *Crusader Castles.* London: Golden Cockerel, 1936.

———. *The Essential T. E. Lawrence.* Ed. David Garnett. New York: Viking, 1963.

———. *A Handbook to the 37-1/2 Foot Motor Boats of the 200 Class.* London: Jonathan Cape, 1993.

———. *The Letters of T. E. Lawrence.* Ed. David Garnett. London: Jonathan Cape, 1938.

———. *The Mint.* New York: Norton, 1955.

——— [T. E. Shaw, pseud.], trans. *The Odyssey of Homer.* Oxford, U.K.: Oxford Univ. Press, 1991.

———. *Revolt in the Desert.* New York: George Doran, 1927.

———. *Seven Pillars of Wisdom: A Triumph.* New York: Doubleday, Doran, 1937.

———. *T. E. Lawrence to His Biographer, Robert Graves: Information about Himself in the Form of Letters, Notes, and Answers to Questions, Edited with a Critical Commentary.* New York: Doubleday, Doran, 1938.

Layton, L. "Vera Brittain's Testament(s)." In *Behind the Lines: Gender and the Two World Wars,* ed. Margaret Randolph Higonnet, et al, 70–83. New Haven, Conn.: Yale Univ. Press, 1987.

Leed, Eric J. *No Man's Land: Combat and Identity in World War I.* Cambridge, U.K.: Cambridge Univ. Press, 1979.

Lendle, Otto. *Kommentar zu Xenophons Anabasis (Bücher 1–7).* Darmstadt, Ger.: Wissenschaftliche Buchgesellschaft, 1995.

Levi, Primo. *The Drowned and the Saved.* New York: Vintage, 1988.

Lewis, Lloyd B. *The Tainted War: Culture and Identity in Vietnam War Narratives.* Westport, Conn.: Greenwood, 1985.

Lifton, Robert Jay. *Home from the War: Vietnam Veterans—Neither Victims Nor Executioners.* New York: Simon and Schuster, 1973.

Litoff, Judy Barrett, and David C. Smith. "Since You Went Away: The World War II Letters of Barbara Wooddall Taylor." *Women's Studies* 17, nos. 3–4 (1990): 249–76.

————. "'Will He Get My Letter?' Popular Portrayals of Mail and Morale during World War II." *Journal of Popular Culture* 23, no. 4 (1990): 21–44.

————, eds. *Dear Boys: World War II Letters from a Woman Back Home.* Jackson: Univ. Press of Mississippi, 1991.

————. *Miss You: World War II Letters of Barbara Wooddall Taylor and Charles E. Taylor.* Athens: Univ. Press of Georgia, 1990.

————. *Since You Went Away: World War Two Letters from American Women on the Home Front.* Oxford, U.K.: Oxford Univ. Press, 1991.

————. *We're in This War, Too: World War II Letters from American Women in Uniform.* New York: Oxford Univ. Press, 1994.

Lloyd, Henry. *The History of the Late War in Germany; With Occasional Remarks.* London: printed for the author, 1766.

Lomperis, Timothy J. *Reading the Wind: The Literature of the Vietnam War.* Durham, N.C.: Duke Univ. Press, 1987.

Long, Patricia. "Growing Up Military." *Psychology Today* 14 (Dec. 1986): 31–37.

Louvre, Alf, and Jeffrey Walsh, eds. *Tell Me Lies about Vietnam: Cultural Battles for the Meaning of the War.* Durham, N.C.: Duke Univ. Press, 1988.

Lynn, Mary C., ed. *The Specht Journal: A Military Journal of the Burgoyne Campaign.* Trans. Helga Doblin. Westport, Conn.: Greenwood, 1995.

MacCurdy, Marian M. "From Trauma to Writing: A Theoretical Model for Practical Use." In *Writing and Healing,* ed. Anderson and MacCurdy, 158–200.

McCain, John. *Faith of My Fathers.* New York: Random House, 1999.

McCubbin, Hamilton I., Barbara B. Dahl, and Edna J. Hunter, eds. *Families in the Military System.* Beverly Hills, Calif.: Sage, 1976.

————, Edna J. Hunter, and Barbara B. Dahl. "Residuals of War: Families of Prisoners of War and Servicemen Missing in Action." *Journal of Social Issues* 31, no. 4 (1975): 95–109.

McDaniel, Norman A. *Yet Another Voice.* New York: Hawthorn, 1975.

Mack, John E. *A Prince of Our Disorder: The Life of T. E. Lawrence.* Boston, Mass.: Little, Brown, 1976.

Mahler, Michael D., Col. (U.S. Army, Ret.), "One Platoon Leader's Catharsis Demeans Those Who 'Gave a Damn,'" *Army* (July 1997): 59–69.

Manchester, William. *Goodbye, Darkness: A Memoir of the Pacific War.* Boston, Mass.: Little, Brown, 1979.

Manfredi, Valerio. *La Strada dei Diecimila: Topografia e Geografia dell'Oriente di Senofonte.* Milan, Italy: JACA, 1986.

Marcus, Laura. *Auto/Biographical Discourses: Theory, Criticism, Practice.* Manchester, U.K.: Manchester Univ. Press, 1994.

Marshall, Kathryn. *In the Combat Zone: An Oral History of Women in Vietnam, 1966–75.* Boston, Mass.: Little, Brown, 1987.

Melling, Philip M. *Vietnam in American Literature.* Boston, Mass.: Twayne, 1990.

Mellown, M. "Vera Brittain: Feminist in a New Age." In *Feminist Theorists: Three Centuries of Women's Intellectual Traditions,* ed. Dale Spender, 314–33. London: Women's Press, 1983.

Meredith, James H. *Understanding the Literature of World War II: A Student Casebook to Issues, Sources, and Historical Documents.* Westport, Conn.: Greenwood, 1999.

Meyers, Jeffrey. *The Wounded Spirit: T. E. Lawrence's* Seven Pillars of Wisdom. New York: St. Martin's, 1989.

Miles, Fern Harrington. *Captive Community: Life in a Japanese Internment Camp, 1941–45.* Jefferson City, Mo.: Mossy Creek, 1987.

The Military Mentor. Being a Series of Letters Recently Written by a General Officer to His Son, on His Entering the Army. 2 vols. London: Richard Phillips, 1804.

Millner, John. *A Compendious Journal of all the Marches, Battles, Sieges and Other . . . Actions of the Allies in Their . . . War against . . . France.* London: n.p., 1733.

Milne, Caleb. *"I Dream of the Day . . .": Letters from Caleb Milne.* Ed. Marjorie Kinnan Rawlings. New York: Longmans, 1945.

Minyard, Charles M. Review of *Baghdad Express: A Gulf War Memoir* by Joel Turnipseed. *Library Journal* 128, no. 8 (May 1, 2003): 136.

Minzesheimer, Bob. Review of *Baghdad Express: A Gulf War Memoir* by Joel Turnipseed. *USA Today,* April 4, 2003.

Mithers, Carol Lynn. "Missing in Action: Women Warriors in Vietnam." In *The Vietnam War and American Culture,* ed. John Carlos Rowe and Rick Berg, 73–91. New York: Columbia, 1991.

Momigliano, Arnold. *The Development of Greek Biography.* Exp. ed. Cambridge, Mass.: Harvard Univ. Press, 1993.

Montgomery, Bernard Law. *The Memoirs of Field-Marshal the Viscount Montgomery of Alamein.* London: Collins, 1958.

Mosse, George L. *Fallen Soldiers: Reshaping the Memory of the World Wars.* New York: Oxford Univ. Press, 1990.

Mousa, Suleiman. *T. E. Lawrence: An Arab View.* Oxford, U.K.: Oxford Univ. Press, 1966.

Myers, Thomas. *Walking Point: American Narratives of Vietnam.* New York: Oxford Univ. Press, 1988.

Natter, Wolfgang. *Literature at War, 1914–1940: Representing the "Time of Greatness" in Germany.* New Haven, Conn.: Yale Univ. Press, 1999.

Newman, John, ed. *Vietnam War Literature: An Annotated Bibliography of Imaginative Works about Americans Fighting in Vietnam.* Lanham, Md.: Scarecrow, 1996.

Newton, John, ed. *Select Passages from the Diary and Letters of the Late John Blackader, Esq.* Edinburgh: John Ritchie, 1806.

Noakes, Lucy. "Making Histories: Experiencing the Blitz in London's Museums in the 1990s." In *War and Memory in the Twentieth Century,* ed. Martin Evans and Ken Lunn, 89–104. Oxford, U.K.: Berg, 1997.

———. *War and the British: Gender, Memory and National Identity.* London: Tauris, 1998.

Norman, Elizabeth. *Women at War: The Story of Fifty Military Nurses Who Served in Vietnam.* Philadelphia: Univ. of Pennsylvania Press, 1990.

Novak, Marian Faye. *Lonely Girls with Burning Eyes: A Wife Recalls Her Husband's Journey Home from Vietnam.* Boston, Mass.: Little, Brown, 1991.

Nussbaum, Felicity A. "Towards Conceptualizing Diary." In *Studies in Autobiography,* ed. James Olney, 128–40. Oxford, U.K.: Oxford Univ. Press, 1988.

O'Brien, Tim. *Going after Cacciato.* New York: Dell, 1975.

———. *If I Die in a Combat Zone, Box Me Up and Ship Me Home.* New York: Dell, 1973.

———. *In the Lake of the Woods*. New York: Penguin, 1994.

———. *The Things They Carried*. New York: Broadway, 1990.

———. "The Vietnam in Me." *New York Times Magazine* (Oct. 2, 1994): 48–57.

O'Donnell, Thomas J. *The Confessions of T. E. Lawrence: The Romantic Hero's Presentation of Self*. Athens: Ohio Univ. Press, 1979.

Ouditt, Sharon. *Fighting Forces, Writing Women: Identity and Ideology in the First World War*. London: Routledge, 1994.

Paden, Lindsay B., and Laurence J. Pezor. "Uniforms and Youth: The Military Child and His or Her Family." In *The Military Family in Peace and War*, ed. Florence W. Kaslow, 3–24. New York: Springer, 1993.

Parke, H. W. *Greek Mercenary Soldiers from the Earliest Times to the Battle of Ipsus*. Oxford, U.K.: Clarendon, 1933.

Parker, Robert. *Memoirs of the Most Remarkable Military Transactions from the Year 1683 to 1718*. Dublin, Ire.: G. and A. Ewing, 1746.

Parks, David. *GI Diary*. Washington, D.C.: Howard Univ. Press, 1984.

Peebles, John. *John Peebles' American War: The Diary of a Scottish Grenadier, 1776–1782*. Stroud, Gloucester, U.K.: Sutton for the Army Records Society, 1997.

Perri, Margaret. *Witnesses to War: The War Stories of Women Vietnam Veterans*. Amherst: Univ. of Massachusetts Press, 1998.

Phillips, Jayne Anne. *Machine Dreams*. New York: Simon and Schuster, 1984.

Plain, Gill. "'Great Expectations': Rehabilitating the Recalcitrant War Poets." *Feminist Review* 51 (1995): 41–65.

Pomeroy, Sarah. *Xenophon, Oeconomicus: A Social and Historical Commentary*. Oxford, U.K.: Clarendon, 1994.

Potter, Israel. *The Life and Remarkable Adventures of Israel R. Potter (a Native of Cranston Island)*. Providence, R.I.: printed for the author, 1824.

Powell, Colin, with Joseph E. Persico. *My American Journey*. New York: Random House, 1995.

Puller, Lewis B., Jr. *Fortunate Son: The Autobiography of Lewis B. Puller, Jr*. New York: Grove Weidenfeld, 1991.

Purcell, Ben, and Anne Purcell. *Love and Duty*. New York: St. Martin's, 1992.

Read, Herbert. *A Coat of Many Colors*. London: Routledge, 1945.

Remarque, Erich Maria. *All Quiet on the Western Front*. New York: Ballantine, 1982.

Rodriguez, Alex R. "Special Treatment Needs of Children of Military Families." In *The Military Family: Dynamics and Treatment*, ed. Florence W. Kaslow and Richard Ridenour, 46–72. New York: Guilford, 1984.

Rogers, Robert. *Journals of Major Robert Rogers Containing an Account of the Several Excursions He Made . . . during the Late War*. London: J. Millan, 1765.

Rowlandson, Mary White. "The Sovereignty and Goodness of God." In *Puritans among the Indians: Accounts of Captivity and Redemption, 1676–1724*, ed. Alden T. Vaughan and Edward W. Clark, 29–76. Cambridge, Mass.: Harvard Univ. Press, 1981.

Roy, James. "Xenophon's *Anabasis*: The Command of the Rearguard in Books 3 and 4." *Phoenix* 22, no. 2 (1968): 158–59.

———. "Xenophon's Evidence for the *Anabasis.*" *Athenaeum: Studi Periodici di Letteratura e Storia dell'Antichità* 46 (1968): 37–46.

Ryan, Maureen. "Pentagon Princesses and Wayward Sisters: Vietnam POW Wives in American Literature." *War, Literature, and the Arts* 10, no. 2 (1998): 132–64.

Ryan-Wegner, Nancy A. "Impact of the Threat of War on Children in Military Families." *American Journal of Orthopsychiatry* 71 (April 2001): 236–44.

Sajer, Guy. *The Forgotten Soldier.* New York: Harper and Row, 1971.

Salter, James. *Burning the Days: Recollections.* New York: Random House, 1997.

Salvatore, M. *Women after War: Vietnam Experiences and Post-Traumatic Stress: Contributions to Social Adjustment Problems of Red Cross Workers and Military Nurses.* Boston, Mass.: Simmons College of Social Work, 1992.

Sams, Margaret. *Forbidden Family: A Wartime Memoir of the Philippines, 1941–45.* Wisconsin Studies in American Autobiography. Ed. Lynn Z. Bloom. Madison: Univ. of Wisconsin Press, 1989.

Sanders, Valerie. *The Private Lives of Victorian Women: Auto-Biography in Nineteenth-Century England.* Hemel, Hempstead, U.K.: Harvester Wheatsheaf, 1989.

Sanger, Ernest, ed. *Letters from Two World Wars: A Social History of English Attitudes to War, 1914–45.* Phoenix Mill, Gloucestershire, U.K.: Sutton, 1993.

Saussure, Ferdinand. *Course in General Linguistics.* New York: Philosophical Library, 1916.

Scarry, Elaine. *The Body in Pain: The Making and Unmaking of the World.* New York: Oxford Univ. Press, 1985.

Schroder, Eric James. "Two Interviews: Talks with Tim O'Brien and Robert Stone." *Modern Fiction Studies* 20, no. 1 (Spring 1984): 147–48.

Schuyler, Philippa. *Good Men Die.* New York: Twin Circle, 1969.

Scott, Caroline F. *Diary of the Siege of Fort William.* Ed. D. M. Rose. Oban, Scot.: reprinted from the *Oban Times,* 1900.

Scott-James, R. A. *Fifty Years of English Literature.* New York: Scribner's, 1951.

Searle, William J., ed. *Search and Clear: Critical Responses to Literature and Films of the Vietnam War.* Bowling Green, Ohio: Bowling Green Univ. Press, 1988.

Shay, Jonathan. *Achilles in Vietnam: Combat Trauma and the Undoing of Character.* New York: Simon and Schuster, 1994.

Sidney, Sir Philip, "An Apology for Poetry." In *The Critical Tradition,* 2d. ed., ed. David H. Richter. Boston, Mass.: Bedford, 1998.

Sinor, Jennifer. *The Extraordinary Work of Ordinary Writing: Annie Ray's Diary.* Iowa City: Univ. of Iowa Press, 2002.

Smith, Angela. *The Second Battlefield: Women, Modernism and the First World War.* Manchester, U.K.: Manchester Univ. Press, 2000.

Smith, James. *An Account of the Remarkable Occurrences in the Life and Travels of James Smith.* 1799. Repr.; Harmondsworth, U.K.: Penguin, 1984.

Smith, Sidonie, and Julia Watson, eds. *Getting a Life: Everyday Uses of Autobiography.* Minneapolis: Univ. of Minnesota Press, 1996.

Smith, Winnie. *American Daughter Gone to War: On the Front Lines with an Army Nurse in Vietnam.* New York: Morrow, 1992.

Southey, Robert. Review of *The Memoirs of the Life and Writings of Percival Stockdale*. *Quarterly Review* 1, no. 2 (May 1809): 386.

Spicer, L., ed. *Letters from My Son, 1942–1944, Roger Lancelot Spicer*. London: Unwin, 1955.

Stanley, L. *The Auto/Biographical I*. Manchester, U.K.: Manchester Univ. Press, 1992.

Stanton, Domna C., ed. *The Female Autograph*. Chicago: Univ. of Chicago Press, 1984.

Statler, Jocelyn, ed. *Special Relations: Transatlantic Letters Linking Three English Evacuees and Their Families, 1940–45*. London: Imperial War Museum, 1990.

Steedman, C. "Women's Biography and Autobiography: Forms of History, Histories of Form." In *From My Guy to Sci-Fi: Genre and Women's Writing in the Postmodern World*, ed. Helen Carr, 98–111. London: Pandora, 1989.

Steinman, Louise. *The Souvenir: A Daughter Discovers Her Father's War*. Chapel Hill, N.C.: Algonquin, 2001.

Stepto, Robert B. "Narration, Authentication, and Authorial Control in Frederick Douglass' *Narrative* of 1845." In *African American Autobiography: A Collection of Critical Essays*, ed. William A. Andrews, 29–35. Englewood Cliffs, N.J.: Prentice Hall, 1993.

Stern, Seth. "New Worry: Kids with Both Parents in Combat." *Christian Science Monitor* 93 (Oct. 2001): 1.

Stevens, Frederic H. *Santo Tomás Internment Camp*. N.p.: Stratford, 1964.

Stockdale, Jim, and Sybil Stockdale. *In Love and War. The Story of a Family's Ordeal and Sacrifice during the Vietnam Years*. Annapolis, Md.: Naval Institute Press, 1990.

Strauss, Leo. "Xenophon's *Anabasis*." *Interpretation: A Journal of Political Philosophy* 4, no. 3 (1975): 117–47.

Stronk, Jan P. *The Ten Thousand in Thrace: An Archaeological and Historical Commentary on Xenophon's Anabasis, Books VI.iii–vi–VII*. Amsterdam, Neth.: J. C. Gieben, 1995.

Styron, William. "A Case of the Great Pox." *New Yorker* (Sept. 18, 1995): 62–65.

Swofford, Anthony. *Jarhead: A Marine's Chronicle of the Gulf War and Other Battles*. New York: Scribner's, 2003.

Tabachnick, Stephen Ely. *T. E. Lawrence*. Boston, Mass.: Twayne, 1978.

Tapert, Annette, ed. *The Brothers' War: Civil War Letters to Their Loved Ones from the Blue and Grey*. New York: Times, 1988.

———. *Dispatches from the Heart: An Anthology of Letters from the Front during the First and Second World Wars*. London: Hamilton, 1984.

———. *Lines of Battle: An Anthology of Letters by American Servicemen in World War II*. New York: Times, 1987.

Taylor, Laura. *Honorbound*. 1988. New York: Jove, 1990.

Thomson, William. *Military Memoirs: Relating to Campaigns, Battles, and Stratagems of War, Antient and Modern; Extracted from the Best Authorities*. London: J. Johnson, 1804.

Tinker, David, and Hugh Tinker. *A Message from the Falklands: The Life and Gallant Death of David Tinker: From His Letters and Poems*. London: Junction, 1982.

Tomibe, Rokuro. "The Secret Story of the War's End." *Bulletin of the American Historical Collection* 7 (1979): 37–45.

La Tregua/The Truce. Dir. Francesco Rosi. Telegraph S.L. (Spain/Italy), 1996; Miramax (U.S.), 1998.

Trodd, Anthea. *Women's Writing in English: Britain, 1900–1945*. London: Longman, 1998.

Truscott, Lucian K., IV. *Dress Gray*. New York: Doubleday, 1978.

Truscott, Mary R. *Brats: Children of the American Military Speak Out*. New York: Dutton, 1989.

Tuplin, Christopher. sv. "Xenophon (1)." *Oxford Classical Dictionary*, 1996.

Turnipseed, Joel. *Baghdad Express: A Gulf War Memoir*. Minneapolis, Minn.: Borealis, 2003.

Tylee, C. M. *The Great War and Women's Consciousness: Images of Militarism and Womanhood in Women's Writings, 1914–64*. London: Macmillan, 1990.

Van Devanter, Lynda, with Christopher Morgan. *Home before Morning: The Story of an Army Nurse in Vietnam*. New York: Warner, 1983.

Vance, Samuel. *The Courageous and the Proud*. New York: Norton, 1970.

Vaughan, Elizabeth. *The Ordeal of Elizabeth Vaughan: A Wartime Diary of the Philippines*. Ed. Carol M. Petillo. Athens: Univ. of Georgia Press, 1985.

Vaughn, Pamela. "The Identification and Retrieval of the Hoplite Battle-Dead." In *Hoplites: The Classical Greek Battle Experience*, ed. Victor Davis Hanson, 38–62. London: Routledge, 1991.

Vernon, Alex. *The Eyes of Orion: Five Tank Lieutenants in the Persian Gulf War*. Kent, Ohio: Kent State Univ. Press, 1999.

———. *Soldiers Once and Still: Ernest Hemingway, James Salter, and Tim O'Brien*. Iowa City: Univ. of Iowa Press, 2004.

———. "Submission and Resistance to Self as Soldier: Tim O'Brien's Vietnam War Memoir." *a/b: Auto/Biography Studies* 17, no. 2 (Winter 2002): 161–79.

Villars, Jean Beraud. *T. E. Lawrence, or the Search for the Absolute*. Trans. Peter Dawnay. London: Jonathan Cape, 1958.

Walker, Keith. *A Piece of My Heart: The Stories of 26 American Women in Vietnam*. Novato, Calif.: Presidio, 1985.

Walsh, Jeffrey, and James Aulich, eds. *Vietnam Images: War and Representation*. Basingstoke, U.K.: Macmillan, 1989.

Walsh, Patricia L. *Forever Sad the Hearts*. New York: Avon, 1982.

Warhol, Robyn, and Helena Michie. "Twelve-Step Teleology: Narratives of Recovery/Recovery as Narrative." In *Writing and Healing*, ed. Anderson and MacCurdy, 327–50.

Warnock, Tilly. "Language and Literature as 'Equipment for Living': Revision as a Life Skill." In *Writing and Healing*, ed. Anderson and MacCurdy, 34–57.

Webster, John Clarence, ed. *The Journal of Jeffrey Amherst, Recording the Military Career of General Amherst in America from 1758 to 1763*. Toronto, Can.: Ryerson, 1931.

Weintraub, Karl Joachim. *The Value of the Individual: Self and Circumstances in Autobiography*. Chicago: Univ. of Chicago Press, 1978.

Weintraub, Stanley, and Rodelle Weintraub. *Lawrence of Arabia: The Literary Impulse*. Baton Rouge: Louisiana State Univ. Press, 1975.

Wells, Maureen. *Entertaining Eric: Letters from the Home Front, 1941–44*. London: Imperial War Museum, 1988.

Wertsch, Mary Edwards. *Military Brats: Legacies of Childhood inside the Fortress*. New York: Harmony, 1991.

White, E. B. *Writings from the* New Yorker, *1927–1976.* Ed. Rebecca M. Dale. New York: HarperCollins, 1990.

Whitmore, Terry. *Memphis-Nam-Sweden: The Autobiography of a Black American Exile.* Garden City, N.Y.: Doubleday, 1971.

Willenz, June A. *Women Veterans: America's Forgotten Heroines.* New York: Continuum, 1983.

Williams, Fenton A. *Just before the Dawn: A Doctor's Experiences in Vietnam.* New York: Exposition, 1971.

Williams, Frank. "Xenophon's Dana and the Passage of Cyrus' Army over the Taurus Mountains." *Historia* 45, no. 3 (1996): 284–314.

Williamson, Adam. *Military Memoirs and Maxims of Marshal Turenne.* London: J. and P. Knapton, 1740.

Wolfe, James. *General Wolfe's Instructions to Young Officers.* London: J. Millan, 1768.

Wood, Edward W., Jr. *On Being Wounded.* Golden, Colo.: Fulcrum, 1991.

Wright, Eddie. *Thoughts about the Vietnam War: Based on My Personal Experiences, Books I Have Read, and Conversations with Other Veterans.* New York: Carlton, 1984.

Contributors

LYNN Z. BLOOM is Board of Trustees Distinguished Professor and Aetna Chair of Writing at the University of Connecticut. In addition to editing Natalie Crouter's *Forbidden Diary* and Margaret Sams's *Forbidden Family* she has written *Doctor Spock: Biography of a Conservative Radical* (1972) and numerous articles on autobiography, coauthored the NEH-funded *American Autobiography 1945–1980: A Bibliography* (1982), and published autobiographical essays such as "Subverting the Academic Masterplot" (1998) and "Living to Tell the Tale: The Complicated Ethics of Creative Nonfiction" (2003).

CHRIS DALEY is completing her Ph.D. at the CUNY Graduate Center in New York City. Her focus is twentieth century literature and cultural studies, specifically Los Angeles literature and alternative religion. She has published fiction as well as criticism, including work on Nathanael West, Zora Neale Hurston, Sylvia Townsend Warner, and feminist desire. She currently runs a collection of graduate programs for the Baruch College School of Public Affairs.

BETTINA HOFMANN teaches at the University of Wuppertal, Germany. She received her Ph.D. from the University of Heidelberg (1996) with the dissertation, "Ahead of Survival: American Women Writers Narrate the Vietnam War."

PAT C. HOY II directs the Expository Writing Program at New York University. A collection of his essays, *Instinct for Survival* (1992), was selected as a "Notable" collection in *The Best American Essays of the Century*. His essays and reviews have appeared in *Agni, Rhetoric Review, Sewanee Review, South Atlantic Review, Virginia Quarterly Review,* and *Wall Street Journal.* Eight of these pieces have been selected as "Notable Essays" in *The Best American Essays* series. He received the 2003 Fellowship of Southern Writer's Nonfiction Award.

MARGARETTA JOLLY is the general editor of *The Encyclopedia of Life Writing* (2001). Her other publications include *Dear Laughing Motorbyke: Letters from Women Welders in the Second World War* (1997) and "The Exile and the Ghost-Writer: East-West Biographical Politics and *The Private Life of Chairman Mao*," *Biography* 23, no. 3 (Summer 2000). She lectures in twentieth-century literature and culture at the University of Exeter.

ROBERT LAWSON-PEEBLES held posts at Oxford, Princeton, and Aberdeen before moving to Exeter University, England, where he is now senior lecturer in the School of English. His work on American environmental history includes *Landscape and Written Expression in Revolutionary America* (1988) and two collections of essays coedited with Mick Gidley: *Views of American Landscapes* (1989) and *Modern American Landscapes* (1995). He has also written on twentieth-century transatlantic cultural history, including *Approaches to the American Musical* (1996). He has published essays on Sir Walter Raleigh, George Washington, Susannah Rowson, James Fenimore Cooper, Henry George, and William Carlos Williams (among others). *American Literature Before 1880*, setting American literature in an international context beginning in the eighth century BC, appeared in 2003. He is currently working on late colonial cultural history. The essay in this collection was written for his father, Cmd. Gen. A. A. Lawson-Peebles.

JOHN W. I. LEE is assistant professor of Greek history at the University of California, Santa Barbara. He received his Ph.D. in history from Cornell University and has held fellowships from the American School of Classical Studies (Athens, Greece) and the Peace Studies Program (Cornell University). Lee's research focuses on the social and cultural aspects of Greek warfare. He has published articles on ancient urban battle and on women in Greek warfare and is currently finishing his first book, *Ten Thousand Greeks without Breakfast: Comradeship and Community in Xenophon's Anabasis.*

JEFF LOEB served as a Marine Corps interpreter in Vietnam (1968–69) and has published over forty articles on African American Vietnam war narratives and on Vietnam autobiographies in general, including pieces in *African American Review* and *American Studies.* He also secured the reissue of and wrote forewords for *Memphis, Nam, Sweden* by Terry Whitmore and *Black Prisoner of War* by James A. Daly. Chapters of his own personal narrative have appeared in *War, Literature, and the Arts.* He has a Ph.D. from the University of Kansas and is chair of English at the Pembroke Hill School in Kansas City, Missouri.

ELISABETH PIEDMONT-MARTON is an associate professor of English at Southwestern University, where she teaches courses in American literature and the Vietnam War, modern poetry, and writing. She received her B.A. from Kenyon College and her Ph.D. from the University of Texas at Austin. Her interest in war narrative began with her dissertation on epic poetry.

ANDREA PETERSON received her Ph.D. from Loughborough University, Leicestershire, England. She currently lectures in English literature at the University of Birmingham, England. She has published on Vera Brittain, war diaries and journals, and feminism and is currently at work on a monograph about Brittain.

TERRY REILLY is an associate professor of English at the University of Alaska, Fairbanks, where he specializes in Shakespeare and Renaissance literature. He has published on Shakespeare, Goethe, Pynchon, Lessing, Young, and trauma theory. His publications in life writing include two articles on Arthur Young's *Travels in France* and another on Doris Lessing's autobiography.

JENNIFER SINOR is an assistant professor of composition and rhetoric at Utah State University. Her professional areas of interest include women's life writing, ordinary (diurnal) writing, and the making of texts. Her book, *The Extraordinary Work of Ordinary Writing* (2002), focuses on the diary of her great, great, great aunt. She has a Ph.D. from the University of Michigan.

ALEX VERNON, an assistant professor of English at Hendrix College outside Little Rock, Arkansas, teaches twentieth-century American literature and writing. His two books are *Soldiers Once and Still: Ernest Hemingway, James Salter, and Tim O'Brien* and *The Eyes of Orion: Five Tank Lieutenants in the Persian Gulf War*. His essays have appeared in *South Atlantic Review; JNT: The Journal of Narrative Theory; a/b: Auto/Biography Studies; Mosaic; Wilson Quarterly; Computers and Composition; War, Literature, and the Arts; Chronicle of Higher Education; Hemingway Review;* and *American Heritage*.

Index